Dynasty

The Astors and Their Times

This book is dedicated
to the memory of Heinz Koppel

*Ich grolle nichte, und wenn das
Herz auch bricht*—Heine

Dynasty

The Astors and Their Times

David Sinclair

BEAUFORT BOOKS, INC.
New York

Copyright © 1984 by David Sinclair

Library of Congress Cataloging in Publication Data

Sinclair, David.
  Dynasty : the Astors and their times.

  Bibliography: p.
  Includes index.
  1. Astor family.   I. Title.
CT274.A86S54   1983   973'.09'92   [B]   84-6467
ISBN 0-8253-0223-4

Published in the United States by Beaufort Books, Inc., New York.

Printed in the U.S.A.   First American Edition

10 9 8 7 6 5 4 3 2 1

Contents

List of Illustrations

PART I

An American Dream

Prologue *A Tale of Two Cities*

I

It is a crisp January evening in the city of New York. The worst of the winter storms will not arrive for almost a month, but some snow has fallen already and the chill north-westerly wind carries the threat of more to come. Despite the cold and the slush underfoot, though, there is a good deal of horsedrawn traffic on the thoroughfares of lower Manhattan, and a small crowd of pedestrians has gathered at the intersection of Fifth Avenue and 34th Street, just across from the vast marble palace built by the late department store tycoon, A.T. Stewart. It is not towards the Stewart house that all eyes turn, however, but towards a four-storey brownstone mansion ablaze with light on the other side of 34th Street, which seems to be the destination of most of the carriages abroad on this winter night.

The brownstone is the town residence of Mr William Backhouse Astor, Jr, but the master is not at home: he is sailing on his yacht somewhere off the coast of Florida, probably in the company of his favourite showgirl of the moment. No, this evening belongs to Mrs Astor – not the only lady to bear that title in the New York of the 1880s, but certainly the one who needs no further identification as far as polite society and much of the rest of the nation is concerned. For this Mrs Astor is far more than the mistress of a Manhattan mansion, chatelaine of a three-thousand-acre estate in Dutchess County and grande dame of a sixty-two-room 'summer cottage' in Newport, Rhode Island. This Mrs Astor is the fount of fashion, the arbiter of taste, the high priestess of manners and etiquette, the chief justice in the supreme court of social acceptability. This Mrs Astor – always to be known as *the* Mrs Astor – is to all intents and purposes the queen of New York, and on one night in January each year her favoured courtiers are called together to pay homage.

For the crowd of stargazers outside the gates of 350 Fifth Avenue, the January Ball provides a living *Who's Who* as America's first families and foreign dignitaries alight from their carriages, the gentlemen stiff in their tailcoats and high collars, the ladies rustling in satins, aglitter with diamonds, heads held erect so as not to disturb elaborate coiffures.

Passing through the great doors of the mansion, the guests enter a large hall, heavy with the scents of roses and orchids, where footmen in blue livery divest them of their coats and wraps and direct them to anterooms in which they may attend to the niceties of their toilette before joining the throng assembled in the three tulip-bedecked parlours on the right-hand side of the great staircase, opposite the ornate reception room where their hostess will formally greet them.

As eleven o'clock approaches, the receiving line begins to form and a thrill of anticipation spreads through the guests. What will Mrs Astor be wearing tonight – white satin set with silver and pearls, or black satin with roses, or red brocade, or regal purple velvet spangled with gold? Will she be displaying all her diamonds, including the famous 'Marie Antoinette stomacher' and the breathtaking sunburst necklace with the two hundred and eighty-two stones? But most important of all, who among her courtiers will be selected for the supreme honour of sitting next to her majesty on the red silk 'throne' set on its dais in the vast ballroom running the full width of the house?

At last, the great moment. The line begins to move and the leaders of New York society are ushered into the presence of the greatest of them all, Caroline Webster Schermerhorn Astor. There she stands, this tyrant of the top drawer, a small, plump woman in a black wig, rather ugly with her big nose, thin lips and heavy-set jaw; gloriously, tastelessly, ridiculously over-dressed by Worth; dripping with diamonds, from the tiara and stars that sparkle in her wig down through the triple fall that encircles her throat, the twelve rows that hang at her breast and that fabulous stomacher that may or may not have adorned the anatomy of Marie Antoinette.

The overall effect of Mrs Astor's excesses would have been supremely vulgar and laughable to a modern eye. Perhaps it can never have been more truly said that a woman was making an

3

exhibition of herself – but for Caroline that was part of the idea. If she was to be the ruler of society, she must display herself like a queen, and to this empty-headed, dull-witted, vain, snobbish and physically unattractive woman, the ludicrous figure she presented to the guests at her January Ball was what a queen should look like. And such was the power she had created for herself that if Mrs Astor said it was so, then it must be so. Instead of laughing, the ruling class marvelled and worshipped and tried to imitate or outdo – as the old French saying goes, 'the world is full of fools and he who would not see it should live alone and smash his mirrors'. Whatever her limitations, Caroline Astor had the ability to be an originator and to make people follow her lead, no matter how silly the direction might seem to a detached observer. With the syco- phantic help of a fat, self-important, clownish little social climber named Ward McAllister (her prime minister, or lord chamberlain, if the metaphor of queendom is pursued), she gave form and structure to the lives of an elite with no centre, no fount of honour, no yardstick by which to measure social standing.

The years B.C. (Before Caroline) in the social history of the United States followed very much the European pattern of class distinction, though of course without the elaborate and instantly divisive hierarchy of titles used by the aristocracy of the Old World – that would have been much too undemocratic. The early settlers had brought with them the ancient concept of nobility, added to which, on the one hand, was the granting of lands and charters by the monarchs of the colonizing nations to favoured or troublesome courtiers and on the other hand the fact that America was the perfect place for the export of the aristocracy's second sons, who at home would inherit the natural superiority of their birthright but not the lands and the fortunes to maintain it. After the Revolution, some of the names may have changed as 'loyalist' families fled or were dispossessed, but the upper stratum of society remained firmly in the hands of the landed gentry, the so- called Old Guard.

During the early part of the nineteenth century, however, an alternative elite began to emerge as the rapid expansion of trade and the acceleration of the Industrial Revolution produced a class of merchants, manufacturers, bankers and entrepreneurs

4

who were proud, ambitious and, most important, wealthy beyond the dreams of many of the mere landowners. At first the Old Guard looked down its nose at these parvenus who had clawed their way up from the ranks of the unwashed: money they might have, but their tastes and manners were certainly not those of gentlemen. For their part, members of the new class cared little whether their 'betters' approved of them or not – they were much too busy making the money that gave them the freedom to do as they liked and the power to influence events irrespective of their manners. But for the heirs of both the Old Guard and the merchant princes, things were different. The sons of the lowly-born wealthy often did not need to work as hard as their fathers, if at all, while the children of the gentry saw marriage into the new class as a way of being maintained in a fashion even grander than that to which they were accustomed.

By the 1870s, therefore, intermarriage had confused the boundaries between the Old Guard and the new class, and the rich and leisured products of such alliances were searching for some kind of definition of their social status.

Nowhere was this more apparent than in New York, which, through the efforts of the businessmen and industrialists, had grown into 'the metropolis of the New World'. According to a contemporary writer, 'New York is one of the most wonderful products of our wonderful western civilization. It is itself a world in epitome... It is the great monetary, scientific, artistic and intellectual centre of the western world ... a great city, a wonderful city. But what it is today is only the beginning of what those who live fifty years hence will behold it. There is still space upon Manhattan Island for twice or thrice its present population and business; and the no distant future will undoubtedly see this space fully occupied, while it is among the possibilities that New York will become, in point of inhabitants and commercial interests, the first city in the world.' Such pride and such ambition, symbolized in 1871 by the start of work on the great Brooklyn Suspension Bridge, which opened twelve years later, required a form of expression honouring those responsible for it, recognizing that New York had the social cachet to match its commercial success.

In the theatre of history, the stage was set for a comedy of manners. All that was lacking was a star. In his self-appointed position as producer of the show, the preposterous Ward McAllister, who in flattering and fawning his way round the capitals of Europe had absorbed the style if not the substance of the real nobility, saw Caroline Astor as the perfect leading lady. As he himself told it: 'At this period, a great personage (representing a silent power that had always been recognized and felt in this community so long as I can remember by not only fashionable people but by the solid, old quiet element as well) had daughters to introduce into society, which brought her prominently forward and caused her at once to take a leading position. She possessed great administrative power and it was soon put to good use and felt by society. I then for the first time was brought into contact with this grande dame and at once recognized her ability and felt that she would become society's leader and that she was admirably qualified for the position.' What he really meant was that Caroline Astor had the status, the motive and, most essential, the money to back, direct and star in his play.

On all counts, McAllister's choice could not have been better. The Astors were certainly not members of the Old Guard, being descended from a penniless German immigrant why by his own efforts had become a multi-millionaire, but by the middle of the nineteenth century they were not only the richest family in the country but their money was also old enough to be respectable. Caroline's position as a 'great personage' rested on more than her rich marriage, though. By birth, she was unquestionably a member of the old Knicker-bocker 'aristocracy',* tracing her descent from one Jacob Schermerhorn, who had arrived in New Amsterdam from Holland only a decade or so after Peter Minuits had purchased Manhattan from the Indians for the equivalent of twenty-four dollars. About 1636, Schermerhorn settled in Beverwyck, which was translated into Albany when the English took it over in 1664, and there he became squire of a substantial estate. Despite some reverses during the time of the Dutch adminis-tration – Jacob fell foul of the imperious governor, Peter

* Descendants of the original Dutch settlers. So-called after Washington Irving's satirical *History of New York*, in which the narrator was 'Diedrich Knickerbocker'.

Stuyvesant, who charged him with gun-running to the Indians and confiscated some of his lands – the Schermerhorns prospered and over time became allied through marriage with some of the leading families of New York: the Van Cortlandts, the Beekmans, the Barclays, the Suydams, the Welleses and the Irvings.

At something less than a million dollars, the Schermerhorns' fortune in Caroline's youth – she was born in 1831 – could not compare with the almost incredible wealth of the new rich who rose to economic if not social prominence in the late eighteenth and early nineteenth centuries, but Caroline's marriage to William B. Astor, Jr, in 1853 gave her the means to acquire the status among the emerging plutocracy that she felt was hers by right of breeding.

If her own sense of natural superiority was not motive enough, Mrs Astor had two further reasons for thrusting herself to the forefront of society. First, although she had married an Astor, she was part of what was very much the junior branch of the family: William B. was the second son in an age when the rights and privileges of primogeniture were absolute. While William was more than well provided for and stood to inherit a considerable fortune in his own right, in the eyes of both his family and the portion of the rest of the world that really mattered he could never hope for the respect accorded to his elder brother, John Jacob III. Thus at first it was John Jacob's wife who was 'Mrs Astor', with all that implied, while Caroline was 'Mrs William'. For a woman with Caroline's pretensions, this simply would not do.

More pressing, however, was Caroline's second reason for wishing to surround herself with an elite who danced to her tune. By the early 1860s, as well as having dutifully produced a male heir, she had four daughters who in due time would be coming out, as the saying goes, displaying themselves to society in order to attract suitable husbands. But in the social muddle of New York, how was the conscientious mother to ensure that her daughters would fall for young men of quality as opposed to the mere possessors of grubby fortunes?

Caroline decided that the only way was to take upon herself the responsibility of judging who was worthy of a place at the dinner table or in the ballroom and who was not, to establish nothing less than a new social code that would distinguish between the true elite and the pretenders and set the standards for polite behaviour. This was no easy task for a woman so signally bereft of natural attributes, mental and physical, and it is doubtful whether she could have achieved it without Ward McAllister, who made up for what she lacked in imagination and style, while Caroline provided both the means to indulge his fantasies and – her one outstanding feature – the force of personality to make other people, often more intelligent and more cultured, accept those fantasies as part of their everyday lives.

McAllister himself was neither *nouveau* nor *riche*, springing from a well-bred family of the antebellum South, where the aristocracy had no doubts about its place but did not always manage to hold on to it. The social life of New York attracted him and at twenty he made his debut on the arm of his godmother, who lived up to his expectations by showing him off in all the right places but fell short of them by failing to make generous provision for him in her will. When an inheritance did come his way it was a mere thousand dollars and, recognizing that so little money was of itself no use to him, McAllister threw it away on an elaborate fancy-dress costume for a ball. That was the last New York saw of him for some time, but he had at least made sure that it would remember him.

With no well-disposed and wealthy relatives on the point of departure, he realized he was going to have to earn his living, and here his family did come in useful. His father and brother were practising law in gold-rich California and they gave him a job. His talents were not of the order that fitted him for the law, but he had strong powers of invention and a natural skill for socializing, so he was put to work wooing clients by entertaining them on a lavish scale, which he did with remarkable success. Within a few years he had acquired a large enough share of the law firm's profits to leave San Francisco and return to the more congenial habitat of the East Coast, where he married one Sarah Gibbons (who was never really heard of again) and set off with her to observe the social habits of the Old World.

The European nobility, with little better to do than compete in the search for novelty, took up McAllister as a curiosity and, since he was careful not to overstep the limits of his position and content to be patronized, he was able to gain entry to some of the most fashionable salons of Italy, France and England, though sometimes only through the servants' entrance.

Armed with all he had learnt about wining, dining and entertaining in the truly grand manner, McAllister returned to America in 1858 and bought a farm at Newport, Rhode Island, summer playground of rich and fashionable New Yorkers, where he began to organize parties – 'as a general would a battle, omitting nothing' – for the elite. In keeping with the season and the surroundings, many of these were outdoor events, *fêtes champêtres* as McAllister insisted upon calling them, and such was his attention to detail that he would even hire sheep and cows to underscore the bucolic atmosphere. His own connexions with gentility (among other things, he was the grandson of a Supreme Court justice) and the success of his parties won him the approval of the upper crust and before long he was being asked for aid and advice relating to some of the great social events of the New York winter season, since he knew a good deal more about the 'right' way of doing things than many of the hostesses and could usually be relied upon to provide style and flair that would make a ball a memorable affair.

In the closed circle of respectable society – it must be remembered that in America, as in Europe, there was a strong undercurrent in nineteenth-century upper class life which was very far from being respectable – the meeting of McAllister and Mrs Astor was inevitable, and when it came about in the early 1870s each recognized in the other qualities that could be put to good use in the drive to satisfy ambition. McAllister was impressed by Caroline's commanding presence as much as by her money, while she admired his taste, his knowledge and his absorption in the finer points of presentation and etiquette. A partnership would clearly contain the ingredients of such stuff as dreams are made on.

II

The Astor-McAllister partnership began in the winter of 1872–1873, the season in which Caroline's eldest child, Emily, 'came out' having attained the age of eighteen. McAllister proposed that the definition of society, with Mrs Astor at its pinnacle, naturally, should be undertaken by the organizing of a subscription ball under strict rules governing the selection of the guests. The subscription dance was already a familiar form in New York society, but the committees which ran such affairs were susceptible to pressure from the nouveaux riches and one could never be sure that the guests were 'genuine' bluebloods according to the Astor-McAllister model that was emerging.

What McAllister had in mind was the sort of ball administered by the redoubtable aristocratic matriarchy of London, which took place at Almack's assembly rooms in King Street, St James's, and to which only those of impeccable pedigree were invited. He was thirty years out of date, of course, since Almack's had seen its greatest days during the time of the Regency and had in fact come under new management in 1840, after which it was used mostly for formal dinners until its closure in 1890. (A persistent legend, which may have originated from its subject, has it that during his Grand Tour of Europe McAllister was introduced to Almack's by no lesser personage than the Duke of Westminster. For this to have been true, McAllister would have had to be no more than twelve years old at the time!)

No matter. New York had never enjoyed the benefits of such tight control over its social life, and to McAllister any European idea, suitably amended, could only be a good thing. In this case the amendment took the form of that deference to maleness which remains so marked in American life even today: whereas in London it had been the ladies who had formed the praetorian guard of society, in New York by McAllister's decree it was to be the gentlemen who held the power of exclusion.

The idea was crystallized in the form of the Patriarchs, twenty-five men who, by virtue of their wealth and backgrounds, were selected by McAllister, Mrs Astor and their appointed committee to lead the New Order. The choice of those twenty-five was not made lightly, McAllister spending many hours burrowing in the ancestral records of the leading families and reporting his findings to Mrs Astor's committee. He claimed that no one could be a Patriarch without four generations of good breeding behind him. This automatically ruled out the Astors, but in the general excitement no one seemed to notice the anomaly when John Jacob Astor III and Caroline's husband both appeared among the ranks of the

Patriarchs. Indeed, the whole list was rather heavily weighted in favour of the Astors and their relatives and the Schermerhorns and theirs, but this was only to be expected since Caroline had set out with the intention of dominating society, and at least it gave the excluded families something to aim for. If one could not aspire to the position of Patriarch, it was still possible to join the magic circle by being included among the two hundred people the Patriarchs were entitled to invite to each of the balls held under their aegis. Even persons of quality from such out-landish places (to Mrs Astor at any rate) as Boston, Philadel-phia, Charleston and Baltimore might hope for distinction in New York by attending a Patriarchs' ball under the provi-sion that a committee could invite up to fifty 'distinguished strangers', also including visiting notables from Europe.

Thus it was that New York became the undisputed social Mecca of America and Mrs Astor's Fifth Avenue mansion its holiest shrine. Phoney as the whole structure was, the elite saw member-ship of the Patriarchs as a source of pride and exclusion from their gatherings as a serious blow to their self-esteem. And, with the advent of the newspaper gossip column, people who would never have the opportunity even to touch a Patriarch's coat tails began to take an interest in the activities of this newly created aristocracy and tried as far as they could to imitate the manners of their 'betters'. The ambitions of one woman and the dreams of one man, vain, self-serving and silly as they were, had somehow been translated into matters of importance.

Sadly, in spite of Mrs Astor's pretensions and McAllister's pompous pronouncements, this new aristocracy that came to be so admired throughout the country was based not on genealogy or on the European concept of nobility, with its overtones of public service and social responsibility, but on the possession of wealth. As McAllister himself once admitted, 'A fortune of only a million is respectable poverty,' adding that his brave new society had no use for a man with nothing to offer but his pedigree, with 'the aspirations of a duke and the fortune of a footman'. This was snobbery of the worst stamp, and the net effect of all the attention the new class attracted during the last quarter of the nineteenth century was to intensify the relentless materialism which has been at once the most powerful driving force and the greatest weakness in modern American life.

Yet what else did the Astor-McAllister elite have to offer? New York, unlike the great social centres of Europe – Paris, London, Berlin, Vienna – was not a national capital and therefore did not automatically command the presence of the great figures of the age to leaven the always rather flat mixture of the leisured classes. Unfortunately, as John Kenneth Galbraith has more recently observed, 'Wealth has never been a sufficient source of honour in itself. It must be advertised, and the normal medium is obtrusively expensive goods.' So it was with the Patriarchs and their acolytes: social success became a vulgar competition to outspend one's rivals and magnificence was measured in dollars.

Of course, the balls and vast dinners of the New York season were perfect showcases for apparently careless displays of wealth, beginning with the jewelry of the hostess and continuing through the extent and extravagance of the floral decorations and food to the costly ingenuity of the party favours, which might be fashioned in gold or silver.

Aided by McAllister, who always suggested the line of most expense, Caroline Astor made her balls and dinners the most glamorous of all. The society scandal sheet *Town Topics* noted that at one dinner for three hundred people, Mrs Astor served champagne costing fifteen dollars a bottle. 'Such plate and crystal can be seen in no other house in New York,' the newspaper commented. 'She has a gold service of 40 pieces and it would be simply impossible to estimate its value. Any one of the dinner plates is probably worth from $300 to $400 [in fact, there is some doubt about this. After Caroline's death the dinner-service was appraised as being gold-plated.] Then there are golden epergnes, candelabra and other articles both for ornament and use... The floral decorations of Mrs Astor's table consist invariably of gloire de Paris roses. Even the young men about town know these cost $1 apiece, and frequently there are 400 of them ...'

Then, of course, there was the food. McAllister had studied French cuisine, and the following menu of nine courses, consumed in about three hours, is his:

Tortue clair (turtle soup)
Mousse aux jambons
Terrapin
Filet de boeuf with truffles

Riz de veau à la Toulouse
Pâté de foie gras en Bellevue
Maraschino sorbet
Camembert cheese and biscuits
Pouding Nesselrode

Clearly, he had not studied gastronomy all that closely. *Riz de veau à la Toulouse*, for example, is a dreadful howler more in keeping with a seedy restaurant than a smart dinner table. But as long as the food was expensive and sounded French, nobody was going to argue about accuracy.

Mrs Astor gave such dinners weekly throughout the New York season and, since the table talk tended to be mundane bordering on crass, the only points of interest were the food and the manner in which it was served. *Town Topics* sneered that 'they do nothing from one week's end to another but arrange themselves about boards that groan with delectable viands, where they open grateful mouths to everything that comes their way; and this they call social intercourse'. It could only lead to 'a race of fat-headed and thick-witted gourmands'.

There was, however, one cultural activity that attracted these swells – the opera – though it must be admitted that the main aim was to see and be seen rather than to appreciate the music. Mrs Astor decided that Monday should be society night at the opera, since the various Patriarchs' balls were also held then, starting at about eleven o'clock, and the rest of the millionaires followed her lead. When the Metropolitan Opera House opened in 1883, its two tiers of boxes quickly became known, for obvious reasons, as the Diamond Horseshoe, with Caroline in Box Number 7 holding most of the attention of the goggling opera-goers and receiving groups of her worshippers there during the intervals. It was a chance for the middle classes to gaze upon their betters, and the management of the opera house thoughtfully included in the programme a guide showing which *grande dame* was to be seen in which box.

The Monday night of all Monday nights, though, was undoubtedly the one in January when up to four hundred people attended the annual ball at 350 Fifth Avenue. Having created a new society, Mrs Astor meant to control it, and the January ball was her most useful tool. More than even the

13

Patriarchs' balls, this was the event to which one had to be invited in order to count oneself among the elite. Over time, those whom Mrs Astor considered worthy of invitations became known simply as 'The Four Hundred' – a generally accepted collective term for everyone who was anyone. How that number was arrived at remains something of a mystery: popular legend had it that the figure was meaningless because it represented nothing more than the capacity of Caroline's ballroom, but since the huge art gallery which served that purpose could and sometimes did hold more than eight hundred people, that theory can be discounted. On the other hand, the decision to limit the number of guests to four hundred was in truth probably no less arbitrary, while the lack of explanation was no doubt a deliberate ploy on the part of McAllister – who invented the term and brought it into currency through the numerous newspaper articles he wrote about high society – aimed at tantalizing those who aspired to membership. The only justification he ever offered was typically pompous and foolish: 'If you go outside that number, you strike people who are either not at ease in a ballroom or else make other people not at ease.'

Nevertheless, the socialites of New York were ready to abide by such sanctions if they offered the opportunity to belong to an instantly identifiable elite, and Caroline Astor was equally ready to apply them if they made her clearly visible as the only queen in the pack. For the Astors of America, descendants of a German butcher's son who had set foot in the New World a mere hundred years before with no more than five English pounds in his pocket, this was their finest hour, and ever afterwards the name Astor would be recognized the world over as a synonym for wealth, luxury and 'class'.

III

If the brownstone mansion at 350 Fifth Avenue was the centre of New York as far as the new elite was concerned, there was within two miles of it another New York which the Astors and their clique did their best to ignore. This was the New York of the poor, the West Side and the Lower East Side, the New York of the tenement, that deformed child of urbanization and the

Industrial Revolution. Below Fourteenth Street lay, according to a contemporary writer, 'a wretched quarter, which extends westward to Broadway and almost indefinitely in other directions... Drunken men, depraved women and swarms of half-clad children fill the neighbourhood, and even the "improved tenement houses", as viewed from the outside, seem but sorry abodes for human beings...'

The tenement had made its appearance in New York as a result of the huge influx of immigrants to the city after 1800. Some indication of the scale of what has been called the greatest migration in history may be drawn from the fact that between 1800 and 1880, the population of New York rose from 60,515 to 1,206,299. The official division of Manhattan's limited space into lots measuring twenty-five feet by one hundred feet made it impossible to provide decent accommodation for this mass of newcomers from Europe and, after the mansions vacated by the rich as they moved to greener pastures uptown had been converted to apartments and filled to overflowing, purpose-built tenement blocks five or six storeys high began to fill up every available inch of space.

A typical tenement building on East Fourth Street was described by a *New York Tribune* reporter in 1879: 'The bedrooms were small and dark with windows 13 by 15 inches in size for ventilation. These opened on stifling hallways and admitted an atmosphere almost as bad as that within... A sick child lay in a rear room gasping for breath while its mother stirred up a fire, the heat of which made the atmosphere terrible ... the yard was unclean as were the closets which gave forth terrible stenches. Under the tenement was a cellar, the rear part of which was occupied [though this was against the law]. The rooms were four in number and were divided by a narrow hallway, the ceiling only seven feet high... There were no windows or other means of ventilation and the apartments could not well be fouler. The walls were cracked and blackened and there was a squalor visible that was revolting...' In that building lived fourteen families, comprising thirty-one adults and forty-one children.

In 1879, under the guise of improvement, there appeared a new horror – the dumbell tenement, so called because of its shape, wide at each end and narrow in the middle so as to allow

15

space for an 'airshaft' between it and its neighbours. These 'great prison-like structures of brick, with narrow doors and windows, cramped passages and steep rickety stairs ... built through from one street to the other with a somewhat narrower building connecting them' were six or seven storeys high with four apartments on each floor grouped round a central hall containing communal lavatories. The flats at the front of the building contained four rooms each and those at the rear three rooms, but few immigrant families could afford the luxury of an entire apartment to themselves at rents of between ten and twenty dollars a month. Consequently, subletting and taking in boarders was the rule. A government commission investigating the exploitation of immigrants was told that 'cots or folded beds and in many instances simply mattresses are spread about on the floor, resembling very much a lot of bunks in the steerage of an ocean steamer'. The only way to determine exactly the population of such buildings, the commission learnt, was 'by a midnight visit, and should this take place between the months of June and September, the roof of the building should not be omitted'.

The American Magazine, in a report on dumbell tenements in 1880, minced no words: 'Had the foul fiend designed these great barracks they could not have been more villainously arranged to avoid any chance of ventilation.' The alleged airshaft was 'a damp, foul-smelling place' and 'the drainage is horrible ... even the Croton [aqueduct] as it flows from the tap in the noisome courtyard seemed to be contaminated by its surroundings...' Furthermore, the magazine pointed out, these tenements were death-traps in the event of fire 'for it would be impossible for the occupants of the crowded rooms to escape by the narrow stairways, and the flimsy fire escapes which the owners of the tenements were compelled to put up ... are so laden with broken furniture, bales and boxes that they would be worse than useless...' In fact, the buildings the magazine writer had seen must have been the better sort, for as late as 1903 fifteen per cent of the tenements in the Lower East Side had no fire escapes at all.

The total population of these hellholes at the beginning of the 1880s was more than half a million men, women and children, according to the *New York Tribune*. 'It is a world in itself,' the paper commented, 'for streams of immigrants ... have been drawn into the seething current... It is a world strained with labour, racked with pain, heartsore from grief, crazed with passion, goaded on to crime, weary unto death yet condemned always to be struggling for life in dark waters...'

A world so near to yet so very far from the daily excesses of the mansion-dwellers on Fifth Avenue, but it was just as much Astor territory, nevertheless. For part of each dollar that Caroline Astor spent on gloire de Paris roses, Worth dresses and French cuisine originated in the squalor and degradation of the tenements. East Fourth Street, East Fifth, East Fourteenth, Fifteenth and Sixteenth, East Twenty-Sixth, Tenth Avenue, West Sixteenth and Seventeenth Streets, First Avenue, Elizabeth Street, West Thirtieth, Avenue A – all these and many more contained rows of stinking, overcrowded, disease-ridden buildings owned by the Astors, the bricks and mortar of their enormous wealth.

The founder of the dynasty, John Jacob Astor I, having made his fortune in the fur business and the China trade, had invested heavily in real estate at a time when Manhattan island was still dotted with farms. His purpose in buying land, when he did not need it to build a house for himself or his children, was simply to own it, nothing more, because he foresaw the unparalleled growth of New York and the wonderful effect such expansion would have on land values. And once acquired, Astor land was not sold, except in single parcels and at vast profits: it was leased to those who cared to develop it.

In those days, of course, the great migration had barely begun and it was John Jacob's heir, the first William Backhouse Astor (Caroline's father-in-law) who so took advantage of the tenement boom that he became known as the 'Landlord of New York'. Taking a lesson from the manufacturers who had realized that quantity was more profitable than quality, William B. mass-produced rents in the way that factory owners were mass-producing goods. One tenement block could generate at least double the rental income of a group of more spacious and less densely populated middle-class dwellings on the same-sized site, even though the rents of the latter would be higher. And if the tenement could be contracted to a sub-landlord responsible for the management of the building, so much the better: it was no concern of the owner what conditions for the tenants were like so long as the ground rent and percentage rolled in regularly. By this method, and by allowing others to erect tenements on vacant lots he had bought or more likely inherited, William B. Astor consolidated a real estate empire that netted about a million dollars a year. Average profits from the tenements ran at about fifteen per cent and in some cases, according to the *New York Times*, slums owned by Astor yielded fifty per cent.

To be sure, the Astors were not the only slumlords grown fat on the miseries of the Irish, German, Italian and Jewish immigrants who poured into New York in their thousands. The fortunes of many other great names – the Roosevelts, Rhinelanders, Stuyvesants and Goelets, for instance – depended to a greater or lesser extent on continually rising incomes from the tenements. But it was the Astors, the richest of them all, who had the most extensive holdings and therefore the strongest interest in holding the landlords' line against repeated waves of protest and rising pressure for reform.

As early as 1845, an investigation into conditions in the tenements concluded that, 'We who claim to be intelligent and civilized suffer our numbers and strength, the bones and sinews and hearts of our people to waste and die away in narrow and gloomy caverns of our own construction, with a rapidity surpassing the combined torrents of pestilence and war.' The inquiry found that a quarter of the children born in New York did not survive their first year, a third died before the age of five and of the remainder, half never attained the age of majority.

A decade later, the *New York Times* was appealing to the consciences of the landlords: '. . . we cannot envy the feelings of the man of wealth, surrounded though he be with luxuries and comforts, whose incomes are reaped from the rents of such houses. To know that I am living in splendid saloons while he who feeds my wealth rots in a pestiferous cellar! To live on the poison of the poor!'

Eventually the State Legislature became involved, recommending official action to curb the excesses of the slumlord, who 'digs deep and from damp foundations, rears his feeble walls far up until they tremble. He measures the height of his ceilings by the shortest of the people, and by thin partitions divides the interior into as narrow spaces as the leanest carpenter can work in.' Laws were passed, restrictions were imposed, but they were powerless against men like William B. Astor who owned the very land on which New York stood and the politicians of the day, as keen to line their own pockets as they were to win votes, were not prepared to interfere with what the upper classes at least regarded as the natural order of things.

Astor and his colleagues took the view that it was none of their business how the poor lived. For one thing, they did not administer the properties themselves, being content merely to collect rents from middlemen. Indeed, their position was underlined in many of the reports on conditions in the tenements: 'The basis of these evils is the subjection of the tenantry to the merciless inflictions and extortions of the sub-landlord. A house or a row or court of houses is hired by some person of the owner on a lease of several years for a sum which will yield a fair interest on the cost. The owner is thus relieved of the great trouble incidental to the changing of tenants and the collection of rents. His income is sure and obtained without annoyance or oppression on his part. It thus becomes the object of the lessee to make and save as much as possible with his adventure...'

Secondly, to a man like Astor whose father had reached New York with little more to his name than any latter-day immigrant, the condition of the tenement dwellers was as much their own fault as anyone else's. Was not America the land of opportunity where every man had the same chance as his neighbour to achieve success and wealth? Had not old John Jacob, product of the German peasantry, risen by his own efforts to challenge and finally surpass the Old Guard aristocracy? His example was there for the new immigrants to follow, and if they did not do so it was because they were idle and degenerate. Easy to say for a man who had never done a day's work in his life.

But there was a third reason why moral indignation at the plight of the poor could do so little to change things – the law of supply and demand. Limited space and an unlimited supply of people to fill it kept land and property at a premium and filled the coffers of the Astors and their colleagues at an ever-increasing rate. All William B. and his heir, John Jacob III, had to do was maintain the status quo and watch their fortunes grow. Both were in their day instrumental in deferring improvements in mass transit and building codes that would have relieved congestion in the slums, made life more bearable for tenement dwellers and at the same time have reduced the profits of the landlords. To the Astors, the city of New York was not a community of souls, but a collection of twenty-five by one hundred foot real estate lots.

While Caroline Astor and Ward McAllister were constructing their new elite, there rang all around them the voices of those concerned with the people at the other end of the social scale. The so-called Tenement House Sunday of 1879 saw preachers joining health officials, architects and radicals in condemnation of the slumlords, and when a disastrous outbreak of yellow fever swept through the tenements that same year, a brigade of health inspectors set out to record the full horror of the 'seething current'. In the heart of the other Astorland they found six people living in three rooms with a total floor area of two hundred and twenty-five square feet; closets undrained or relying on waste water from nearby taps; women and children sleeping and living in hallways; men making cigars in unventilated, unlit living rooms with their families around them – 'a fearful picture of misery and dirt', a *Tribune* reporter called it.

'This house is owned by Astor,' one immigrant told a Board of Health inspector, as if by way of recommendation.

'More's the pity,' the official replied.

Although the state of the market continued to give them the advantage, Astor and the other land and property owners did not much care for the sort of publicity their holdings were receiving. Piously, they signed an appeal for reform and, in 1880, dug into their pockets to provide $260,000 for the construction of a 'model' tenement on First Avenue, well away from the Lower East Side. Bathrooms were provided in the new building and every room had a window – but with the 'economic rent' fixed at fifteen dollars a month for four rooms, no slum dweller was likely to be able to take advantage of the improvements. Caroline Astor, meanwhile, was in the process of spending two million dollars on redecorating the 'cottage' her husband had just bought so that they could spend the summers in the invigorating air of Newport. And the following year, Caroline's brother-in-law, John Jacob III, joined the other big landlords in raising the general level of their rents by ten per cent. So much for improving the lot of the poor. As Mrs Alexander had written in her *Verses for Little Children*:

> The rich man in his castle,
>   The poor man at his gate,
> God hath made them, high or lowly,
>   And order'd their estate.

Thus far it seemed that the Astors might justifiably claim that God was on their side. But the ordering of their estate was very far from over.

1 *Founder's Day*

For almost the whole of the nineteenth century and at least the first half of the twentieth, the name of Astor was synonymous with vast wealth, power and privilege. The Astors of New York had become the richest family in America, leaders of society, confidants of presidents and virtually landlords of the fastest-growing city in the world. Their cousins in England had not only created a new branch of the aristocracy but also sat in Parliament and gained control of two of the nation's oldest, most respected and most influential newspapers. On both sides of the Atlantic, people looked upon the Astors with awe and perhaps envy. They were living proof of one of the basic principles of old-fashioned capitalism: that any man, however humble his origins, could become a millionaire if he was prepared to work hard and to organize his efforts according to the laws of the marketplace.

The antecedents of the Astors were humble enough. The founder of the transatlantic dynasty had started life as the fourth son of an improvident village butcher in southern Germany. The Astors were not originally German, however. A persistent legend within the family has it that they are descended from one Pedro d'Astorga, a Castillian knight killed during the Crusades who is supposed to have taken his name from his coat-of-arms, which featured a hawk – *azor* in Spanish. More likely, the mysterious Pedro hailed from the ancient town of Astorga in Castile's neighbouring province, Leon, but in any case his link with the Astors who were to be found in the village of Walldorf, near Heidelberg, some five centuries later is extremely doubtful. More certain is the connexion between the Walldorf Astors and one Jean-Jacques d'Astorg, who appeared in the area in the late 1680s and married a Walldorf girl, Anna Margaretha Eberhard, in 1692.

Where this d'Astorg got his name from is unclear, though since he came from Savoy, the precarious little duchy between France and Italy, and he spoke Italian as well as French, it is possible that he had Italian blood. There were certainly Astorgas in southern Italy before the seventeenth century. At any rate, it is known that Jean-Jacques d'Astorg was a Protestant, almost certainly a member of the Waldensian sect, a heretical movement that sprang up among the Alpine valleys during the Middle Ages, broke with the Church of Rome and later allied itself to the Protestant reformers of Switzerland and Germany. The Waldensians of Savoy had been protected to some extent against repeated persecution on behalf of successive Popes and Catholic kings of France, but the revocation of the Edict of Nantes in 1685 and the fact that the then Duke of Savoy, a boy of ten, was no more than a vassal of King Louis XIV, made even the remote duchy unsafe for the individualistic sectarians. D'Astorg was one of many who fled in search of places where they would be free to worship as they pleased. Heidelberg was a natural choice: as the headquarters of the Calvinist movement it was a refuge for Protestants of various shades who, despite doctrinal differences, united in their opposition to the Catholic hierarchy. And if it was peace that Jean-Jacques sought, he could hardly have chosen better than Walldorf. Though only about eight miles from the university city of Heidelberg, the village nestled sleepy and unchanging amid the farms and vineyards of the Neckar valley on the edge of the Black Forest.

D'Astorg must either have salvaged some of whatever wealth had been his in Savoy or else have taken a wife with a substantial dowry, for he is pictured as a minor landowner of the district, with income to keep him in something approaching gentlemanly style. But if this was truly the case, there was certainly some dissipation after his death in 1711, for his grandson – an entirely Germanized Johann Jakob Astor (or Asdor, or Ashdour, or Ashtour), born in 1724 – could do no better than an apprenticeship to the trade of butchering. The butcher in the rural Germany of the eighteenth century was a far cry from the jolly fellow in the straw boater and striped apron we might picture today: Astor would tour the local farms when required to slaughter and dress the animals selected and

23

fattened to provide the domestic food supply. It was hard physical work, not very pleasant, not very regular and certainly not likely to make the practitioner rich. But none of that worried Johann Jakob. What little is known of him portrays a man apparently content with his lot in life, given to the way of the flesh rather than the spirit, prepared to work hard when he had to and otherwise to maintain his strength by repeatedly raising a beer tankard to his lips. A simple man, with simple needs, no ambition and not much sensitivity.

By the age of twenty-six, Johann Jakob was doing well enough to marry and in 1752 his first child, George, was born. Three more sons and two daughters followed, then in 1766 his wife, Maria Magdalena, died, probably in her mid-thirties. A man with six children to rear could not be without a wife, so Johann Jakob married a second time, though this proved to be of little benefit to his offspring since he went on to father six more. Recollections have dealt rather unkindly with the second Frau Astor, but it must be said that whatever her character she would have been hard pressed to provide the care and attention the children of her predecessor felt they deserved when she had so many babies of her own to bring up. Maria Magdalena's brood, however, seem to have resented both the stepmother and the second family, for as soon as they were able they tended to leave what had become an overcrowded home – the girls to marry, of course, the boys to seek their fortunes elsewhere. Domestic considerations apart, the older boys could see that Walldorf was never going to be anything more than a backwater: even the once magical Heidelberg had lost some of its glitter, the Elector of the Palatinate having moved his court from there to Mannheim.

George, naturally, was the first to go, an uncle in London securing him a job in a company making musical instruments with which he was connected. The second son, Henry, seemed more likely to stay at home since he was learning butchering from his father, but in 1776 he seized his opportunity when the German princelings began to raise mercenary regiments to help the Hanoverian King George III of England to suppress a rebellion in the colonies of America. By September of that year Henry was in British-held New York, not as a soldier but as a sutler, acquiring and preparing meat to feed the Regiment of

Hesse: his father's training had paid off, though not in quite the way Johann Jakob had intended, and would do so more handsomely in the years to come.

In the spring of 1777, the third brother, John Melchior, aged seventeen, disappeared quite suddenly, turning up later in the service of a nobleman in a distant province. The two girls married as soon as they could. That left the youngest boy, born on 17 July 1763 and named John Jacob after his father. He it was who would imprint the name of Astor – and indeed of Walldorf – on the map of history.

John Jacob was now fourteen, well built and strong like his father but with an alert mind said to have been inherited from his mother. He was rather self-contained, even a little morose, and possessed of a quiet determination that stirred dreams in him even as he uncomplainingly heaved carcases in the barn with his unsympathetic father.

Many years afterwards, reminiscing as old men will, John Jacob Astor would talk of having tramped as much as forty-five miles in a single day – presumably from Walldorf to Mannheim and back – to collect the letters his brothers sent from England and America. The boy's imagination was excited by George's descriptions of life in the great city and even more by Henry's stories of the vast, untapped and underpopulated land in which he found himself and where he was beginning to see his future. But it was to be London that gave John Jacob his first taste of freedom. Among the letters he collected was one from George suggesting that John Melchior should join him in the musical instrument business, and since John Melchior had decided to go his own way Jacob asked that he be allowed to take his brother's place. So it was that in the spring of 1779 the sixteen-year-old butcher's boy left his native village and set off on the first part of a journey that was to take him farther than anyone in Walldorf could possibly have dreamed of.

A little way out of the village on that fateful day, John Jacob paused for a moment beneath a tree and, according to a story which he himself probably originated, laid down three rules for the life on which he was embarking: that he would be honest, that he would be industrious and that he would never gamble. Hard working he most certainly was: a gambler he was not, except once and then only in a business sense. As to his honesty, there may perhaps be differing opinions about that.

The river Neckar joins the Rhine not far west of Walldorf, near the town of Speyer, and it was to this confluence that John Jacob made his way, knowing that the great artery of Europe offered the quickest route to the North Sea coast. He joined the crew of one of the vast rafts of Black Forest timber that were steered down the Rhine for export and in little more than two weeks he was in Holland with enough money in his pocket to book a passage to England. Arriving in London, he contrived to find his way to the Broadwood musical instrument factory where his brother worked and in no time at all he was settled in both a job and lodgings which George obtained for him.

Details of young Astor's life in London are sparse and unreliable. His first task, obviously, was to learn English and he would later boast of being reasonably proficient in the language after six weeks (though he never lost a heavy German accent). He had a secure job and a reasonably comfortable existence, and there were undoubtedly opportunities for advancement in the musical instrument business, particularly in view of his family connexions; yet this was a slow and frustrating course to a youth fired with ambition, and besides his background was a serious handicap in class-ridden England. America, where the rebel colonists, who now seemed to be winning their war for independence, had declared against the yoke of birth – that was a place where a man might achieve all he was capable of. Henry's letters from New York continued to be encouraging: he had by now abandoned military life and gone into business for himself, obtaining meat from whatever source he could and selling it to whoever would pay. His younger brother, whether or not he had originally seen London as no more than a first step, determined to make his way to America as soon as possible. He saved as much money as he could, working from dawn to dusk making instruments, but some indication of the handicap his ambition suffered may be gained from noting that in four years John Jacob managed to accumulate only about fifteen pounds in savings – this at a time when a guinea would hardly buy a man a decent wig and a respectable suit of clothes would cost at least five pounds.

Nevertheless, John Jacob considered those savings substantial enough to set him on his way to America and during the very month when the British finally evacuated New York, November 1783, he set sail from Liverpool having negotiated a steerage passage for the sum of five pounds. Among his meagre baggage were seven Broadwood flutes, which had cost him a further five pounds but which he reckoned would be marketable goods in America (and they were at least easy to transport). These expenses had reduced his capital to the equivalent of twenty-five American dollars, which meant that when his ship became icebound in Chesapeake Bay towards the end of January 1784, John Jacob could not afford to take one of the coaches that eventually came out over the ice to convey the voyagers to Baltimore, and he had to wait almost two months before he could set foot in what was to be his adopted country.

The delay was not without value, however, since John Jacob fell in with a young German who had some experience of the American fur trade and who told the hopeful immigrant of the huge profits to be made from pelts that were sold for next to nothing by Indians. Through this man, Astor also became acquainted with officials of the century-old Hudson's Bay Company who were travelling in the same ship, and from them he learnt how a great fur trading operation was conducted. From such conversations, it must have become clear that the fur business was one in which the enterprising individual trader was on almost equal terms with a large, established corporation. Moreover, the amount of capital required to get into the market was not beyond the realms of possibility. John Jacob stored away such impressions for future reference.

At this point, the story of Astor's arrival in the New World becomes somewhat confused, which is hardly surprising since very little documentary evidence of his progress has survived and what is 'known' is based on the sketchy recollections of contemporaries elicited many years later. One version has it that when his ship eventually did make port, John Jacob went ashore to explore and met a Swiss shopkeeper named Tuschdy who volunteered to sell his flutes for him at no commission. Impressed by such a welcome, the story goes on, John Jacob remained in Baltimore until the instruments were sold and then departed for New York with a well-filled pocketbook. Another account, however, pictures Astor travelling to New York by coach in the company of his German fur-trading friend and spending almost all his remaining twenty-five dollars in the process.

Of the two, the second version seems more likely, for if he had been flush with cash when he reached New York Astor would not have felt compelled immediately to take a lowly job as a delivery boy and street hawker for a German baker in the Bowery, which he certainly did and which appears to have been something of an embarrassment to him in later life. In fact, when looking back John Jacob liked to give the impression that fur trading had been in his mind even before he left London and that, emboldened by the advice of his German travelling companion, he had quickly sold the 'merchandise suited to the American market' which he had brought with him and invested the proceeds in peltry. Thus the tale of the Swiss flute-seller of Baltimore may have been an attempt to gloss over his early struggles and to point up the shrewdness and extraordinary capacity for business dealing for which he had become justly famous. After all, in his mature years Astor had the reputation of possessing almost magical business acumen and if he flattered himself that he had carefully plotted his path to fortune from the very beginning, people would have believed him, just as they apparently accepted that when still a boy in Walldorf he had had a premonition that one day he would be master of enormous wealth.

In all probability, then, Astor arrived in New York virtually penniless, with no real thought of the actual way in which he was to make his fortune and little idea of how to begin. Obviously, his first move was to find brother Henry, by now an established meat trader in the Fulton Market – in spite of having been officially on the 'wrong side' in the revolutionary war. A living example of the principle that the true businessman has no friends and no enemies, only customers, Henry had cheerfully purveyed viands to both sides in the conflict, careless of whether the animals he slaughtered had been obtained legitimately or were the products of rapine by the British raiding parties that forayed into the countryside. Indeed, there are suspicions that Henry may have indulged in a little thievery himself when demand outstripped supply in those confused times. Still, when the British troops and those Americans loyal to King George finally withdrew, Henry did not hesitate to throw in his lot with the builders of the new republic and he was rewarded by steadily growing prosperity. He married the stepdaughter of a fellow German immigrant and left her to mind the market stall while he travelled about buying livestock and investing his profits in land.

Not surprisingly, Henry offered John Jacob a start in his own business – after all, butchering was something they both knew about – but that was definitely not what the younger Astor had in mind. For one thing, he could have been a butcher back in Walldorf and for another he had already rejected the slow climb to modest prosperity offered by George in London. Though he would certainly accept help, he knew that he must strike out on his own if he was to take full advantage of this land of opportunity.

Going it alone, however, was not something John Jacob could do right away, and at Henry's suggestion he went to work for a German baker named George Dietrich, who had a shop in Queen Street (which was renamed Pearl Street some time later) at the bottom of the Bowery. Adding his voice to the cacophony of street cries that characterized the Bowery was even less promising than selling meat with Henry, but at least it gave Astor the chance to become acquainted with New York and its ways, as well as providing free bed and board. Legend has it that while John Jacob was exploring the city, he passed a row of elegant new houses on Broadway and promised himself: 'I'll build, one day or other, a greater house than any of these in this very street.' He would never be able to fulfil his boast as a baker's boy, but that job was to last no more than a few weeks for in his travels around the Bowery Astor had noticed something that was too much of a coincidence to be ignored: the premises of a fur merchant who needed a clerk. The conversations aboard the ship from England came back to him, the talk of Indians prepared to sell for a few beads and trinkets, the limitless demand of the European market, profits out of all proportion to capital outlay. He applied for the job and got it.

His employer, an elderly Quaker named Robert Bowne, offered two dollars a week with board and lodging and, to Astor's delight, there was not much clerking to be done. Beating furs to keep moths out of them (a back-breaking and thoroughly unpleasant task), rummaging through piles of pelts brought from the north by schooner, negotiating prices, selecting the best skins for shipment, John Jacob soon began to learn all there was to know about the business side of the fur trade. His keen wits, diligence and enthusiasm impressed Bowne to such an extent that in the autumn of 1784 the merchant trusted his young assistant to go bartering for pelts with the farmers of the hinterland, and by the spring of the following year Astor was journeying north up the Hudson River into Indian country to acquire furs at source.

Even in the midst of the modern muddle of expressways, parkways, thruways and interstates with which twentieth-century civilization has blighted the countryside, it requires no great leap of the imagination to picture upstate New York as it appeared to John Jacob Astor on that first journey – a wild, dangerous land of primeval forests, broad rivers, rushing torrents and deep, silent lakes. Barely beyond the crowded confines of New York city, the sheer Palisades tower at the edge of the Hudson, which broadens farther on into the moody magnificence of Tappan Zee and Haverstraw Bay, while the gloomy Catskills and the Blue Mountains are mere curtain-raisers for the lonely, lake-dotted splendour of the Adirondacks, stretching almost to the shores of the mighty St Lawrence. Away from the cities and the dormitory towns with their spacious frame houses, it still looks like frontier country, which it certainly was when John Jacob travelled through it.

It must have been breathtaking to the young German immigrant as he set off that spring, with the trees in leaf, the rivers and lakes well filled from the winter snows. Probably he did not venture very far into the wilderness on this occasion, but far enough to gain some insights into the ways of the proud and suspicious Iroquois Indians and of the half-savage white fur trappers who shared the life of the native 'long house'. And he undoubtedly penetrated far enough to discern both the abundance of fur-bearing animals and the fact that emergent America was being robbed of a precious natural resource.

The fur trade at that time was monopolized by the British colonists of Canada and the centre of its operation was Montreal. So important was fur as a source of revenue to British businesses and the Crown that the government in London continued to ignore part of the Treaty of Ghent, by which the revolutionary war had been officially ended, and retained a line of forts stretching eastward from Detroit to Lake Champlain, within what was ostensibly American territory. This military presence ensured that furs collected in the Great Lakes region went north into Canada and thence directly to London, rather than south to New York. The monopoly was controlled by the venerable Hudson's Bay Company and the Northwest Company, an association of previously independent traders set up to end the disastrous and often bloody competition which had followed the expulsion of the French and their fur trading system from Canada in 1762. The two companies maintained strings of trading posts around the Great Lakes to which the Indians could bring their pelts, and also financed expeditions by groups of white and half-breed trappers, who received a commission for their services.

But, as John Jacob was quick to see, this monopoly organization was far from being tight. It depended upon two factors that could hardly have been less reliable – the Indians and the *coureurs des bois*, or 'forest rangers', as the trappers were romantically called.

The Indians of the Great Lakes and St Lawrence region were roughly divided into two main, mutually antagonistic groups, the Algonquins and Iroquois. At first, both groups had savagely resisted white settlement but since the Europeans had shown no signs of departing, the Indians had begun to form alliances with the various nationalities colonizing North America, depending on which seemed the most likely to help them in their own tribal conflicts. The French, for example, entered into a pact with the Algonquin tribes, though that succeeded only in infuriating the more powerful Iroquois who, trying to preserve the dominion of their Six Nations (Mohawks, Senecas, Tuscaroras, Cayugas, Oneidas and Onondagas) over what is now New York State, sided first with the Dutch and then with the British and ultimately became a decisive element in the defeat of France in North America. With the British in control, however, the Iroquois realized that they had helped to crush one form of tyranny only to see it replaced by another, and they began to feel a growing sense of bitterness which the War of Independence merely exacerbated since it dashed forever any hopes of the Six Nations returning to their former supremacy.

Thus, while the Indians had to trade and to maintain relations with the white man in order to survive, they did so with no great relish, while for their part the British and Americans regarded the natives as barbarous and untrustworthy savages whose only value lay in being exploited.

As for the fabled 'forest rangers', many of them were of French extraction and therefore unlikely to be very fond of the British companies which had taken over the fur trade, while all were men of fiercely independent spirit, acknowledging no loyalty other than to the precarious and harsh freedom of the woods. It mattered not to them whether it was the Northwest Company or the Hudson's Bay Company that bought their pelts, as long as they received payment enough to buy clothing and equipment and provide an occasional sampling of the delights civilization had to offer.

Such, then, were the weak links in the chain of the British fur monopoly, and John Jacob Astor saw clearly how a shrewd and determined outsider could break them. Already he was skimming a little of the British companies' profits through purchasing directly a few of the furs that otherwise would have been shipped to Montreal, but it was obvious that by winning the confidence of the Indians and forest rangers and by establishing a network of agents such as Hudson's Bay and Northwest had, he could in time push the British entrepreneurs off American soil.

Astor began to dream of a new fur trading monopoly, based in New York and with himself at its head. He had left Walldorf to make his fortune and, like many another aspiring capitalist, he discovered that the easiest way of achieving his aim was to fix upon a plentiful natural resource that could be obtained very cheaply and was so much in demand as to fetch vastly inflated resale prices. In short, he had hit upon what would prove to be one of the main foundations of American success.

II

Great wealth was not the only dream shimmering on the horizon when John Jacob Astor and his pack of furs were borne down the Hudson aboard an Albany sloop as spring turned to summer in 1785. He had fallen in love with a Bowery girl, Sarah Todd, and had hopes of marrying her before the year was out. Sarah was no raving beauty, but she had a winning smile and big dark eyes – added to which she came from good, hard-working, down-to-earth (if not rather dour) Scottish stock and her commonsense attitude to life matched John Jacob's own. They met, so the story goes, during Astor's first weeks in New York, when he was selling cakes for Dietrich. Sarah helped her widowed mother to run a boarding house at 81 Queen Street, which was near both the baker's shop and the premises of Astor's second employer, Robert Bowne.

John Jacob thought Sarah was pretty; for his part, he had a certain quality which seldom failed to impress people and he was also tolerably good looking. Sarah encouraged him to call on her, and he quickly won the approval of Mrs Todd with his frankness, diligence, ambition and irrepressible confidence. In spite of his heavy accent, he talked well and he could entertain on the piano as well as the flute. He had no money, of course, but Mrs Todd would not have been alone if she had sensed that John Jacob Astor was a young man who would go far – besides which, Sarah seemed to be completely besotted with him.

After his successful trip upstate, Astor received a pay rise from Robert Bowne and began to make plans for his marriage. First, however, his employer dispatched him to London with a consignment of furs. The actual date of this journey is uncertain. Astor himself placed it in 1784, but that would appear unlikely since he had barely started to work for Bowne then and knew little of buying and selling pelts. Such evidence as exists is entirely circumstantial, but it points to the year 1785 for the voyage. For one thing, Bowne would have felt much more confidence in his clerk's ability to sell furs once Astor had proved his shrewdness in buying them. Secondly, Astor married Sarah in September 1785 and they set up home in two ground-floor rooms at 81 Queen Street, where Astor went into business for himself the following spring. The implication is that having made contact with some of the great merchants in London and having seen for himself the enormous profits that fur shippers were making, John Jacob returned to New York more determined than ever to go into business on his own account rather than working so hard to make someone else rich.

There is yet a further reason for believing that Astor made his journey to London some time during the summer of 1785. Until March of that year he had been advertising 'Flutes of Superior Quality' (presumably those he had brought with him from England) for sale at the offices of the *New York Packet*, the weekly paper in which his advertisement appeared. By May 1786, the *Packet* offered the information that 'an elegant assortment of Musical Instruments, such as pianofortes, spinnets, the best of violins, German flutes, clarinets, hautboys ... strings, music books and paper' had recently been imported from London and were to be obtained at 81 Queen Street. This points to John Jacob having visited Broadwoods in person to arrange for shipment of more instruments to sell. It is highly unlikely – even allowing for the influence of brother George – that such a deal, almost certainly involving long-term credit, could have been struck by letter.

The musical instrument business was to be the foundation of Astor's operations for some time to come. He was well aware that fur trading, still largely ignored by American entrepreneurs in view of the difficulties of competing with the British, offered him the best chance of success, but he needed time and financial support to build up his enterprise to the point where he could buy a stake in the bulk market of Montreal. He was both acute enough to seize the opportunity to import musical instruments into a country where they were in short supply and lucky enough to have a family link with manufacturers that allowed him to trade on favourable terms. Also, Astor was a pure businessman in the sense that he would deal in anything likely to show a profit. The fact that his first fortune (there was a second, greater one to come) was made in the fur trade signifies only that it was where he saw the prospects of the greatest profit. In that, perhaps, lay part of the secret of his early success against the monopolists north of the border: for them, the so-called *seigneurs* of the lakes and forests, buying and selling furs was not just a business but a way of life.

With musical instruments to provide a base income and Sarah to mind the store in her mother's front room, Astor's adventures in the fur trade got their start from the dowry of three hundred dollars his wife brought him. This he used to equip himself and buy trade goods for expeditions into the interior, to cover transportation of pelts back to New York, to buy shipping space across the Atlantic and so on. In the spring of 1786 he took ship up the Hudson for the first time on his own behalf, having undertaken a second trial run as Bowne's representative the previous autumn and no doubt having cannily remained in the Quaker's employ throughout the winter while he laid his own plans. During the next few years his stocky, five-foot-nine frame, square-jawed face and yellow hair would become a familiar and even welcome sight on the forest trails, in the Indian villages and among the growing white settlements of New York state.

'He began his career,' his friend Washington Irving wrote, 'on the narrowest scale; but he brought to the task a persevering industry, rigid economy and strict integrity. To these were added an aspiring spirit that always looked upwards; a genius bold, fertile, and expansive; a sagacity quick to grasp and convert every circumstance to its advantage, and a singular and never wavering confidence of signal success.'

To the residents of Albany, Astor was almost a harbinger of spring, arriving with the first sloop to get through from New York as the ice melted each year. In the early days, he would strike out on foot along the Indian trail snaking westward through Schenectady, Utica, the Onondaga settlement that was to become Syracuse, Rochester, and finally Buffalo, at the northern tip of Lake Erie. This journey of more than two hundred and fifty miles, which can now be covered by car in about four and a half hours on Route 90, would have taken Astor two to three weeks, depending on the weather and the length of time he stayed in the towns, villages and encampments through which he passed. It was fraught with difficulty and danger. A sudden spring blizzard could cover the countryside with several feet of snow, or a torrential rainstorm make streams impassable and cause landslides. There was always the possibility of encountering savage beasts or hostile Indians, and some of the wild forest rangers thought no more of killing a competitor than they did of slaughtering muskrat or beaver. John Jacob needed all his persevering industry, sagacity and singular confidence to face such a trek.

But face it he did, and survived it, and prospered from it. His uncertain health in later life may perhaps be attributed to these early hardships, but as a strong young fellow in his mid-

35

twenties he shouldered his heavy pack – never less than sixty pounds of barter goods – strapped on his powder horn and hunting knife, picked up his musket and made the ways of the wilderness his own. Unlike most of the other small traders he did not revel in the freedom of the forest or the rough cameraderie of the trail. He embarked on his overland expeditions simply because they represented the cheapest way of obtaining pelts and therefore of maximizing the profits from their sale, and he took care to maintain good relations with the trappers and dealers he met because he knew that their experience could benefit him. Also, he was earning the respect of the Indians, coureurs and traders who, he felt sure, would be working for him in the not-too-distant future. So he pushed on, west towards the Great Lakes or north into the Adirondacks, bringing back bundles of pelts which at journey's end had to be unpacked, beaten, sorted, graded and repacked. It was a back-breaking life, but Astor had never been afraid of hard work and at least he could console himself with the knowledge that few other small businessmen could count on a return of up to one thousand per cent on their goods.

At first, Astor sold most of his furs through the regular auctions in Albany, though some of the rarer ones he would ship downriver for Sarah to sell in the shop. It was not long, however, before his efforts began really to pay off, not only financially but also in terms of his ambitions. Although he always drove a hard bargain, the fur trappers seemed to like dealing with him, partly, no doubt, because they knew he had first-hand knowledge of the trade, but mainly because they received from him the full value of their pelts, rather than having to settle for whatever the powerful Hudson's Bay or Northwest agents gave them or to rely on the paltry commissions from company-backed expeditions. In time, therefore, Astor was able to arrange for his suppliers to bring their furs to collection points in the trailside settlements – usually general stores, like that of his friend Peter Smith in Utica – which meant that instead of footslogging two hundred and fifty miles he could travel by wagon and thus purchase pelts in larger quantities, since he did not have to carry them on his back. More and more bundles with Astor's name on them began to be loaded on the Hudson River sloops, and by the beginning of

1789 the little shop in Widow Todd's front room had a new line to advertise:

> John Jacob Astor At No. 81 Queen Street, Next door but one to the Friends' Meeting House, Has for sale an assortment of Piano Fortes of the Newest Construction, made by the best makers in London, which he will sell at reasonable terms.
>
> He gives cash for all kinds of Furs And has for sale a quantity of Canada Beavers and Beaver Coating, Raccoon Skins, and Raccoon Blankets, Muskrat Skins etc., etc.

By that time, Astor was mixing with the highest and mightiest in the fur trade. Two years previously he had had the good fortune to meet Alexander Henry, a legendary Canadian trapper and frontiersman who also happened to be one of the sixteen major shareholders of the Northwest Company. Henry had been impressed by the young German's grasp of his business, and not least by the spirit which had led Astor to take to the forest tracks himself, and had invited his new acquaintance to the annual meeting of the Northwest Company held at Fort William, a small town on the northern shore of Lake Superior, almost two thousand miles west of Montreal. Washington Irving described well the importance and style of this meeting:

> To behold the Northwest Company in all its state and grandeur . . . it was necessary to witness an annual gathering at the great interior place of conference established at Fort William, near what is called the Grand Portage . . . Here two or three of the leading partners from Montreal proceeded once a year to meet the partners from the various trading posts of the wilderness, to discuss the affairs of the company during the preceding year, and to arrange plans for the future . . . Here, in an immense wooden building, was the great council hall, as also the banqueting chamber, decorated with Indian arms and accoutrements, and the trophies of the fur trade . . . The councils were held in great state, for every member felt as if

sitting in parliament, and every retainer and dependent looked up to the assemblage with awe, as to the House of Lords. There was a vast deal of solemn deliberation, and hard Scottish reasoning, with an occasional swell of pompous declaration.

These grave and weighty councils were alternated by huge feasts and revels, like some of the old feasts described in Highland castles. The tables in the great banqueting room groaned under the weight of game of all kinds; of venison from the woods, and fish from the lakes, with hunters' delicacies, such as buffaloes' tongues, and beavers' tails, and various luxuries from Montreal, all served up by experienced cooks brought for the purpose. There was no stint of generous wine, for it was a hard-drinking period, a time of loyal toasts, and bacchanalian songs, and brimming bumpers.

This was an order of business very different from what young John Jacob Astor was used to, and an introduction to it by the great Alexander Henry was a wonderful opportunity. Accordingly in 1788 – the year his first child, Magdalen, was born – Astor journeyed to Montreal and thence by one of the Company's huge cargo canoes to Fort William. Impressive as the ceremonial must have been, John Jacob was struck much more forcibly by the sheer scale of the Company's operations, which brought home to him the fact that annual tours of upstate New York were never going to place him in the front rank of fur dealers: he must establish a network of trading posts and let the pelts come to him and, while he could still turn a handsome profit supplying the domestic market, he must get into the export business, where the real money was to be made.

Astor learnt something, too, about trading with the Indians when he visited Michilimackinac, an island at the eastern end of the straits between Lakes Huron and Michigan, which was one of the places still held by the British in defiance of the peace treaty with America and was the location of the Northwest Company's main depot and trading post. Most of the thousands of furs stored at Michilimackinac came from the North-West Territory, but Astor noted that canoes loaded with cheap liquor were heading south towards the Indian villages of the American mainland. Northwest agents explained that the Indians would sell almost anything in exchange for alcohol and were also much easier to deal with (that is, to exploit) when tipsy. The British government forbade the sale of liquor to Indians in the territories it controlled but, as the Northwest men pointed out, those territories did not include the region south of the Great Lakes. Astor stored away the information against the day when he would need a competitive edge.

On the long journey back to Manhattan, John Jacob began to formulate his strategy for capturing a significant portion of the international fur business. Volume was the key: he must buy more to sell more in order to increase his profits and still compete with the Northwest Company on price. It would take time to build up the network of suppliers such quantities would demand, and while he was doing that he would have to buy in bulk from Montreal for the export market. The problem with that was the British government's insistence that furs bought in Canada could only be exported to London and the American government's ban on direct imports from the British colonies, but Astor reasoned that if he bought furs in Montreal and sold them in London, he could use his profit both to finance his own fur-gathering operations and to buy other goods in Britain which he could import and sell in America, thus making a further profit.

He could also, of course, re-export some of his pelts from London for sale in America, and he may well have made such an arrangement on his way back through Montreal towards the end of the summer of 1788, which would have been another reason for his advertisement in the *Packet* in January the following year. Probably he also collected furs from Albany as he passed through. However he did it, he appears to have had a good year, for the records show that on 18 May 1789 he was able to follow the advice of his brother Henry, who had begun to invest in Manhattan real estate, and sink $250 of his profits into several parcels of land in the Bowery which Henry happened to be selling. Many years later John Jacob was to say, with hindsight, that he should have bought every foot of Manhattan. Such a remark reinforces the impression of him as a man whose main interest in life was making a lot of money and who would turn his hand to whatever line of business was likely to show most profit.

For the time being, however, Astor was devoting himself to the fur trade, and early in 1790 he moved his family out of Widow Todd's boarding house and into larger premises he had bought at 40 Little Dock Street (which later became part of Water Street). The ground floor of this building was a shop and there was ample living space, with three bedrooms, above it. John Jacob needed the extra space for the increased quantities of furs he expected to be handling and also because Sarah was pregnant again – in fact, the child, a girl, died in infancy, but Sarah began her third pregnancy later that year. That he could afford to pay $850 for his new quarters was an indication of how well he was doing. He had made his first big purchase in Montreal, was beginning to ship regularly to London and was importing a variety of barter and other goods either for retail sale in New York or for his growing number of agents upstate to use in trade with the Indians. Just how favourable the terms of business were may be seen in contemporary records. A dealer could sell a beaver pelt in London at about twenty-five shillings (roughly equivalent to three dollars); for the same price he could buy a musket for which, in trading with the Indians, he could get ten first-quality beaver skins. A 'point' blanket, so called because the number of skins required in exchange was shown by lines of stitching at the edge, would fetch between six and ten pelts according to size.

It is hardly surprising, then, that at a time when $750 (or in England about £300) a year allowed a man to live comfortably and even with a degree of style, Astor was prosperous enough to invest a little less than $7,000 in his real estate sideline between 1789 and 1791. Not that John Jacob bothered very much in those days about the style in which he lived. He had his own home and shop, and his family – which by 1791 included two children, a girl and a boy – was well fed, but there were no luxuries. Indeed, the richer he became the more Astor pleaded poverty, and although he no longer tramped the trails of the wilderness he would spend at least half of each year journeying to and from Montreal to buy his main supply of furs in person, would still sort and beat the pelts in his shop, and would sometimes be found among the docks of South Street helping to load or unload a ship so that he might be in a position to count his profits a little bit sooner.

But while he was still prepared to do hard physical work, Astor was now moving out of the shallow waters of mere trading and into the main current of New York business. He sensed that although the hand of the old colonial, land-owning elite remained on the tiller, the fuel that would make America surge forward was money and that those who were making the money would be the ones actually to set the course, which would naturally lead towards the horizons that best suited them. Accordingly, John Jacob began to frequent places where the leading businessmen gathered, going so far as to purchase in 1792 a share of the Tontine Coffee House, a favourite meeting place of the mercantile class. Through that and becoming a Mason (joining the same Lodge as Governor George Clinton and the powerful state chancellor, Robert R. Livingston, who had helped to draft the Declaration of Independence), Astor gradually made connexions, rubbing shoulders with the likes of Stephen Van Rensselaer and the future vice-president, Aaron Burr. He was to make good use of such men later on.

It may seem surprising that at this comparatively early stage in his career, the obscure butcher's son with the heavy accent, who had thus far spent more time in the canoe and the Indian lodge than in the drawing room, should be accepted into the company of the most influential businessmen and politicians in New York. Indeed, earlier writers – picturing Astor as a boorish, ill-mannered, socially ignorant peasant – attribute his success in attracting rich and powerful friends to some almost magical quality in his character. Forceful and charismatic he undoubtedly was, but a moment's reflection will show that his social rise was not as startling as all that.

For a start, the manners of the eighteenth century were far less rigid and stilted than the Victorian inventions we have inherited and adapted, and furthermore there is no reason to suppose, as more credulous chroniclers have, that John Jacob would have been unable to hold his own in polite society. It is somewhat romantic to picture an awkward German country boy shocking the New York nabobs with his social gaffes yet being tolerated and even fawned upon to some extent, but it must be remembered that as well as having received a solid education, Astor had spent four years in London, where he could hardly have failed to become aware of what was considered acceptable behaviour. Moreover, the evidence for his supposed lack of social graces comes from a highly unreliable source: the vain, snobbish and rather foolish James Gallatin, son of President Jefferson's treasury secretary, Albert Gallatin (of whom more later). The younger Gallatin sneered at John Jacob's table manners, noting in his diary that at dinner Astor had eaten both peas and ice cream with a knife, which is an almost impossible feat demanding an extraordinary degree of manual dexterity. Later, in a journal peppered with pretentious French phrases, Gallatin recorded his horror at an incident during a family luncheon attended by Astor in Paris: 'Really Mr Astor is dreadful... He came to *dejeuner* today; we were simply *en famille*, he sitting next to Frances [James Gallatin's sister]. He actually wiped his fingers on the sleeves of her fresh white spencer. Mamma in discreet tones said, "Oh, Mr Astor, I must apologize; they have forgotten to give you a serviette." I think he felt foolish.' He probably did feel foolish, having no doubt, out of the corner of his eye, mistaken the white material of the young lady's bodice for the napkin the servants had failed to provide.

Possibly Astor did not know or care about the finer points of etiquette, but at a time when large quantities of food and drink were consumed by the wealthy with very little ceremony, and when it was not unusual for a man to blow his nose without benefit of handkerchief, or to break wind or pick his teeth without embarrassment, his manners would not have caused much comment except among people, like James Gallatin, of exceedingly delicate sensibilities. A greater obstacle in his attempts to win friends and influence people would have been the fact that he had no background. Even the elder Gallatin felt that the 'peddler of furs' was out of his class. But here Astor's path was smoothed by his rather mysterious friendship with the rich and highly respected New York merchant William Backhouse, the American representative of a British mercantile, banking and coal-owning family.

It is not clear precisely when, why and how William

Backhouse took up the young immigrant. Some have said it was Backhouse, himself a dealer in furs, who convinced John Jacob that prosperity was to be found in pelts. This seems improbable, since Astor started to work for Robert Bowne very soon after his arrival in New York and would have been unlikely to have come into contact with a businessman of Backhouse's standing in the days when he was a cake seller. Bowne may have known Backhouse and have introduced him to his bright new clerk, or Astor may have sold Backhouse some of the rarer varieties of pelts in which he dabbled independently while working for Bowne. Most probably, though, John Jacob had dealings with Backhouse's brother Thomas, a leading London furrier, during his early excursion across the Atlantic on Bowne's behalf and was given an introduction to the New York branch of the family.

At any rate, Astor appears to have made a considerable impression on the elderly Englishman, who entertained him in his Broadway home, offered help and advice – perhaps even financial aid, which John Jacob frequently sought as his business outgrew his capital – and provided an entrée to the New York business community. As well as outstanding business acumen, John Jacob displayed a remarkable gift for making the right contacts (at least in his early years – later on, he simply bought them). But there must have been a genuine feeling between him and Backhouse, for John Jacob named his third child after his mentor, a second son born on 19 September 1792, just a few weeks after the death of William Backhouse.

By the time of William Backhouse Astor's birth, his father had moved out of Little Dock Street and into even larger quarters at 149 Broadway, where the more conservative leading citizens still lived among the maples and tulip trees, although the great migration uptown had already begun. The Astors continued to live above the shop, but the process of what modern social scientists have labelled 'upward mobility' – always a potent driving force in American life – was well and truly under way. A couple of years later that process was to accelerate as a result of one of those developments that tend to favour the well-placed businessman in an emergent nation.

America's relations with Britain had been at best uneasy since the signing of the peace treaty in 1783, particularly in view of the British refusal to honour one of the articles of that treaty requiring withdrawal from the border forts, but matters worsened in 1793 when America's ally France declared war on Britain, and the British – who had steadfastly refused to enter into a trade agreement with the United States – began to seize American ships headed for French ports. In April the following year, the House of Representatives began to debate a bill to impose an embargo on trade with Britain until the north-western forts had been evacuated, but President Washington, fearing a new war with the former colonial power, dispatched John Jay (chief justice of the Supreme Court and one of the negotiators of the original treaty) to London to reach the most satisfactory accommodation he could. The mission itself, let alone any potential treaty, was considered treacherous by the Republican Party, so the agreement with which Jay returned to New York in May 1795 was kept secret even after its ratification by the Senate, until it was leaked to the public.

There was a tremendous outcry, during which Jay was burnt in effigy and the Federalist leader Alexander Hamilton was stoned, but Jay's Treaty, as it came to be known, was finally voted into operation by a very narrow margin. The old bitter feelings against Britain having been sufficiently vented, the public began to see the value of the treaty and businessmen welcomed it since it offered some protection to their European cargoes.

Among those who welcomed Jay's Treaty with most enthusiasm was John Jacob Astor. The main concession of the British was that they would vacate their north-western forts by 1 June 1796: the stranglehold of the Northwest Fur Company on the rich hunting grounds south of the Great Lakes was thus broken.

'Now', said Astor, 'I will make my fortune in the fur trade.'

The way was open for him to become the first great monopolist and the richest man in America.

2 *Boundaries of Empire*

I

By the time Chief Justice Jay left America on the mission that was greatly to contribute to the wealth of John Jacob Astor, the thirty-one-year-old fur dealer had already placed what were to be the hardest years of his life behind him. With a net worth estimated at something more than $50,000, Astor had become one of the foremost merchants of New York and – reflecting his new status – had gone so far as to commission the artist Gilbert Stuart to paint his portrait in 1794. Apparently, the magical quality of Stuart's brushwork did not impress his dour client, who refused to pay the fee until the artist produced something more to his taste. Desperate for money as always, Stuart obliged with a second portrait, now in the Mansell Collection, which depicted Astor as a rather princely figure with somewhat more refined looks than contemporary descriptions imply. As well he might have been, Astor was pleased with such a flattering picture (which incidentally bears a passing resemblance to one of Stuart's later portraits of George Washington that made the artist so famous) and paid up. But however much he was pressed to enhance the physiognomy of his subject, Stuart could not disguise the sharp perception of his eye and there is an unmistakable hardness and lack of sympathy about the personality emerging from his canvas. The eyes – fixed, like those of the Mona Lisa, upon the viewer from every angle – are cold and impenetrable, even a little contemptuous, while the mouth with its thin upper lip has the cast of a man set on reorganizing the world to his own advantage and strong enough, both physically and mentally, to achieve his ambitions.

Thus far, he had done exceptionally well in furthering his ambitions, and the implementation of the Jay Treaty appeared to remove any limits on his horizons. Simply by ending the American-imposed ban on imports from Canada and removing the British requirement that furs bought in Montreal be shipped to London first, the treaty served to increase Astor's profits. He could now import directly to serve a rapidly growing domestic market (the population of New York City, for example, was in the process of doubling every ten years) as well as being able to export to wherever he chose, at the time most convenient and profitable to him, and without having to pay middlemen. This alone was enough to bring gold pouring into the Astor coffers in almost embarrassing quantities, but the rise in profits was not matched by a significant increase in the scope of John Jacob's fur-gathering operations, because the British evacuation of the border forts was not accompanied by any curtailment in the Northwest Company's activities. Though no longer guaranteed a monopoly, Northwest was not actually banished from American soil and its agents were so entrenched and well organized that competing with them was difficult. Astor put his own men into the Great Lakes country, but they made little headway and – much to Astor's disgust – there was no support from an American government still warming its feet by the embers of post-revolutionary idealism. Indeed, the sainted George Washington proposed in the waning years of his presidency that an attempt be made to regulate the fur trade by government intervention, with the establishment of official trading posts on what amounted to a non-profit basis and a ban on the sale of liquor to the Indians. This paternalistic attitude helped nobody, since the Canadian dealers simply carried on in their old ways, frustrating American merchants and, in the words of Albert Gallatin, preserving 'a most dangerous influence over our Indians'. Astor could only grit his teeth and wait for the day when he could tackle the Northwest Company on what remained for the time being its own ground.

Meanwhile, he was buying ever greater numbers of furs in Montreal and casting about for alternative ways of building up his business. He was still importing and selling musical instruments and other goods he obtained in Europe (including powder and shot, muskets, pistols, carbines and even cannon) with the returns from his fur sales there, but the great expansion of his enterprise, which helped to give him a fortune of a quarter of a million dollars by the early 1800s, was his entry into the China trade.

John Jacob's first venture in Far Eastern commerce is obscured by one of several romantic legends that blossomed around him during his rise to wealth and fame. This particular one appears to have begun with Astor himself, in old age, and may reflect his childish satisfaction at his own cleverness and success. It enjoyed wide currency among the contemporaries of his later years and was often repeated by his children and grandchildren.

The story goes that in 1799 Astor sailed to London with a valuable cargo of furs, following his principle of never paying a middleman for what he could do himself. To add spice to the tale and credence to the many canards of his miserliness, it was said that Astor travelled steerage – if that information came from him, I suspect it was intended either to reinforce the reputation for financial caution of which he was so proud or as a little joke on behalf of one who was by then the richest man in America. At any rate, having disposed of his cargo, Astor scoured the City of London for premium import goods, visited brother George at the musical instrument factory and spent a lot of time broadening his contacts among the City merchants. In the course of his perambulations, he happened upon the headquarters of the East India Company, that temple to capitalism and imperial power, and through conversation with the porter discovered that the Governor of the company was a German immigrant with a name that sounded familiar. On impulse, John Jacob asked the porter to announce him to the Governor, was admitted to the presence of the nabob and recognized him as someone he had known during his boyhood in Walldorf.

Here in the story we may detect again the shadow of Astor's self-image, which endowed his younger self with what modern hagiographers would call charisma – a natural ability to attract favourable attention and to impress people who mattered. It seems that the high and mighty Governor of the East India Company duly succumbed to the Astor spell, invited John Jacob to dinner and offered to help him in any way he could. Overcome with uncharacteristic shyness, Astor declined the dinner invitation on the ground that he did not have a thing to wear in such exalted circles and informed the Governor that there was nothing the company could do for him at present.

The Governor insisted that Astor call upon him before he left London and when he did so, John Jacob was presented with a package containing two documents which he was told might be of value to him. The first paper was an East India Company trading permit, No. 68, which allowed any ship carrying Astor goods to sell its cargo through ports controlled by the company; the second document was a list of 'prices current' for trade goods in Canton.

According to the legend, it was Permit No. 68 that gave Astor the key to the riches of the Orient, but when he first received it he had no conception of the treasure it represented: the credit for that, interestingly enough, goes to Sarah Astor. John Jacob appears to have idolized his wife, honouring her as the best judge of furs in the business and claiming to have paid her the preposterous sum of five hundred dollars an hour for grading pelts, as well as recalling for the benefit of his grandchildren that he had married the rather sour old woman who sometimes terrified the youngsters 'because she was so pretty' – though 'pretty' was not a word contemporaries would have used to describe her. Perhaps such recollections of an invaluable helpmeet who died sixteen years before her husband were gilded by nostalgia or the familial sentiment that was always so strong in John Jacob. On the other hand, his habit of giving so much emphasis to Sarah's contribution tended to sustain the providential quality with which he liked to imbue the details of his rise. Whatever the reason, the story of Permit No. 68 is as much Sarah's as John Jacob's. She is said to have asked to examine the permit and list of Canton prices and to have noted that one of the commodities in demand by the Chinese was fur. Then, it is suggested, Sarah persuaded her husband to go into partnership with a New York shipowner on a China cargo, though Astor's investment was to be no more than the precious permit. Despite John Jacob's caution, a deal was struck with the shipowner, a certain Mr James Livermore, and early in 1800 a vessel left New York for Canton. A year later, Astor collected his share of the profits – a tidy fifty-five thousand dollars.

That, at least, is how it was told. There are, however, a number of dubious aspects to the legend. For one thing, no record of any deal between Astor and Mr Livermore has ever come to light: the only evidence for it comes from a highly suspect source, the pseudonymous Walter Barrett, who goes into great detail in his glaringly inaccurate collection of gossip entitled *The Old Merchants of New York*. Even if there really was some kind of arrangement between Astor and Mr Livermore, the latter would have had to be a very inexperienced shipowner indeed to have entered into a contract for the China trade to which his partner's only contribution was a trading permit from the British East India Company. In Canton, Permit No. 68 would have been worth less than the paper it was written on, since the choice of which merchant should be allowed to fill the godowns of the great port with cargo lay entirely with the officials appointed personally by the Chinese emperor. To be sure, the East India Company had a base in Canton, but in no sense did it wield any authority. Furthermore, American shipping was not subject to the restrictions placed on British vessels with regard to trading in ports that actually were controlled by the East India Company, so they sailed happily and without hindrance to Bombay, Rangoon, Calcutta, Madras and Colombo. In the circumstances, it is hard to see any real value in the Governor's gift to Astor, other than to indicate a market he might profitably explore.

As if that were not enough to discredit the legend, Astor must have been a dull-witted and ill-informed merchant (which he was not) to have been unaware that the traders of Boston and their sea captains had been enjoying a flourishing trade with China for the best part of twenty years, exporting mainly silver coin and the fabled aphrodisiac ginseng in return for teas and silks but also dabbling in ... furs! In fact, the first American ship to sail round the world, the *Columbia*, had carried seaotter and other pelts to China in 1788. It is inconceivable that John Jacob and his partner, if indeed there ever was one, did not themselves know all this.

The very durability of the tale does suggest, however, that it may have had some basis in fact, and it is possible that Astor was given a document by the Governor of the East India Company, though it would have been of no real value, as the Governor himself must have known. For his part, John Jacob may well have been impressed at first – he had up to that time never traded outside Europe – and, on discovering the paper's real worth (or lack of it), have sought to cover up his naivety by investing Permit No. 68 with the magical qualities described. After all, even businessmen have some imagination.

There was nothing imaginary, though, about the voyage of the *Severn* in 1800, which seems to mark Astor's real entry into the China trade. John Jacob was part of a consortium which, records show, loaded the good ship *Severn* with more than thirty thousand seal, beaver, otter and fox skins, as well as the by then traditional ginseng and silver coin, and sent her in the wake of the Bostonian vessels round Cape Horn and across the Pacific to Canton. A little more than a year later, the ship returned with a cargo of silks, satins and nankeens, chinaware and tea on which Astor and his friends made a considerable killing. John Jacob invested his profits back in the China trade, buying one ship outright and taking a share in several others.

According to the gullible Walter Barrett, Astor's own ship accidentally discovered an important new source of revenue when she put in to the Sandwich Islands to take on food and water: 'They also laid in a large stock of firewood. When the ship reached Canton a mandarin came on board and, noticing their firewood, asked the price of it at once. The Captain laughed at such a question, but signified that he was open to an offer. The mandarin offered five hundred dollars a ton, and every part of it was sold at that price. That was *sandal*wood.'

Alas for Mr Barrett, he had apparently never heard of Captain John Kendrick, a Bostonian pioneer of the Canton trade, who carried the first cargo of sandalwood from 'Owyhee' to China in the mid-1790s, after which it became a standard item aboard the so-called North-westers plying between Boston and the Far East. Compounding his ignorance, the author blundered on: 'For seventeen years Mr Astor enjoyed that lucrative sandalwood trade without a rival. No other concern in the United States or England knew the secret. Nor was it discovered until a shrewd Boston shipowner detailed a ship to follow Mr Astor's, and observe the events of the voyage.'

Such stuff as myths are made on! The only thing that can be said in defence of Barrett is that he was merely repeating stories, gossip and rumour current among the New York business community – in this case, thirty years or more after the events recalled. Astor neither discovered the profit potential of sandalwood nor did he hold a monopoly in its sale. What he did do was precisely the thing he had done when he first entered the fur business, which was to enter an established area of commerce and, by dint of vision, shrewdness and hard work, develop it far beyond the limits previously envisaged. Many a Boston merchant grew rich in the China trade, but none as rich as John Jacob Astor. He was one of the earliest prophets and practitioners of 'big business'.

Reminiscing after Astor's death, Philip Hone – auctioneer, friend and business associate of John Jacob, socialite, sometime mayor of New York and generally reliable diarist – noted: 'The fur trade was the philosopher's stone of this modern Croesus, beaver skins and muskrats furnishing the oil for the supply of Aladdin's lamp. His traffic was the shipment of furs to China, where they brought immense prices, for he monopolized the business; and the return cargoes of teas, silks, and rich productions of China brought further large profits; for here, too, he had very little competition at the time of which I am speaking... All he touched turned to gold, and it seemed as if fortune delighted in erecting him a monument of her unerring potency.'

There is a certain amount of exaggeration in that passage for which Hone must be forgiven because, as he looked back, it must have seemed that Astor did monopolize the fur trade with China, though this was never actually true. He certainly traded on a far greater scale than anyone else in America, his main competitors being Russians, who had the advantage of the rich storehouses of Alaska and the Pacific North-west almost on their doorstep, and he gave even them a run for their money.

In a brief biographical sketch of John Jacob, his great-grandson, William Waldorf (later Viscount) Astor, quoted the founder as saying that by the end of the eighteenth century he had 'a million dollars afloat, which represented a dozen vessels'. It was another example of the old man's advancing the timescale of his rise to wealth and fame (he also claimed, for instance, that he was a millionaire long before anyone would have guessed, which is hard to swallow), but there is no doubt that his boast was fulfilled before much of the nineteenth century had passed. By 1803 he was having his own ships built, the first called the

Beaver, appropriately enough, and the second named for his daughter, Magdalen. These sleek three-masters could make the round-trip to Canton in a year or less – the *Beaver* did it in nine months on her maiden voyage – which served to increase Astor's profits that much more quickly.

The *Magdalen* figures in one of the early stories of John Jacob's meanness, which was to become a subject of much gossip over the years. It seems that the master, Captain John Cowman, informed Astor that the ship must have a chronometer. That, the wily merchant replied, was the responsibility of the skipper, not the owner; ships sailed perfectly well without chronometers. Cowman insisted: not only would a chronometer save money on insurance but it would also be a useful aid to seamanship and reduce the length of a voyage, thus paying for itself in a very short time. Astor reluctantly agreed, but when a bill for five hundred dollars reached him he refused to pay for the chronometer, and Cowman stormed off the ship. Astor found another captain, Cowman another employer and six weeks after the *Magdalen* sailed for Canton, her former skipper followed suit under a different flag – bringing his ship back into New York within a few days of the *Magdalen* and smartly unloading his cargo of tea, which helped to produce a glut and a resulting $70,000 loss for Astor, who had held his tea in the *Magdalen's* hold in expectation of a rise in prices. But, the story continues, Astor was not one to hold a grudge and promptly gave Cowman back his ship . . . with a chronometer.

This particular story does actually seem likely to have been true. Although an accurate and reliable chronometer had been developed some forty years earlier, its cost (about £450) had discouraged widespread use in spite of the navigational benefits. By the turn of the century, cheaper models were available and had been taken up by the more progressive shipowners and skippers. As we have seen, however, Astor was not a man to throw his money about unless he could see a material return on it. The only point about which one might quibble is the size of John Jacob's loss, since the average investment in a China cargo at that time was about $60,000 and the profit margin roughly fifty per cent – presumably the tea involved in the tale was not a complete write-off.

Rather less believable is another captain story involving two pipes of Madeira and several thousand pounds of tea. John Jacob had apparently sent the wine on the voyage to China in accordance with the well-established tradition that sea air and the motion of a ship assisted in the process of making Madeira 'fine'. Upon the vessel's return to New York, Astor discovered that the wine had been stowed under the bulk of the tea cargo, which was destined in this case for the European market. John Jacob therefore asked the captain to liberate the casks without unloading the tea, promising him a demijohn of the Madeira in consideration of all the extra work involved. After two days the wine was unstowed and delivered to Astor's home. The ship sailed to Amsterdam with its tea, returned to New York and subsequently set off for Canton without any mention being made of the Madeira the owner had promised his captain. A further China voyage followed, after which the skipper took it upon himself to broach the subject of the wine. It was not yet 'fine', Astor told him. A year later, following yet another trip to Canton, the captain inquired again: the wine was still not 'fine' – and as far as the captain was concerned, it never would be.

This tale has been offered as an example of Astor's meanness, his reluctance to part with anything that belonged to him unless it went to a member of his family. Yet it raises a number of questions. Would the captain really have put all that tea on top of his employer's precious wine? Would the Madeira have been stowed in the hold at all? And why was it so important to Astor? He cared nothing for the niceties of viticulture and indeed hardly ever drank wine.

I suspect that if the whole thing was not a sailor's grog-shop yarn it was the invention of either a competitor of Astor's or someone who knew him only in his later years, when – as will become apparent – his reputation for miserliness, harsh dealing and callous disregard for others was well deserved. The Madeira incident dates from a period when John Jacob's contemporaries, while admitting that he was a shrewd and aggressive entrepreneur, saw him as a good employer and straight dealer. John Robins, a contemporary of Astor and for many years the leading draper in New York, once recalled how easy it was to do business with John Jacob: 'He said what he meant and he meant what he said. He had one price, a fair one, gauged on the market, and you could take it or leave it.' Such a man would surely have offered the going rate for the extra work involved in shifting the cargo to release his wine – and he would probably only have wanted it in such a hurry if he had had a buyer ready to take it off his hands at a good price.

Good prices were usually what Astor got in his ship-owning days. The Canton trade and its concomitant import-export business in Europe produced plenty of capital with which he could gradually and almost unnoticeably develop his fur-gathering operations at a time when any attempt on his part to stand toe-to-toe with the Northwest Company would have been disastrous. The pelts he bought either in bulk from Montreal or from his own suppliers went to Canton and were exchanged for tea and other goods to be sold on the domestic market, or re-exported to Europe where the profits were invested in trade articles used to obtain more furs. Apart from this neat circle of commerce, there remained very valuable outlets for furs in London and in Leipzig, the clearing-house for the trade in continental Europe. The large profits that Astor made enabled him methodically to increase the numbers of his fur agents in Indian country and at the same time to build up his capital base for the day when the big push against the Canadians might be feasible.

In this exercise he benefited from, or rather took advantage of two factors with which history presented him. The first was the American government's decision to seek rapid expansion of overseas trade by deferring the payment of import tariffs for up to eighteen months. A merchant like Astor, therefore, could sell, say, tea as soon as it was unloaded and take his profit of about fifty per cent as well as collecting from the buyer duties of as much as two hundred per cent which he was not required to remit to the government until more than a year later. The average investment of $60,000 would yield $210,000 gross, of which $120,000 – the import duty – was the shipper's to do with as he pleased within the time allowed before the revenue collector called. That sum would finance two further voyages to China, generating another $60,000 in profits and saving the shipper interest charges of perhaps four per cent a month which would have applied to borrowed capital. The duty on the first shipment could be paid by half the deferred duties on the second and third, and so on. In effect, the merchant who successfully completed one Canton run could finance the expansion of his business largely with money 'on loan' from the government. It has been estimated, again not entirely reliably, that John Jacob Astor had the use of more than five million dollars in deferred revenues during his boom years in the China trade: the profits that amount of capital brought him can easily be imagined.

It was the second example of historical intervention, however, that was to prove more important to Astor in the long run. In December 1803, the size of the United States almost doubled when President Thomas Jefferson completed the purchase from France of almost a million square miles of territory west of the Mississippi river. The Louisiana Purchase has been rightly called the greatest bargain in American history: for about twenty-seven million dollars, the government obtained the rich land comprising the modern states of Louisiana, Missouri, Arkansas, Iowa, North and South Dakota, Nebraska and Oklahoma, as well as by far the larger part of the country now covered by Kansas, Colorado, Wyoming, Montana and Minnesota. This vast area – theoretically stretching westward to the Pacific but in fact bounded by the physical barrier of the Rocky Mountains* and the political confines of British claims to what are now the states of Washington and Oregon and Spanish possession of Texas and California – was of incalculable worth in terms of natural resources, and no one was more acutely aware of this than Astor. He had heard trappers' tales of countless hordes of fur-bearing animals inhabiting the unmapped and, for all practical purposes, unexplored regions beyond the Mississippi and he realized that whoever held the key to that great storehouse could control the fur trade of virtually the entire continent.

Astor's agents and the brigades that supplied them had moved steadily farther west as he had cautiously expanded his business, but he had not been unopposed. A Canadian outfit, known as the Mackinaw Company and formed by several directors of Northwest, had established itself at Michilimackinac (though it was actually in American territory) and had sent

* At the time of the Louisiana Purchase they were known as the 'Stony Mountains', a title subtly less evocative.

trappers into the Mississippi basin, while a number of smaller companies had based themselves in St Louis, which by 1800 was a firmly founded settlement with a population of about a thousand, having been a frontier post of the fur trade for some forty years. The Louisiana Purchase, by moving the frontier from the Mississippi to the Rockies and beyond, revealed the most tempting prize that could have been offered to a fur dealer, and Astor determined that it should be his. The Mackinaw Company was actually in the best position to begin the race, but John Jacob outclassed the Canadians in financial stamina. Emboldened by the vast profits he had made in the import-export business, he forgot the promise he had made himself on the day he left Walldorf and prepared to embark upon the first and only great risk of his career. That comes later in the story, though. In the meantime let us see how John Jacob was developing his commercial base – and his social position.

II

By 1803, the year of the Louisiana Purchase, John Jacob Astor was definitely to be numbered among the leading citizens of New York. He even lived cheek by jowl with them, having paid $27,000 for the spacious former home of the leading Federalist politician Rufus King at 233 Broadway, on the block above Vesey Street opposite the site where City Hall now stands. No longer was there any question of living above the shop: he had his business premises four blocks south at 71 Liberty Street, within easy walking distance of the South Street piers. Furthermore, like other prominent New Yorkers he now owned a country estate, though today it is hard to imagine the eastern river frontage of Manhattan as a rural retreat for the rich, with the East River Drive running through what would have been their front gardens. Astor's country house was called Hellgate (the more mealy-mouthed referred to it as 'Hurlgate') and its grounds sloped down towards the strait of that name between Wards Island and Long Island which the transatlantic shipping had to negotiate on the way downriver to the docks. His neighbours there included such Old Guard notables as the Rhinelanders, Crugers, Schermerhorns and Gracies (whose mansion remains), and the banker Nathaniel Prime from whom

Astor had once been obliged to raise capital at the exorbitant rates of interest then prevalent.

But Astor's property interests were considerably more extensive than the buildings he and his family used. From the modest beginnings suggested by his brother Henry, he had gone on buying city lots at the rate of several thousand dollars a year. Now he turned his attention to the surrounding country-side and began to purchase farms, estates and even parcels of grazing land. Where he could not buy, he assumed mortgages and before long he had almost half a million dollars invested in out-of-town real estate. Many businessmen said he had more money than sense, but they and their heirs would have cause to regret that they did not follow John Jacob's lead. With his uncanny ability to profit from the march of history, he sensed that New York was destined to grow into a great city – though even he, as he somewhat ruefully admitted years later, was surprised by the scale and speed of the development.

In 1803 Astor and a partner paid $25,000 for seventy acres of the Eden Farm, on the north-western outskirts of New York, which had fallen into the hands of a spendthrift heir. Later John Jacob acquired the entire property, and to his great-grandson that land was worth in excess of twenty million dollars – it happened to lie almost at the junction of what became Broadway and 42nd Street, running north along Times Square!

His speculation in land and property brought Astor into close contact with some of the leading figures of the day, previewing in some cases an uncomfortable relationship be-tween politics and business which remains evident today. Among Astor's 'clients' was the flamboyant and wayward Aaron Burr, Jefferson's Vice-President. Burr was one of those politicians who believe that their reward for public service should be a grand and gracious style of living and, like many of his successors at Tammany Hall,* Burr always had an eye for the main chance.

---

* The name Tammany is used as a symbol of and synonym for political corruption. The Tammany Society of New York (descendant of many such patriotic groups founded at the time of the War of Independence) was notorious for its baleful and corrupting influence on city and even national politics during the nineteenth and early twentieth centuries. Tammany Hall, the society's building on 14th Street, was leased to the Democratic Party of New York as its headquarters, and the web of corruption thus spread to

An opportunity to line his pocket presented itself in 1797 when popular feeling arose against the Trinity Church Corporation, which seemed to many democratically minded people to be an unwelcome reminder of the episcopacy's power in pre-revolutionary days. A republican government determined that no established church should ever again grow fat on the proceeds of landowning had limited Trinity's income to $12,000 a year, but there were suspicions that the corporation's dealings were less innocent and law abiding than they seemed. A committee was formed to investigate Trinity's financial affairs and Burr (not yet Vice-President) contrived to have himself made chairman – emerging as the lessee of the church-owned King's Farm, some four hundred acres and a colonial mansion in Ionic style, near what is now Greenwich Village, at a ridiculous $269 a year. Nothing more was heard of Trinity's financial accounts.

Burr quickly raised a loan of $38,000 against the property, but this was not enough to keep him in the style to which he wished to become accustomed and in 1803 he sold the lease of half his holding to Astor, with whom he had been acquainted for some time, for $62,500. Those lots included the house, Richmond Hill, which Astor promptly sublet to another leading political client (and fellow Mason), Governor George Clinton.

The following year saw the beginning of Burr's fall from grace. On 11 July came the infamous duel with Alexander Hamilton, in which Hamilton was mortally wounded, and Burr – desperate for money – sold another lease to Astor for $8,000. A couple of years later John Jacob obtained the remainder of the property when Burr fled to Paris having been tried for treason:* the price was $32,000 plus the residue of Burr's original mortgage from the Bank of Manhattan. Astor shrewdly subleased the land for sixty years, which meant that in 1866 it reverted to his heirs with all the improvements tenants had made and with a right of renewal of the master lease from Trinity on advantageous terms. The technique of buying land

include the Democratic leadership. The word Tammany is derived from the name of the Indian chief Tammanend, who signed a treaty of friendship with William Penn, founder of the Pennsylvania Colony.

* Burr was acquitted in spite of an embarrassed President Jefferson's attempts to 'hang him', but suspicion continued to cling to him.

and letting others develop it was thus established, to become standard practice among successive Astor landlords.

When Burr later saw how Astor had profited from what should have been his own property, he attempted to reverse the transfers he had effected, but John Jacob was too careful to have left any loopholes and Burr had to accept his loss. Far from feeling any bitterness over the affair, the former Vice-President admired Astor's skilful handling of the deal and the two men remained friends, a fact that was to benefit both of them a few years later. It is not difficult to see what drew them together, despite their very different personalities and modes of living – Astor, the solid, respectable and rather dull business and family man, against Burr the sharp lawyer, socialite, intriguer and amorous adventurer. Both raised the principle of self-interest to the level of a philosophy and each claimed for himself a natural superiority over his less able and less powerful fellow men, a sort of God-given right to exploit the world and its inhabitants for his personal gain. This was not mere cynicism, but a genuine belief that in some way they were among the chosen people for whose convenience and advancement life was ordered. To use a modern American phrase, they saw themselves as 'movers and shakers' and considered anyone who could not be placed in that category as nothing more than fodder for their ambitions. Such people – and we can recognize their like only too easily today – make history, but they also pervert it in human terms because their world and the codes that govern it have nothing to do with morality. Burr's own mercurial personality occasioned an untimely exit from the political stage, but Astor's more circumspect and calculated activities over a much longer period made a deep and lasting impression, and not a particularly savoury one.

A shameful example of these two egotistical and amoral spirits working in collusion is provided by the Morris case, which involved a tract of land comprising near on a third of Putnam County, New York. This 51,000 acres belonged by inheritance to Roger and Mary Morris, high Tories who were dispossessed by the Revolution and fled to England. The new state government of New York seized the Morris's lands, along with many others', divided them into manageable agricultural lots and sold title at modest prices to seven hundred farmers, who prospered over the years on the fertile soil of the district. Until 1809, that is, when a smart lawyer – and there is a strong case for that lawyer having been Aaron Burr, who happened to be in London at the time – discovered by accident that the Morrises had held only a life interest in the Putnam County estate, which upon their deaths was to have passed in perpetuity to their heirs.

This was a pretty legal tangle: the state government had sequestrated land which did not belong outright to the people it wished to dispossess and in effect it was now punishing the Morris heirs for political 'crimes' for which they could in no way be held responsible. On the other hand, a community of more than three thousand people had blossomed on land that its present occupants had purchased in good faith, believing that they were acquiring absolute title. The government could not afford the political price of evicting all those people and returning the land to foreign citizens descended from 'traitors' to the Revolution. How many lawyers would have loved to get their hands on such a case!

For the three Morris heirs to have pressed their claim, however, would have been a costly and long-drawn-out procedure. Clearly, they would not actually get back the land, and indeed they would not have known what to do with it if they had, so it was from their point of view a simple matter of compensation. The lawyer who advised them – and we assume it was Burr, partly because he was identified by several contemporary sources and also because of the subsequent course of events – suggested that the best way to profit from the government's error was to sell their interest in the land for ready cash. There was one man in New York who had not only the money to buy out the heirs but also the energy, the determination and the resources to press the claim on his own behalf: John Jacob Astor (and if this was not Burr's advice, whose was it?) was approached in 1809 and responded with an offer of $100,000 for the heirs' interest, a windfall which the Morrises quickly accepted.

John Jacob felt he had pulled off quite a coup, acquiring a considerable parcel of prime agricultural land at less than two dollars an acre. He could not collect on it immediately because Mary Morris was still alive, but since she was eighty years old

Astor reasoned that it would not be long before he came into his 'inheritance' – as he noted cynically himself, 'the life of Mrs Morris, according to calculations, worth little or nothing'. With this in mind, he asked the state of New York to buy outright title to the Morris land for $300,000, having first sold minority interests to a group of his business associates so that he should appear as the principal of a partnership rather than what he actually was, a greedy and impatient land speculator. The state legislature was not impressed, however, apart from which it was under pressure from radicals to reform the system of landholding surviving from colonial times which opponents branded as feudal. Astor's application disappeared into some file marked 'pending' on the ground that no decision could be made while Mary Morris lived.

The old lady's life proved to be worth a good deal more than Astor had bargained for. It was sixteen years before she did him the favour of passing away, and throughout that time John Jacob continually pressed the state to settle his claim, while the unhappy farmers who lived on and worked the land remained in limbo, uncertain whether they could bequeath to their heirs all they had worked for, and unable to sell their properties or raise mortgages on them. Their mental anguish must have been considerable, but John Jacob was not a man to be concerned with such things: to him this was a straightforward business exercise and all that mattered was the money he would make.

Finally in 1827, two years after the death of Mrs Morris, the New York legislature was forced to make a decision in the face of a successful eviction suit brought by Astor against one of the farmers (with Aaron Burr, long back in New York and established in legal practice, advising but not appearing in person). Among the defending counsel in the case was Daniel Webster, senator, leading constitutional lawyer and future Secretary of State, who argued that the plaintiff's claim was 'for lands not in their wild and forest state, but for lands the intrinsic value of which is mingled with the labour expended upon them'.

In one of the flights of oratory for which he became famous, Webster continued: 'It is no everyday purchase, for it extends over towns and counties and almost takes in a degree of latitude. It is a stupendous speculation. The individual who now claims it has not succeeded to it by inheritance; he has not attained it, as he did that vast wealth which no one envies him less than I do, by fair and honest exertions in commercial enterprise, but by speculation, by purchasing the forlorn hope of the heirs of a family driven from their country by a bill of attainder. By the defendants, on the contrary, the lands in question are held as a patrimony. They have laboured for years to improve them. The rugged hills had grown green under their cultivation before a question was raised as to the integrity of their titles.'

But respecter of property and the law as he was, Webster must have known that his defence was no more than rhetoric. Astor's lawyer could reply with absolute confidence that 'Mr Astor bought this property confiding in the justice of the State of New York' – right, no matter how wrong in human terms, was on his side in the legal sense. Indeed, similar cases occur from time to time even now and, in the United States, it is usual when buying property to take out title insurance against the possibility that the vendor has no absolute right to sell.

Recognizing the difficulty of its position but unwilling to admit its error in such circumstances, the administration in Albany told Astor that he must bring four more eviction suits and that if the Supreme Court found for him in three of the total of five cases the state would buy him off. Of course, Astor won and the state 'bought' the Morris lands for more than half a million dollars' worth of five per cent New York stock. Astor's legal expenses added up to about $50,000, though what Burr got out of it is anyone's guess. At all events, Astor did not celebrate his victory. 'I had much trouble and little profit by this transaction,' he observed dourly. Probably he would have preferred to evict all the three thousand or so people on 'his' land and to have then sold it – its value on the open market had been assessed at one and a half million dollars.

Whatever one may think of his morality in this case, Astor cannot be faulted on his observance of the law. That, however, was simply because the law in question happened to benefit him. On other occasions he was perfectly happy to brush aside the legislation of his adopted country if it did not work to his advantage and more especially if it stood in his way. He got away with it because he was rich and because he took care to cultivate leading politicians – that is, if he did not already hold something over them in the form of loans, mortgages or land. Apart from his dealings with Burr, he bought land from George Clinton, advanced a mortgage to James Madison and had financial or business associations with President Monroe and Albert Gallatin. To James Monroe, for example, Astor advanced large sums of money on easy terms – with $5,000 for openers in 1814 – while the Virginian was secretary of state and during his two terms in the White House, but after Monroe's retirement (in other words, when he had ceased to be useful) Astor was foremost among the creditors who obliged the former statesman to sell his home near Leesburg and seek what amounted to charity from the Congress of the nation he had served so well.

The most notable occasion on which Astor used his political contacts to line his pocket at the expense of both his competitors and the law was in 1808, during President Jefferson's unpopular embargo on foreign trade, which was designed to punish the warring powers of Britain and France but succeeded mainly in ruining American businesses that depended on import and export. Astor's fur and property interests were substantial enough to sustain him very comfortably through the inconvenient suspension of the China trade, but he chafed at the thought of large and comparatively easy profits lying unclaimed through a political dispute in which he had no stake. He was not alone in his frustration; many businessmen openly talked of defying the Embargo Act. But it was Astor who had the effrontery and the influence to do it with impunity.

In the summer of 1808, his ship the *Beaver* sailed 'for China', as the *Commercial Advertiser* reported. The business community was astounded: with navy frigates turning back any vessel which did not have certification showing its trade to be confined to coastal waters and whose owners had not posted bond against unlawful intercourse with foreign ports, how had Astor got his ship away, and so blatantly? Government collusion seemed to be the only answer, and before long federal officials and congressmen were being harried by angry merchants demanding to know why they should not be favoured in the way Astor had been.

Under pressure, the whole murky tale came out. The

Beaver's voyage, officials explained, was not a commercial one but rather a favour for a visiting Chinese dignitary who would otherwise have been prevented by the embargo from returning home. A mandarin in New York? Experienced China traders smelled a rat. It was well known that the Chinese regarded Westerners as barbarians and did not wish to sully themselves through contact with them any more than was strictly necessary. In any case, such an exotic visitor would have been bound to excite interest and comment, yet nobody had heard of him. But it was all open and above board, insisted the New York senator Samuel Mitchell: why, he himself had seen the nobleman, one Punqua Wing-chong, who had asked the senator to petition the government on his behalf so that he might be allowed to take ship for Canton. The obliging senator had given the mysterious mandarin a letter to President Jefferson stating that Punqua Wing-chong 'came to New York about nine months ago on business' and now wanted to go back to China, 'where the affairs of his family and particularly the funeral obsequies of his grandfather require his solemn attention'. The distinguished visitor had taken the senator's letter to Washington, but since Jefferson at the time had been at his country home in Virginia, he had himself written to the President requesting permission to engage a ship.

So far so good. But out of all the ships available, why had the *Beaver* been chosen? The answer, it emerged, was that it had not been Punqua Wing-chong who had approached Senator Mitchell but John Jacob Astor; it had been Astor's 'client', James Madison, the Secretary of State, who had urged Jefferson to grant the mandarin's request; and it had been Astor's close friend Albert Gallatin, Secretary of the Treasury, who had officially approved the arrangements the President had agreed to. Furthermore, along with Punqua Wing-chong on his voyage to Canton had gone 45,000 dollars' worth of specie, ginseng, furs and other cargo.

There was an outcry from the merchants and shippers, a group from Philadelphia writing to Gallatin with the information that some of then who had actually lived in Canton could identify the great Wing-chong as no more than 'a petty shopkeeper'. A gleeful Press, then as now delighted at the prospect of embarrassing the government and exposing a scandal, quoted other merchants as saying that the 'mandarin' was a dock loafer smuggled out of China 'who had departed from that country contrary to its laws and would be saved from death on his return only by his obscure position', or that he was a Chinaman picked up in a park, or even 'an Indian dressed up in silk and adorned with a peacock fan'.

The *Commercial Advertiser* went so far as to make a personal attack on Jefferson, who had written to Gallatin that he considered Wing-chong's case as one 'of national comity' which 'may be the means of making our nation known advantageously at the source of power in China'. Astor, unusually for him, was stung into defending both the President and himself in public and wrote to the editor of the *Advertiser* promising a full statement of the facts, which would show that 'the government has not been surprised by misrepresentation in granting permission, and the reputation of those concerned cannot be in the slightest degree affected'.

No such statement was forthcoming and nothing further was heard of Punqua Wing-chong after his return to China. Albert Gallatin ruefully admitted in a letter to Jefferson that, 'I apprehend that there is some speculation at bottom.' How right he was. The *Beaver* returned to New York 'with a full cargo of teas, silks and nankeens' and Astor made a killing in a market denied such blessings for more than a year, clearing something between one hundred and two hundred thousand dollars.

It was the first time that the activities of John Jacob Astor attracted unwelcome public comment, but it was certainly not to be the last. Neither was it the last time Astor thumbed his nose at the law, or cynically exploited the political aspirations of emergent America for his own gain. And therein lies his tragedy, if indeed it is permissible to use such a word in connexion with a man who was so conspicuously successful by most accepted standards. He had the instincts of an empire builder but not the vision or the necessary vein of altruism. The scope of his ambition, to be sure, was much broader than that of most of his contemporaries in business, but how much wider it might have been – and how much greater his achievement – if he had been able to range beyond the pale of the profit motive. He saw the potential of the Louisiana Purchase and the

65

development of the West, but he saw it only in terms of himself and his personal fortune. He failed to appreciate (though he pretended to) that the fusion of his image of empire and America's dream of expansion 'from sea to shining sea' could produce something of immense benefit to both himself and his country. His imagination impelled him to reach out into what was literally unknown territory, but its lack of an essential element made it inevitable that his one great gamble would culminate in his one great failure.

The first step in his grand but flawed design was taken in the spring of 1808 when Astor founded the American Fur Company with the object – at least as he expressed it in a letter to Jefferson – of ensuring that control of the vast fur-harvesting potential of the wilderness west of the Mississippi should be placed firmly in American hands rather than falling by default to the Canadian robber barons of the Northwest and Mackinaw companies. He spoke in nicely judged patriotic terms of 'extending the American domain' and even 'adding new states to the Union', pointing out that such an undertaking 'would require a greater capital than any individual or unincorporated association could well furnish'. Jefferson encouraged the project 'with the assurance of every facility and protection which the government could properly afford' and the American Fur Company was duly incorporated by the State of New York on 6 April 1808.

Even at that early stage, however, it would have been apparent to anyone interested enough to investigate the matter that Astor had been lying in his teeth when he had written to Jefferson. This was unintentionally made clear by Washington Irving in his book *Astoria*, a history of the enterprise written later at Astor's request. Portraying John Jacob as a man who relied on no one but himself, Irving wrote that the company's entire capital of one million dollars came from his own pocket and 'though he had a board of directors, they were merely nominal ... he, in fact, constituted the company ... the whole business was conducted on his plans and with his resources...' Or as his great-grandson, William Waldorf, first Viscount Astor, put it, the corporation was nothing more than 'a fiction intended to broaden and facilitate his operations'.

John Jacob cared not at all whether the new empire in his

mind's eye was American, or Canadian or, for that matter, Roman, just as long as he himself was running it and pocketing the proceeds. Far from helping his country, a later commentator noted, he sought 'to concentrate the western fur trade in the hands of only such American citizens as had been born in Walldorf, Germany, in 1763 and had arrived in the United States from London in the spring of 1784'. Indeed, one of his first acts under his new company's charter was to cut in a number of Northwest luminaries as partners in a subsidiary called the Pacific Fur Company, which intended to exploit the great forests between the Rockies and the ocean, recently explored by the historic Lewis and Clark expedition. Only one of the stockholders in that consortium was a native American. Shortly afterwards, in 1811, he again combined with Canadians to buy out the Mackinaw Company, which as the Southwest Company became another subsidiary of American Fur.

These moves were intended to be part of a great double-cross in which Astor would later press for legislation banning foreign nationals from holdings in American companies and, having won it, would assume full control of all the large-scale fur business south of the Great Lakes, in the Louisiana Territory and in the disputed lands of the Pacific Northwest. As a vision of empire it was unique in its day, but since Astor had no genuine nationalistic sentiments himself – viewing the whole scheme purely in terms of dollars and cents – he failed to appreciate the patriotic motives of his new partners from the north, and in that lay the root of his undoing.

The key to Astor's plan was the establishment of the first American settlement in the Pacific Northwest. It was to be sited at the mouth of the Columbia river, in the Oregon Territory, and it was to be a clearing-house for furs gleaned from the region – either through trappers engaged by Pacific Fur or by trade with the Indians – which were then to be sent directly across the Pacific to China, the world's best market. Goods purchased in China with the fur profits would be imported via New York, completing a perfect circle of trade. And since New York would continue to be Astor's centre for the domestic and European markets, the American Fur Company and its subsidiaries – divested of Canadian participation – would enjoy a coast-to-coast monopoly of the business, large enough and powerful enough to crush any attempt at competition, whether from north of the border or from the smaller American companies which had sprung up in the Louisiana Territory.

Of course, Astor was not the only one to see the opportunity. The Northwest Company, on whose behalf Sir Alexander Mackenzie had made the first 'official' transcontinental journey of discovery as long ago as 1793, had already established some trading posts in what was known as New Caledonia, an area lying between the north-western territory claimed by America and the Russian possessions in what is now Alaska. The Canadians had severe problems of supply and communications, however, since there was no good harbour nearby – everything had to be hauled overland to and from Montreal, a costly and time-consuming business. Astor's planned base at the broad mouth of the Columbia (which had been charted by a Captain Gray of Boston in 1792 and later explored by the great English navigator George Vancouver) would thus give him tremendous advantages, including the possibility of a trading agreement with the Russians to the north, who also had difficulties in transporting the furs from that remote outpost of their empire: such an association would further squeeze the Northwest Company and hasten Astor's achievement of monopoly.

Here Astor was moving into the realms of diplomacy and high politics; relations between America and Britain were tense and a move into the Pacific Northwest might appear to the British as an aggressive act; furthermore, any deal with the Russians would require official sanction. John Jacob wrote to Jefferson outlining his scheme and once more presenting himself as a patriotic citizen, according to what he told Washington Irving, who faithfully reported:

> He was already wealthy beyond the ordinary desires of man, but he now aspired to that honorable fame which is awarded to men of similar scope of mind, who by their great commercial enterprises have enriched nations, peopled wildernesses, and extended the bounds of empire. He considered his projected settlement at the mouth of the Columbia as the emporium to an immense commerce; as a colony that would form the germ of a wide civiliza-

tion; that would, in fact, carry the American population across the Rocky Mountains and spread it along the shores of the Pacific, as it already animated the shores of the Atlantic.

This emporium, this colony, this vanguard of a spreading civilization was to be named Astoria.

III

President Jefferson readily gave his approval to the Astoria project. He wrote: 'I considered, as a great public acquisition, the commencement of a settlement on that point of the western coast of America, and looked forward with gratification to the time when its descendants should have spread themselves through the entire length of that coast, covering it with free and independent Americans, unconnected with us but by the ties of blood and interest, and enjoying like us the rights of self-government.'

John Jacob Astor, his own private and materialistic dream reinforced by the vision of the philosopher prince of the American Revolution, swiftly put his plans into effect. Having carefully studied the account of the Lewis and Clark expedition written by one of its members, Patrick Gass – it was published in 1807, ahead of the official report commissioned by the government – Astor had already determined that to ensure the success of his venture two parties of 'colonists' should set out from New York. One would travel overland, following the trail blazed by Lewis and Clark, establishing friendly relations with the Indians and setting up staging posts on the way. The second group would reach the mouth of the Columbia by sea to begin construction of a fortified trading centre and generally to make arrangements for business to begin as soon as the overland trekkers arrived.

The leader of the overland expedition, and ultimately Astor's chief agent in the west, was to be Wilson Price Hunt, the only American partner in the Pacific Fur Company and its largest stockholder after Astor (though Hunt held only five of the one hundred shares against John Jacob's fifty). Since Hunt was a businessman with no experience of the wilderness, he was to be accompanied by Donald McKenzie, one of the five Northwest Company veterans Astor had taken into partnership, each holding four shares in the company. The other four Canadians – Alexander McKay, Duncan McDougal, David Stuart and Robert Stuart, David's nephew – were to be joint leaders of the seaborne group. All Astor had to do was raise the finance for the project and then sit back to wait for the profits to roll in. With his fifty shares in Pacific Fur, he stood to gain considerably more than anyone else involved. On the other hand, he also had by far the most to lose.

Hunt and McKenzie left New York in June 1810 and travelled to Montreal to engage a band of voyageurs and gather supplies for their journey. This was the first mistake: as soon as the Northwest Company learnt that Astor's men were recruiting it put pressure on the best voyageurs to prevent them from joining the expedition, with the result that Hunt was forced to pay exorbitant advances and wages to the least prepossessing members of the Canadian fur fraternity. McKenzie should have been able to do better in this respect, with ten years in the Northwest Company behind him, but he appears to have chosen not to help much, for reasons which will become apparent.

At the end of July, Hunt moved his unimpressive crew to Michilimackinac on the first stage of the journey to St Louis, starting point of their westward excursion. He hoped to strengthen the party through the addition of some better-class voyageurs, but the Mackinaw Company – still a year away from Astor's coup – took the same dim view as Northwest had done in Montreal, and it was some time before Hunt could attract even one experienced hand. In the end it was McKenzie who made the breakthrough. Frustrated by his partner's inability to put together a proper team, and no doubt unwilling to embark upon such a risky venture without reliable support, McKenzie appealed to the childish pride of the voyageurs by offering recruits cockades of feathers and ostrich plumes which they could flaunt in the faces of the swaggering Northwest and Mackinaw brigades. Within days a force of thirty or more men had been assembled, though still at a very high price.

Hunt was all for making the best of the brigade he had and

pushing on with the expedition, but one of his Michilimackinac recruits, Ramsey Crooks, offered a word of caution. Crooks, a Scottish-American whose name would later become a by-word in the fur trade, was an experienced trapper and trader who had worked for Northwest before going into business on his own. He had recently returned from the Louisiana Territory and he told Hunt hair-raising stories of the warlike Sioux and Blackfeet Indians, pointing out that a force of thirty men would be too small to deter attack – indeed, small enough to encourage it – and recommending that the party be doubled in size. Crooks's advice was supported by McKenzie, but there was nothing to be gained from remaining in Michilimackinac, with the onset of winter not far off, so it was decided that the expedition should progress to St Louis, within striking distance of the serious part of the journey, where there was at least a chance of hiring voyageurs who knew something about the territory they were to cross.

In the second week of August, the Astorian brigade moved out – though 'it was with the utmost difficulty that they could be extricated from the clutches of the publicans, and the embraces of their pot companions' – and paddled or hauled their huge birch canoes from Michilimackinac across Lake Michigan to Green Bay, down the Fox River and overland to the Wisconsin, joining the Mississippi at Prairie du Chien and arriving at St Louis on 3 September.

They stood now at the gateway to the West, but the year was too far advanced for them to go much farther, since they had no wish to be caught by the snow in the unfamiliar and forbidding foothills of the Rockies. On the other hand, there were two good reasons why the brigade should not winter in St Louis. The first was the liveliness of the town itself, with its strong French and Spanish connexions: voyageurs were not men likely to resist the temptations of the flesh, and months of inactivity in a place providing plenty of scope for diversion could seriously reduce the numbers of the expedition as well as costing its promoters large sums of money in bar bills.

The second reason for an early departure was, in the eyes of Hunt at least, even more pressing – the Missouri Fur Company, a St Louis outfit run by a shrewd and resourceful Spanish-American named Manuel Lisa, who operated a number of trading posts in the Missouri valley and had established good relations with some branches of the Sioux and other local tribes. Lisa and his associates were not about to relinquish any part of the growing business for which they had worked so hard, and they did everything they could to obstruct the Astorians. After the experiences in Montreal and Michilimackinac, Hunt knew that he could not risk giving a rival company a long winter in which to suborn the members of his brigade, so on 21 October men and supplies were loaded aboard two barges and a keelboat and the expedition set out to get as far along the Missouri as it could before ice made the river impassable. By 14 November the brigade had covered four hundred and fifty miles; they made camp at the mouth of the Nadowa river just two days before the ice closed in. As soon as the encampment had been secured, Hunt took Ramsey Crooks and a small group of men back to St Louis to buy more supplies and recruit more voyageurs. Before he left, he made the second significant mistake of the expedition – he effectively demoted his co-leader, Donald McKenzie.

There had been tension between Hunt and McKenzie almost from the start. The former Northwest man regarded Astor's appointed chief lieutenant as a rank amateur who knew nothing of the sort of men he had been chosen to command and even less of the kind of journey on which he was expected to lead them. Hence McKenzie's lack of support during the difficulties in Montreal. For his part, Hunt suspected that his Canadian partner had not entirely forsworn his previous allegiance, to which he was inclined to attribute the early recruiting problems. McKenzie, of course, was much more at home in the company of the rough, proud and untameable voyageurs, and the high proportion of Canadians among them made Hunt feel particularly vulnerable. The American was anxious about leaving such alien spirits to their own devices while he was away in St Louis, not knowing what he might find when he returned, so he saw it as a fortunate deliverance when a messenger from Astor arrived with instructions for Hunt to assume sole charge of the expedition. He immediately appointed as his deputy Joseph Miller, a former American army officer taken into partnership in St Louis, and before leaving the camp made it clear that McKenzie was now very much a subordinate. Thus were the seeds of disaster sown.

It may be that Hunt had communicated his suspicions of McKenzie to New York, but John Jacob Astor had a much stronger reason for wishing to diminish the influence of the Scotsman: he had convincing evidence by this time that his four Scottish partners with the seaborne expedition were not acting in his interest. For one thing, he had learned that none of the landing party brought from Canada had complied with his request that they should become American citizens before they sailed. Worse was to come.

McDougal, McKay and the Stuarts had sailed from New York on 8 September 1810 aboard the *Tonquin*, a small but solid ship of two hundred and ninety tons carrying ten guns and a crew of twenty. Barely was the *Tonquin* out of coastal waters when a dispute broke out between the captain and his principal passengers. The skipper, Lieutenant Jonathan Thorn, seconded from the United States Navy at Astor's request, issued an order for 'lights out' at eight o'clock in the evening; the four Scottish partners were incensed by this imposition and refused to obey, maintaining that as senior officials of the Pacific Fur Company, which was bearing the cost of the voyage – including Thorn's salary – they were entitled to do as they pleased. An ugly quarrel ensued, but although eventually tempers were cooled by the more moderate members of the party and a compromise was reached, an atmosphere of hostility had been created which was to last throughout the voyage and contribute greatly to its tragic conclusion.

Lieutenant Thorn has taken a good deal of the blame for the miserable fate of the Astoria project, one writer going so far as to describe him as a psychopath and a sadist. He certainly was a martinet, and a man with his fair share of faults, but pseudo-Freudian judgments are on shaky ground. Thorn was no Captain Queeg, rather a pretty typical specimen of the career naval officer of his day – brave, simple-minded, fanatically loyal to his superiors, tyrannical in the obsession to maintain 'a tight ship'. These were the very attitudes and qualities that impressed Astor, yet they were also precisely the reason why Thorn was the wrong man for the *Tonquin*. He was too narrow-minded, too inflexible and inclined to live by the rule book, too much concerned with the management of his ship rather than the overall purposes of the expedition. A merchant skipper would have been much more suitable. For a start, he would probably have been a better seaman – navy officers of the time, with some notable exceptions, were not famous for the brilliance of their seamanship, and Thorn was not among the exceptions, as will become clear. Secondly, a merchant captain would have been more inclined to make distinctions between command and counsel, treating the landing party differently from his crew: he would always bear in mind that his position depended upon the goodwill of his employers and the success of the voyage.

In the end, then, it is Astor who must bear the responsibility for what happened. Unused to being involved in real risks, he was afraid of what his Scottish partners and their wayward voyageurs, whom he held in some contempt, might do once they were out of his sight, so he appointed Thorn as his captain because he knew that all the lieutenant's instincts and training would impel him to carry out to the letter any instructions Astor gave him and that his loyalty would be absolute. Of course, John Jacob was right in this assessment, and he was also right to be suspicious of the four Scotsmen, who had designs other than the enrichment of a German immigrant in a country hostile towards their own, but in setting up an inevitable conflict of both powers and personalities he created an impossible situation. The arrogant Thorn, who expected to be obeyed without question, and the proud, touchy, aggressive Scots simply did not mix.

Thorn quickly made clear in his reports to Astor his assessment of the Pacific Fur Company partners and their employees. They were 'lubberly' poseurs, full of pride and vanity on shore but completely useless at sea, 'the most worthless beings that ever broke sea-biscuit'. They apparently complained about the food, though the *Tonquin*'s table was graced by the sort of fare Thorn would have considered almost indecent aboard the warships he was used to. At first the landsmen were seasick, but once they had recovered they began to treat the voyage as a holiday cruise, loafing about the deck smoking and singing, eating and drinking everything they could get their hands on, yarning, making notes in journals and signally failing to keep themselves and their quarters shipshape

74

and Bristol fashion. From time to time the captain would descend without warning on the 'lubber nests' and root out the inhabitants with orders to stir themselves and clean up both their persons and their berths. None of this was conducive to good relations.

The first landfall was made on 4 December, when the *Tonquin* was obliged to put in at the Falkland Islands because the ship was very short of water. McDougal and McKay went with a boat party to find an anchorage and locate a spring, but neither was available and Thorn signalled the party to return to the *Tonquin*. The Scots, however, decided to go exploring and did not come aboard until nine o'clock in the evening. Thorn said nothing, but when the pair went ashore again the following morning he warned them to be alert for recall since he was waiting only for a shift in the wind. Once more his order was ignored, as McKay and McDougal went goose-hunting and it was not until they saw the *Tonquin* under sail that they felt obliged to rejoin the ship, which cost them some hard rowing. The captain received them coldly, but kept his peace.

A couple of days later the *Tonquin* dropped anchor in the natural harbour of Port Egmont, Saunders Island, where she was to remain while repairs were carried out and the water casks filled. The 'lubbers' had a marvellous time, shooting game, boating and discovering traces of the then abandoned settlement founded by Commodore Byron in 1765. On the morning of 11 December all was ready for departure and Thorn was furious to learn that eight of his passengers, including McDougal again, had failed to respond to the signal calling them back aboard. It was the last straw for the captain, who made sail and put to sea, leaving the errant passengers to 'shift for themselves' on the barren island. McDougal and the others, seeing the ship under way, leapt into a twenty-foot boat and rowed off in pursuit, but it was three and a half hours before they caught her, and they would not have done so then but for a sudden change in the wind.

So the uncomfortable voyage went on, Thorn acting ever more high-handedly as his contempt for the partners grew and his notion of his duty hardened, while the Scotsmen vowed that once they had established themselves on the Columbia they would assume their rightful powers and quickly put this petty dictator in his place. Thorn undoubtedly took a tougher line than was necessary, bearing in mind that it was not a military undertaking subject to normal military rules, but it seems equally certain that the four Scots, puffed up with their own importance, and released for once from the hierarchical constraints imposed by the Northwest Company, were happy to make free with Astor's money. After all, if they consumed all the provisions and had to buy more, it was not at their cost; if they delayed the construction of Astoria by dallying on exotic isles, it was not their loss. Astor had agreed to finance the operations of the Pacific Fur Company for five years, up to a maximum amount of $400,000: to his partners, what difference did a few months or a few thousand dollars make? Of course, John Jacob expected to see returns on his investment long before he had put in almost half a million dollars, and one of the reasons he had hired Thorn was to make sure that time and money were not wasted. That the captain had specific instructions to keep the Scotsmen in check is made clear in Washington Irving's account – after all the time Astor had spent in Montreal, he well knew the Northwesters' capacity for extravagance.

But, as with the overland expedition, Astor created confrontation by a perverse division of control, appointing McDougal as his business proxy. McDougal was 'an active, irritable, fuming, vainglorious little man, and elevated in his own opinion, by being the proxy of Mr Astor'. As far as he was concerned, the interpretation of Astor's instructions was his overall responsibility and the skipper of the *Tonquin* was his servant. He therefore seized every opportunity to challenge Thorn's attempts to impose his will and encouraged his partners to ignore the captain's orders almost as a matter of course. Nor was McDougal's megalomania by any means confined to his relations with the captain. As the partners eventually settled down to planning their trading post and fort at Astoria, furious and sometimes violent rows broke out among them, with McDougal brandishing his letter of appointment from Astor as a badge of authority.

The captain's regular dispatches detailing the difficulties he was having with McDougal and his colleagues made John Jacob Astor nervous, particularly when Thorn intimated that he believed the Scots were plotting against him. Astor began to have second thoughts about the wisdom of relying on so many non-Americans – hence his instruction to Hunt to take sole command of the overland party. But there was nothing he could do about the state of affairs aboard the *Tonquin*.

On Christmas Day 1810, the 'ship of fools' rounded the Horn and ploughed across the Pacific, reaching Hawaii in the second week of February to take on supplies and recruit more men. The beauty of the Sandwich Islands, and especially their amorous female inhabitants, proved to be a great attraction to the 'lubbers' and their visit lasted three weeks. When they left the tension between captain and passengers was if possible greater than before, since Thorn had heard rumours in Hawaii of impending war between the United States and Britain. When the partners began to distribute arms to their men (a perfectly normal procedure, given that their next landfall was to be on a possibly hostile coast), the lieutenant's suspicions of imminent mutiny became obsessive, making him even more watchful and unapproachable: any reasonable relationship between him and the Scots was now beyond the realm of possibility.

It was in this unpromising mood that the party arrived off the mouth of the Columbia on 22 March 1811. The sight that met their eyes was both awe-inspiring and menacing – a great estuary, more than four miles across, guarded by a low landspit on the south side and a promontory called Cape Disappointment to the north, with between them a sandbar over which the sea broke in monstrous plumes of spray. Beyond the shoreline was mile upon mile of gloomy forest, giving way to apparently endless chains of snow-girt, cloud-capped mountains.

Forbidding though this prospect was, it was known that previous expeditions had successfully navigated some miles upriver. Clearly there must be a serviceable channel into the estuary: it was simply a question of finding it. Here, though, one might begin to doubt Lieutenant Thorn's judgment as a seaman. He was wise enough not to risk his ship closer than eight miles from the shore, but he ordered the whaler to be launched in conditions that were, to put it mildly, unfavourable, with a fresh north-westerly whipping up the waves as they careered towards the rocky coast. His first mate protested, but Thorn was adamant. The whaler and her five-man crew, including the mate and three Canadian voyageurs, were never seen again.

This was a bad start, but worse was to follow. Though the weather moderated, Thorn lost a second boat and three more men – and narrowly avoided losing the *Tonquin* herself – before he abandoned the attempt to find a channel and anchored in the safety of Baker's Bay on Cape Disappointment.

And still the arguments between the captain and the fur traders continued. Excited by the prospect of ridding himself of such troublesome passengers, Thorn immediately began to unload their equipment, and built a shed at Baker's Bay to house it. McDougal, however, wanted to establish his base on the southern shore of the estuary and chose a site with a safe harbour at Point George – it was not ideal, but he was as keen to see the back of Thorn as the lieutenant was to be on his way. Accordingly, on 12 April the *Tonquin* put into the little bay and the foundation of Astoria began in earnest.

McDougal quickly established friendly contacts with the Chinook Indians of the region, so work on the fort and trading post proceeded unhindered by fears of attack. Nevertheless Thorn became impatient at what he considered slow progress by the shore party which was delaying his departure on the second part of his mission, to cruise northwards along the coast and barter pelts from the natives (he complained in a letter to McDougal of the time wasted by 'sporting and smoking parties'). By 5 June, however, the Astorians were satisfied that they no longer needed the *Tonquin* and she sailed away, taking Alexander McKay as supercargo and one of the clerks to assist him. She was never to return.

At just about the same time, in June 1811, Wilson Hunt and his overland party, now grown to sixty-four men, were preparing to cross the 'Great American Desert' – the wide prairies which now produce enormous quantities of wheat but which in those days were 'a vast uninhabited solitude, seamed by ravines, the beds of former torrents, but now serving only to tantalize and increase the thirst of the traveller . . . this immense wilderness of the far West, which apparently defies cultivation, and the habitation of civilized life'. The men recruited in St

Louis were seasoned frontier hands, and mainly Americans,* which made Hunt feel more comfortable but did nothing to ease the strains within the brigade. Joseph Miller's appointment as deputy leader had already split the party into Canadian and American factions, with the former continuing to look to the disgruntled McKenzie as their chief. Indeed, Hunt was sought out in St Louis by five American trappers who had followed him from Nadowa to complain about the constant feuding at the camp.

Hunt lacked the leadership skills to reconcile these differences and soothe the petty jealousies, while McKenzie had a definite interest in maintaining divisions – he would make Astor realize his error in appointing a novice as leader instead of a hardened frontiersman. Perhaps, too, the Scotsman was already looking for an excuse to break away from the main party and strike out with his own men in a sort of race to reach Astoria. Altogether it was hardly a promising atmosphere for the perilous trek that was about to be undertaken, and further pressure was placed on the expedition by the activities of Manuel Lisa and his Missouri Fur Company colleagues. Hunt and Lisa came into open conflict in St Louis when the former hired as interpreter Pierre Dorion, a halfbreed Sioux who worked for the Missouri Company and owed a large sum of money to the company store in respect of the liberal quantities of whisky he was inclined to consume. Lisa issued a summons for debt, but this merely had the effect of strengthening Dorion's resolve to leave and he took to the woods to escape arrest, promising to meet Hunt's party on its way back to Nadowa.

At the same time, however, Lisa approached Hunt with the information that he himself was about to send a brigade into the Missouri valley: he offered to join forces with the Astorians, but Ramsey Crooks advised Hunt that the Spaniard was not to be trusted, giving as a reason his strong, but unsubstantiated, suspicion that Lisa had incited a Sioux raiding party to attack him on a previous foray into the wilderness. As a result, Hunt became obsessed with the notion that he must get a head start on the Missouri Company and gathered his small band together for a hasty departure from St Louis. In spite of unseasonal

* Though they included two British naturalists and adventurers: John Bradbury, who later wrote *Travels in America*, and Thomas Nuttall, author of *Genera of American Plants*.

flooding caused by early spring rains, the party made its way to Nadowa by boat, arriving at the encampment on 17 April. On the way they were joined by the fugitive Dorion (who insisted on bringing along his wife and child) and by John Colter, one of the pioneer explorers of the West, discoverer of what was to become Yellowstone National Park, and a man with knowledge of the Oregon Territory from his service with Lewis and Clark.

Still looking over his shoulder for Lisa's men, and anxious that they would stir up hostile Indians against him, Hunt moved out his brigade as soon as the rains stopped and by the end of the month they were six hundred miles west of the Mississippi. Several independent trappers had by now joined the party and these men, who were familiar with the terrain that lay before the expedition, suggested continuing by water to an Arickara Indian village on the edge of the plains and then leaving the river and heading directly west across the prairies towards the Rocky Mountains, through which they would find passes more accommodating than those encountered by Lewis and Clark on their more northerly river route. The Arickaras had horses to sell and, more important, were hospitable to white men. Hunt decided to head for their settlement with all haste, partly because their route would take them through the domain of the fierce Sioux Tetons, but mainly so that he could come to terms with the Arickaras before the arrival of Lisa, who was only four days behind and had already sent a messenger with another offer of cooperation – which of course was treated with suspicion.

As it happened, however, the Sioux encountered by the brigade were peaceable and anyway Lisa's men overtook the Astorians before they reached the Arickara village, the two parties sailing along opposite riverbanks, separated not only by water but also by mutual antagonism, which occasionally erupted into violent confrontation. At the settlement Lisa offered to buy Hunt's boats and pay for them in horseflesh. A deal was made, but Hunt remained doubtful about Lisa's intentions and was angered by the Spaniard's openly expressed opinion that the Astorians would never reach their goal, which damaged the brigade's morale so badly that several members had to be dissuaded from deserting by a mixture of threats and inducements.

It was with some relief, therefore, that Hunt took his leave of the Arickaras and the Spaniard on 18 July, though no one was encouraged by the attitude of the Missouri men on the day of departure, since they made it clear that they never expected to see the Astorians again. The first part of the journey went well, however. They rode across the prairies, finding plenty of buffalo and other game to feed them, then made their way through the arid sandstone passes of the Black Hills in what is now South Dakota. By September they were in the Rockies, following Indian trails, crossing the Bighorn River and eventually reaching Fort Henry, the most westerly outpost of the Missouri Fur Company. The post was deserted, since its trappers had journeyed eastward with their pelts to meet Lisa, but the Astorians welcomed the shelter of its log cabins.

In this place of safety and relative comfort, the dissensions among the party, which had flared up sporadically on the journey, now became open and serious. The Canadian *engagés*, happier on water than on land, insisted that the time had come to take to the rivers again. Hunt opposed this course, but the majority – including his deputy, Miller – was against him and he had to agree to the construction of canoes from the abundance of birch trees on the heavily wooded slopes: he assumed in any case that having conquered, as he thought, the feared mountains, the remainder of the journey would be swift and easy. How wrong he was. A series of tactical errors and Hunt's inability to inspire confidence in his men turned an expedition that was already a failure into a travesty.

The mission had failed in the sense that, although the brigade had spent almost half its time since leaving St Louis in camp, they had neglected to establish a single one of the planned staging posts along the route, so that much of the purpose in setting up Astoria at all had been lost. At Fort Henry, Hunt decided he had better remedy this omission. Here he had a ready-made post at his disposal, so he organized some of his party to begin the work they had travelled so far to do. A small group of trappers was detached from the main body to collect furs, which were to be stored at the fort (without any apparent consideration as to what the reaction of the rival Missouri men might be when they returned). But at this point the brigade was shocked by the announcement of Joseph Miller that, tired of the petty bickering and lack of coordination among the so-called businessmen, he was renouncing his partnership and opting for the rough simplicity of the wild forest life – he was going with the trappers. Despite the remonstrances of his partners, he left the fort with four experienced hunters on 10 October 1811. He was soon to regret his impetuous decision. Indian attacks that robbed the hunters of virtually all their possessions, months of aimless wandering in the wilderness and repeated periods of near-starvation convinced Miller that the trapper's life was not for him, and he was glad to return to civilization the following year. At least he came back alive – his four companions in adversity were all to perish at the hands of marauding Indians.

Miller's defection left Hunt in sole charge of the expedition, with McKenzie sulking in his tent, so to speak. It was a state of affairs that was not to last long. Having lost one voyageur and a canoe on the downstream journey from Fort Henry, the party halted above an impassable whirlpool on the upper reaches of the Snake River and immediately fell into a dispute about what they should do next. It was clear that the canoes, which had taken two weeks to build, would have to be abandoned, but all the horses had been left at the fort and the country that lay before them was a bare and trackless waste they would have to traverse on foot. Hunt was for pressing on regardless – carrying what they could on their backs and caching the bulk of their supplies on the banks of the Snake – on the grounds that since the great barrier of the Rockies had been crossed, nothing now barred their way to the sea. McKenzie, veteran of many forays into unexplored territory, was not so sure: he was for turning north to find the headwaters of the Columbia and then proceeding by canoe. The decision was crucial and no compromise was possible. On 9 November McKenzie and five followers left the main body to find a route through the mountain passes, meeting on the way two small scouting parties sent out by Hunt who decided to throw in their lot with the Canadians. Their experiences in the wintry wastes were terrible, but they were to fare better than Hunt's men.

After the realization, reinforced by the loss of three more canoes, that the upper reaches of the Snake were unnavigable, it began to dawn on Hunt that the expedition was in a desperate situation – lost among mountains in which no white man had ever set foot, short of food and facing the onset of winter, when snow would block the narrow passes. It was a trap that had to be sprung quickly, but how? Hunt decided to divide such resources as he had and set Ramsey Crooks, with eighteen men, to search one side of the river for a way out while he and the remainder explored the other side. For weeks, as the weather worsened, with incessant rain gradually turning to snow, the two groups blundered about the inhospitable slopes, meeting only a few half-starved Indians and completely unable to find game to feed themselves. They were reduced to gnawing on boiled beaver pelts, while thirst drove some of the voyageurs to drink their own urine. (There were rivers and streams aplenty, to be sure, but their banks were so precipitous that the water could not be reached.) Several men died, others became so crazed with hunger that they simply wandered away to their doom. A number of the remainder, including Crooks, fell ill and were abandoned in the wilderness to follow on later if they survived. It was a sorry, emaciated and ragged little band that finally found a route into the lush lowlands of the Umatilla Valley and emerged from the mountains on 18 January 1812, to discover from some friendly Indians that the Columbia was only a few miles away.

They camped by the Umatilla for two weeks, recovering their strength and hoping that some of the stragglers would find them, but as none of those left behind appeared and their fate remained unknown, the party pushed on to the Columbia, where they built canoes and were borne by the strong current on the last leg of their journey, reaching Astoria on 15 February. McKenzie and his men had arrived at the fort a month before, but old animosities and recriminations were forgotten in the celebration of reunion.

When the joy subsided, though, the leaders of the expedition sat down to consider their position and found it very different from the one John Jacob Astor had envisaged. Hunt had lost many of his men and virtually all his supplies. Moreover, he had done nothing to establish a trade route to the east or even to make a return journey less hazardous and uncertain than the trek he had just completed. That, however, was nowhere near the full extent of the expedition's failure: it had now no means of sending out furs or even communicating with civilization by sea, for the *Tonquin* was no more. Hunt listened in horror as his partners told the story carried to Astoria by the ship's interpreter, the only survivor of Lieutenant Thorn's last voyage.

The *Tonquin* had sailed north as planned and put into Neweetee, Vancouver Island, where the Indians were accustomed to trading with white men. Thorn had been warned by Astor that these particular natives were untrustworthy – the captain had been instructed to treat them courteously but not to place any faith in their professions of friendship and never to allow more than a small group of them aboard his ship. Astor, however, was a long way from Vancouver Island and Thorn's patience, not an asset he had in abundance, had been severely tried by months of harassment by the businessmen for whom he felt a disgust matched only by his contempt for Indians. He considered that his employer's interests had not been well served thus far and, in his fanatical zeal to do his duty, he took it upon himself to redress the balance. While his supercargo, McKay, was ashore accepting the hospitality of a tribal chief, Thorn attempted to begin trading with groups of curious Indians who came out by canoe to visit the ship.

Sensing that Thorn was not used to trading, one chief demanded exorbitant barter for sea-otter skins. This enraged the captain, who finally picked up one of the pelts and rubbed it in the chief's face, ordering all the Indians off his ship. Such behaviour was a serious insult to the natives and it appalled McKay when he returned: he advised Thorn to weigh anchor immediately and get out while the going was good, but the lieutenant replied that with a well-armed ship and heavily stocked armoury he was not going to run away from a few ignorant savages.

The following morning the Indians were back, indicating that they carried no weapons and were now ready to trade in earnest. Forgetting Astor's injunction and ignoring the counsel of the anxious McKay, Thorn allowed the natives to swarm over the ship and, amazingly, to trade their pelts for knives. Soon every Indian aboard was armed, and Thorn began to see the danger he was in. He barked an order to make sail and tried to herd the natives off the *Tonquin*, but it was too late. The

Indians sprang to the attack, slaughtering Thorn, McKay and the entire crew save four men and the company's clerk, Mr Lewis, who barricaded themselves in the cabin then opened fire with muskets, killing a large number of Indians and sending the rest fleeing for the shore.

For the rest of that day and throughout the night the *Tonquin* lay with sails flapping and no sign of life aboard, while the Indians kept an anxious eye on her lest her cannon were suddenly to open fire. By the next morning, however, the natives' confidence had increased and they approached the ship cautiously in their canoes. As they drew near, the figure of Mr Lewis, blood-spattered from a mortal wound sustained in the attack, appeared on the deck and beckoned them aboard. Excited at the prospect of plunder, the warriors clambered over the side. The ship's Indian interpreter, who had escaped the massacre by mingling with the attackers, noticed there was no sign of the other survivors from the crew and soon Mr Lewis also disappeared. The reason quickly became clear. As the Indians thronged the decks squabbling over their booty, the *Tonquin* blew up: Lewis, knowing that he was going to die anyway, had decided to exact a terrible revenge on the murderers of his shipmates and had set light to the powder magazine. More than a hundred Indians were killed outright and scores of others were fatally mutilated.

The interpreter must have been a lucky fellow, for he survived the second bloodbath, too, being thrown uninjured into the water by the explosion. He witnessed the slow, agonizing deaths of the four other white survivors, who had left the *Tonquin* under cover of darkness but had been captured by the Indians after their small boat had been blown ashore. And eventually he stole away and brought news of the tragedy to Astoria.

Of course, the loss of the *Tonquin* came as a severe blow to the Astorians, yet in the circumstances there was nothing for them to do but carry on with their enterprise. When the first log cabins and storehouses were completed, a stone barracks was built and the whole settlement was surrounded by a palisade which, with the siting of two four-pounders, secured the settlers against Indian attack. The Indians of the Columbia estuary, however, were more interested in trade than in war.

Before long the new storehouses were filling up with good quality pelts, trappers were at work in the woods of the interior, and a small outpost had even been established upriver. The arrival of McKenzie and his men, later Hunt's party and later still – about April 1812 – Ramsey Crooks and some of the stragglers who had survived, increased both confidence and the level of activity at Astoria. For a time it looked as if the project might be made to succeed after all. But history, which had up to now been John Jacob Astor's chief ally, was about to play him false.

Back in the autumn of 1811 John Jacob had sent his ship *Beaver* to Astoria with supplies and reinforcements for the settlers. Increasing talk of war with Britain had made him realize the risk he was running with such a high proportion of British subjects in his expedition, so the new Astorians were almost all native Americans. But that was not the only reason for the voyage of the *Beaver*: she was to load whatever furs had been gathered at the settlement and make the inaugural run from Astoria to Canton, pausing on the way in Alaska to pick up Russian pelts under an agreement Astor had made with the imperial government. John Jacob was not so worried about the composition of his settlers that he would be willing to spend money for no other purpose than to redress the balance. At the time the *Beaver* sailed, of course, Astor knew nothing of the situation at Astoria – the loss of the *Tonquin* and the difficulties and delays that were troubling the overland expedition. What he did know, from sources in Montreal, was that the North-west Company had sent men south from its bases in western Canada to set up a trading post in the wilderness north of the Columbia. It was therefore imperative that Astoria should begin operations as soon as possible and the arrival of the *Beaver* would both encourage the settlers and serve as notice to Northwest that Astor was in earnest.

It was all too late, however. Within a month of the *Beaver*'s arrival on the Columbia the United States was at war with Britain in a misconceived and tragic sideshow to the greater conflict in Europe. Astor fretted and fumed and waited for news from the west coast, but all he heard was information that the Northwest Company now intended to send an armed ship to Astoria to claim the settlement in the King's name. John

Jacob's response was to dispatch his fastest ship, the *Lark*, in March 1813 to warn the Astorians of the danger they were in. He wrote to Hunt, once again appealing to the spirit of patriotism: 'Were I on the spot, and had the management of affairs, I would defy them all; but, as it is, everything depends upon you and your friends about you. Our enterprise is grand, and deserves success, and I hope to God it will meet it. If my object was merely gain of money, I should say, think whether it is best to save what we can and abandon the place; but the very idea is like a dagger in my heart...' In fact, the real dagger was the enormous loss he would suffer if Astoria was abandoned.

The shadow of disaster which had clouded the whole project almost from the start showed no sign of lifting. Hunt had left Astoria in the *Beaver* in the summer of 1812 and nothing further had been heard of him, leaving McDougal and the others to speculate that the ship might have gone the same way as the *Tonquin*. In fact, the *Beaver* had gone to Canton, having dropped off Hunt in the Sandwich Islands where he was vainly trying to hire a ship to replace the *Tonquin*. Eventually he found one, and returned in August 1813, but by then his partners had been visited by a small Northwest brigade with news of the war and, in the face of their threats, McDougal had signed a document turning over to the Canadians his main trading post in the interior, at Spokane, and announcing his intention of leaving Astoria by 1 June 1814 if no ship arrived from New York in the meantime. McDougal explained his actions to Hunt by saying that the Northwesters were expecting the imminent arrival of a company ship escorted by a British frigate and had offered him the choice of either cooperating with them or seeing Astoria destroyed by cannon-fire. Faced with this *fait accompli*, Hunt decided all he could do was try to salvage everything possible before the arrival of the British. He persuaded the skipper of the ship he had hired to take him back to the Sandwich Islands, where he would engage an empty cargo ship to transport the furs which had been collected by the Astorians in what had been a particularly good season. He left the settlement on 26 August, just six days after his arrival, giving McDougal authority to act on his behalf. Of all the mistakes Hunt made in the course of the expedition, this was to be the fatal one.

In New York, meanwhile, Astor had also heard the story that a British warship was bound for his small colony. He immediately applied to the government for aid and, thanks to the support of his friend Albert Gallatin, was promised the escort of a navy frigate for a third ship of his, the *Enterprise*, which he intended to send to Astoria. But the administration had other things on its mind, since the war was going badly for the Americans, and shortly before the two ships were about to sail, the naval crew was transferred to the Great Lakes fleet. Astoria would have to look after itself.

What was really happening, though, was that McDougal was looking after himself. He had already given up Astoria for lost and he persuaded his Scottish partners that in view of the war they had no choice but to reach an accommodation with their former colleagues in the Northwest Company. Some of the Scots wavered, but the strength of McDougal's position was reinforced in October 1813 when a band of Canadian seventy-five strong appeared at Astoria and camped just outside the stockade, raising the Union Jack over their tents. The 'invaders' brought a letter to McDougal from his uncle, a principal in the Northwest Company, informing him that a British naval squadron was on its way to 'take and destroy everything American on the Northwest Coast'. When this letter was read to the Canadian members of the settlement, any doubts about where their loyalties should lie were dispelled. By the time the British arrived off the mouth of the Columbia at the end of November – they came, incidentally, in a single frigate, not a squadron – Astoria had already been handed over to the Northwest Company, its furs sold to the Canadians for less than half their true value.

Hunt returned in February 1814 to find the British flag flying, McDougal comfortably installed as a partner in the Northwest Company, and Astoria renamed Fort George. There was nothing for him to do but take off the men who did not wish to throw in their lot with the Canadians and return to New York with the sorry news for Astor. (David Stuart and McKenzie, finally disgusted with McDougal's duplicity, had decided to make their way to St Louis overland.)

Astor was badly shaken, both financially and emotionally, but his phlegmatic nature refused to admit defeat. 'We have been sold, but I do not despond,' he wrote. 'While I breathe and so long as I have a dollar to spend I'll pursue a course to have our injuries repair'd.' He was to live up to that promise with ruthless efficiency, but he was never tempted to undertake such a gamble again and the fact that the Astoria affair rankled him ever afterwards may be assumed from the commission he gave to Washington Irving in the 1830s, since the resulting book was nothing if not a defence of the actions of John Jacob Astor.

3 'This Land Is My Land'

The years immediately following the War of 1812 have been described as among 'the barrenest in American history'. After the Treaty of Ghent in 1815 the Federalist Party, midwife at the birth of republican government, went into decline because its opposition to the war came to be perceived as pro-British Tory and anti-democratic. With the party's gradual extinction, 'scandal, intrigue and personal criticism became the most marked characteristics of American politics'.* Economically, too, everything was 'up for grabs'; financial crises were continual; fortunes were made and lost almost from day to day.

For John Jacob Astor it was a time of consolidation rather than expansion. Apart from the fact that the war had helped to keep the prizes of the West out of his reach, both the fur and tea trades inevitably went into recession between 1812 and 1815. Indeed, the second Embargo Act in 1813 – the notorious 'Damn-bargo' introduced by President Madison to keep American ships in port and prevent further clashes with the European combatants – virtually put an end to an import–export business already severely restricted by a British blockade.

As was so often the case, Astor fared better than most merchants in adversity, notwithstanding the huge financial sacrifice of Astoria (estimated at almost a million dollars). Before the Embargo he landed two highly profitable tea cargoes and in 1813 he pulled off a reprise of the Punqua Wing-chong trick, though in this instance the credentials of the passenger were impeccable: he was the celebrated French general Jean Victor Moreau, hero of the Revolution and of the battle of Hohenlinden in 1800. Having supported Napoleon Bonaparte both militarily and politically, General Moreau had fallen from

* Alexander Johnston in *American History 1763–1876*.

the Emperor's favour and had been banished from France on a trumped-up charge in 1804, settling in New Jersey. Disgusted by the grandiloquent posturing of his former chief, he had remained active in exile politics and had come to the notice of one of the New York representatives of the Tsar of Russia, Britain's ally against Napoleon. The Russian diplomat was also in contact with Astor, concerning the fur-transporting arrangement planned for Astoria, and these two saw a way of obtaining mutual advantage through Moreau. The general was persuaded to offer his considerable military skills to the Russians, who were at that time pursuing Napoleon's army westward across Europe, and Astor offered Moreau a passage to London in one of his ships. The American government could hardly refuse a permit for such a voyage and the British navy off Sandy Hook was not inclined to bar the passage of a vessel on the business of an ally (Astor even flew the Russian flag), so the ship, *Hannibal*, came safely to London. Of course, she also carried several hundred tons of furs, and Astor was able to report 'a good Market – I have done very well on the voyage'. As for Moreau, he joined the Tsar's general staff at the battle of Dresden, where he had his legs shot off in the cannon-fire of his former colleagues and died on 2 September 1813.

Astor's other wartime activities were no less amoral and sometimes verged on the treasonable. To be sure, he subscribed two million dollars to the American war bonds (on which he was to make a profit of fifty per cent), but he also offered a loan of $50,000 to the British authorities in Montreal. Furthermore, he gave the Canadians immediate warning of Madison's declaration of war, which allowed them both to prepare to meet surprise attacks along the border and to seize the American base at Mackinac – his reason being that he had furs stored in Canada which he wanted to get across the border before the disruption of fighting began. Some of his employees were later caught smuggling pelts into the United States in collusion with a bribed customs inspector, but Astor himself was never actually indicted.

One reason why suspicion of Astor's lack of loyalty to his adopted country remained no more than that was his support of the war bonds issue, and he used this to protect himself while he lobbied for an early end to the conflict, which he naturally saw as economic suicide. To his friend and client James Monroe, the Secretary of State, he wrote (and I leave his spelling intact in this case as an indication of the way he wrote and must have pronounced English):

'Senice I had the pleasure to See you at Washington I have Recd a Letter from Gottenbourg and an other from London boath are from very Inteligent Merchants after Speeking an the Subjict of commerce thy bouth give it as thire apinian that Great Britain will not make Peace with this country unless we acknowladge thea Right of theire coming an Board of aur Ships to take thire Seamen or Subjicts – the Englishman Says if your government of the publick mind is not prepard to Conseed this point the war will go on untill thy are it is to me Some what Singular that two merchants the ane in Londan & the other in Sweedne Should at the Same time write & express opinions so Leik each ather.'

The implication is clear: in Astor's view commerce was considerably more important than national integrity or global politics. Thus, when he realized that the temper of the government and of most of the population would suffer no talk of peace, he made what use he could of the situation without reference to the wishes of his countrymen. Shipowners who could not afford to have their vessels lying idle would sell them at bargain prices, and Astor always had ready cash. Other merchants, their businesses temporarily ruined by the depredations of the British or the legal injunctions of their own rulers, were keen to raise money by mortgaging their property and selling their land, and Astor was never one to reject a choice piece of real estate, especially if he could advance a mortgage with the prospect of foreclosure in the near future. In this way, while others faced bankruptcy, he tightened his hold on Manhattan and at the same time positioned himself to get a head start on the competition when trade revived at war's end.

For politics, he had no use at all. Those who practised that peculiar art were important, as far as he was concerned, only in as much as they could help to increase his fortune. The main foundations of his life were his business and his family, each as dear to his strange, narrow soul as the other. Sarah had borne him eight children, five of whom had survived, three girls and two boys. The eldest boy, born in 1791 and named John

Jacob II in the dynastic manner, had proved tragically unable to fulfil the role expected of an heir. As he had grown, disturbing evidence had emerged that there was something desperately wrong with him. He was subject to sudden and apparently unprovoked changes of mood, behaving sometimes like a normal lively boy but at other times merely staring vacantly into space, beyond everyday communication. A strong, healthy child, he was also prone to fits of violent rage in which he could be a danger to himself and to others.

In the absence of any psychiatric thought, a bitterly disappointed John Jacob at first clung to the belief that his all-important firstborn son was only a slow developer, but as time passed and no appreciable improvement could be detected he came to the conclusion that the boy was mentally deficient, an idiot. Accordingly, John Jacob II was kept quietly at home, his parents hoping all the while that the best of care would somehow make him better and insisting that the other children treat their eldest brother as if nothing was wrong. Eventually it seems to have dawned on them that mental disturbance rather than imbecility was the root of the trouble and doctors were consulted, but in those pre-Freudian days the only options available to them in the way of 'treatment' were confinement in an institution or a secure and protected domestic environment under constant medical supervision. An asylum and a clinic were tried briefly, but at last John Jacob accepted the inevitable and built a house for the unfortunate, staffing it with servants, hiring a live-in physician and committing his son to at least a materially comfortable life of seclusion and care. John Jacob II lived on until 1869, sometimes lucid and able to write verse, but for the most part trapped in his disordered inner world.

In the circumstances, it may be imagined with what anxiety Jacob and Sarah watched over the early years of their second son, born in 1792 and christened William Backhouse Astor, as I have said, in honour of the merchant who helped John Jacob to develop his fur business. William was a handsome, fresh-faced boy, rather on the shy side, and notable for that childish earnestness which is sometimes called 'old-fashioned'. Learning came naturally to him and the eight years he spent at the fashionable boarding school presided over by the Reverend Mr Smith at Stamford, Connecticut, were not wasted. Armed with a thorough knowledge of Greek and Latin, he was sent to complete his education first at Columbia College, then at the University of Heidelberg and finally at Göttingen University, the pre-eminent school of Classics under its world renowned Professor of Eloquence, C.G. Heyne.

Göttingen suited William very well. Of a serious and scholarly bent, he enjoyed studying the history, languages and philosophies of the ancient world and made a lifelong friend in the brilliant Christian Bunsen, a year older than himself, who explained the beginning of their relationship thus: 'I am now in a very convenient position, residing altogether with the son of an American merchant named Astor, boarded and lodged in the best manner, and am to receive between this time and Easter 30 louis d'or for which I give him instruction in German and other things...' It was normal practice for older students to be selected as tutors for younger ones, but as well as helping Bunsen to earn his keep the arrangement provided him with an opportunity to improve his English, which was to be an advantage in later years when, as Baron von Bunsen, he was ambassador to the Court of St James's. If the friendship – they soon abandoned the formal German second-person pronoun 'Sie' for the more intimate 'Du' – was instrumental in making Bunsen an Anglophile, it also brought William's Germanic background into focus: years afterwards he would recall with affection his time at Göttingen with Bunsen, and throughout his life he would always converse with his children in the language of the old country, just as his father did.

During the long vacation in the summer of 1811, Astor and Bunsen set out to tour Germany, visiting Gotha, Weimar and Jena, Leipzig and Dresden. The following year William had to return to New York and begged his friend to accompany him, but Bunsen refused. Instead, they embarked early in 1813 on a journey intended to cover Vienna, northern Italy and Paris, but they got no further than Frankfurt when the military confusion following the French defeat at Leipzig overtook them and the German frontiers were closed.

'William is no more!' John Jacob cried when he heard news of the situation in Europe. At length, however, a letter from William reached New York and the anxious father replied at once that he should return home with all speed. The ship

Hannibal, which carried poor General Moreau to his fate, somehow contrived to pick up William from the Continent on the return journey and conveyed him safely across the Atlantic. Not that William was particularly pleased to be back. He preferred the leisured intellectual life of Europe and could hardly wait to rejoin it. Almost as soon as the peace treaty was signed in 1815 he headed for Paris and the following spring met Bunsen for a tour of Italy. In the course of their wanderings among the Roman ruins, the pair decided that they would see for themselves the great sites of the ancient world they had studied so closely and began to make plans for a grand tour of Greece, the Levant, Persia and the Near East. Alas for William, his father had other ideas and the Astor heir was summoned to New York again, this time for the purpose of learning how to manage the fortune he would in due time inherit. It was the end of everything he wanted from life; before he had the chance to see his beloved Europe again he would be an old man; instead of talking philosophy with the likes of Bunsen and his friend Arthur Schopenhauer, he would have to speak of the fur trade and the tea market and the returns on real estate; rather than studying the mysteries of the ancients, he would be forced to pore over balance sheets and rent rolls and bills of lading.

All this William accepted stoically, for he was endowed with both his mother's compliant fatalism and his father's respect for money, though he lacked John Jacob's ruthless genius for amassing wealth – 'William will never make money, but he will keep what he has,' said his father. But if William was contented and comfortable with the life his father had decreed for him, none among his acquaintances would have described him as a happy man: happiness, as we shall see, was not a commodity generally available to the heirs of John Jacob Astor.

Things should have been different for the distaff side. After all, the responsibility of Astor women did not extend to minding the millions but only to spending them, as far as they were allowed. Yet here, too, the Astor legacy would weigh heavily on personalities, taking different forms in successive generations. Magdalen Astor, John Jacob's first child, named in honour of his sainted mother, was indulged almost from the day she was born in 1788 and grew into a wilful, self-centred and ultimately bitter woman. No beauty, even as a young girl, she was nevertheless sought after as a bride owing to her father's fortune, and many well-britched parents would entertain the Astors to dinner with an alliance in view for one of their sons. Perhaps Astor, too, had an eye to a liaison that would benefit him, for when Magdalen reached the age of eighteen he began to take her with him to Montreal to sample the hospitality of the fur magnates.

In the event, though, it was neither an American nor a Canadian who captured Magdalen but a Dane, Adrian Bentzon, governor of Santa Cruz in what was then the Danish West Indies. Bentzon impressed John Jacob, who described him as the ideal son-in-law at the wedding in 1807 and even went so far, when Bentzon was deposed by the British, as to make him his business representative with special responsibility for political and diplomatic ventures. It was Bentzon who hovered over the delegates to the peace conference that ended the War of 1812 so that Astor should have the first news of its conclusion, and Bentzon who hung about in Washington when his father-in-law was lobbying for the winding-up of the government's attempts to regulate trade with the Indians.

The marriage, however, was not blessed and indeed was marred by tragedy – the Bentzons' first child, a boy given the forenames of John Jacob Astor, was drowned at the age of ten and their second, a girl named Sarah, died in infancy. Magdalen's temper, never very stable, deteriorated further and her husband, on his frequent travels for Astor, sought solace with other women. The end came in 1815, when Britain returned Santa Cruz to Denmark and Bentzon was asked to take up residence in the governor's mansion once more. Magdalen, who liked nothing better than to see New York's high society genuflecting at the altar of her family's wealth, refused to accompany her husband so he went on his own, no doubt greatly relieved at being able to place such a distance between himself and his shrewish wife.

The conventional thing, in those days when marriages were considered to be indissoluble except in extreme circumstances, would have been for Magdalen to have remained a separated wife, finding comfort and sexual companionship discreetly where she might. But, as time was to prove over and over again, convention was no bar to the Astors and, amid a good deal of scandal, John Jacob used his considerable influence to obtain a divorce for his daughter in 1819, Bentzon having cooperated willingly by announcing his adulteries – a small price to pay for his freedom. Within the year Magadalen was married again, at the age of thirty-two, this time to an Englishman, John Bristed, sometime clergyman, lawyer and a dabbler in literature and magazine journalism.

Bristed fared no better than his predecessor, soon realizing the basis for the society gossip that he had been chosen because there was not a red-blooded New York male who would have taken Magdalen on. He stayed just long enough to father a child then made his escape to England, unable, according to Henry Brevoort (Magdalen's cousin on her mother's side), 'to bear the matrimonial yoke any longer with the Lamb of Bellzebub... She is certainly a maniac'. The twice-deserted Magdalen was left to the care of apparently the only man who could love her, the doting John Jacob, and the company of her son, christened Charles, who was to find himself a most favoured grandchild.

Both Magdalen's marriages ended in disaster, but as far as John Jacob was concerned that of his second daughter, Dorothea, began that way. Born in 1795 and named for her aunt, Henry Astor's wife, Dorothea was a plain, plump girl sometimes referred to unkindly as 'fat Dolly'. When she was eighteen her father began to cast around for a suitable husband, but Dolly had a mind of her own and settled matters by eloping with the 'handsome and fascinating' Colonel Walter Langdon, five years older than herself, whom she met while on a visit to the Gallatins in Washington. Albert Gallatin warned John Jacob of the liaison, pointing out that Langdon came with every recommendation but no money; nothing could dissuade Dorothea, however, not even the threat of being disinherited, and after the marriage her father did in fact disown her.

So sentimental a family man as John Jacob, though, could not bear such a rift for ever and in due time Dorothea and her husband were welcomed as full members of the Astor clan. Legend has it that the reconciliation came about when Astor was at a children's party in a friend's home and his attention was caught by a pretty little girl who seemed somehow familiar.

'What is your name, little girl?' John Jacob is supposed to have asked.

'Sarah Sherburne Langdon,' the child replied.

Whereupon Astor, emotion welling in his breast, said with a sigh: 'For your sake, I shall have to forgive your father and your mother.'

Be that as it may, the Langdons did emerge from the shadows of parental displeasure and began to enjoy the benefits of Astordom. John Jacob set them up in a palatial town house in Lafayette Place, while his generous, if delayed, marriage settlement enabled Colonel Langdon to purchase the Hyde Park estate in the Hudson Valley and take up the pursuits of a country squire. Some have suggested that he was a fortune-hunter, but if so he was an extraordinarily patient one and the marriage between him and Dorothea was happier than might have been expected. Whether it would have been as happy if Dolly had not been restored to her inheritance cannot, of course, be determined, but the indications are that it would have been. As it was, Dorothea enjoyed a life of contentment and eight admirable children.

Dolly's sister Eliza, youngest of John Jacob's surviving children, was certainly no rebel, though there may have been a time when she thought seriously of defying her father. By common consent the prettiest and perhaps also the cleverest of the Astor girls, she was said to be very much her father's favourite. As she reached maturity it was rumoured that John Jacob had it in mind to marry her to James Gallatin, who would be given a position in the prospective father-in-law's business. 'I doubt whether he will easily be brought into the plan of marriage,' one gossip-monger opined, a conclusion hardly surprising in the light of young Gallatin's view of Astor, which has already been noted. Eliza herself apparently fell in love with a dentist named Eleazar Parmly, who came from Vermont but had established a very successful practice on Broadway not far from the Astors' home.

Parmly, according to one writer, had 'a secure place in the history of American – or, indeed, European, dentistry'. He was a man of 'culture, charm, probity and extraordinary skill ... largely responsible for lifting the profession to its present level. Eleazar died worth three million dollars, and possessed an international reputation...' A descendant of Parmly's partner, Solymon Brown, added: 'It cannot be questioned that Eleazar

Parmly stood at the head of the dental profession in this country for some thirty years, and that no dentist before or since has occupied such a prominent position here, reputation with the laity and professional brethren being taken into account.' Nevertheless, to a man like Astor he was only a dentist, and therefore not a suitable match for his darling daughter. The romance must be stopped, and John Jacob sought to achieve this by taking Eliza with him on a prolonged trip to Europe (he was not going to risk a second elopement in the family). In any case, he had already selected a most suitable husband for his youngest daughter: Count Vincent von Rumpff, a Swiss who held the position of minister in Paris for the Free German Cities of the Hanseatic League and was thus a valuable contact for a merchant wishing to expand trade in Europe, as well as having direct access to most of the royal courts of the continent.

The account of what followed depends upon contemporary rumour, the testimony of Parmly's partner and some vague references contained in poems written by the dentist, who – in the fashion among young men at the time – had a penchant for versifying. It seems that Sarah Astor, knowing full well that it was useless to argue with her husband, let John Jacob take Eliza away and then wrote to Parmly urging him to follow his beloved to Paris and, since he was already unofficially engaged to her, carry her off and marry her. In one of his verses written in 1825, the dentist speaks of his plans to travel to 'far-distant countries', and the story goes that he set out for Paris in the autumn of that year, arriving shortly after the marriage of Eliza and von Rumpff on 10 December. Returning dejected to New York, he was sent a thousand dollars by Sarah to reimburse his expenses.

None of this has ever been completely verified, and indeed there is evidence to suggest that Parmly did not go to Paris until two years after Eliza's nuptials, when he had already been married himself for a year. Yet why did the new Countess von Rumpff suddenly became something of a religious fanatic, founding Sunday schools for children and presiding over 'religious soirees' that began with ninety minutes of prayer and Bible reading? And why was it that her health markedly deteriorated shortly after her marriage, to the point where she died at the age of only thirty-seven? There is a suggestion in some of Eleazar Parmly's later verses that Eliza died of a broken heart and it is said that, although apparently happily married himself, Parmly twice travelled to Rolle, in Switzerland, to visit the villa where she died and to stand in contemplation by her grave in the little churchyard. On the other hand, the death of a beautiful woman was a favourite subject of amateur versifiers of Parmly's generation, so his outpourings can hardly be taken as fact, while a curious volume published in 1839 by an obscure author named Robert Baird spared no effort in showing what an exemplary man von Rumpff was and how perfect was his marriage to Eliza.

What is certain is that much of the last years of Eliza's short life was spent in the company of her father. If the story of her broken romance with Parmly is true, John Jacob's attention can be construed as at least partly guilt from having made his daughter marry for advantage rather than love, but there are several other reasons why Astor would have wanted to spend so much time in Europe and since he was there it was only natural to him that he should see as much as possible of his daughter.

In the first place, Astor's business at this period required less of his direct intervention than previously. William's eye for detail and inherited canniness with money made him an ideal partner for his father, a sort of super-clerk who took the responsibility for day-to-day administration while the broad policy and commercial decision-making remained firmly in John Jacob's control. A second reason for Astor's long sojourns in Europe was provided by Count von Rumpff, who presented his father-in-law to the various German princelings and introduced him to Court circles in Paris, Vienna and Naples. John Jacob's pride and self-satisfaction at mixing with the nobility of Europe is easy to imagine: it was not every village butcher's son who found himself on familiar terms with the sort of people at whom he had once gazed in wonder as they drove by in their carriages. This was social acceptance of a kind simply unavailable in New York, whose class structure Astor did not in any case fully understand. He had been brought up to respect emperors and kings, princes and grand dukes, counts and landgraves rather than people who claimed superiority on the basis of nothing more than Dutch or English surnames.

More to the point, though, and perhaps the underlying reason why Astor chose to pass so many of his first years of freedom from everyday business worries in Europe – to the extent of paying $50,000 for his own villa, Genthod, near Lake Geneva – was a sentimental attachment to the Old World of a kind which is still noticeable among American immigrant families today, when bumper-stickers proclaim 'God Smiles on the Irish' or 'It's Great to be Polish', the 'hyphenated American' is a common phenomenon, and a great deal of time and money is spent on genealogical research. How much sharper this sense of belonging somewhere else must have been in the early years of the United States, and particularly to a man like Astor, who had chosen to go there simply because it seemed to afford him the best chance of making his fortune. He had no special commitment to democracy, no sense of building a new order – indeed, if anything, his ambition was to secure for himself by the acquisition of wealth a place among the old order which was given to others by right of birth. He became an American citizen, of course, in the days when a man was either for the victorious revolution or against it, and when it suited him he was vociferous in denouncing foreigners who sought to share in the great natural bounty that America had to offer, but we may suspect that at bottom he felt a certain amount of contempt for his fellow Americans.

It was probably no accident that one of his chosen friends and associates was Albert Gallatin, a man born and raised in Europe who emigrated to America some three years earlier than Astor and who possessed a talent for finance and diplomacy that matched John Jacob's ability to make money. Gallatin was Astor's first choice as a business partner and it was his refusal to accept the offer that prompted the sudden recall of William to New York to share his father's burdens. (Gallatin's integrity and extreme probity prevented him from compromising his position as a public servant by involvement in commerce – added to which, he knew Astor well enough to see that his proposed partnership would be nominal only.) Unwilling to take an American so far into his confidence, John Jacob began the process of handing over the business to his heir rather sooner than he might otherwise have done.

Nor was it accidental that so many foreigners were selected

for the expedition to Astoria. Apart from wishing to harm the Northwest Company by poaching some of its most experienced men, Astor had no confidence in American fur traders, regarding them as lazy, undisciplined and altogether too individualistic. He wanted men who would follow orders, and he felt he could not trust Americans to do that. He failed to see that Americans would at least be more likely to have the interests of their country at heart, but then the interests he himself held most dear were his own.

In sum, Astor's view seems to have been that he had little in common with his adopted countrymen. A lover of music and, in his youth at least, of books, he thought of Americans as uncultured, such intellectual pleasures as there were in New York being only poor imitations of what any of the great European cities could offer: much of his time in Paris and Vienna was spent at the opera houses and concert halls. He also saw Americans as naive and crass, lacking in subtlety – how else can one explain his effrontery in arranging the mandarin stunt and then repeating it with General Moreau?

No, John Jacob Astor was never an American, except in name. To him the United States was not a country, but a commodity to be bought and sold. He was an early example of the kind of mentality that would wipe out a civilization, make entire species of 'useful' animals extinct, turn prairies into dustbowls, cynically and thoughtlessly exploiting everything that would show a profit. And, sadly, his distorted vision and lack of commitment to anything outside himself would be passed on through generations of his descendants, isolating them from their contemporaries and warping their lives, until outside influences and changed circumstances combined to break the Astor mould.

II

The entry of William Backhouse Astor into the family business coincided with developments that were to establish the American Fur Company as the first great American monopoly. The postwar economic slump had a serious effect on international trade, and John Jacob reasoned quite correctly that the way to keep the profits coming in was to concentrate on his domestic operations, which meant the fur business. 'It is a trade by which I have lost money,' he told an associate, 'yet ... I have not lost my hopes, but that ere long I shall participate to a considerable extent in its goods and its evils.' There was another powerful reason, though, for turning his eyes inward: he intended to make good his vow to repair the injury of Astoria, and his method of doing this was simply to eliminate all competition both outside and within the United States.

Naturally enough, his earliest efforts were directed against the Northwest Company, which in Astor's eyes had robbed him by stealth of his cherished base on the Pacific. Using his political friends and his position as one of the prime movers of the recent war loan, not to mention the residual anti-British feeling in the country from the humiliations of the war, he ceaselessly lobbied the administration and the Congress for an Act excluding Canadians from fur trading on American soil. As an incentive to the government he offered the prospect of renewing the attempt to colonize the North-west. Albert Gallatin later recalled that in the spring of 1816 'you mentioned to me that you were disposed once more ... to re-establish Astoria, provided you had the protection of the American flag; for which purpose a lieutenant's command would be sufficient to you. You requested me to mention this to the President, which I did. Mr Madison said he would consider the subject, and, although he did not commit himself, I thought that he received the proposal favourably.' Madison had too many other things on his mind, however, and Astor never did get the support he asked for. But he did get his law barring Canadians from the American fur trade, and in 1821 he had the supreme satisfaction of seeing the Northwest Company disappear altogether. As *Silliman's Journal* reported: 'The Northwest Company did not long enjoy the sway they had acquired over the trading regions of the Columbia. A competition, ruinous in its expenses, which had long existed between them and the Hudson's Bay Company, ended in their downfall and the ruin of most of the partners. The relict of the company became merged in the rival association, and the whole business was conducted under the name of the Hudson's Bay Company.'

Northwest's demise may be attributed directly to Astor's revenge. Unable to compete with the Hudson's Bay Company in the Canadian Northwest, it had nowhere to go when the American Congress closed the frontiers. Astoria was abandoned and burned, the Canadian trappers and their dependants withdrawing to Fort Vancouver, but by then John Jacob had lost interest in it and the oldest American settlement on the Columbia was left to others to develop into a thriving port and a centre of the salmon fishing and lumber industries. It was chartered as a city in 1876, when it had a population of some five thousand.

Of course, Astor was delighted at the collapse of the Northwest Company and he immediately gave orders to Robert Stuart, who had been rewarded for his loyalty at Astoria by being placed in charge of the main trading post at Michilimackinac, to take over the whole of the Canadians' former territory in the Great Lakes region before any American competition could be organized. Stuart reported to his immediate superior, Ramsey Crooks, now manager of the American Fur Company, that Astor – 'the Old Cock', Stuart called him – 'is digesting a very extensive plan for establishing all the Indian Countries within the line of demarcation between G.B. and the U.S. and the probability is that a considerable time may elapse before that object can be brought to full maturity, as he wants an exclusive grant or privilege.' That Astor as an employer was neither exactly loved nor entirely trusted is clear in a later part of Stuart's letter: 'You can very readily draw your own conclusions regarding his views, which I really believe are as friendly toward us all as his own dear interest will permit, for of that, you are no doubt aware, he will never loose sight until some kind friend will put his or her fingers over his eyelids.'

Perhaps this last was a reference to the fact that John Jacob cared little for those under his control, regarding them as resources to be exploited just like the animals whose pelts they collected. He wanted results, and he did not much care how they were achieved, what methods were used, which laws were flouted, who was harmed – and if his agents got into trouble trying to meet the quotas and the targets he imposed, that was nothing to do with him. So why did his employees stay? The simple answer is that there was nothing else for them to do, other than go into another business, because the main plank of Astor's strategy was to either close down or buy up any competing company, or as Crooks himself put it, 'to annihilate their opposition entirely'. The American Fur Company thus became hated along the length and breadth of the American frontier, according to the leading historian of the fur trade, Hiram M. Chittenden, who added: 'Many are the stories, largely exaggerated, no doubt, that have come down to us of its hard and cruel ways. Small traders stood no show whatever and the most desperate measures were resorted to without scruple to get them out of the way. Many an employee, it is said, who had finished his term of service and had started for St Louis with a letter of credit for his pay fell by the way and was reported as killed by the Indians.' And President Zachary Taylor, whose early soldiering had brought him into contact with Astor's agents on the Mississippi, considered the American Fur Company as 'the greatest scoundrels the world ever knew'.

There were those who did attempt to stand up against the company, such as the government's Indian Agent at Mackinac, a certain Major Puthuff, who tried to turn the anti-Canadian law against Astor himself. The point was that since Canadians were not allowed to operate fur companies in the United States, it followed that there should also be an embargo on their working for American fur traders. Astor, however, was keen to use to his advantage the numbers of Canadian voyageurs who had been thrown out of work by the fall of the Northwest Company. Ramsey Crooks summed up his chief's attitude thus: 'The Canadian boatmen ... are indispensable to the successful prosecution of the trade. Their places cannot be supplied by Americans ... although the body of the Yankee can resist as much hardship as any man, 'tis only in the Canadian we find that temper of mind to render him patient, docile and persevering. In short they are a people harmless in themselves whose habits of submission fit them peculiarly for our business and, if guided as it is my wish they should be, will never give just cause of alarm to the Government of the Union'. The exclusion law, therefore, contained provision for the import of Canadian trappers by licence if the President judged it to be in the public interest. James Monroe was now in the White House, the recipient of loans from Astor with easy repayment terms: sensibly, the President decided that in this case he was not best placed to make a judgment on the public interest and the authority was passed down the line to Lewis Cass, Governor of the Michigan Territory, with the comment that the American Fur Company should be aided in every possible way.

Cass saw where his duty lay and instructed the Indian agents to grant licences to Astor while taking care not to give too many to his competitors. At this point, Major Puthuff enters the story. Upon receiving Cass's order he took up his pen and wrote: 'I wish to God the President knew this man Astor as well as he is known here. Licences would not be placed at his discretion to be distributed among British subjects, agents or pensioners. I hope in God no such licence will be granted. His British friends here calculate confident on his success in this matter, that they may be disappointed is my most sincere wish. Should they succeed incalculable evil will assuredly grow out of the measure.'

Cass was furious, Puthuff was sacked and Astor got his licences. Almost a century later the writer Gustavus Myers discovered in a yellowed, crumbling American Fur Company ledger the record of a payment of $35,000 to Governor Lewis Cass on 3 May 1817 as compensation for unspecified services. (Myers reported seeing the ledger in 1909, while it was exhibited at the Anderson Galleries in New York before being auctioned. It subsequently disappeared and attempts to trace it have so far failed.)

Astor had the workers he wanted and he had control of the Great Lakes region. There remained two obstacles to complete monopoly – the independent traders in the South-west and to the west of the Mississippi, and the American government's own trading posts in Indian country, 'a system,' according to Chittenden, 'which if followed out as it should have been, would have led the Indian to his new destiny by easy stages and would have averted the long and bloody wars, the corruption and bad faith, which have gained for a hundred years of our dealings with the Indians the unenviable distinction of a "century of dishonor".' But of course the system was not 'followed out', and one of the main reasons why not was an all-out attack on it by the American Fur Company.

John Jacob had railed against the government posts at the

time of their creation in 1796; now he had the money and the power to destroy them. His agents were instructed to do everything they could to tempt the Indians away from trade with officials. The chief temptation was liquor, which could not be sold by the government men (and which was in any case prohibited in Indian country, though none of the private traders took any notice of that). The selling of whisky and rum to the Indians had another advantage in that it was a highly profitable exercise: the cost of its manufacture was approximately five cents per gallon, while its selling price was fifty cents a bottle – and the Indians were not exactly discriminating customers, as the following recipe shows:

'Take two gallons of common whiskey or unrectified spirits, add to thirty gallons of water and to this add red pepper enough to make it fiery and tobacco enough to make it intoxicating, and you have a decation that will cause the Indian to give everything he possesses into the hands of the white man.'

This appalling concoction had the desired effect, and trade at the 'dry' government posts gradually fell away until, with a good deal of persuasion from Lewis Cass, the administration seemed to be on the point of abolishing them. Then there was a hitch. The Indian trade department came up with a plan to make the posts more effective and asked the Congress to vote extra money for them. In the winter of 1821–22, while Astor was away enjoying the delights of Europe, a full-scale battle took place on the floor of the Senate. Chief among the apostles of free trade with the Indians was the newly elected senator from Missouri, Thomas Hart Benton, who in his loud and overblown style waxed eloquent on behalf of the private trader and helped to win the day for those who sought abolition of the government posts. He just happened to be the attorney for the American Fur Company, though in this case of course he was doing no more than his public duty, upon which Ramsey Crooks was quick to congratulate him: 'You deserve the unqualified thanks of the community for destroying the pious monster . . . the country is indebted to you for its deliverance from so gross and holy an imposition.'

The conduct of the American Fur Company now became as gross as the government posts had been 'holy'. In trade with the Indians of the border country, liquor became the chief medium of exchange, sold against future deliveries of furs so that the tribes, demanding more and more 'firewater' as their dependence on it increased, became trapped in an upward spiral of debt to the company. To be fair, this disgusting trade cannot be blamed entirely on Astor, who once wailed that 'without ardent spirits, there is no competition'. It was the Hudson's Bay Company that first used alcohol to maintain its fur monopoly, and that example was followed by the independent traders who sought to secure a corner of this most lucrative business. In his usual way, Astor merely outdid the opposition.

A Senate investigating committee of the 1830s discovered that the Winnebagoes, Sacs and Foxes were in debt to the American Fur Company to the extent of $40,000, and their 'line of credit' was increasing at the rate of some $10,000 a year. A similar situation was found among the Sioux, Cherokee, Pawnee, Chickasaw and other tribes. Thomas L. McKenney, the head of the department of Indian trade who had tried to save the government posts, told the committee that company agents routinely cheated drunken Indians by weighing their pelts short and that for a bottle of whisky a brave would even sell his wife or daughter.

In what has become something of an American tradition, laws were enacted with Christian concern and then largely ignored. At first, after the closure of the official trading posts, alcohol could only be introduced to Indian country for the use of the white agents, trappers and clerks. This prohibition was ridiculous: all the companies had to do was inflate the numbers of their employees, and on official forms the sizes of hunting brigades began almost to look like their military equivalents. Not all the federal Indian agents were as conscientious as the unfortunate Major Puthuff.

But the condition of the Indians deteriorated so rapidly under the influence of alcohol that the government was obliged to take further steps. One writer, Arthur D. Howden Smith, expressed it this way: 'Alcohol killed the Indian's soul, making him a slave more surely than the easy credit the post factors allowed. He was as unsalted to it as he was to the white man's diseases. It paralysed every virtue barbarism had inculcated in him, accentuated every vice and lust he knew or could learn from the white trappers, who were only too willing to teach him.'

By the mid–1820s there were fears that the activities of the fur factors were seriously undermining the government's policy of keeping the Indians peaceful. Reporting that the American Fur Company's area manager at Mackinac had taken delivery of 3,300 gallons of whisky and 2,500 gallons of fortified wines during 1825, the military commander of the Detroit region wrote to his superiors in Washington: 'The neighbourhood of the trading houses where whisky is sold presents a disgusting scene of drunkenness, debauchery and misery; it is the fruitful source of all our difficulties, and of nearly all the murders committed in the Indian country ... It is true there are laws in this territory to restrain the sale of liquor, but they are not regarded.' And the officer, a Colonel Snelling, ventured the opinion that 'an inquiry into the manner in which the Indian trade is conducted, especially by the American Fur Company, is a matter of no small importance to the tranquillity of the border'.

After the Senate inquiry of 1832, a law was passed forbidding the importation of liquor into Indian territory, but it made no difference. For one thing, there was no general agreement on exactly what constituted 'Indian country', and for another, since the law prohibited the *importation* of alcohol the traders simply built their own stills and made it themselves. The Indian trade department did seize some of the flat kegs, suitable for concealment in saddle-bags and underneath trade goods in wagons, in which liquor was transported, and on at least one occasion an American Fur agent was prosecuted and came close to losing his licence to trade. But federal officials, even if they were honest, could not cover all the forest trails – and in any case, the Secretary of War, charged with supervising Indian trade, was by this time Lewis Cass. Not only was Cass apparently in the pay of Astor, but his attitude towards the Indians was less than friendly: in defiance of a Supreme Court ruling upholding treaties made by the government with the Cherokees, Cass was personally responsible for the forced emigration of that tribe and others from the territories west of the Mississippi.

The American Fur Company was certainly making progress. The entire Great Lakes region floated into its grasp on a sea of liquor, and Astor was able to devote his attention to the new frontiers in the South and West, which were the best sources of the still sought-after beaver skins. However, these territories, because of their wildness and the lack of settlement, were most popular with small American outfits and free trappers who ranged far and wide with the nomadic Sioux and Pawnee, Cheyenne and Blackfeet, Apache and Arapaho. Neutralizing the opposition here was not going to be easy, but John Jacob found a man equal to the task: Pierre Chouteau, Jr, who had all the arrogance of the Louisiana French and an attitude towards competitors summed up by the instructions he gave to his subordinates: 'Coûte que coûte ... Ecrasez tout opposition.' (Again, here is an example of Astor's underlying, perhaps unconscious view of Americans – all his chief lieutenants were of foreign birth or extraction, Crooks, Stuart and now Chouteau.)

Manuel Lisa and his Missouri Fur Company, which had caused so much anxiety to the Astoria expedition, were still very much in evidence, spreading out from St Louis to open trading posts farther and farther west. Operating even deeper in the wilderness was the Ashley-Henry Outfit, formed by two military men-cum-explorers who, from a base on the Snake River, discovered bountiful new beaver streams in the lush valleys west of the Rockies. There were Canadians in the game, too, controlling their business through proxies because of the law Astor had shepherded through Congress and trading under the name of the Columbia Fur Company; there was an association of independent trappers from Louisiana called the French Fur Company, and there were numerous partnerships of adventurers such as that masterminded by Jed Smith, the trail-blazer of California. None of these groups could command anything like the resources of American Fur, but what they lacked in capital was more than compensated for by their pioneering spirit, and through constantly opening up new hunting grounds they traded with a high degree of success and profitability.

Yet in the very success of the smaller associations lay the means of their destruction. Having lost the taste for finding new territories to conquer on his own behalf, Astor fell back on the method that had served him so well in the past – letting others break the virgin ground and then moving in from a position of financial strength to take over. Chouteau pursued this policy with a ruthless efficiency worthy of his employer, and there were several elements to it. Where rivals were buying furs from the Indians, the Astor company on the one hand offered the tribes better terms of trade (or large quantities of alcohol) and on the other hand took steps to absorb the firms supplying barter goods so that competitors were obliged to buy from it on credit and therefore were forced to sell their pelts to American Fur on whatever terms they could get. If the competing outfit was trapping on its own account, Chouteau was quite happy to encourage local Indians to attack the hunters, at the very least stripping them of all their equipment. Otherwise, he was empowered to bribe, threaten and generally suborn the loyalty of voyageurs in the direction of his own company.

Sometimes entire partnerships were bought out by Astor, as in the case of the Columbia Fur Company. The Canadians were offered extremely favourable terms to throw in their lot with American Fur, a district of their own in which to operate more or less independently of their parent and, of course, a guaranteed outlet for their pelts. One of their number, Kenneth McKenzie, was among the first factors to introduce a still for home-made whisky after the anti-liquor law of 1832, and in his capacity as manager of the upper Missouri region he began a steamboat service to transport furs to the main clearing house in St Louis. The French Fur Company, after holding Astor off for three years, also sold out to him – though one of its number, a man called Leclerc, could claim a small victory over American Fur. At the time of the merger, Leclerc decided to strike out on his own, and a very good job he made of it, too. Pierre Chouteau tried once more to buy him off, and failed – but the agent he had sent to do the bargaining noted that Leclerc had liquor among his trade goods and promptly confiscated it on the ground that it was illegal. When Leclerc protested, Chouteau's man 'arrested' him. Leclerc sued for wrongful interference and won $9,000 in damages ... then gave up the fur trade anyway. What happened to the overzealous American Fur agent is not recorded.

The Missouri Company, faced with competition from

McKenzie and his hooch, also allowed itself to be taken over and the Ashley-Henry Outfit faded away when William Ashley decided to liquidate his fortune of about $100,000 and go into politics. Piece by piece, John Jacob Astor's vision of national monopoly in the fur trade was being put together. In large measure he now influenced the international market in the most popular pelts. Since he controlled one of the two most important sources of supply, prices in Europe, for example, would fluctuate according to the numbers of furs he chose to export at any given time. Thus, when the market was glutted by deliveries from the Hudson's Bay Company, Astor could ensure that price levels were maintained by withholding his own pelts. Or, if he chose, he could undercut his British competitors, damaging them while sustaining his own profits through volume.

And what profits they were. In answer to an official inquiry in 1831, William B. Astor wrote to the Secretary of War: 'You may estimate our annual returns at half a million dollars.' The beauty of it was that to obtain that sort of return, the Astors took no risks – they were left for the traders in the field to deal with, and few of them made their fortunes. Having capitalized and established a complete structure that worked to his advantage, all John Jacob had to do was sit back and watch the money pour in, making slight policy adjustments as required, while William kept the books and ensured the smooth running of the collection and distribution machinery.

But while Astor & Son, the holding company that now embraced all John Jacob's interests, was rapidly filling its coffers by means of the fur business, the situation in the Canton trade had deteriorated sharply by the mid-1820s. Once the postwar recession had abated, merchants rushed to meet the revived and growing demand for imported goods and commodities, but in the haste to make profits again certain areas of the market – such as China tea – became glutted, with a resulting drop in prices. Wealthy importers like Astor tried to stabilize price levels by purchasing and storing hundreds of tons of excess tea, but in 1826 an event occurred that came close to ruining the market altogether.

Apart from Astor, two of the main tea importers in America were Thompson & Company of Philadelphia and Thomas H.

Smith of New York. All had been helped considerably by the United States government's generous attitude towards tariffs, but in the case of Thompson the temptation offered by an eighteen months' delay in the payment of import duties proved to be too great – he attempted over a period of years to swindle the government through what is now euphemistically called 'creative accounting'. The fraud was exposed in 1826, when the United States Treasury collector in Philadelphia rejected Thompson's bonds against duties owed for tea imports. Thompson argued that if he was not permitted to sell his tea he would be quite unable to make good his tax debt, so the authorities relented to the extent of placing his shipments in the Custom House and allowing him to withdraw them only when he had buyers and had already paid the duty covering the amount he wished to sell. Thompson agreed, but with bankruptcy breathing down his neck he resorted to even more desperate measures. Each certificate of withdrawal he received from the Treasury officials was falsified before being handed to the customs officers so that Thompson was able to release much more tea than had been allowed and to place the illegal excess on the New York market. Most of it was bought by Astor and Smith, who were trying to maintain prices in the face of competition from quick-turnover speculators with no thought for the future of the market.

Eventually the Treasury realized what Thompson was doing and he was sent to jail (where he died in misery a few months later), but that left the authorities in Philadelphia with hundreds of tons of tea locked up in the Custom House. They decided to offer this to wholesalers for no more than the cost of the duties owing, with the bonus of a debenture certificate which meant that if the tea was re-exported the duty would be repaid – in other words the tea would be free to any merchant who could find a market for it overseas. Astor and Smith were both best placed to deal with this and most interested in ensuring that the tea was not dumped on the domestic market, so between them they bought it all.

Unfortunately the glut affecting the United States had also reached a peak in Europe. It was months before the tea could be disposed of, and even then the supercargoes had to let it go for prices that did not cover the cost of transportation and foreign import taxes. The effort proved to be too great for Thomas Smith, who found he could not pay two million dollars in outstanding government duties and was forced to give up his company. The tea market entered a period of uncertainty and stagnation that caused even the great Perkins company of Boston to restrict its operations – and John Jacob decided he had had enough of it. The days of the windfall profits in the Canton trade were over: apart from the difficulties of an oversubscribed tea market, the sandalwood business had virtually disappeared, thanks to the careless greed of Hawaiian rulers, and the Chinese authorities were cracking down on the sale of opium, in which Astor, along with most other Canton traders, had dabbled over the years. As far as John Jacob was concerned, the game was no longer worth the candle, and in 1827 he began to wind up his Far East business and sell off his fleet. Furs were what he had started with and it was in furs, by virtue of his shrewdly and ruthlessly established monopoly, that the real money was to be made now.

Yet there was perhaps another reason for Astor's withdrawal from the China trade. At the age of sixty-four, and feeling the effects on his health of the ceaseless labour which had marked his rise, he neither had the energy nor felt the need to engage in the daily round of mercantile activities. By this time he may well already have been the richest man in America, and that meant he was no longer a mere merchant but a businessman in the fuller sense of the word, a capitalist able to let his money do the work. Indeed, the whole basis of American economic life was changing in line with Adam Smith's dictum that the degree of specialization in business reflects the breadth of the market, or in other words the extent of demand. As the number of consumers increased through immigration, the economy expanded and earnings rose, entrepreneurs appeared to take over the secondary functions previously carried out by merchants themselves – such things as transportation, advertising, the provision of credit, insurance and so on. Therefore the exporter, for instance, need no longer be a shipper in his own right or even take a share in a ship, since there was a specialized freight company that would transport a cargo on his behalf for a fee. Freed from such peripheral responsibilities, the merchant could employ that portion of his operating surplus not required to finance the continuance of his primary undertaking by investing it in someone else's company in the hope of sharing in another profit-making enterprise.

With his vast reserves of liquid capital, John Jacob Astor was in a strong position to make investments. The 1820s marked the beginning of the age of rapid transit by water and rail: Astor invested a million dollars in six per cent stock for the Ohio Canal and was an enthusiastic founder director of the Mohawk & Hudson Railroad, which was to grow into the New York Central. He also bought stock in a number of insurance companies and in 1817 sank $200,000 into the Second Bank of the United States, though that was to prove an unwelcome institution to his fellow New York businessmen a couple of decades afterwards. Later on he went into federal and state securities and subscribed to banks chartered by the state of New York, one of which involved Albert Gallatin.

But in the end the investment that appealed most to him, and with which his name and the names of his descendants would be most closely associated (not to say reviled) down the years, was the one first suggested by his brother Henry: real estate. That, not the furs, not the China trade, was to be the true basis of the Astor fortune. And the yoke that would weigh so heavily upon so many of the heirs of John Jacob Astor.

III

Between 1800 and 1820, John Jacob Astor invested $715,000 in real estate on the island of Manhattan. During that time the population of New York more than doubled, from 60,515 to 123,706, and the city spread rapidly northward. 'In 1820,' a nineteenth-century writer noted, 'the surveying and laying out of Manhattan north of Houston Street, after ten years of labor, was completed.' The demand was for building plots, and Astor's careful purchase of what others had dismissed as wasteland began to pay off. One illustration of this comes in an anecdote concerning a house on Wall Street which John Jacob sold for $8,000. The buyer, thinking he had outsmarted the legendary businessman by obtaining the property at a favourable price, pointed out that in a year or two it would be worth half as much again. Astor's reply put him in his place: 'With

$8,000 I'll buy eighty lots above Canal Street. By the time your lot is worth $12,000, my lots will be worth $80,000.'

Buy the acre, sell the lot – that was his philosophy. But as the city developed, he sold less and less, preferring to offer twenty-one-year leases on vacant land that the lessee could build on and otherwise improve, thereby becoming liable for any taxes due. At the end of the term, the land reverted to Astor without penalty and the leaseholder could renegotiate, or remove within ten days any buildings he had erected, or sell the whole to the landlord at a price determined by an independent committee of arbitrators. Under this system Astor's rental income amounted to $27,000 in 1827 and was increasing at the rate of almost $8,000 a year. By 1840 the three hundred-odd leases he held brought in $128,000 annually and the figure was still rising: it would reach almost a quarter of a million in the year John Jacob died. In some cases, Astor increased his real estate revenues still further by advancing mortgages to lessees so that they could build on the land they rented from him. He simply couldn't fail to make a lot of money, sometimes more than he bargained for. If mortgage interest was not repaid when due, he had no hesitation in foreclosing, getting back his land with whatever improvements had been made at no cost to himself.

Of course, the new land of the free did not take kindly to the importation of such traditional (some might say feudal) European notions of land tenure. The journalist Horace Greeley, founder of the first weekly *New Yorker* and of the *Tribune*, spoke for many people when he inveighed against 'land speculators like Mr A.' who 'should be checked in their dealings by a statute forbidding any man from holding or acquiring hereafter more than six hundred or a thousand acres, or a certain quantity within the city . . .' But Greeley recognized that there was not much hope of preventing men like Astor from making fortunes on the backs of their hardworking tenants as long as the policy of the United States government was to 'protect Mr Astor's houses, lands, ships, stocks, etc., and yet to exact no taxes from him according to his income.' The legal basis of landholding, said Greeley, positively encouraged real estate speculation – and old John Jacob did not need much encouragement when large profits could be seen on the horizon (quite literally, in this case).

116

Indeed, the returns from land and property in Manhattan were so great that in the 1830s Astor decided to renounce commerce altogether and concentrate on his investments, particularly in realty.

There were a number of factors influencing this final withdrawal from the marketplace. As with the China trade in the previous decade, the fur business in the early 1830s had seen its best days. Overproduction, combined with the movement of fashion away from beaver hats and a growing suspicion that the pelts might be responsible for spreading cholera, pointed to a decline in profits that was to be accelerated by the development of industrial processes for the manufacture of, for instance, warm woollen fabrics which would reduce the demand for furs. Furthermore, as *Silliman's Magazine* pointed out in 1834: 'The advanced state of geographical science shows that no new countries remain to be explored. In North America the animals are slowly decreasing, from the persevering efforts and the indiscriminate slaughter practised by the hunters, and by the appropriation to the uses of man of those forests and rivers which have afforded them food and protection. They recede with the aborigines before the tide of civilization...'

There would still be a fur trade, of course, but it would necessarily be limited. That was not for Astor. Let others be content with smaller profits and all the problems associated with a declining industry. Growth was his watchword.

But there were other, more personal reasons for Astor's desire to get out of the fur trade. By the time he reached his seventies, his various infirmities were becoming burdensome and, while his passion for making money was no less intense than it had been in his youth, the spirit that drove him could no longer be matched by his physical capacity. Although William could deputize for him in the everyday matters of business, John Jacob could not trust his son to take over completely the administration of a trade he knew only at second hand – and perhaps, too, Astor's assessment of William as a man lacking the flair to make money played a part. How much better to leave as his legacy something self-perpetuating, like property, rather than a commercial venture that was subject to the vagaries of the market and could be brought to ruin by the mistakes of an untalented operator. As his will was to show,

117

John Jacob Astor intended to leave a fortune that his heirs could not easily dissipate through either ignorance or intemperance.

Finally, the spur to his abandonment of the American Fur Company – which Ramsey Crooks once described as 'to him like an only child' – was the need to put the past behind him through a new and absorbing interest. In 1832 he had gone to Europe in a vain attempt to recover his health and while there had received news of the death of his eldest daughter, Magdalen. Worse was to come. In Europe again the following year, he heard of the death of both his brother Henry and his half-sister Elizabeth. Intimations of his own mortality rose up before him on the voyage home aboard the packet *Utica*, commanded by one of his former China skippers. On the first night out of Le Havre the ship encountered a fierce storm in the English Channel and a terrified Astor offered the captain a thousand dollars to be put ashore, a request Captain De Peyster refused, saying he could not risk it in darkness. The ferocity of the tempest increased and as the ship was buffeted out into the Atlantic John Jacob, almost beside himself with fear, raised the stake to $10,000 if the ship would put about and head for the nearest port. De Peyster, who was to make much of the story later, protested that such an action would invalidate his insurance, and in any case the other passengers might object.

Astor skulked in his cabin while the gale raged, but as the day went on the weather moderated and the captain, who seems to prove the adage that every man has his price, changed his mind: he would turn back if Astor would give him a promissory note for ten thousand dollars. John Jacob presented a piece of paper, but De Peyster could not read the handwriting and suggested, 'Let me write it out for you, then you can sign it.' Now it was Astor's turn to have second thoughts – it was that note or nothing, he said. So the uncomfortable voyage continued, with John Jacob making a further attempt to escape when the *Utica* encountered another vessel in heavy weather off the Grand Banks, and it was with considerable relief that the old man watched from the rail as the ship tied up at her moorings in New York harbour ... until William came on board with the news that his mother had just gone to her grave.

John Jacob was shattered: first Magdalen and now Sarah, his

wife of almost fifty years. 'He appears feeble and sickly,' Philip Hone noted when he saw Astor shortly afterwards, adding that he doubted whether the ailing millionaire could live much longer. But Hone misjudged his man. John Jacob Astor was a long way from being finished. If the loss of Sarah was fundamentally to alter his life, then he might as well take the opportunity to change everything. He sold the American Fur Company to partnerships headed by Ramsey Crooks in Mackinac and Pierre Chouteau in St Louis and with what energy he had remaining embarked on the creation of a new empire much closer to home.

In fact, home itself was about to change. Some years earlier, Astor had developed an obsession to build the finest hotel in New York as a sort of monument to himself and the dynasty he had founded. Why he should have chosen to commemorate himself through a hotel is a matter for conjecture, though it may have had something to do with the image of a butcher's son being in a position to entertain the great and famous of the world – while making a profit at the same time, of course. At any rate, the Astor House, or the Park Hotel as it was first called, was to be a large and splendid building and the site John Jacob had in mind for it was the very Broadway block, between Vesey and Barclay, on which he had lived for twenty-five years or more. The district had become rather less fashionable as the city had spread to the north and there had been little difficulty in persuading almost all the other occupants of the block to move into the newer areas above Canal Street. One estimate put the average purchase price of the houses at no more than fifteen thousand dollars. However, the last home on the block, number 227 Broadway, was owned by a wealthy man named John G. Coster who did not want to move into the newer, trendier quarters. Successive offers over a number of years failed to dent his resolve and the great hotel project remained in abeyance. But Astor was accustomed to getting what he wanted, and two versions have been handed down of how he did it in this case. Walter Barrett, in *The Old Merchants of New York*, tells how John Jacob, having kept to himself his plans for the block while buying the property of the other residents, finally revealed the nature of the project to Coster.

'You can build a palace with the money I will pay you,' he

119

told the reluctant vendor. 'I wish you to name two friends and I will name one. The three shall fix the value of Number 227. When they have done so, add $20,000 to it and I will give you a check for the total amount.'

The other story, however, has it that it was not Coster but his wife who held out, capitulating only when Astor allowed her to name her own price – which turned out to be $60,000, perhaps three times the market value of the property.

Whichever way it was arranged, the Costers moved uptown to the 500 block of Broadway and Astor promptly ordered demolition squads into the old neighbourhood. By the end of June 1834 the site had been cleared and on 4 July the stone-laying ceremony took place in the presence of leading citizens and municipal officials. The building work proceeded rapidly under John Jacob's constant supervision – his enthusiasm for the project was a powerful antidote for his grief at Sarah's death – and the massive, six-storey, stone-faced structure became one of the first man-made wonders of the New World. To modern eyes, the squat, rectangular building with its ranks of flat windows and troops of chimneys would have appeared too solid and boring, lacking in style, incongruously fronted by heavy Doric pillars and altogether overly respectable, like a pretentious surburban bank. Contemporary New Yorkers, though, like Philip Hone, considered it 'a *palais royal* . . . splendid edifice . . . an ornament for the city'. And to its well-heeled patrons (they had to be rich to pay a rate of two dollars a day) the Astor House was the last word in luxury and elegance, with its three hundred bedrooms, seventeen bathrooms, black walnut furniture and shopping arcade. Its service, which aimed to rival that of the great hotels of Europe, included innovations like the now-familiar pigeonhole system at the front desk for keys and mail, an ingenious device for summoning room service, bootblacks continuously stationed in the lobby, and washstands with free soap in every room. If such gracious living might have been a little out of place in a city where the streets were paved with rubbish and the pedestrian had to be wary of roaming pigs, it was only foreigners who noticed.

Not that John Jacob himself took on the role of hotelier, though. When it was completed in 1836 he gave the Park Hotel, as it then was, to William in return for 'one Spanish milled dollar, and love and affection' and it was immediately leased at an annual rent of $20,500, later increased to thirty thousand. But its identification as 'Astor's House' and eventual change of name left no doubt that he intended it to be a monument, and it began a tradition that was to survive in the Astor family, on both sides of the Atlantic, for more than a century, as well as helping to establish the word Astor in the public consciousness as a synonym for a pampered and luxurious style of living. During its eighty years of existence the Astor House attracted celebrities from all over the world – political leaders, kings and princes, socialites and even literary folk. Charles Dickens stayed there several times during his successful American tours and the renowned editor Nathaniel Parker Willis actually lived there for a while, entertaining among others Edgar Allan Poe on an awesomely lavish scale. The hotel restaurant was famous for its literary and political dinners (kidneys in champagne and vanilla custard were among its specialities) while the lounges were thronged with 'highly dressed ladies' and the sumptuously decorated corridors were known as 'flirtation galleries'.

Of course, the building of the hotel left John Jacob without a home in town, but he remedied that by building a four-storey brownstone mansion up at Broadway and Prince, in the block immediately below Houston Street, and provided himself with a small office building behind the house, which was at 85 Prince Street. Not wishing to live alone, he took in his grandson, Charles Bristed, Magdalen's boy, and began to educate him in the ways of a gentleman. In due course, the fortunate Charles took Astor as his middle name and inherited his grandfather's country estate at Hellgate, but meanwhile he and the old man had their every need attended to by a multi-racial staff of servants against a background of furniture, paintings, antiques and objets d'art garnered from Europe and the East.

But there was more to celebrate the achievements of John Jacob Astor in 1836 than his new hotel and his stately home, for that year saw the publication of *Astoria*, the book he had commissioned Washington Irving to write in homage to and justification for that ill-fated transamerican venture. The idea had first been mooted in the autumn of 1834, as Irving explained in a letter to his nephew, Pierre, in September of that year:

John Jacob Astor is extremely desirous of having a work written on the subject of his settlement of Astoria ... something that might ... secure to him the reputation of having originated the enterprise and founded the colony that are likely to have such important results in the history of commerce and colonization.

The old gentleman has applied to me repeatedly in the matter, offering to furnish abundance of materials in letters, journals, and verbal narratives, and to pay liberally for time and trouble...

In an interview which I had with Mr Astor, a day or two since, in which he laid before me a variety of documents, I accordingly stated to him my inability at present to give the subject the labor that would be requisite, but the possibility that you might aid me ... in which case I should have no objection to putting the finishing hand to the work...

Mr Astor is a strong-minded man, and one from whose conversation much curious information is to be derived. He feels the want of occupation and amusement, and thinks he may find something of both in the progress of the work...

Washington Irving had 'no care about it for myself', but on the other hand it was easy work, a chance to gain some employment for his nephew, and a potentially profitable piece of hackery. Astor, who had known the Irving family for some years, had suggested that Washington and his nephew should live in style at Hellgate during the preparation of the book and that he himself sought no profit from its publication. Pierre jumped at the chance and a month later his uncle was able to report: 'I have ... fixed your compensation at *three thousand* dollars. Mr Astor has his papers all arranged, so that you would be able to get to work immediately ... I think you may find it ... very interesting and agreeable ... and may accomplish it within the space of a year.'

And so it was agreed. The Irvings moved into Hellgate and Pierre began his researches while Washington concentrated on his other literary work and made arrangements for the con-

John Jacob Astor, the German butcher's son who became the richest man in America. Engraving after a portrait by Gilbert Stuart.

John Jacob in later life — a cartoon published by the London *Spectator* to accompany Astor's obituary in 1848.

John Jacob Astor II: his mental illness condemned him to a life shut away from the rest of the world.

An unknown artist's impression of Astoria, John Jacob's ill-fated trading post in the Pacific North West. The engraving dates from about 1871.

William Backhouse Astor, known as 'the Landlord of New York'.
Through careful management of his real estate holdings, he doubled the
Astor fortune.

Hub of the empire: the Astor Estate Office on Prince Street, between
Broadway and Mercer Street, from which first John Jacob and later
William managed their real estate.

John Jacob Astor III, the first head
of the family who never had to
work for his living. Haughty and
imperious, he was powerful enough
to remain untouched by his
involvement in the Tweed
corruption scandal.

William Backhouse Astor Jr,
younger brother of John Jacob III.
More interested in women and
yachting than in business, William
remained in the background as his
wife, Caroline, dominated New
York society.

Caroline Astor, the queen of New York society in the 1880s and 1890s.
Under this portrait by Carolus Duran, Caroline would stand to receive
guests arriving for her grand balls.

An engraving of Brooklyn Bridge, symbol of New York's pre-eminence
among American cities and a link between Manhattan and the mainland
that helped to increase the value of Astor real estate holdings.

John Jacob Astor IV and an artist's impression of the sinking of the
Titanic, in which he died.

John Jacob Astor VI, half-brother to Vincent, at the time of his scandalous engagement to Eileen Gillespie.

Vincent Astor, son of John Jacob IV and 'the richest young man in the world' when he inherited his father's fortune in 1912. Thrice married but without an heir, he left most of the fortune to charity when he died.

October 11, 1937

Newsweek

10 ¢ — The Magazine of News Significance

Who's Ahead,
Lewis or Green?

Who Wants
to boycott
Japan?

Will
screwballs win
World Series?

A cover of *Newsweek* magazine in 1937, the year Vincent Astor became
its chief proprietor.

struction of his soon to be famous cottage (now a museum) at Tarrytown on the bank of the Hudson north of New York City. The first draft of *Astoria* was completed in the fall of 1835 and Washington spent that winter revising it. He made it clear to anyone who wanted to know that he received no payment himself from Astor, only the copyright to the book and any royalties accruing. This was not a bad deal by any means: Carey and Lea paid Irving $4,000 for the American publication rights and he got £500 from the London firm of Bentley for the British rights.

Astoria was published in October 1836 and became a bestseller at once. Though grateful for the addition to his fame, Washington Irving was a little nettled: he had never taken the book very seriously (with good reason, for it is a poorly constructed and carelessly written work) and it was therefore with a note of complaint that he wrote, 'I have heard more talk about this work, considering the short time it has been launched, than about any other that I have published for some time past', and he was inclined to disagree with the London *Spectator*, which called it his *chef d'oeuvre*. No doubt he was right to be suspicious of the praise heaped upon the book, for what appealed to the reviewers was not so much the skill of Washington Irving as the grand design and the personality of John Jacob Astor. The *Spectator* again:

'Astoria' is the history of as grand and comprehensive a commercial enterprise as ever was planned with any well-grounded prospect of success, and which was prosecuted among scenes as vast and nations as wild, gave rise to incidents as ludicrous, as interesting, as appalling, and developed characters and manners as marked and striking as anything on record respecting the adventurous explorers of the Middle Ages, or the hardy discoverers of the modern days.

And the *Westminster Review*:

The plain merchant assumes the character of the founder of

123

an empire and his enterprise appears a great scheme for the aggrandizement of a nation rather than a private mercantile operation to increase his own fortune.

And in America, the *Quarterly Review*:

From an obscure stranger [Astor] has made himself one of the celebrities of the country ... he has comprehended the ends of the earth in his schemes and filled them with his agents and made them acquainted with his name. Nations have taken cognizance of his individual enterprises, statesmen have studied them and labored to favor or thwart them ...

But perhaps it was Longfellow who summed up the appeal of the book: 'The remarkable form of John Jacob stands out like a statue of granite. A sublime enterprise.'

Whatever Irving's reservations, it was all that Astor could have hoped for, and more besides. In the book he was presented exactly as he wished to be, taking all the credit for the conception of the Astoria enterprise and none of the blame for its failure, posing as a dedicated patriot rather than the acquisitive, self-interested disciple of Mammon that he was. His old bones were warmed by the comforting glow of hero-worship generated by Irving's uncritical efforts. America was at his feet.

As for Manhattan, more of that – much more – was about to fall into his hands. The great financial panic of 1837, caused mainly by the excesses of the 'hard money' supporters of Andrew Jackson and their attack on the theory of paper currency as exemplified by the doomed Bank of the United States, led to thousands of business failures, many of them in New York. The Administration had suspended land dealing except on payment of specie, so the city was flooded with paper money that became temporarily worthless when the state banks, fearing complete collapse, refused to pay depositors in coin. Astor's vast wealth and extensive property holdings not only insulated him from the effects of the crisis but also allowed him to make substantial gains in real estate as mortgagees ran out of cash and defaulted on their interest payments. He foreclosed on sixty mortgages in 1837–38 and bought all the land he could get his hands on as prices fell through the floor. A reputed million-dollar parcel in Harlem (though it was probably overvalued by some fifty per cent) was knocked down to him for a mere two thousand, while a sizeable chunk of East Side building land, ideal for tenement lots, cost him just twenty thousand.

When the financial crash reached its nadir in 1837, he invested $224,000 in the Manhattan real estate market. There could be no doubt now that he was the richest man in America, though nobody – not even Astor himself – knew just how rich, and it was equally certain that he was by far the largest landholder in New York. The recovery from the crisis served further to increase his wealth as immigrants poured into the city and real estate values soared out of sight in a period of expansion unprecedented even by New York's standards. All he had to do was sign leases, advance mortgages, collect rents and sometimes go to court for a foreclosure order.

Yet as Astor grew richer, the stories of his parsimony also increased. He had no new challenges for the future and no occupation for the present; whereas the American Fur Company had formerly been 'like an only child', now there was simply money, and the more he had the more jealously he guarded it. Charity, except to members of his family, was not among his virtues. As he himself once said: 'The disposition to do good does not always increase with the means.' At least he was honest about it, and in view of his own achievements he sincerely believed that if a man was poor it was his own fault.

The anecdotes of his meanness are legion, beginning with one concerning the great naturalist John James Audubon, to whom Astor had – presumably in a weak moment – promised a thousand dollars towards the production costs of his classic *Birds of America*, published between 1827 and 1838. When Audubon arrived to collect the pledged sum, Astor told him: 'You come at a bad time. Money is very scarce. I have nothing in the bank. I have invested all my funds.' Five visits later, the old man was still saying the same thing. 'William,' he called to the next room, 'have we any money at all in the bank?' Either the younger Astor was somewhat naive or else he had a conscience, for he replied: 'Yes, father. We have $220,000 in the Bank of New York, $70,000 in the City Bank, $90,000 in the Merchants' ...' John Jacob cut him short, and Audubon finally got a cheque for his thousand.

Fitz-Greene Halleck, the poet who served as Astor's confidential secretary for sixteen years from 1832, recalled that he once teased his employer into making a charity donation by offering to underwrite a small bank draft. Halleck frequently joked with Astor about his wealth, but it was John Jacob who had the last laugh. The poet once said to him: 'Mr Astor, of what use is all this money to you? I would be content to live upon a couple of hundreds a year for the rest of my life, if I was only sure of it.' With what was described as 'bitter satire', Astor's will contained a provision for the payment of an annuity to Halleck – of two hundred dollars a year.

Another paid companion of Astor's later years, the editor and bibliographer Joseph Green Cogswell, was also not above making sport of the old man's stinginess. He recorded that when he visited a hotel with his employer, the latter expressed the opinion that the owner of the establishment would never make a success of it. When Cogswell asked why this should be so, Astor said: 'Don't you see what large lumps of sugar he puts in the bowl?' And when Cogswell hired a boat to take Astor on a harbour cruise he amused himself on the walk to the pier by informing the old man that he estimated the boat's waiting time was costing twenty-five cents a minute, whereupon Astor, who could walk only with difficulty, attempted to break into a run.

But at least Joseph Cogswell could claim the credit for having talked Astor into the only important philanthropic act of his life. Whatever else he may have been, John Jacob was certainly no philistine: he loved music and the theatre (one of the buildings he owned was the Park Theatre in New York) and was fascinated by both the work and the conversation of literary men. During the years of his semi-retirement, his Broadway home became a meeting-place for writers and poets who were entertained to splendid dinners and fine wines, and he employed Cogswell partly so that he could have a man of letters to read to him as his sight failed and partly to have an

126

expert on hand to buy books for the private library he intended to establish. Cogswell, however, saw his position as an opportunity to advance his own cherished ambition of establishing in New York the country's finest public library. Astor, he once told a friend, 'is not a mere accumulator of dollars, as I had thought. He talks well on many subjects and shows a great interest in the arts and literature.'

As he spent more and more time with John Jacob and finally moved into his home – often sitting up at night with the old man, who suffered terribly from insomnia – Cogswell implanted the idea in his employer's mind that it would be a great thing for the richest man in America to be remembered as the founder of such a notable institut'on as a public library, which would serve as a memorial even more permanent and well known than the Astor House hotel. Anxious to please a companion upon whom he had come to rely heavily, Astor assented to the proposition, but as always there was the difficulty of actually persuading him to part with money so that the project could begin. Cogswell was nothing if not persistent and he kept up the pressure for years. He recalled: 'Had I not foreseen that this object would never have been effected unless someone had been at the old gentleman's elbow to push him on, I should have left New York long since.'

Eventually, coincidence came to his aid. Through Astor he had become friendly with Washington Irving, and when Irving was appointed American minister to Spain in 1842 he asked Cogswell to accompany him as secretary to the American legation. Philip Hone takes up the story: 'But Mr Cogswell does not go. Mr Astor, who enjoys his society, has bribed him to remain. He is willing to pay as much for the velvet cushion on which it is his pleasure to rest his head as the secretaryship would have produced, and it comes in the shape of a permanent salary to Mr Cogswell as librarian of a great public library which Mr Astor has signified his intention to establish and endow in this city, which he proposes now to anticipate. Cogswell wisely determines to receive his equivalent and stay at home, write articles for the 'New York Review' and accompany his patron in his daily drives from Broadway to Hell Gate. Maecenas keeps Horace with him, and Horace knows when he has a good thing.'

An exultant Cogswell pressed Astor to select a site for the library building from among his prodigious holdings, commissioned an architect to draw up plans, and threw himself with unbounded enthusiasm into the task of buying books. But it was not to be accomplished as easily as that. First, Astor havered over which plot of land he could give up with least pain – then he hit upon a further consideration, as his nephew, Henry Brevoort, discovered: 'Dr Williams . . . told me a good story about the old boy. . . He consulted the Dr as to what items of property he might conscientiously conceal from assessment. The Dr thought the Library legacy was a fair one for exemption – Oh! said Money-bags, I had tought of dat & so he continued to every proposition of the Doctor's. At this rate the Legacy, if the old man holds out long enough, will turn out a profitable speculation.'

Thus John Jacob had a very good reason for not proceeding too quickly with Cogswell's plans. Apart from constantly changing his mind about where the library should actually be built, he delayed consideration of the architect's drawings, finally throwing them into a chest when he learnt from Cogswell that expenditure in the first year would amount to sixty-five thousand dollars. Of course, he could not risk dampening Cogswell's ardour too much, so he allowed him to carry on collecting books and compiling a catalogue for the as yet non-existent public benefaction. This seemed to satisfy the bibliophile, which was just as well since it was not until Astor's death in 1848 that work could finally begin on the library project: John Jacob's will contained a bequest of $400,000 to cover the site in Lafayette Place, the building, the purchase of books and an endowment of $10,000 a year. Even then, Astor's reluctance was obvious. The legacy was completely inadequate, and it was left to William to honour in full the promise his father had made. It was not until six years after John Jacob's death that the library opened, and ten more years before its catalogue appeared.

But none of this made any difference to Cogswell, the real founding spirit of the Astor Library. The years of waiting, the frustrations of continual delay, merely served to make the eventual realization of his dream all the sweeter. By the time the library opened its doors, he had packed the building with a hundred thousand books, twice as many as the Library of Congress in Washington and more than even the great collection at Harvard. In what became the New York Public Library, Joseph Cogswell ensured that John Jacob Astor was to have a permanent memorial almost in spite of himself.

Such a thought, however, did not trouble the old multi-millionaire himself as he entered his last years of senility and decrepitude. The centre of his life, the very wellspring of his being, seemed to be the fortune he knew that he must sooner or later leave behind, and he was as reluctant to part with money through death as in any other way that would not show a profit. McKenney, from the department of Indian affairs in Washington, wrote of Astor in 1846: 'I am told by those who know him that his relish for wealth is as keen as ever. That gone, he is gone.'

A couple of years earlier, Philip Hone (who else?) had noted in his diary: 'Mr Astor ... presented a painful example of the insufficiency of wealth to prolong the life of man. This old gentleman, with his fifteen millions of dollars [a conservative estimate, as it turned out], would give it all to have my strength and physical ability... He would pay all my debts if I could insure him one year of my health and strength, but nothing else would extort so much from him. His life has been spent in amassing money and he loves it as much as ever. He sat at the dinner table with his head down upon his breast, saying very little, and in a voice almost unintelligible, the saliva dropping down from his mouth, and a servant behind him to guide the victuals which he was eating, and to watch him as an infant is watched ... there are some people, no doubt, who think he has lived long enough.'

By 1847, racked by palsy, his digestion so disordered that he fed only at the breast of a wet-nurse, Astor had to be tossed in a blanket each day to keep his circulation going. Yet his rent collectors still reported to him personally, and one source, James Parton, in his *Life of John Jacob Astor* (1865), tells of him arguing with an agent who had failed to collect rent arrears from a particular tenant.

'She can't pay it now,' the collector said. 'She has had misfortunes and we must give her time.'

Astor cried: 'I tell you she can pay it and she will pay it. You don't know the right way to work with her.'

The agent mentioned the affair to William, who gave him the appropriate amount of money with instructions to present it to John Jacob as if it had come from the recalcitrant tenant.

'I told you she would pay it if you went the right way to work with her,' said Astor triumphantly when the money was handed to him.

Poor William – bent to the will of his father for fifty-six years, and not even to be freed by the eventual death of the old tyrant. He was the first to feel the cold steel of the double-edged Astor legacy.

PART II
The Lords of New York

4 Heirs and Graces

I

When William Backhouse Astor succeeded to the title of 'the richest man in America' on 29 March 1848 he was by all accounts as dull and unprepossessing as his father, in his youth and middle age, had been vital and charismatic. Tall and well built, with a stoop that gave the impression of a man bowed down by care, William was cold and taciturn, slow to respond, uneasy in company and generally withdrawn. Like John Jacob he was absorbed in his business affairs, but he did not follow the parental example of warmth towards his family and a delight in good conversation. The mind which had been formed in the habit of study turned in upon itself when the stimulus of a classical education was so abruptly removed by his recall from Europe. Accustomed to losing himself in the intricacies of ancient history, language and literature, he found it impossible to disengage from a scholarly mode of thinking, and the fact that he applied it to the mundane details of the fur trade and the real estate business made him intensely boring.

'He knew every inch of real estate that stood in his name,' it was said when he came into his inheritance, 'every bond, contract and lease. He knew what was due when the leases expired and attended personally to the matter.' He could also recite his rent rolls from memory. Perhaps such attention to minutiae was William's way of making bearable the life his father had decreed for him, but if it actually made him happy he seldom showed it. A portrait of him at about the time of his father's death shows a morose-looking, heavy-set face with a blank expression in the eyes and a thin-lipped, downturned mouth. Lord Rosebery, visiting the United States in 1873 (the future British prime minister was then aged twenty-six) was 'shewn' William Astor at Trinity Church one Sunday and described him as 'a hard dreary looking old man'.

Even in early manhood William appears to have been neither handsome nor lively, an acquaintance describing him as 'the richest and least attractive young man of his time', but of course his wealth was a great attraction in itself for the well-bred young spinsters of New York, most of whom, according to a visiting Englishman, were 'the most heartless worldly b[itche]s that can be imagined'. Fortunately for William, though, it was not one of the hard-eyed socialites who captured him but 'a country girl' who matched him perfectly in diffidence, plain looks and deep Christian conviction (unlike his father, William was a regular churchgoer). Luckily, too, the prospective bride had a pedigree to match John Jacob's social ambitions for his children: Margaret Rebecca Armstrong – eighteen years old when William met her during a business visit to Albany – came from a distinguished military-political family and was also related, through her mother, to the illustrious Beekmans and Livingstons.

Margaret's father, General John A. Armstrong, had won honour during the Revolution, had served in the Senate representing Pennsylvania and as minister to France, then had been appointed Secretary for War by President Madison in 1812. By the time his daughter moved into the Astor orbit the crusty old general had been politically disgraced and was playing the squire on his portion of the Livingston acres in upstate New York, but his social credentials were such that John Jacob Astor was pleased to sanction a marital alliance – in spite of the fact that both he and his friend Albert Gallatin had been branded as traitors to the United States in Armstrong's vituperative reply to those who had criticized his handling of the War of 1812 and forced him from office.

Not that the elder Astor, though, was dazzled by this brilliant connexion: ever the pragmatist, and with the dissolution of daughter Magdalen's marriage to Adrian Bentzon very much in mind, he proposed to General Armstrong that Margaret should renounce her entitlement to a share in William's patrimony in return for a cash settlement on marriage. Blue blood may have been better than red, but in John Jacob's spectrum the most important colour was banknote green. Armstrong, having more class than money to support it, readily agreed to the generous figure mentioned by Astor and

133

signed away his daughter's legal dower right to one-third of the many millions of dollars William was eventually to inherit. The practice thus established was to be a source of regret to several Astor wives in the future.

In the case of William and Margaret, however, John Jacob need not have worried about the possible dissipation of the Astor fortune. The marriage was to last for more than half a century, and anyway William outlived his wife by two years. They were married in 1818 in suitably fashionable style and with an Episcopalian ceremony, as befitted the bride's Old Guard background. John Jacob gave them a house at Broadway and White Street, eleven blocks north of his own home, and took his son officially into partnership. William settled down into what would become the routine of the rest of his life, rising early to deal with his correspondence, breakfasting at nine o'clock, then walking to his office, where he tended to spend the day working like any clerk, and walking home again. In the evenings the Astors would often entertain, and Margaret's connexions assured them a steady attendance of the best guests – Livingstons, of course, and Stuyvesants, Jays, Kents, Crugers, Schermerhorns and Brevoorts, the young, rich and more or less idle foundations of a social register with which the Astors were soon to become so closely associated, adding or subtracting names at will. But the entertainment at White Street, and later in Lafayette Place, was not all that entertaining, given William's unsociable attitude and his wife's bucolic lack of style, so that even the old gossip Philip Hone could find nothing much to say about it, confining himself merely to recording the dates.

Left to themselves, however, William and Margaret could indulge whatever passions lay buried deep within them, and such evidence as there is suggests that their relationship was a happy and healthy one. William unbent so far as to invent for his wife a nickname, 'Peachy', a compliment to her exceptionally fine complexion – which seems to prove that he was not insensible to Margaret's physical charms. Margaret herself, outwardly quiet, strong-minded and pious, was underneath it all something of a romantic who delighted in the gothic novels and mystical poetry of the period and seems to have found a trace of the imaginary hero in William. (Although he did not have the good looks demanded by contemporary fiction he certainly possessed the required wealth and social standing.)

Within a year of their marriage the couple's first child was born, a girl named Emily by her mother after the heroine of Mrs Radcliffe's *The Mysteries of Udolpho*. During the next twelve years Margaret bore six children, which appears to indicate that she and William enjoyed an active sexual relationship. All the children save one, a girl named Sarah, survived to adulthood, although poor Emily was to die in her twenties.

By the time of Sarah's birth in 1832 Margaret's bloom was fading and her husband had settled into plodding middle age, but she was still able to pursue at least some of her romantic fantasies, aided no doubt by William's inheritance in 1833 of a million dollars from his childless uncle, Henry the butcher. A change of house, to something grander, was indicated and William built a magnificent red-brick mansion on a lot owned by his father in Lafayette Place, a short and leafy street near the intersection of Broadway and Bowery where the Vauxhall Gardens had once been. After the fashion of the great houses that featured in the English novels she loved, Margaret staffed her new home with servants dressed in livery and even went so far as to hire a valet for William, though most of her class considered that an effete European affectation. (The valet did not last long, however: William did not care either for his appearance or, more particularly, for spending money on it, and his body servant became so disgusted with what he considered his master's slovenliness that he left to work for President Van Buren.)

As was to become normal practice a generation later, the leaders of New York society followed the example set by an Astor and Lafayette Place was transformed into a millionaires' enclave. The Schermerhorns took the plot adjoining William's – with consequences as yet unforeseen for the Astor dynasty – on the eastward side of the street backing on to the Bowery, and scions of the other first-rank families moved in all around. William's sister, Dorothea Langdon, restored by now to her father's favour after her elopement, was presented with a palazzo copied from the style of Florence on another Astor site at the corner of Lafayette and Art Street, which was in due course to be renamed Astor Place, which identifies it still today.

But the sudden windfall provided by the decease of Uncle Henry set Margaret Armstrong Astor's thoughts working in another direction, too. She yearned for a place in the country such as she had known in her youth, where she could indulge her interest in gardening and where the children could escape the enervating humidity and frequent outbreaks of disease that marked the city's summers. As it happened she got precisely the place of her girlhood memories – her father's estate by the Hudson. The old general had fallen on hard times but could not bear to give up his farm, so William bought it, extended the house (adding an entire wing and a tower with superb views towards the river and the Catskills) and allowed both Armstrong and his bachelor son Kosciusko* to continue living and farming there. The estate was known as La Bergerie, reflecting Napoleon's gift of a flock of merino sheep to General Armstrong at the end of his diplomatic service in Paris, but in another flash of romanticism Margaret renamed it Rokeby, after Sir Walter Scott's poem of that title set in the north-east of England, traditional Armstrong country. Even here the Astors were not removed from New York social life, for the 1830s saw the beginning of the trend among the wealthy to build country homes on Hudson Valley farmland grown unprofitable through the expansion of transport which could bring agricultural products from the fertile Midwest. And of course Dorothea and her family were not far away at Hyde Park.

But it was the private rather than the social life at Rokeby that appealed most to William and Margaret. He built himself a large octagonal library – though his innate meanness got the better of him and instead of the traditional panelling he had plaster painted to resemble wood – and liked nothing better than to sit by its fire in the evening reading German lexicons and reference books, of which he was an avid collector. She had her garden and her houseplants and eventually a greenhouse. 'My mother is a good deal of a farmer,' her eldest son, John Jacob III, once said.

By 1838 William and Dorothea were the only surviving children of John Jacob Astor, apart from the mad John Jacob II, and between them they had thirteen children who would,

* Presumably named for the Polish general who fought with the American side in the War of Independence.

they hoped, bring added social cachet to the family by marrying well (they certainly did not need to marry for money). First to the altar was Sarah Shelburne Langdon, the girl alleged to have charmed her parents' way into the affections of John Jacob, who emulated her Aunt Eliza von Rumpff by capturing a European nobleman. Her bridegroom was Baron François Robert Boreel, chamberlain to the King of the Netherlands and first secretary of his country's legation in Paris. The couple settled in The Hague but were given a house on Broadway as a wedding present and were bequeathed the City Hotel in New York by John Jacob.

William's eldest child, Emily, made a glamorous but slightly disappointing match, disappointing at least as far as her family was concerned. Emily was a most unAstor-like girl, pretty and vivacious, with a well-developed sense of humour, and she found a complementary character in the dashing Sam Ward Jr, heir to a banking fortune, who was famous for his wit, charm and love of good food and wine. William looked askance at this altogether too flashy young man who was wooing his favourite daughter. The Wards were certainly rich, but not in the same league as the Astors, and their social standing was by no means that of a Livingston or Cruger. But Sam was as astute as he was colourful and embarked on a campaign to win over not only Emily's father but also John Jacob, whom he correctly saw as the real arbiter of the family's affairs and who doted upon the blue-eyed beauty Sam was determined to make his wife. He disarmed William by sending a large box of fine grapes out to Rokeby, and as for John Jacob 'he was full of jokes for the old man', according to a friend. 'He once brought a ventriloquist to the estate at Hellgate in secret' with the facetious intention of making Astor believe that he had 'a cat in his belly'. Ward commented at the time that the Astor family required his 'constant attention'.

Both William, who reassured himself with the thought that 'a man who has a million is as well off as if he were rich', and John Jacob gave their approval and the couple were married in 1838. The wedding, said Sam's sister Julia,* was 'the most cheerful I

---

* Julia Ward Howe, minor poet, social reformer and campaigner for women's rights who became famous as the composer of *The Battle Hymn of the Republic*.

ever saw' and the newly-weds moved into a large house on Bond Street, running between Broadway and Bowery just a little way south of Lafayette Place. All who knew them expected them to settle down to a life of public glitter and private bliss. Emily became pregnant immediately and late in 1838 gave birth to a girl named Margaret Astor Ward, always to be known as 'Maddie'. But her second confinement in 1841 ended in tragedy: she died during the birth and the son she bore was dead within a few days.

William and Margaret were devastated. The grieving father sought solace in his relationship with his eldest son – though he paid scant attention to the rest of his children – but Margaret never quite recovered from the shock of Emily's premature death. At first she kept to the house, but when her doctor counselled that she must go out she took to walking with her two youngest daughters, dressed as she insisted that each of the girls should be in a floor-length mourning veil. From a generally good-humoured woman 'she changed into a stern, quiet one – she could never bring herself to mention Emily's name again'.

Margaret was, however, to have the consolation of bringing up her grand-daughter, Maddie, even if it did come about in a rather unpleasant way. The ebullient Sam Ward did not suffer his bereavement for long, marrying – horror of horrors for the upright Astors – a beautiful Creole girl called Marie Angeline Grymes who was known as 'Medora' to the New York fast set. William Astor was incensed (he ordered Sam's bemused sister Louisa out of his house when he first heard the news of the marriage) but his anger was soon eclipsed by the blind fury of his father when Sam took the ill-considered step of turning over the Bond Street house to his new wife. Henry Brevoort was on hand to record John Jacob's feelings:

An untoward event has just happened in this family, which has stirred his ire; a thing which always does him good. Master Sam W—— has married Miss Medora Grymes and settled upon her *his* house in Bond Street, which house had been purchased & previously given or settled upon his first wife, but by our laws, became his, after her decease. This affair sticks deep into the old gentleman's gizzard. He views it as a sort of impeachment of his accustomed sagacity; a sort of outwitting & overreaching in the art of bargaining . . . the resentment of the A's is, I think, carried beyond all just bounds.

Well, there was property involved, wasn't there? Astor property, it appears, which had fallen into the 'wrong' hands by the accident of death. Or was there? The traditional assumption, to which Brevoort clearly subscribed, was that Sam and Emily had been given the Bond Street house by the Astors, hence the chagrin when the former Miss Grymes got her hands on it. Yet other records seem to indicate that it was Sam's father, the successful banker, who made the gift. This would seem logical, since old Sam Ward lived in Bond Street himself and it might have been expected that if the Astors had been involved the young couple would have been settled in Lafayette Place, where a regular Astor enclave was being established. Yet if that were the case, why the fury when Sam did what he was perfectly entitled to do with his own property by putting it in his second wife's name?

Was it the fact that the house, which would in the ordinary way have come down to Emily and her half-Astor offspring, had been placed beyond the reach of the foremost landowning family in New York? Or was it simply that the ultra-conservative Astors could not bear the prospect of Maddie being present while the popular Medora held court in what was now her own house for the more raffish (by Astor standards) elements of metropolitan life? Even more curious is that Sam actually agreed to hand over Maddie to William and Margaret. Again, the standard explanation is that John Jacob threatened to sue for the return of the house if his demand for the transfer of Maddie was not met. But if it had not been his house in the first place . . . ? Presumably Sam was either offered an inducement or placed under some kind of pressure. His later conduct suggests that he did not willingly part with his daughter: he complained to William at one point that Maddie did not seem to be writing to him very often and he hinted to friends that the Astors had turned the girl into a religious fanatic. Subsequent relations between him and the Astors were tense in the main, with William taking legal action to sell some of Sam's property against taxes due and to secure official guardianship of Maddie, while Sam protested that he was being kicked when he was down (the collapse of the family bank having sent him off to California with the Forty-niners to seek a new fortune).

In the end no one was really the loser in this mysterious state of affairs. Maddie brought much pleasure to her grandmother and eventually credit on the family through a 'good' marriage. Sam's life, though mercurial and touched from time to time by unfriendly influences, ended in a warm glow of appreciation by most people who knew him. His second marriage was an on-off business, more or less according to the state of his finances, and he outlived both his wife and the two sons of the union. He moved in a wide and influential circle of politicians, writers and journalists, eventually becoming one of the most famous and successful political lobbyists in Washington after the Civil War and at the same time earning the reputation of 'the most hospitable of entertainers that the United States boast'. He died in Italy in 1884, but not before he had been honoured in verse by his warm friend Longfellow, whose umbrella was apparently mislaid after Sam had borrowed it and left it at the Somerset Club in Boston. The 'tale of the lost umbrella' began thus:

> A messenger rides up and down,
> Through Beacon Street in Boston town;
> From Craigie Hall unto the Club
> Of Somerset; there at the Hub,
> Where is my umbrella!

In the eyes of the priggish Astors, however, being 'a character' as Sam was, no matter how well liked, was no distinction and they could well have done without the Ward connexion, which as we have seen William would have liked to break. So too, at first, with the liaison formed by Dorothea's third daughter, Louisa. Sarah had married well, of course, and so had her younger sister Eliza, born in 1818 – her husband, Matthew Wilks, was an English country gentleman with an estate in Ontario, Canada, where he took his bride to live. Louisa, though, was cast in the mould of her mother, and that spelled trouble. A story handed down from one branch of the

Astor family tells what happened.

Eliza and Louisa, it seems, were out driving one day when the younger girl happened to mention that she needed to do some shopping at Peisers, the drapery store. The carriage pulled over and Louisa alighted, saying she would just be a minute. Eliza waited patiently but after some time had passed began to wonder what her sister was doing. She went into the shop and discovered that Louisa had walked straight through it and out the back door. Mystified, Eliza drove back to Lafayette Place for lunch, where with the pudding came the news that Louisa had eloped with Oliver DeLancey Kane, descendant of a 'treacherous' pre-Revolutionary Tory family whose lands had been confiscated by a bill of attainder. Louisa's father, Colonel Langdon, reacted in precisely the same way as his father-in-law had done when he had eloped with Dorothea – perhaps what upset him most was that the Kanes had been on 'the wrong side' during the War of Independence! He disinherited Louisa and persuaded William Astor to do the same. In this case, however, there was no time for a reconciliation, for the colonel died suddenly in 1847, but Louisa and her husband were not entirely left out of the Astor inheritance. Probably at the insistence of the good-natured Dorothea, they were readmitted to the circle just in time to be included among John Jacob's bequests, receiving a seventh share of real estate, stocks and cash worth two million dollars at the time and considerably more as tenements blossomed on the land they had been left.

The remaining daughters of the two families made marriages that shamed no one. The most brilliant was that of Laura Astor, William's second girl (born in 1824): a rather homely young woman, she caused a good deal of envy among the socialite sisterhood by capturing Franklin Hughes Delano, heir to a Massachusetts whale oil fortune and said to be 'one of the handsomest men of his day'. At the time of their wedding in 1844 a rumour circulated to the effect that the bride had been given by William a cheque for a quarter of a million dollars, but this turned out to be a $200,000 trust fund, which in the end was worth considerably more. William also bought the couple an old Dutch farm, Stein Valejte, next door to Rokeby – adding some of his own land to form a quite substantial estate – and John Jacob, not to be outdone, gave them a home in Colonnade

Row, an elegant terrace of town houses on the western side of Lafayette Place.

In the face of such largess, Delano retired from the shipping business in which he had been a partner and lived the leisured existence of a gentleman, only occasionally soiling his hands with commerce. He and Laura became keen collectors of art, china and particularly jewelry, a passion aroused in Laura by her elder sister Emily, who had sought to take the bitter edge off her favoured position in the family by showering her little sister with precious gifts. The marriage was long and happy, but clouded by an inability to have children, which meant that the couple took an abiding interest in their many nephews and nieces. When they moved to Europe in their later years two of the daughters of Maddie Astor would often be sent to stay with them, and the girls recalled such visits with affection. Franklin died in Europe, but Laura lived long enough to see him commemorated in the naming of a son born to one of her Delano nieces – the boy was, of course, Franklin Delano Roosevelt, who in the following century would be close to the then head of the Astor family in America.

The youngest daughters of both William and Dorothea married foreigners and withdrew to the periphery of the Astor group, though neither was quite forgotten when it came to dividing the spoils. Cecilia Langdon's husband was a Swiss, Jean de Nottbeck, and in due course she inherited John Jacob's villa by Lake Geneva. Mary Alida Astor, born in 1826, followed her cousin Eliza in marrying an Englishman, which pleased her family (they always admired English manners and customs) and brought her a dowry of $200,000 with an additional hundred thousand in property.

Thus did the Astor influence burrow into the roots of American society, but of course it was towards the central figures of the dynasty, the heirs in the male line, that most attention and care was directed. Daughters were expendable, but sons would in time become guardians of the fortune. William had three boys, but like his father he subscribed entirely to the principle of primogeniture and favoured John Jacob III – always known as 'Junior', an indication of how completely the flawed John Jacob II was ignored – to the detriment of the other two. Indeed the youngest son, Henry, born in 1830, was almost as much of an outcast as his great-uncle John Jacob, and for a similar reason.

Henry Astor was not mad, but he was certainly very strange, with a violent streak in his nature and an uncontrollable temper. Like John Jacob II he was a large and powerful man, with a deep chest and thick neck, and to add to his awe-inspiring appearance he sported a luxuriant red beard. His favourite activities were boxing, wrestling, horse racing and chasing women, and in him his father's lack of interest in social intercourse was raised to the level of total aversion. It was to the family's relief, therefore, and no doubt with some solemn encouragement from William, that in early manhood Henry withdrew to Rokeby, spending even the winters there with no company other than that of the servants and the neighbouring farm lads, with whom he liked to indulge in sport (not to mention what he got up to with the farmers' daughters). To make matters worse as far as his family was concerned, he was generous to a fault and, since he had been reasonably well provided for in his grandfather's will, he was able to lend money to his less wealthy neighbours over terms and at rates of interest no businesslike Astor would ever have considered.

Although his fortune was founded upon and increased by the Astors' real estate holdings in New York, Henry took absolutely no interest in the business and enjoyed his life of splendid isolation until, when he was forty, he exploded into the consciousness of his family. On 4 May 1871 he ordered his carriage and set off through the country lanes, accompanied by a minister, to the cottage of the Dineharts, transplanted German peasants, whose 'handsome, blooming', twenty-seven-year-old daughter Malvina he married on the spot. Though Henry tried to keep the marriage secret, the news of it soon reached the Astors in New York and a conference was hastily convened at the estate office in Prince Street. After much wailing and hand-wringing, William dashed off to Dutchess County to interview his son, returning with the unwelcome news that Henry and his $30,000 a year were irrecoverably lost, since Malvina Dinehart had signed no marriage contract relieving her of her dower rights.

William and the rest of the family were furious, fearing that they would be held up to ridicule by the whole of New York society, particularly when it was revealed that Malvina's ancestors had been bondsmen of the high and mighty Livingstons. What was to be done? Henry had already been stripped of the management of his estate in favour of family trustees following an unfortunate incident involving in-laws of the Dineharts: during a bout of drunkenness he had beaten Josephine Ash, the four-year-old daughter of the Rokeby farm manager, and the girl's father had been prevented from attacking Henry only by the swift action of Mrs Ash. This new scandal demanded further action in the interests of protecting the rapidly growing bounty of the Astor properties. William's will must be changed.

The enraged father, writing a new codicil to his testament that reduced Henry's patrimony from $150,000 to $30,000 and revoked two trust funds worth a total of four hundred thousand, made the following comment: 'My son Henry, having recently formed a matrimonial connexion under peculiar circumstances without my knowledge and in such a rank in life as that the large property derived by him under deeds executed by my father, and the beneficial use or income of which is absolutely secured to him, will be more than adequate for all useful purposes of himself and any family he may have in the condition of life he has chosen for himself, I think it proper to revoke and annul to the extent hereinafter specified the disposition in his favor or for his benefit or for the benefit of his issue.'

Heaven forbid that any of the wealth – or at least any more of it than could not be saved – created through the efforts of a German peasant's son should ever find its way into the hands of German peasants! And to complete Henry's ostracism, the family trustees resigned, being replaced by the Astor Estate's lawyer and other employees.

Henry was unrepentant: why should he worry what the family thought of him as long as the cheques arrived each quarter-day? During his lifetime he was to see the annual income of his property rise to three-quarters of a million dollars, far more than he could possibly spend. The family might have cut him off, but old John Jacob had guaranteed him a life of leisure and comfort. In 1874, seeking even greater solitude than he already enjoyed, he bought a farm at West

Copake, Columbia County, on the Massachusetts border near what is now the Taconic State Park. One room of the large house he paved with silver dollars and in the two-hundred-acre grounds he built his own racetrack. The Dineharts lived off him, of course, but their in-laws, the Ash family, decided that they should have a share of the fortune so they sued Henry over his attack on their daughter, claiming that Josephine had suffered permanent damage.

The case was heard at Poughkeepsie, loading further embarrassment upon the New York Astors. Counsel for Ash entertained the court with an outline of Henry's eccentricities, describing how he would don a surplice and 'preach in the house whether anyone was present or not – did it for a pastime more than anything else – had made the Bible a study' and would punctuate these sermons by hitting a bell with a crowbar. He was frequently drunk, the lawyer alleged, and on one occasion his wife had expressed the opinion that 'the red-eyed hound ought to be hung' (though Malvina denied this in her evidence). Another time, in his cups, he had locked Mr Ash and Malvina in a room together. Henry's lawyer, on the other hand, suggested that the suit was nothing more than an attempt at extortion prompted by jealousy over the Dineharts' good fortune: 'Mr Astor didn't do much marrying, except in form and ceremony; they married him ... the millions and acres which Astor now owns will be swept into the same pool into which he has married.' But the court was less than sympathetic to the plight of such a rich man and awarded the Ashes twenty thousand dollars.

Once the sensation of the trial was over, Henry and Malvina retired from public view to their estate in the Berkshires and lived long and peacefully, their only contact with the Astors being visits from Henry's kind-hearted sister, Laura Delano, and his great-nephew Vincent, who in time would develop some eccentricities of his own that would have a profound effect on the dynasty.

There was nothing eccentric about the marriages of William Astor's other sons. Both chose as brides extremely acceptable daughters of Lafayette Place neighbours: Charlotte Augusta Gibbes in the case of John Jacob III and Caroline Webster Schermerhorn in that of William Backhouse Jr. These two wives were to raise the status of the Astors to unprecedented heights, the first as mistress of most of the millions, the second as queen of New York society. But at the same time, their husbands were to play their parts in what proved to be the dynasty's long, slow decline.

II

The event that was entirely to alter the character of the Astor dynasty occurred on 29 March 1848. That day, Philip Hone wrote in his diary: 'John Jacob Astor died this morning, at nine o'clock, in the eighty-fifth year of his age; sensible to the last, but the material of life exhausted, the machinery worn out, the lamp extinguished for want of oil. Bowed down with bodily infirmity for a long time, he has gone at last, and left reluctantly his unbounded wealth. His property is estimated at twenty million dollars, some judicious persons say thirty million dollars; but at any rate, he was the richest man in the United States in productive and valuable property; and this immense, gigantic fortune was the fruit of his own labor, unerring sagacity and far-seeing penetration. He came to this country at twenty years of age; penniless, friendless, without inheritance, without education, and having no example before him of the art of money-making, but with a determination to be rich, and ability to carry it into effect.'

A trifle exaggerated perhaps, since Astor had been neither entirely friendless nor uneducated upon his arrival in America, but in essence an accurate summary of how John Jacob was judged by the American upper class. More important, though, was Hone's point about Astor's wealth having been the product of his 'own labor, unerring sagacity and far-seeing penetration'. His descendants would never be able to claim that: John Jacob had organized matters so that none of his chief heirs would have to do a day's work in their lives, except by choice, and would need neither sagacity nor penetration in order to build on their inheritance. In fact, the provisions of his will seemed to make it clear that the last thing any future head of the family must do was employ any initiative or judgment he might possess.

Of course, outside of the Astors' own social stratum there were people who took a rather dimmer view of John Jacob's achievements than did Philip Hone. James Gordon Bennett,* owner and editor of the New York *Herald*, expressed the opinion of many when he editorialized: 'If we had been an associate of John Jacob Astor ... the first idea that we should have put into his head would have been that one-half of his immense property – ten millions at least – belonged to the people of the City of New York. During the last fifty years of the life of John Jacob Astor, his property had been augmented and increased in value by the aggregate intelligence, industry, enterprise, and commerce of New York, fully to the amount of one-half its value. The farms and lots of ground which he bought forty, twenty, and ten and five years ago, have all increased in value entirely by the industry of the citizens of New York. Of course, it is as plain as two and two make four that the half of his immense estate, in its actual value, has accrued to him by the industry of the community.'

What prompted Bennett's outburst was the publication of John Jacob's will, with its meagre crop of public bequests – the product of a man the editor described scathingly as a 'self-invented money-making machine'. In all, Astor bequeathed half a million dollars to charitable purposes, and if that seems like a lot of money it should be noted that the sum represented just two and a half per cent of the estate. The Astor Library, of course, received $400,000, thanks entirely to the long-applied pressure of Cogswell. Among the other legacies were $25,000 to the German Society for an immigrants' counselling service designed to prevent them from falling into the traps 'to which strangers without knowledge of the country or its language may be exposed'. Astor's native village, Walldorf, was given $50,000 to build a house 'for the use of the poor' and $37,000 of the remainder went to New York charities for the blind, orphans and destitute children and 'respectable aged indigent females', and to the Lying-in Asylum.

'Poor, mean and beggarly,' snapped Bennett, pointing out that if Astor had left only ten million to his family that amount would have been 'quite enough for any reasonable person, of any rank, in this country'.

It has been argued that Bennett's was very much a minority

---

* The *Herald*, which sold daily for a penny, became a prototype for the sensational, mass-circulation newspapers of the following century.

view and that to criticize now the low level of philanthropy in Astor's will is to judge it by modern standards, ignoring the fact that at the time social conscience was not a notable feature of life. Astor, it is claimed, was acting no differently from other members of his social class. The fact is, however, that John Jacob was in a class of his own, better placed than any man to show some gratitude to the country which had given him the opportunities to amass a fortune – and a fortune the like of which had not been seen outside the greatest families of Europe. Furthermore, he had less excuse than most for the absence of social conscience. He had not been raised as a member of the upper class, insulated against and ignorant of the conditions of ordinary life; he knew poverty, hardship and labour. He had lived among the working classes for much of his life and, though he pretended to endorse the fashionable 'Christian' view that if people were in need it was their own fault, he must have known how hypocritical that was, must have been aware in his heart that his own success had depended upon luck and other people as well as on his own work and skill. One must conclude that John Jacob Astor's lack of charity was born not of apathy or ignorance but of greed. His meanness was of the spirit.

It is, moreover, idle to suggest – as have several apologists for Astor – that America's social conscience was notable for its absence in the middle years of the nineteenth century. During that period there was a great flowering of radical thought and a growing pressure for wide-ranging reform. True, the forces of entrenched privilege were to hold the line for a further half-century, and more, but even among the rich there were enlightened men and women. Nor was James Gordon Bennett alone in his criticism. The Whig elements and their mouth-pieces, as was natural, tended to praise Astor with a lavish-ness bordering on sycophancy, but the Democrat press as a whole leaned towards the view of the *Herald*. In the *Tribune*, for example, Horace Greeley wrote the lesson of Astor's life as, 'Lay not up for yourselves treasures on earth,' and an Irish immigrant leader, who knew at first hand the misery of those who lived in the foul tenements on Astor land, was considerably more forthright. 'How many men,' he asked in a radical paper called *The Subterranean*, 'one hair of

whose head is worth more than [Astor's] whole soulless car-
case, have come into the world without a shirt and without a
penny, that are daily destined to go out of it worse than they
came in?'

And even so famous a Whig as Horace Mann, leader of the
party in Massachusetts and known as the 'father' of the public
school system, was moved to deplore the spectacle of a man
'hoarding wealth for the base love of wealth, hugging to his
breast, in his dying hour, the memory of his gold and not of
his Redeemer; gripping his riches till the scythe of death cut
off his hands and he was changed, in the twinkling of an eye,
from being one of the richest men that ever lived in this
world to being one of the poorest souls who ever went out
of it'.

In a pamphlet entitled *Thoughts for a Young Man*, the great
reformer continued: 'Nothing but absolute insanity can be
pleaded in palliation of the conduct of a man who was worth
nearly or quite twenty millions of dollars, but gave only some
half million of it to any public object... In the midst of so
much poverty and suffering as the world experiences, it has
become a high moral and religious duty to create an overwhelming public opinion against both the parsimonies and the
squanderings of wealth.'

Mann drew a parallel between Astor and Stephen Girard, the
Philadelphia banking, insurance and real estate magnate whose
life story bore some similarity to that of John Jacob. Born in
France, Girard had spent his early years in the hard life of the
sea and having emigrated to America in 1775 had laid the basis
of his fortune in shipping during the Napoleonic wars. Like
Astor, he had abandoned commerce and directed his attention
towards investment and by the time of his death in 1831 had
amassed what was for the time a huge fortune of six million
dollars. He was also like Astor in the sense that his business
methods were open to question on ethical grounds, and his
personality was rather less attractive than John Jacob's, but his
great redeeming feature was his devotion to philanthropy on a
grand scale. He spent his last years carefully planning how his
estate would be distributed (he had no immediate family) and
the bulk of his fortune went to the state of Pennsylvania and the
city of Philadelphia for public improvement programmes, with

a large endowment set aside to found Girard College, a school for orphan boys.

Mann was, admittedly, something of an exception among Whigs, though *Harper's* was being less than complimentary (even if unintentionally) when it declared that 'to get all that he could and to keep nearly all that he got' were the laws of Astor's being. Yet Mann's attack so incensed John Jacob's grandson, Charles Astor Bristed, that one feels it must have touched a nerve very near the surface. Bristed, who had done very well by Astor's estate, rushed to his benefactor's defence, claiming that his grandfather had left only eight million dollars and attempting to reply in the same terms as Mann by pointing out that 'Girard left the greater part of his fortune to establish a college for orphans, into which no minister of any religious denomination was ever to set foot . . . which always struck me as a very ingenious, diabolical contrivance for the increase of knowledge without virtue.'

Even John Jacob III, who as we shall see felt himself to be very much above the common run of life, was so stung by the criticism of his grandfather that he commented, 'It is enough to make one wish to abandon such a country' – a thought that his even prouder eldest son was to take very seriously.

The attacks, then, were not to be lightly dismissed. Yet oddly enough, the critics were really aiming at the wrong target. It was too easy for radicals to look at the will and scorn its scant regard for the public good: much more important, however, was the way in which Astor had packaged the bulk of his fortune that was passed on to his family, and more particularly to his chief heir. 'To keep nearly all that he got,' *Harper's* had said, was one of the laws of his being, and in his will he did his best to make sure that he retained control of the money he had made even from the grave.

This was entirely contrary to the spirit of democratic America, which did not want to see the growth of vast, self-perpetuating fortunes on the model of the European landowning aristocracy. Laws had been passed limiting not only the practice of leaving property to eldest sons but also the devices that could be used to prevent the disposal of an estate, such as trusts. After several attempts, John Jacob found a way round those laws.

At first Astor directed that the main part of his property –
that remaining after the bequests to the various branches of the
family – should go to William in trust, managed by six men of
whom the beneficiary was one. Changes in the law, however,
raised the possibility that such a will might be declared invalid,
so John Jacob compromised. William could do as he wished
with half of his inheritance but received only the income from a
trust covering the other half, and that he could only use to
increase the value of the portion he held absolutely. When
William died, the half of the estate in trust was to go directly to
his children and could not be disbursed in any other way.

Not only, therefore, did John Jacob decree what should
happen to his own fortune, but he even laid down the terms for
a substantial part of his heir's estate. Thus was constructed the
foundation of a dynastic inheritance which the man who
created it clearly intended should last forever.

As if he was attempting to disguise the main measures he had
taken to protect his twenty-million-dollar estate, Astor began
his will with what were, in view of the total amount involved,
the minor bequests. The very first section covered Dorothea
Langdon, 'fat Dolly', who had so disappointed her father by
eloping, but even here there was a clue as to John Jacob's
intentions. Dolly received outright her house and land in
Lafayette Place and the furniture from her father's home on
Broadway, 'also the use, during her life, of all my silver plate,
my new service of plate excepted'. The rest of her bounty,
though, was all tied up in trust: $100,000 in New York
municipal bonds, $25,000 invested with the New York Life
Insurance and Trust Company, five hundred shares in the Bank
of America and a thousand in the Manhattan Company; then,
in a series of codicils, more property in what had become the
Astor neighbourhood, a further $100,000 in investments, and a
provision that if the income from the shares and bonds proved
to be under $15,000 a year she could take the interest on the
two $100,000 trusts.

For the Langdon children there was $25,000 each, with an
additional $25,000 apiece for the three boys when they reached
the age of thirty; $50,000 to be divided equally among the seven
of them and, in a codicil, a further $100,000. And then there
was the property – such property as would make them all

millionaires. A hundred lots of the land John Jacob had bought from George Clinton all those years ago and which was now a valuable part of the West Side; Broadway real estate between Prince and Houston streets; five prospective tenement lots in the Lower East Side; houses on the east of Lafayette Place near William Astor's home; and, for the sons only, eight lots on Broadway just above Canal Street. As if that was not enough, the young Langdons also got half of the estate left by their aunt, Eliza Astor von Rumpff, which comprised thirteen hundred shares in two banks, the Merchants and the Mechanics, and $75,000 worth of securities.

Altogether it was a pretty good haul for a family which, because of the 'unauthorized' marriage of the parents, had once risked being cut out of the will. But the bequest looked paltry beside the fifteen million dollars that was going to William and eventually to his children and the resentment this discrepancy caused was increased by the fact that both Dorothea and her errant daughter Louisa were obliged to take legal action in order to receive what was rightfully theirs.

Not content with her properties and investment income, Dolly sought the interest on her two trust funds, claiming that the return on the stocks and bonds she had been left fell below the $15,000 specified in the will. Brother William, who took the view that Dorothea was doing very nicely on what she already had, refused to touch the trusts – and the Langdons sued. The legal wrangle lasted for nine years and was finally settled by the Court of Appeal in Dolly's favour. She did not really need the money and William had no excuse for holding on to it: the real winners, as so often in such cases, were the lawyers.

Louisa provided still more lucre for the legal profession. Upon her own elopement with Oliver de Lancey Kane, not only had her father and William Astor cut her out of their wills but John Jacob had, while stopping short of disinheriting her, reduced by half her portion of the property he had allotted to the Langdons and seen to it that she would not share in other Astor estates. The death of Colonel Langdon and Dolly's campaign to have her daughter reinstated brought a codicil in John Jacob's will restoring to Louisa fifty per cent of what had originally been taken away, meaning that she received a third less than her sisters. This did not satisfy Louisa and she again followed her mother's example by going to court. After a complex series of hearings, appeals and counter-appeals, an equally complex judgment was handed down which fixed Louisa's 'fine' for disobedience at $50,000, giving her otherwise the same settlement as her siblings.

It was not surprising that legal eagles loved to hover around the Astors, but there were to be no more pickings for them among the beneficiaries of John Jacob's will. Twenty-six-year-old Charles Astor Bristed, for instance, was hardly likely to complain about his share: the old man's house at 485 Broadway and his estate at Hellgate; the inevitable lot in Lafayette Place and another on Broadway; property in Houston Street, in Avenue A on the East Side, in Eighth Avenue on the West Side, and a sizable piece between 37th and 40th streets west of Broadway, in what became New York's famous Garment District. For his spending money he could rely on the interest from a trust fund of $115,000 and a quarter share of Aunt Eliza's estate. John Jacob had always intended that his favourite grandson should live as a gentleman, and a cultivated one at that. Having sent Charles to Harvard and even to Cambridge University – thus forming his personality along the right lines and developing in him a taste for literature and leisure – old Astor gave him in 1848 the wherewithal to indulge the civilized habits he had learnt.

The grandchildren in William's family were settled much less generously, but after all one of them would eventually assume responsibility for the bulk of the fortune and the rest were not exactly going to suffer deprivation and hardship. Henry was a problem, of course, but the rents from the properties he was bequeathed would at least keep him in comfortable isolation, away from the sneers of the New York nabobs. John Jacob III and William Backhouse Jr shared in the same ten-block-deep tract of property running north from 42nd Street and west between Broadway and the Hudson, not to mention lots on Lafayette. They also divided the remaining quarter of Eliza's estate $37,500 in bonds plus six hundred and fifty bank shares) and to the eldest went 'my new service of plate'. Their sisters got nothing from John Jacob: after two attempts to provide for them while guarding against their acquisition of 'unsuitable' husbands, he passed on the responsibility to their father.

Of course, John Jacob Astor had other family, too, much less exalted than the branch he had founded, and being a sentimental German he could not overlook them in his will. George Astor, the musical instrument maker, had died leaving seven children – his widow received an annuity of £200 and four daughters were given $20,000 each. When it came to the sons, Astor was more discriminating. George Jr had worked for him in New York, apparently without much enthusiasm or success, so he got a mere $3,000; William Henry had become a musician, a profession not noted for its financial sagacity, and his uncle felt that $10,000 was all he could manage. The eldest, Joseph, had remained in London and seemed a steady enough fellow, for which his reward was twenty-five thousand dollars. These dispositions had clearly been difficult for John Jacob, the number of codicils they consumed being no doubt a reflection of the struggle between family loyalty and his customary caution in parting with money. Other relatives, both in America and in Germany, received anything from ten thousand to one thousand dollars each.

There were two sections of the will in which William Astor felt obliged to intervene, apart from the bequest for the foundation of the Astor Library. The first was that scornful two-hundred-dollar annuity for Fitz-Greene Halleck, a 'shabby affair' which many of the poet's literary friends felt he should reject. Halleck, always the gentleman, did not agree. 'I had no claim on Mr Astor,' he said. 'I was not of his blood; I had rendered him services and he had paid me for them. If he had any bequest to make, it was for him to judge its magnitude, not me; and the annuity is as acceptable as it would have been had it been ten times its present size. It evidenced the respect of Mr Astor, and it does not become me to denounce it... Mr Astor treated me like a gentleman. For years he paid me handsomely for my services and now he pays me the compliment of remembering me as a friend in his will...'

But either John Jacob had not been serious about this annuity, and had made his son a party to the sour joke, or else William (a man not celebrated for his sense of humour) thought his father had treated his former secretary and companion unfairly, for he immediately increased the bequest. One source has it that Halleck was given an ex gratia payment of $10,000, which according to the recollection of a cousin he lent to a friend without security and subsequently lost. More probable, however, is the Astor version, which says that the annuity was raised to fifteen hundred.

William's second intervention was in the matter of his insane elder brother, John Jacob II, who in 1838 had been installed in his own house at Ninth Avenue and Fourteenth Street, well away from fashionable society and surrounded by a high fence enclosing an extensive garden. His father had decreed that $5,000 a year should be set aside as the salary of the doctor who lived with John Jacob II and seemed to be the only person who could control him, wagging his finger and admonishing: 'Astor, be a man.' William, however, took the view that such a service was not worth $5,000 a year and that his brother could be dealt with equally well by someone less expensive. He sacked the doctor but, according to a contemporary account, he had failed to realize the extent of his brother's awareness. John Jacob II was enraged and stamped about his house scattering furniture and smashing windows. When his fury had abated, he simply threw himself on his bed and burst into tears. William was deeply shocked and guilt-ridden. He immediately asked the doctor to return, but the latter replied: 'I'm not coming back. I'm a free man for the first time in years.' His resolve weakened only when William offered him a salary of $10,000, double what John Jacob had set aside.

As for the Astor Library, John Jacob's only act of philanthropy of any magnitude, William had to dip into his inheritance to support it right from the start, otherwise the bequest would never have brought it to the point of opening. Then, as soon as it did open in 1854, William was called upon to add a new wing, sacrificing another precious Astor plot of land. Indeed, the Astor Library proved to be a drain on William throughout his life, but it was what his father appeared to have wanted (even if he had not been all that keen on paying for it) and William was nothing if not a dutiful son.

But the institution did have the effect that its founder must have desired. It was the only reference library in the city (the idea of circulating libraries was still in its infancy) and many well-known writers – including the visiting Dickens and Thackeray – were thankful for it. Ralph Waldo Emerson was full of admiration for what he called a great public bequest and

Washington Irving's *Life of George Washington* was written in the library. The politician Charles Sumner, one of the earliest advocates of equal rights for blacks, told a friend: 'I range daily in the alcoves of the Astor: more charming than the gardens of Boccaccio and each hour a Decameron.' For those with less literary inclinations, the Palladian halls of the library were one of the sights to be seen in New York by distinguished visitors such as the Prince of Wales (later King Edward VII), who was entertained in the city in 1860.

By 1875, the year of William Astor's death, the library contained almost a quarter of a million books and was undoubtedly the most comprehensive assembly of reference works in the continent. Yet it was so short of money that the heating was completely inadequate, there was no lighting, it was unattended at night and its array of magazines was not provided with binders. It was, said the *New York Times*, 'a sadly impecunious establishment' reserved for a select few and by no means the great public institution that the city needed, to which supporters of the library's trustees replied that it had never been intended to encourage 'the indulgence of an idle habit of intemperate and promiscuous reading'. The truth was that the Astor Library had been founded reluctantly and was maintained with reluctance. As a memorial to John Jacob it was inappropriate because it did not show a profit, unlike, say, the Astor House hotel. Three generations of the family gave money to the library, but forty years after its opening the endowment produced an income of only $47,000 a year: it was a raindrop compared to the deluge of five million dollars Andrew Carnegie was to pour into the establishment of New York's lending libraries at the turn of the century. The Astor, huffed the New York *Tribune*, was 'a refuge for a few supercilious officials and a few ornamental trustees' with 'an old reputation for churlishness and indifference'.

Finally, in 1895, the institution was merged with the Tilden and Lenox collections to become part of the New York Public Library, which moved to the present building on Fifth Avenue in 1911, and the alcoves of academe in Lafayette Place were turned over to the Hebrew Sheltering and Immigrant Aid Society. Probably the Astor would never have been founded if old John Jacob had not been blackmailed into it by Cogswell, and as far as the Astor heirs were concerned it was no more than a convenient receptacle for public bequests they must have otherwise found it hard to make.

In any case, and perhaps typical of the Astors' ambivalent attitude towards the America which had made them rich, it was neither the Astor Library nor the Astor House hotel that William saw as the real memorial to John Jacob, but the Astor Haus in dear old Walldorf – built at a cost of $7,000, under the personal supervision of John Jacob III, and endowed with $50,000 to provide for 'the sick or disabled, or the education and improvement of the young, who may be in a condition to need the aid of such a fund'.

William was quoted as saying: 'I take great pride in the Astor House of New York, but a greater pride in the Astor Haus at Walldorf. The massive granite blocks and pillars of the former may crumble and fall to the ground or its columns and corridors become choked with weeds, but the latter will continue in existence while the town of Walldorf exists and there are any poor people in it.'

In the end, though, it was with the luxury of hotels rather than the comfort of the poor that the name of Astor was to be most closely associated.

III

The extent of William Astor's real estate holdings earned him the title of 'the Landlord of New York', but few of his lessees or tenants would have recognized him if they had encountered him in the street. He did not figure prominently in the press, though some of the less savoury properties that stood on his land were beginning to attract public attention, and in spite of the power conferred by his wealth he took no active part in politics, seeing the purpose of that doubtful art as solely to maintain the status quo. With few interests, little in the way of emotion, a very small number of friends, and neither taste nor talent for the kind of aggressive commercialism in which his father had indulged, it is hard to guess what William clung to as the foundation of his life, unless it really was the cramped little office on Prince Street with its ledgers, leases, tenant lists and street plans.

Did he ever think back with regret to the blighted promise of his student days, ever curse the fate that had conspired to rob him of virtually everything that might have been his own and had transformed him into a mere cipher of his father's invention? At this distance it is impossible to tell, for William rarely vented his feelings. A certain amount of nostalgia is discernible for the lost pleasures of his youth, particularly his time in Europe, but there is no evidence of any resentment at being forced to play the monkey to his father's organ-grinder – none, that is, except for William's almost incredible lack of *activity*, which may indicate that his heart was not really in it. John Jacob had made sure that William would be required to do nothing, and that is precisely what he did. As a journalist once noted, it was 'as if Napoleon in the fullness of power had used his whole strength to make himself a safe and decorous sovereign in some small corner of his possessions – had made a warm cloak of his purple robe and a handsome crutch of his sceptre'.

John Jacob, looking down on the scene from his private and no doubt well-appointed paradise, must have been pleased with what he had wrought. His greatest fear had been that the fortune he had worked so diligently to accumulate should be dissipated by heirs who lacked his own perspicacity, but from that point of view he could have wished for none better than William, who seldom exercised his judgment or if he did it was strictly in accordance with the principles his father had laid down. Indeed, the only major land purchase William made was in 1826, when John Jacob was still very much in evidence. That was the old Thompson farm, which William acquired for $25,000 and which was to sit nicely between Fifth Avenue and Madison at 32nd Street, facing what became part of 'millionaires' row' and ultimately the Empire State Building. Otherwise it was a matter of assessing which way the city would expand – a fairly easy task considering that skeleton street plans, neatly divided into lots twenty-five feet by one hundred, had already been prepared by the authorities to cover ground as far north as Harlem – and of following John Jacob's rules for the purchase and management of land, of granting leases and mortgages, collecting rents, letting others develop and improve what they could never own. Much more than his father, William was a money-making *machine*, because his operations were directed by another hand. 'He sat in his office as though it were a house of detention to which his father had condemned him for life.'

Overall Astor owned about three of every hundred acres comprising the city of New York, which placed him well ahead of the Rhinelanders, Goelets, Roosevelts and Stuyvesants, the other chief landlords. Most of his holdings were in prime locations, yielding an annual return of anything between seven and fifteen or twenty per cent. Simply by holding on to what he had, he could earn upwards of a million dollars a year. Ironically, it was the poorest districts of the city that made him richest. Between 1840 and 1860 half a million people – the overwhelming majority immigrants from Ireland and central Europe – swarmed into New York and the demand for accommodation sent realty values soaring in lower Manhattan. Tenements sprouted like weeds, poisonous at their roots but offering golden fruits to those who owned the land on which they grew.

The *New York Times* said: 'Of course many – perhaps the majority of those who own these houses – know nothing of how they are used. Their agents let and underlet and hand the proceeds to the landlords. Still with a humane man even ignorance is no excuse. He *should* know.' Given William's attention to detail and knowledge of his properties, it is difficult to believe that he did not know how the buildings he owned below Fourteenth Street were being used. No doubt he had never actually seen them, but he could read about them in the newspapers and in official reports such as the one published by the state legislature in the 1850s: 'Of all the avenues through which avaricious selfishness reaches and takes from the poor, there is not one in which its operations are so profoundly manifested in populous cities as landlordism.'

Of course Astor was not a builder: what rose up on the land he owned was left to tenants and sub-landlords. But under the leasing system introduced by John Jacob, those buildings were technically controlled by the Astor Estate and indeed would eventually fall into its ownership as the leases expired. If he leased a standard-sized plot on, say, Third Street, William must have known to what use it would be put, indeed encouraged that use because of the high return it would surely bring. A simple clause in the lease, perhaps limiting the height of the building or restricting the numbers of occupants, would have prevented the construction of a tenement on a site. But this was the age of laisser-faire and in any case the multitude had to be housed somewhere – if it had not been in the rat-holes of the Lower East Side it would have been the shanty towns disfiguring what were then the upper reaches of Fifth Avenue; but the shanties ceased to be an option as the mansions of the rich and the villas of the growing middle class moved farther and farther away from the noisome, diseased and crime-ridden heart of the 'old' city.

The state legislature's report on the slums concluded that 'the avarice of capitalists renders governmental interference for the protection of the poor and unfortunate an absolute necessity'. Street orators, inspired by the Paris Commune of 1848, railed against the landlords of New York; the newspapers condemned the greed and exploitation that forced people to live in 'the vilest and most abominable sites ever inhabited by swine'; even a man so far removed from the seamier aspects of life as Philip Hone was forced to concede that America, the land to which so many of Europe's poor and oppressed looked for their salvation, often proved 'for the deluded emigrant a land of broken promise and blasted hope'. And yet for almost thirty years after the first expressions of alarm about the conditions of life for the labouring classes of New York, nothing was done.

A shiver of fear ran through the more comfortable quarters of the city in 1849 when a mob went on the rampage just a few yards from the Astors' enclave in Lafayette Place. The official explanation for the Astor Place riot was that it arose from the bitter and much-publicized rivalry between two famous actors, the English tragedian William Macready and America's first home-grown stage star, Edwin Forrest, but the roots of the violence lay much deeper than that. Social historians have seen the fighting outside the Opera House, where Macready was appearing, as a symbol of the simmering resentment felt by the poor towards those whom they saw as their oppressors, the purveyors of their misery. The very sight of musket-carrying militiamen should have been enough to calm the passions of people arguing over a theatrical performance, but in the event the riot grew worse after the state troops were called out and the militiamen opened fire, killing thirty-two people and wounding thirty-six more. This was no mere clash between partisan fan clubs – how many people would be prepared to die out of admiration for an actor? – but an explosion of wrath and outrage that the land forged on the principle 'that all men are created equal and independent' had been allowed to fall into the grasp of an elite richer and more powerful than its former colonial rulers. The old European hierarchy of the classes might have been swept away by the Revolution, but the gulf between rich and poor had if anything become wider than ever in the officially endorsed free-for-all that followed.

The riot in Astor Place ('Massacre Place', it was dubbed by the slumland agitators) was one of several that shocked the solid citizens of New York, but although the voices of social reformers began to be heard there was naturally no enthusiasm for change among those who could see only that they might stand to lose by it. Liberty was all very well so long as it meant the freedom to create wealth by any method that offered itself and at whatever cost to others. Fortunately for the Astors and their kind, the political masters of New York subscribed to the view that wealth was not something to be shared and devoted their efforts, when they were not busy making themselves rich, to the support not of the people who elected them but to those who contributed most to their campaign chests.

William Astor was hardly the most generous of men, but along with his peers he gave financial support to the confidence tricksters, gangsters and placemen at City Hall because he believed that their overweening self-interest complemented his own. In 1855 he went so far as to offer public endorsement to Mayor Fernando Wood, a handsome, charming, unscrupulous wheeler-dealer who was being challenged by his Republican opponents because of alleged corruption in the city police force. A rousing orator and brilliant publicist, Wood organized a mass meeting to be addressed on his behalf by many of New York's leading businessmen: although William Astor did not actually appear on the platform, his name topped the list of sponsors for the gathering. The following year, an election one, Wood was opposed even by a faction within his own Democratic Party and feared he might lose the nomination, so he composed for public consumption a glowing testimonial that portrayed him as a man of honour and probity, dazzling administrative ability and unparalleled public service. Every merchant, banker, landlord and other businessman who depended upon the goodwill of city officials was asked to sign the document, and prominent among those who did was William Astor.

Why did Astor do it? Well, he certainly gained real estate, receiving at knockdown prices waterfront properties previously owned by the city and with the bonus of having landfill carried out at the taxpayers' expense. On the other hand, Wood required in return for continuing goodwill not only support and electoral finance but also contributions to his personal fortune – over the years Astor forked out thousands of dollars' worth of property settlements for the mayor's benefit. Nor did it stop there; many a Tammany Hall politician lined his pocket with tribute exacted on city assessments, which greatly affected Astor as the leading landowner. As the historian James Parton put it: 'Year after year he saw a gang of thieves in the City Hall stealing his revenues under the name of taxes and assessments but he never led an assault upon them nor gave the aid he ought to those who did. Unless he is grossly belied, he preferred to compromise, not fight, and did not always disdain to court the ruffians who plundered him.' It was clearly a case of better the devil he knew. Who could tell what might happen to the rich pickings of the tenements if the radicals and social reformers were to win control of the city? At least Mayor Wood and his cronies could be counted upon to nip in the bud such suggestions as laws to control the proportion of the standard city lot that could be taken up by a building. Or even if they did sometimes, for political reasons, give way to some of the do-gooders' demands, they could make sure that such statutes were never actually enforced.

This mutual aid society worked so efficiently that the landlords were even able to withstand the after-effects of the so-called 'draft riots' of 1863, when on the provocation of compulsory registration for the Union Army to fight the Civil War the slums revolted and embarked upon an orgy of murder, arson and looting which was ended only after five days by the intervention of regular troops. (The touchstone for the violence was the announcement that a man could avoid the draft by payment of three hundred dollars, which was seen as a concession to the rich at the expense of the poor.) William Astor had the effrontery to propose that his son, John Jacob III, and son-in-law Franklin Delano serve on a 'citizens' association' intending to investigate living conditions in the tenements. An impression of grave official concern was spread abroad through stories in the newspapers of the way the other half lived, and sincere medical men were invited to submit detailed reports on the iniquities of tenement-building, but no new regulations were passed or even promulgated as a result of all this activity.

It was not until 1867, after yet another official report, that the first legislation governing the construction of tenements was reluctantly enacted, and that made very little difference. The law required that a building should cover not more than sixty per cent of a standard lot, but the Astors and their friends fought a strong rearguard action against it, claiming that since almost half of each site would be useless, tenants would have to pay higher rents. Not only that, but with the flood of immigrants continuing every foot of building land was needed, and it was simply perverse to insist that forty feet in every hundred should be thrown away. The legislature was persuaded by the force of these arguments but unwilling to take the political risk involved in repealing the act; so a compromise was reached – the sixty per cent rule would remain but the board of health would be given power to vary the ordinance on application by the builder or landlord. From that date new tenements covered a mere ninety to ninety-five per cent of their lots.

The pressure for social justice, then, did not greatly affect William Astor. What did worry him, towards the end of the 1850s, was the decline of Whig politics and the rise of the Republican Party on the tide of the anti-slavery movement. The Whig faction virtually disappeared from the scene when President Millard Fillmore failed to secure the party's nomination for the 1852 election. Astor supported him again in 1856 when he ran on what was called the Native American (otherwise dubbed 'Know Nothing') ticket, but Fillmore received only eight electoral votes and the Democrat James Buchanan went to the White House. Buchanan was opposed to slavery on

163

moral grounds but felt obliged to support the ruling of the Supreme Court that states could not be prevented from permitting the institution of slave-owning. The stand split the Democratic Party and allowed the Republican outsider Abraham Lincoln to win the presidential election of 1860.

William Astor and many other men of wealth and property in New York were convinced that Lincoln's election would mean war: they campaigned feverishly before polling day, Astor himself being involved in publicizing last-minute attempts to compromise with the slave states of the South and helping to organize a conference that called for the maintenance of the Union at any price. This was hardly surprising. Wall Street held some two hundred million dollars in debt from the Southern states and viewed with alarm the prospect of that money disappearing through secession and war, a consideration that easily overcame whatever point of view individuals might hold about slavery. So desperate were the businessmen that on Lincoln's inauguration in January 1861 many of them supported Mayor Fernando Wood's plan for Manhattan, Long Island and Staten Island to secede from the Union themselves and become a free city under the name of Tri-Insula, a scheme which was even approved by the city council.

But the nation as a whole was in a mood for war, almost as if it felt the need to be cleansed by blood, and the attack on Fort Sumter, South Carolina, by the Confederate states in April 1861 swept aside all Wall Street's fears. The Tri-Insula proposal was quietly dropped and, as is so often the case at the beginning of a war, commerce entered a boom period underpinned by fat government contracts and war loans. Even the property market entered an upward curve as the government printed money and inflation forced up rents. Big business suddenly became Republican.

But war inevitably breeds change, and the 'draft riots' of 1863 were but one manifestation of the pressures building up on the society which had grown out of revolution and now saw – or at least those who controlled it did – the prospect of another revolution, unwanted this time, looming in its shadows. 'We have,' said the *New York Times* after the Civil War, 'a seething, ignorant, passionate, half-criminal class which possesses no property and can get none ... let this mighty throng hear that there was a chance to grasp the luxuries of wealth, or to divide the property of the rich, or to escape labor and suffering for a time and live on the superfluities of others, and we should see a sudden storm of communistic revolution in New York such as would astonish all who do not know these classes.' The mob had to be kept down, and men such as Astor found themselves supporting politicians whose talents for demagoguery were able to soothe the slum-dwelling masses whilst their self-interest and greed led them to play along with the attempts of the rich to maintain their position.

William himself struck a blow for his class by challenging the income tax which had been levied to pay for the prosecution of the war by the Union side. As the richest man in the country, earning perhaps $1.3 million a year, he took his case to the Supreme Court and won the judgment that the tax was unconstitutional: it was to be nearly half a century before the rich could legally be forced to give financial support to the country that had for so long supported them, and in the meantime the gap between the upper and lower classes in the land of natural equality was to become even wider and more glaringly obvious in a display of ostentation and 'conspicuous consumption' for which a new generation of Astors would set the pace.

There was, however, nothing ostentatious about William Astor's way of life. He did not smoke, drank little and took no pleasure in entertaining or indeed in being entertained. His chief pleasure seemed to lie in the Astor Estate office, doing what in large part was a clerk's work – because 'if we do it ourselves we know that it is properly done'. He was, in the words of one biographer, a 'mole capitalist, burrowing his way undramatically through land to more wealth without benefit of newspaper headlines, showy splendor or outward political pomp. He never went to Wall Street ... his name was connected with no great or novel enterprise... Although he was the city's leading landlord, no building he erected was noteworthy.'

He did not even, as his father had done, make use of his later years, when his son could take over the running of the business, to travel and enjoy himself. His only trip abroad was to Europe in 1857, when he was sixty-five, but he was not stimulated by the scenes of his youth observed anew, though his old friend Bunsen reported that, 'Astor's faithful attachment to me and the impression we received of his excellence give us true pleasure.'

By 1870 William was the last Astor of his generation. His sister Dolly had died almost twenty years before and in 1869 poor John Jacob II finally cast off his particularly unfortunate mortal coil, most of his estate passing to the Langdon children, who had considered themselves rather hard done by in the division of the spoils after the death of the first John Jacob. William was now semi-retired, still going daily to the office but spending only a few hours there while his eldest son ran the business. He withdrew even farther in 1872 when Margaret died: unable to carry on living in Lafayette Place without his wife, he moved uptown to Fifth Avenue, which was becoming the new ghetto of the wealthy. In any case, Lafayette was not the leafy backwater it had once been – Colonnade Row had been converted into a hotel, the Astor Library had expanded and there was a good deal of both carriage and pedestrian traffic through the Place. Most of the Astors had already moved out. William Backhouse Jr had led the migration to Fifth Avenue, closely followed by his brother, their twin mansions being the talk of the town; Laura, Alida and Maddie, with their respective husbands, had settled on Madison Avenue; only Langdons and Wilkses remained in the old neighbourhood, and they were quite definitely poor relations, though 'poor' was a relative term for anyone in the Astor constellation.

Within a year or two of his wife's death, William's mind began to wander somewhat and his temper grew shorter, but at least he would not suffer the physical collapse which had darkened the last years of his father. Then end, when it came, was mercifully quick. He caught a chill in the late autumn of 1875 and took to his bed, but within a couple of days he knew he was dying. 'I might have lived another year,' he said, 'if I had not caught this cold, but I am satisfied to go now. I am eighty-four years old [he was actually eighty-three], long past the allotted time of man, and at my age life becomes a burden.' He died early in the morning of 24 November as unobtrusively as he had lived. The obituary notices in the press were at once less critical and less laudatory than those for his father – there was little to criticize and even less to praise. In London, the *Spectator* wondered 'why one feels a slight contempt for a career like this – a contempt deepened rather than lessened by the charm which very great wealth, like very great power, has for the imagination... A man is not bound to be lofty, if loftiness is not in him, but there is in the career of Mr Astor, excellent person that he is always reputed to have been, a want of greatness which power like his would in some natures have called forth.'

In New York, *Appleton's Journal* was more specific: 'Mr Astor, it is said, counted his buildings by the thousands. The stranger wandering through the city would naturally expect to find at least a few architectural piles erected by the taste and munificence of the wealthiest man in the country. With the exception of the Astor Library, there are none. No schools, no academies, no churches, no public pleasure grounds bear his name. The wealth of this great millionaire is not even evidenced in useful or economical things. The best form of house for the laboring man is one of the problems of the day. Mr Astor, with all his great resources, made no effort to solve it. No model tenements went up under his inspiration; no pretty or tasteful rows of cottages were devised by his hand; no contribution whatever toward the solution of questions in the economy of the home ever came from him. He made no experiments, acquired no experience, contributed no results, set no needed example even in the domain of house building, into which his accumulated wealth ever steadily went.'

E.L. Godkin, the Irish-born editor and publisher of the *Nation*, deplored Astor's refusal to use the power he wielded as a lever for social and political reform. 'The property which the late Mr Astor possessed,' he wrote, 'would have enabled him, had he felt inclined, to make the attempt to exercise a very large share of the political power of the city in which he lived but his political life and ambition were confined to a quiet resolution that whatever party or ring might be in power it should not harm his capital or income. Within these limits submission to the ruling powers, no matter of what stripe, was his simple plan and was adhered to as steadily as if he had been living under a despotism instead of in a free country.' Quite simply, said Godkin, ever the moralist, Astor had ignored what was his duty as the leading citizen of New York.

Others felt that William had been derelict in his public duty, too, when he had drawn up his will. His estate, at between forty and fifty million dollars, was worth twice that of his father, yet William's charitable offerings added up to no more than John Jacob's, some five hundred thousand dollars. That amount was broken down as follows:

$450,000 for the Astor Library
$10,00 for the American Bible Society
$5,000 for the Society for the Relief of Respectable Aged
Indigent Females
$5,000 for the Institute for the Blind
$5,000 for the Lying-In Asylum
$5,000 for the Ladies' Depository
$10,000 for the Exempt Firemen's Benevolent Fund
$2,500 to each of four employees of the Astor Estate.

During his lifetime, William had, it is true, donated $50,000 for the building of St Luke's Hospital, but his general attitude towards philanthropy was summed up in an anecdote published at the time of his death. A clergyman who had been at school with him visited him one day at the Astor Estate Office to be received with a cold stare and the equally cold question: 'Can I do anything for you?' After looking at William across the big desk for a moment the minister replied, 'No, sir,' and left. Indeed, there is even a hint of irony in the fact that when asked to contribute to the Association for the Improvement of the Poor the man who made much of his living from the wretched inhabitants of the New York slums pledged a mere hundred dollars a year.

Receiving the details of the will 'with regret if not with surprise', the New York *Post* sniffed: 'The testator was the representative of an old New York family; the vast estate which he controlled was situated within the city; its growth had been dependent upon the growth of the city. It may have been expected, therefore, that local public institutions would have been remembered liberally in the disposition.' It would have been less insulting to the city, the *Post* suggested, if instead of leaving half a million to charity Astor had left nothing at all.

But, as the *Sun* pointed out, 'selfish motives are powerful, unselfish ones weak'. And the *Independent* magazine gave a riposte to anyone who might be inclined to justify Astor's position: 'Compared with ordinary men, his benefactions were large,' it admitted, 'but when his vast opportunities are remembered, his returns to the public from whom his wealth was derived seem very small.' That was the rub – while all businessmen must make their profits at the expense of somebody, the Astors were perceived as dipping their hands directly into the pockets of those who could least afford to support them in their lives of luxury. The landlord has to work twice as hard as anyone else to earn public esteem, but then William never did care very much about what other people thought of him.

Of course, as far as his family was concerned there was no cause for complaint in his will. Yet, though he adhered strictly to the rules of primogeniture and carried out what were clearly his father's wishes, he felt obliged to justify the inevitable discrepancy between the $1,100,000 he left to each of his daughters, Laura and Alida, and the vast residue which was divided equally between John Jacob III and William Jr (though the former had a larger share of the whole estate because of bequests the first John Jacob had made).

'I declare', William wrote, 'that the inequalities between the property appropriated to them and that to my sons John and William are not owing to any difference in my affections, respect, esteem and regard for them but inasmuch as they all receive very ample fortunes, I have intended to relieve them from the care and exposures which a larger fortune would carry with it.' In other words, that was all mere women could handle. Originally the explanation had been intended to apply also to the wayward Henry, but it was superseded in his case by the ninth codicil, written after Henry's marriage in 1871, which reduced his patrimony to thirty thousand dollars.

William, the dutiful son, followed faithfully the founder's safeguards against wasteful heirs. The half of the estate he had received absolutely was passed on in trust to John and William, while the portion John Jacob I had left in trust was given absolutely to the brothers. 'Has any man,' the *Independent* asked, 'the right to leave his eldest son twenty or thirty millions

169

of dollars? The man who has twenty millions cannot eat more oysters, or drink any more wine, or wear any more clothes than the man who has one million.'

In their own peculiar ways both John Jacob III, the new titular head of the family, and William Jr knew just what to do with and how to safeguard the fortunes handed down to them. Nevertheless, the Astor inheritance was soon to be dissipated. The founder had been, in a sense, lucky in having only one son to consider, because of the mental incapacity of John Jacob II. William, however, had two sons, so the inheritance was split irretrievably – a matter of little consequence at the time, but one which would become important in the next generation, when the two main branches of the family would see themselves as being in competition.

5 *The Ruling Class*

I

The accession of John Jacob III opened a new and ultimately destructive phase in the history of the Astor dynasty in the United States. (Greater glory was to be won in Britain, but of that more later.) He was the first head of the family to have been born and raised against a background of luxury and leisure. William, of course, had been able to remember the days when home had been more or less a fur warehouse – though there is probably no truth in the legend that his father had set him to work beating pelts – but when John Jacob was born in 1822 the scent of animal skins came no nearer than the New York docks, and by the time he was in his teens the beaver, otter and muskrat were things of the past. Indeed, this Astor was not even required to be acquainted with the rudiments of commerce, since the nature of his inheritance and the provisions of the wills that controlled it ensured that the family fortune increased without any effort on the part of its beneficiaries. The head of the family must therefore be less of a businessman and more of a gentleman, and that fact was to play a prominent part in the decline of the American Astors over the next three generations.

John Jacob III has often been described as the first Astor aristocrat, a product of inherited wealth and blue (Livingston) blood who accepted his privilege as a right. Certainly his appearance seemed to indicate that here was no ordinary man. Six feet tall, with keen grey eyes and a florid complexion framed by Dundreary whiskers and distinguished by the classic Victorian moustache, he might, as one American writer noted, 'have stepped out of an English Tory Cabinet'. Yet looking at portraits of him in later life one sees no trace of nobility: hauteur, dignity, imperiousness, perhaps, but an unmistakable impression of the crude self-importance and vulgar confidence of Trollope's less admirable capitalists or Dreiser's millionaires. Had he been in an English Tory Cabinet, he would doubtless have come from a rotten borough.

His father apparently saw in John Jacob III a proxy for his own blighted dreams of a quiet, cultured life. Unfortunately the boy lacked William's academic abilities and inclinations and 'failed of distinction' at Columbia. Nevertheless his father determined that Johann, as he was called at home, should attend his old university, Göttingen. Accompanied by Joseph Cogswell, who was spending sixty thousand of old John Jacob's dollars on books for the yet to be endowed library, Johann spent two years in Europe, acquiring an unhealthy (in American terms) respect for the traditional class system of the Old World and just enough education to enable him to survive a year at Harvard Law School. After Harvard he spent a further year working in a law office – specializing in property, no doubt – and then, upon reaching his majority, he was overtaken by the fate decreed for the firstborn, the Astor Estate Office.

Since, unlike his father, John Jacob III apparently had no youthful ambitions of any kind, the dull routine of property management was not as stultifying and frustrating as it might have been. Though he accompanied his father to the office every day and shared William's passion for economy, he was much less absorbed in the business side of his life. 'Work hard, but never after dinner,' he was fond of saying. One wonders whether he really had any idea of what hard work was. His attendance at Prince Street was more of a comfortable habit than a business obligation – after all, it gave him something to do, provided his life with a framework it would otherwise have lacked.

It was his wife who really taught him to behave in an aristocratic manner. Charlotte Augusta Gibbes, whom John had known since childhood because her family were Astor neighbours on Lafayette Place, had all the refinement of her South Carolina forebears (they claimed kinship with the English King John!) and that sense of *noblesse oblige* which so marked the Southern gentry. She was warm-hearted, charming, generous and possessed of what was for her times an unusually well-developed social conscience. Augusta appreciated, too, the social obligations that went with the position of the richest family in America and under her guidance John learnt to overcome the ingrained Astor 'separateness' and to be a gracious host, an art collector and, where it did not interfere with business, something of a public benefactor. 'I think they are fairly well matched,' commented Julia Ward Howe when the engagement of John and Augusta was announced. 'One can only say that each is good enough for the other.' What that meant was that Astor had the money while Augusta had the class: her family fortune was not what it had once been, but her father had been one of the founders of the exclusive Union Club in New York.

The wedding took place in 1847 and of course Philip Hone was there to record the event. 'The better sort have been regaled of late by a grand wedding. Mr John Jacob Astor ... has married Miss Augusta Gibbes... The wedding was attended at the house of her father by all the fashionable people of the city. Last evening my daughter and son went to a grand party at Mr Astor's, and I also was tempted to mix once more in the splendid crowd of charming women, pretty girls and well-dressed beaux. The spacious mansion in Lafayette Place was open from cellar to garrett, blazing with a thousand lights. The crowd was excessive; the ladies (such part of their exquisite forms as could be distinguished in the melee) elegant and tastefully attired with a display of rich jewelry enough to pay one day's expense of the Mexican war.'

Augusta appeared at first as a model Astor wife, dressing plainly, displaying commendable thrift in household matters and within a year producing the required heir, named William Waldorf in memory of the homeland (though the misspelling has never been explained). He was to be her only child, though the reason for that was probably gynaecological rather than economic. As the years went by, however, she applied quiet pressure on her husband to raise the tone of their life in keeping with her Southern notions of gentility. In this she was aided by Caroline Schermerhorn Astor, wife of John's brother, William Backhouse Jr, whose one aim in life was to lead New York society. When Caroline decided that Lafayette Place was becoming too congested and altogether common and bullied her husband into begging from his father a portion of the old Thompson Farm site on Fifth Avenue, Augusta enthusiastically claimed the same favour for John. Thus the year 1859 saw the completion of two identical brownstones of four storeys on either side of a large garden and surrounded by high brick walls. The more northerly mansion, on the corner of 34th Street, occupied by Mr and Mrs William Astor (though practically speaking less often by Mr), became the social hub of the city, while in its twin, Augusta – smiling wryly at the vulgar ambitions of Caroline – entertained a more refined and, she hoped, rather more cultured section of the elite.

There was barely time to settle into this glamorous new existence, however, before the nation careered headlong into civil war and John was called to what he later remembered as the most exciting and enjoyable period of his life. While old William pleaded for calm, saw nightmare visions of his fortune crumbling to ashes and considered Fernando Wood's scheme for the secession of New York, John wholeheartedly supported Abraham Lincoln and prepared himself to defend the Union with every means at his disposal. What was immediately to hand, of course, was money, and Astor is credited with having been the first New Yorker to dig into his pocketbook on behalf of the Union. When the Confederacy attacked Fort Sumter, John donated $3,000 for the arming of the appropriately named tugboat *Yankee* which sailed to relieve the island garrison.

Astor's second attempt to pay for Union munitions, in May 1861, was peremptorily rebuffed by Lincoln's inefficient and soon to be removed Secretary for War, Simon Cameron, but John's patriotic ardour was undimmed and in the winter of that year he volunteered for military service. As befitted his social status, he was given the rank of full colonel and dispatched to Washington as an aide-de-camp to Major General George McClellan, the 'Young Napoleon' who led the Army of the Potomac and who, in November 1861, was appointed commanding general of all the Northern forces. Though Astor continued to appreciate his home comforts – renting a house in the capital complete with butler, valet and chef – he found military life exhilarating, particularly when after a long period of training the Army of the Potomac moved south with the intention of laying siege to Richmond, Virginia, the Confederate capital, with the colonel in charge of river transport.

Back in New York, Augusta Astor, in spite of her Southern

ancestry, rallied enthusiastically to the Yankee cause. In fact she so far forgot South Carolina as to participate with other grand ladies in the raising of a negro regiment, the 20th, to which she presented colours with a rousing speech: 'When you look at this flag and rush to battle, or stand at guard beneath its sublime motto, "God and Liberty", remember that it is also an emblem of love and honor from the daughters of this great metropolis to her brave champions in the field, and that they will anxiously watch your career, glory in your heroism, and minister to you when wounded and ill, and honor your martyrdom with benediction and tears.'

Colonel John Jacob, meanwhile, was 'intent on learning his duties and carrying them out', as an army friend put it. 'You would have imagined him a young subaltern dependent for his future on his prospects in the service.' His duties were mainly clerical, it seems, and he was denied the experience of battle even when McClellan besieged Yorktown, since the Confederates decided to abandon the city without a stand-up fight. Reporting on this almost bloodless victory, Astor was warm in his regard for McClellan's skill and shrewdness, but he was backing a lost cause. Republican 'hawks' in Washington already suspected that the Democrat 'Little Mac' was deliberately pulling his punches and after Robert E. Lee forced the numerically superior Army of the Potomac to retreat before Richmond in the so-called 'Seven Days' battles, McClellan was replaced as commanding general. (McClellan was reinstated after General Pope's humiliation at the Second Battle of Bull Run in the summer of 1862, but after his own failure to defeat Lee with vastly superior numbers at the bloody encounter of Antietam he was relieved of all his commands.)

Astor immediately resigned his commission: the charitable view is that he realized McClellan, in his diminished role, had less need of aides-de-camp, but it might be that having come under enemy fire during the retreat from Richmond the colonel felt that his duty had been done, particularly since his anxious father had actually forbidden younger brother William to volunteer for active service. It is perhaps significant that when, as a result of his financial contributions to the war effort, he received the brevet rank of brigadier general he paid little attention to the honour, preferring to remember his eight

175

months as a colonel when he attended regimental reunions.

The war over, business boomed in New York, but John Jacob III was not the man his grandfather had been and could not measure up to the challenge of aggressive entrepreneurs like the former ferryman Cornelius Vanderbilt, who was rapidly becoming the city's and indeed the nation's transport tycoon. Finding landlordism a bit of a bore, John had dabbled in railroad companies and had, with partners, amalgamated several prospective lines into the New York Central, which linked Albany and Buffalo and made a handsome profit. But Vanderbilt, owner of the New York & Harlem Railroad, had plans for a monopoly and needed the Albany connexion. Astor and his friends had failed to realize the potential of a service running from New York to Buffalo via Albany and had allowed the line from the city to the state capital to remain in the hands of the Hudson River Railway, contenting themselves with merely accepting transfer passengers at Albany. They became alive to the danger their railroad was in only when Vanderbilt bought control of the Hudson company, and by then it was too late. The wily ferryman forbade Hudson's men to connect trains or cars to New York Central rolling stock and engines, and refused to accept freight to or from the rival line. Since the Hudson terminus and the Central station at Albany were half a mile apart, Buffalo passengers found themselves having to lug their baggage that distance to change trains, and the profits of the New York Central began to suffer, as did its stock on Wall Street.

John and his partners had no reply to the kind of business methods old John Jacob Astor had pioneered, and in the end they virtually begged Vanderbilt to take over their company: 'The undersigned ... are satisfied that a change of administration of the company and a thorough reformation in the management of its affairs would result in larger dividends to the stockholders and greatly promote the interests of the public. They, therefore, request that you will receive their proxies for the coming election and select such a board of directors as shall seem to you to be entitled to their confidence. They hope that such an organization will be effected as shall secure to the company the aid of your great and acknowledged abilities.' And then, adding insult to injury, Vanderbilt merged his New York–Buffalo railroad with the Lake Shore & Michigan Central line to provide an unchallenged service all the way to Chicago. No doubt it was the humiliation of the New York Central that caused John's sister-in-law, Caroline Astor, to exclude the Vanderbilts from her inner circle for so long. But not even *the* Mrs Astor could stop the march of the new capitalists whose fortunes would soon eclipse that of what had once been the richest family in America: the business ability which had placed the Astors on top was no longer present.

At the time, though, the loss of the New York Central meant little to John Jacob III other than mild embarrassment. The Civil War and its aftermath had increased the demand for housing in New York, particularly in the poorer sections, enabling Astor and the landlords' cartel to raise rents in the tenements by ten per cent. By 1880 the Astor Estate was earning five million dollars a year and the family was worth eighty million dollars, double the amount William had left in his will. Half of this belonged to the eldest son.

In spite of all this wealth, effortlessly earned, the waste of even a penny in his business dealings remained anathema to John (the richest man in America was known to edit telegrams personally so that they should cost not a dime more than was absolutely necessary). Yet he accepted without question the expenses involved in maintaining social eminence, bearing in mind Caroline's excesses in the mansion next door. The nabobs were now migrating to Newport, Rhode Island, during the summer months – 'America's First Vacationland' the Newport County Chamber of Trade calls it in publicity material these days – and Augusta felt it was incumbent upon the Astors to be in the vanguard of the trend, so they were among the first to buy a summer cottage in the new resort, the 'cottage' being in fact a mock French chateau named Beaulieu. Of course, Caroline had to go one better, and her sixty-two-room cottage, Beechwood, became the wonder of its age, as we shall see.

Each summer Beaulieu was the scene of a grand ball, which would have disgusted John's forebears as a meaningless extravagance, but that was by no means the limit of Augusta's un-Astorish frivolity, in which her husband seemed cheerfully to indulge her. She had a passion for fine lace and persuaded John to buy hundreds of yards of it, much of which she was never able actually to wear – her collection can now be seen in the

Metropolitan Museum of Art in New York. She also loved jewelry and it was not unusual for her to appear at a great social occasion glittering like a chandelier in three hundred thousand dollars' worth of diamonds – tiara, necklaces, earrings, bracelets and rings.

More significant was the fact that Augusta was the first Astor to donate large sums of money – her husband's, of course, in this case – to charitable causes. Orphans, prostitutes, the chronically sick and even, by a curious quirk of fate, Indians who had once sold their souls for a bottle of adulterated Astor liquor, were recipients of Augusta's beneficence. The favourite charity was the debutant Children's Aid Society, founded by Charles Loring Brace, which in the 1880s picked up waifs and strays living literally in the streets of New York and packed them off to the Golden West, where life was healthier if not always better (some unfortunates became little more than slaves to the farmers who took them in). 'It is so little I can do for them,' Augusta said, but each Christmas she would spend $2,000 on sending a hundred orphans out West by train, having first equipped them with shoes, warm clothing and Bibles. The records of other organizations dedicated to helping the poor show regular donations of anything from one hundred to five hundred dollars from Mr and Mrs Astor, and John endowed a six-cents-a-night lodging house for street urchins – known with some irony as the Astor House – as well as building the West Side Hostel for boys and supporting a school for the children of German immigrants who wished to learn a trade.

The Astors' largest single donation, however, was almost a quarter of a million dollars for the initial building of the Memorial Hospital for the Treatment of Cancer. Augusta's own fragile state of health gave her an understandable if perhaps somewhat morbid interest in hospitals and the sick, and as well as being a supervisor of the Memorial she helped to found she was on the board of the Women's Hospital, to which she sent the flowers that adorned her grand entertainments and the fruit and other food left over from them.

Such concern for what Augusta called 'the large and needy class' was praiseworthy, no doubt, but of course with exemplary nineteenth-century hypocrisy it completely ignored the true nature of the city's social problems. If John Jacob III had been a real philanthropist, he could have improved the plight of the poor at a stroke by responding positively to what became a widespread campaign to alleviate the appalling conditions in the tenements. Instead he, or rather his lawyers, resisted and often blocked in the courts every official attempt to relieve the suffering of the slum-dwellers. The view taken in John's new Astor Estate Office on West 26th Street (more elegant and imposing than the two-room, nondescript building the first John Jacob had erected) was that vote-catching politicians and unscrupulous contractors were out to victimize the innocent landlord by raising his tax assessments and forcing him to carry out uneconomic improvements to his properties. Was America a free country, or was it not? In case after case, the Astor Estate challenged the right of government to tinker with the basic machinery of capitalism, and most times the judgments favoured the businessman.

For twenty years the Astors stood in the way of tenement reform and they also opposed municipal plans for rapid development of the still-green acres in the northern part of Manhattan. The more congested the lower portion of the island, the greater the demand for tenements and the better the returns from them. Only when the city reached, and indeed passed, bursting point within its established limits would Astor release his northern lands, for then they would be more valuable because more needed. The concept of an extensive and efficient public transport system – subway or elevated railroad – was also a threat to the Astors: what would happen to property values downtown if people could actually choose to live elsewhere in the knowledge that a train could carry them rapidly to their workplaces? It did not help that most of the elevated railway schemes discussed in the 1870s were based on tracks running along Broadway, the heartland of the Astor empire. (In this case, though, it is not difficult to sympathize with the landlords; the New York 'El' is not a pretty sight.)

At first the Astors opposed rapid transit schemes on grounds of the disturbance the digging would cause, arguing that property might be irreparably damaged. Then they turned to the constitutional argument, claiming that provision of public transport was not one of 'the legitimate purposes of govern-ment': it was for the businessman to provide services if he chose to do so. It was on constitutional grounds that the Astors were able to delay subway construction in New York until the very end of the nineteenth century.

Legal action, however, was not always necessary to prevent the encroachments of politicians – they could usually be bought, particularly when it came to the matter of fixing tax assessments. Whereas national politics in America was and is an occupation for rich men, local administration has often been seen by the unscrupulous as a means of getting rich, and nowhere was this more obvious a hundred years ago than in New York. Men like Astor were only too happy to help city and state legislators to make their fortunes if it meant that they themselves could keep the fortunes they had already made or, as in the case of Astor himself, inherited. It was all too tempting and too easy. Having been swept into power on a tide of rhetoric aimed at the voting masses, the enterprising (i.e. crooked) politician could feather his nest most comfortably with the blessing and partly at the expense of the business community so long as he kept up the flow of oratory and kept down the taxes of the wealthy. No one knew this better than the New York 'boss' of the 1860s, William Marcy Tweed, with whom the name of John Jacob Astor III was to become scandalously linked.

'Boss' Tweed, who had grown up in the Manhattan slums, was perfectly happy to see his former neighbours festering in dark and incendiary hell-holes (John Jacob III once pointed out that it was cheaper to let a tenement burn to the ground than to pay for the installation of safety measures against fire) so long as he himself could afford to build a mansion on Fifth Avenue that rivalled and even outshone the twin brownstones of the Astors. His actual role in the ring of corruption that has been recorded in history bearing his name is not entirely clear. It may be that political enemies pushed on him blame that should properly have been shared by others. But there is no doubt that the men who were robbing the city blind were part of the political machine Tweed controlled from his comparatively lowly position as a county supervisor: the mayor, A. Oakley Hall; the financial controller, Richard 'Slippery Dick' Connolly; and the city chamberlain, Peter Barr Sweeney. Furthermore, Tweed must have obtained his mansion-building money from somewhere.

That the Tweed Ring was pillaging the city treasury was common knowledge, but no one knew exactly how and few were disposed to speak out against it. The landlord class was protected against the excesses of zealous reformers while the poor were fed palliatives and a few pennies. In fact, when in 1870 the *New York Times* voiced its unease over what was going on at City Hall and urged public scrutiny of Controller Connolly's account books, the paper's campaigning editor, Henry J. Raymond, was roundly criticized for besmirching the fair name of New York. The *Times*, however, struck near enough to the bone to worry 'Boss' Tweed, facing an election that year, and he felt obliged to concoct a response to the editor's charges. He announced that a committee of six prominent business tycoons and bankers would be invited to examine the municipal ledgers and publicly reveal their findings. The chairman of this committee was to be none other than John Jacob Astor III.

Just how Tweed suborned Astor and his colleagues is a matter for speculation. They were unlikely to have been open to financial inducements, since between them they could have bought the entire city, and they were powerful enough to withstand any threats Tweed would have been capable of carrying out. That they naively thought all was well with the city's fiscal affairs does not bear examination, and any susceptibility to blackmail seems equally unlikely – in their own way they were all honest men. Probably it was simply that their consciences were firmly placed in their bank accounts, that Tweed had only to raise the spectre of radicals marching to elected office under the banner of public resentment for the sensitive capitalists to clutch their wallets in alarm and agree to anything that would prevent the reformers from rampaging through City Hall, which would have meant the end of civilization as the upper crust knew it.

In all seriousness Astor and his five committeemen presented themselves at Connolly's office and were seen to go inside. When they emerged they had no difficulty in signing a statement which concluded that 'the financial affairs of the Controller are administered in a correct and faithful manner'. This endorsement, published two days before the election, propelled Tweed and his Tammany cohorts to a resounding victory, though it did not silence the mutterings of the *Times*.

Astor and his committee, Henry Raymond wrote, were living illustrations of the saying that, 'There is nothing so mean as one million of dollars except two millions... They have made themselves parties to a great fraud and if we are not mistaken they will live long enough to repent it... Instead of combining for mutual protection against the unscrupulous officials of the Ring, they sneak off one after another to the Tax Commissioners' office to beg for a petty reduction of the assessment of their property.'

Astor was much too grand to stoop to swapping blows with the *New York Times*, but the literary tastes of his cousin Charles Astor Bristed prompted that worthy to express in suitably pretentious prose the tender feelings of the seigneur. 'The rich,' wrote the favourite grandson of John Jacob I, 'are prone to belong to the *parti de l'ordre*, as a Frenchman would say – in other words to acquiesce in the party in power. If that party is composed of arrant knaves, still they will try to keep on good terms with them as a Russian gentleman tries to keep on good terms with the Russian police though knowing them to be the vilest wretches. They say to themselves: "It is true, these are terrible scoundrels. We would give a great deal to see them all hung and the balance sent to State Prison. But the public won't back us and what can we do by ourselves against the Ring with its array of foreign ruffians and native renegades and priests and what not – above all, with its appliances and opportunities for making war at the enemy's expense? *Si populus vult spoliari, spolietur*. Every man must make the best terms he can for himself."' There, if you like, is an elegant case for laisser-faire: the Astor philosophy in three languages!

But the *Times* was not about to let things be, and in the summer of 1871 Raymond got his chance to stop muttering and shout from the housetops, to nail the Ring and Astor's cover-up committee. A disgruntled official handed over actual pages from Connolly's books which showed that in a little more than two years Tweed's men had stolen thirty million dollars from the people of New York and increased the city's fiscal debt by fifty million through inflated payments to business associates.*

* Connolly, the chief embezzler, escaped abroad taking six million dollars with him, but Tweed was sent to prison, where he died.

One member of the Astor committee confessed that it had been 'used as a cover and shield by those who were robbing the city', but John Jacob himself remained impassive and aloof. An aristocrat such as he was not to be soiled by the sordid workings of democracy: that was for ordinary people. As he brooded in the exclusive Knickerbocker Club, which he had helped to found in response to the importation of undesirable nouveau riche elements into the Union Club, the thought might well have crossed his mind that America would be a much healthier nation were it still part of the British Empire. They ordered these things better in England; people knew their place.

The British way of life (that is, in the manner of the aristocracy) became ever more appealing to John Jacob as he grew older, and he spent longer and longer periods in London. He might have been the American ambassador there – the post was offered to him by President Rutherford B. Hayes in recognition of services to the Republican Party and of his role in obtaining the presidency for Hayes – but he could not countenance the prospect of leaving the Astor Estate to look after itself, particularly since brother William refused to have anything to do with the management. So he continued to live in America, though he became increasingly remote from the mainstream of its life, especially after Augusta's death in 1887, when a bad heart restricted his activities and a phobic fear of publicity, no doubt occasioned by the drubbing he had received in the press over both the Tweed affair and the condition of his tenements, drove him to limit even his correspondence.

When he died on 22 February 1890, some commentators noted an unfulfilled quality about his life ('pathetic', the *Spectator* called it), but most recalled his upright Episcopalian principles, his unwavering sense of duty, his financial probity and prudence and above all his air of nobility. 'The great fortune which he commanded could not have been put into better hands,' said the *New York Times*, and no one could argue with that. Yet what did John Jacob Astor III actually achieve with his great fortune? A few office blocks in the financial district, a few miles of terraced brownstone houses indistinguishable from any others, a few acres of land in Harlem and the Bronx which anyone with the money to do so would have bought in the certain knowledge that their value would soar as New York eventually expanded under pressure from below. Even his much-vaunted acts of charity, in any case largely inspired by his wife, added up throughout his life and at his death to no more than two million dollars, in percentage terms precisely the same as his illustrious namesake had given away.

In sum, then, there was little to remember him by. Yet he earned his place in history just by living, not only because he was the richest American of his day – and probably the third richest man in the world* – but also because he was the last of the great American Astors. His son, even prouder and more conscious of his superiority, would abandon a country that dared to criticize its own aristocracy, and within three generations the Astor family would be virtually finished as a potent force in American life.

In his eulogy for John Jacob III, the Rector of Trinity asked 'Who can fill his place?' He could not have known it then, but the answer was, nobody.

II

The main difference between nearly all the descendants of John Jacob Astor and the founder of the dynasty was that while he was a man of action they were content to accept their passive role, allowing what John Jacob had created to remain the wellspring of their lives without adding to it anything of their own – a situation which the old man had deliberately set up out of the fear, possibly justified, that the family fortune would be dissipated by some future generation. What John Jacob did not foresee in his obsessive desire to keep what he had made was that the lack of some central activity in the lives of his children and grandchildren would inevitably result in style becoming more important than substance as the successors sought to justify their existence in ways unrelated to the business that supported them inexorably without ever really needing their attention.

William Backhouse Astor filled his life with the minutiae of

* At the time of Astor's death the *Spectator* estimated that only the Czar of Russia and the Prince of Hohenzollern-Sigmaringen exceeded his wealth.

management; John Jacob III divided his time between the estate office and the smoke-filled back rooms of Republican politics, but unlike his father he also 'wasted' time and money on stocking his library with fine books and his cellar with fine wines, on entertaining in the grand manner and on becoming a patron of the arts. Already the style of Astor life, the idea of behaving like a millionaire, was beginning to assume importance. In the life of John's brother, William Backhouse Jr, however, style was to become everything. If John was the last of the great American Astors, William was destined to be the first of the decadent ones. He had his reasons, as we shall discover.

The first misfortune to befall William was his birth in 1830, or at least the order of its occurrence in a family that placed primogeniture above everything. Had he been the firstborn son, there is every chance that William would have made at least as good a job as John of managing the Astor fortune, assuming that the weaknesses which later appeared in his personality were external in origin rather than inborn. He was certainly cleverer than John, maintaining a high standard at school and graduating second in his class at Columbia, and where his elder brother was shy, solemn and withdrawn, William was outgoing, spirited, polished and charming. With a little encouragement he might have been as dashing and successful as old John Jacob, but it was his fate to spend his life in the shadow of others more forceful than he – his father, his brother and later his wife.

In spite of his academic distinction, William was not sent to Göttingen, but he was allowed to travel widely in the Middle East, Greece and Turkey (at least, one supposes, it kept him happy and out of the way while the firstborn settled unchallenged into a chair at the Astor Estate Office). His journey gave him a breadth of outlook rare in the America of his time, but when he returned home he found that there was little use to which he could put this new dimension. His father virtually ignored him and it soon became clear that any inclination he had to make a contribution to the family business was less than welcome. In a more dynamic character this would have spurred a desire to show what he could do on his own, but William, brought up to see himself as a second son and therefore a second-class Astor, simply opted out and left the administration of the empire to his 'betters'.

William's second piece of bad luck was his marriage to Caroline Webster Schermerhorn, who, like John's bride, was a Lafayette Place neighbour. One can see the appeal of such a match to Caroline: her family had impeccable antecedents but a certain want of financial underpinning, and William was after all a handsome and dazzling young man. It is harder to understand why William should have settled for this dumpy, empty-headed, plain and insufferably vain girl whose one aim in life was to acquire for herself the social status which she believed her lineage deserved. When she married William in 1853 she was twenty-two, getting on in years for a bride at that time and in those circles. William was twenty-three, young for a husband, and his youth might help to explain this mismatch. Many a man has married early and unwisely in order to both prove his maturity and escape from a home of baleful influences. William probably felt that in his own house, with his own wife and his own children growing up around him, he could show his father and brother that he could amount to something on his own. It was certainly easier than standing up to them on their own ground.

In the event, both partners were to be disappointed in their expectations of the marriage. Caroline fulfilled her duty – without much pleasure, it seems – in ensuring the survival of the species, producing children at regular intervals until in 1864 the fifth turned out to be the desired male heir, John Jacob IV. But she did not share her husband's interest in literature and the arts, or his love of sailing and horses, and she tended to exclude him from the upbringing of the children, particularly the girls. For her part, Caroline felt cheated when she discovered that her Astor was an inferior brand, lacking both power over the fortune, of which his brother had received the lion's share, and status within the family. Her response was to replace substance entirely with style, insisting on a grander house, a summer place in Newport, more exclusive clothes, more brilliant jewels, more lavish entertaining. If the family would not recognize the importance of this Astor branch, graced as it was by an Old Guard Schermerhorn, then Society would be made to give it the respect it deserved. Caroline even demanded that William drop the Backhouse from his name – apart from the fact that to her the word had the unpleasant connotation of 'outhouse', she felt that 'Mrs William *Backhouse* Astor' drew a false distinction between her and the main line of the dynasty. After all, William was just as much a direct male heir as John Jacob IV. So 'Mrs William Astor' it became and eventually simply 'Mrs Astor'.

Mr Astor, meanwhile, decided to meet indifference with apathy. He would leave his brother and his wife to their petty concerns, if that was what they wanted, and follow his own desires. He bought himself a splendid yacht, the *Ambassadress* – and later an even more luxurious one – where he could indulge the lusts of the flesh far away from prying eyes (Caroline seems never to have been enthusiastic about the physical side of their relationship, and the birth of their son might well have meant that she felt she no longer needed to submit). William also bought a magnificent estate called Ferncliff on the banks of the Hudson near Rhinebeck in Dutchess County, where he played the farmer and bred racehorses. His life settled into a pattern of absence.

Caroline, becoming ever more involved in the construction and administration of her very own stratum of high society, apparently sighed with relief every time she watched her husband's figure disappear into the distance. 'Dear William has been so good to me,' she would confide to friends. 'I have been so fortunate in my marriage.' Fortunate in that William chose to ignore it most of the time. One of his grand-daughters, Caroline Drayton Phillips, described him as 'a very trying and disagreeable man. He drank and had affairs with second-rate women.' (The epithet second-rate was charitable.) When Caroline Astor gave a ball on one of the rare occasions when William was in New York she would arrange with one of her husband's friends to keep him late at his club, for if he chanced to arrive home in the midst of the merriment he would throw out the orchestra and order his children to go to bed. Caroline Phillips's brother Harry was actually afraid of his grandfather's gruff manner and tended to burst into tears in his presence, at which William would growl, 'Turning on the water pipes again? Take him away.'

William's drinking became notorious among those who knew him. He was once described wryly as 'a one-man temperance society dedicated to destroying all spiritous liquor even if he had to drink it all himself'. But at least that and his unsavoury amours were carried on well away from home. One of his favourite watering-holes, if that is the appropriate term, on his ceaseless journey of escape was Florida, where he became something of an institution. He bought a block of commercial property in Jacksonville, opened a railroad and made plans to establish the largest orangerie in the world (though the scheme came to nothing), which earned him a land grant of eighty thousand acres from the state governor. It was even suggested that many Floridians would have liked to see Astor as their representative in the Senate in Washington, a fascinating prospect to contemplate.

Despite the gulf between them, William and Caroline were alike in dedicating their lives to the creation of an all-pervading illusion that they both, in their different ways, found more acceptable than reality. But Caroline was much more ambitious than her husband: he was content to cocoon himself in a world of his own making; she insisted on reorganizing in her own image the entire structure of upper-class life in New York.

What precisely motivated Caroline in her ultimately over-weening desire to be the social queen of the city is not at all clear. She always claimed that her main interest lay in seeing that her daughters made 'good' marriages, but that justification does not really bear close examination. Actually not all the marriages that were made by Caroline's children were good (indeed one of them was to end in an almighty scandal). Probably her assault on the pinnacle of the establishment was influenced by a number of factors. By 1872, the year when she first began to make her presence felt, her children had reached ages at which they could safely be left in the care of servants, so that Caroline had time on her hands. That year, too, Margaret Astor, her mother-in-law, died and the position of leading lady fell vacant. It should have been filled by Augusta, but although she was a competent and admired hostess there was a certain eccentricity about the people she chose to entertain: writers, artists, actresses, people with no 'background'. She was, wrote a contemporary, 'a brilliant woman full of social and intellectual attainment', but that was too much for most of the uneducated, uninterested and uninteresting great ladies of New

York in the 1880s – in the 1920s, perhaps, Augusta would have been a star – and Caroline felt that the Astors' social position would be undermined by vulgar newcomers like the Vanderbilts if someone did not strike a blow for the old values (whatever they were). And finally, 1872 was the year in which Ward McAllister appeared on the scene, fresh from his social studies in Europe and ready to amaze New York with his savoir faire.

Between them McAllister and the heavy, ugly woman he called 'The Mystic Rose' planned a social code that was to revolutionize the high life of the city. There was absolutely no basis for it other than the needs, pretensions and prejudices of the pair who devised it. For example, they decided that a 'gentleman' must have at least three generations of wealth and position behind him in order to qualify for the title. Why three generations? Why not four? Or two? Well, the Astors could claim three generations and the Vanderbilts only two. Yet such egocentric stupidity was immediately accepted by the people Caroline wished first to impress and then to dominate. So uncertain of themselves were the socialites of New York, so desperate to find something that would endow them with an importance to match their money, that they allowed a vain, pretentious woman and a pompous little gasbag of a man to rule their lives.

It might be that McAllister's role in this was far more significant than has commonly been supposed. He seems, in retrospect, such a ridiculous figure that it is easy to assume his part to have been a minor one. However, it must be remembered that McAllister lived off Society just as he had once earned his keep by entertaining clients of his family's law firm and perhaps it was he, rather than Caroline Astor, who was the puppet-master. He knew how to play upon the vanity of his patroness, how to inveigle her into spending more and more money, and there is no doubt that he was indispensable to her success. Maybe, then, it is not stretching the limits of possibility to suggest that McAllister deliberately set out to make Caroline the queen of Fifth Avenue for his own purposes and that without his manipulations she would never have embarked upon her project. In the end, of course, his own bluster got the better of him and he began to live up to all the claptrap he had spouted, so that in making his self-important pronouncements on the nature of Society he pushed his credibility too far. By that time Caroline had learnt the techniques of manipulation herself and no longer needed him.

Caroline Drayton Phillips, who was a child at the height of Mrs Astor's reign in the 1880s, retained a strong impression of her grandmother. 'She was very worldly and quite a snob. She lived for parties and bought endless Worth dresses and was covered with jewels...' Those dresses led to difficulties with the Treasury Department, which suspected that such large quantities as accompanied Caroline every time she returned from a trip to Paris must be destined for sale since one woman could not possibly intend to wear them all! On one occasion, customs inspectors imposed a duty of $1,800 on Caroline's new clothes and when William challenged them in court it was ruled that unworn clothing was indeed liable to duty. But William was not going to lose almost $2,000 without a fight – he was an Astor, after all – and he took the Treasury to the Supreme Court, which finally ruled in his favour, saying that any monetary advantage obtained through buying clothes was 'but an incidental advantage attendant upon the opportunity to go abroad'. Perhaps if there had been an income tax in those days William would have been able to claim that his wife's wardrobe was deductible as a business expense.

Certainly the administration of the new society was more or less a full-time job for Caroline, requiring the employment of a secretary. Once the hierarchy had been established through McAllister's invention of the Patriarchs in 1872 there were always important decisions to be made as to who should and should not qualify for inclusion, and on what grounds, as well as what rules of conduct should apply in formal surroundings and how the pattern of social events should be organized. All this required a great deal of thought: Caroline had to remain one step ahead so as to continually identify standards that others might rise to. Nearly every day letters would arrive from social climbers seeking inclusion in the charmed circle, and then there was the problem of arranging balls and dinners and nights at the opera so that no two important occasions should clash.

Furthermore, Caroline was by no means unchallenged as

Society's sovereign and rivals such as the Belmonts* and Vanderbilts, excluded from the Patriarchy but too rich and well established to ignore altogether, were perfectly capable of arranging their own entertainments to eclipse anything Mrs Astor might have in mind. 'Very rich and purse-proud,' Lord Rosebery was told of August Belmont before visiting New York in 1873. 'A snobbish little Jew – with nice (but cold) wife and daughters.' Nevertheless his Rothschild connexions made him sought after by visiting European nobility and his wife was able to surround her dinner table with figures far more imposing than any that Caroline Astor could boast of. But it was Alva Vanderbilt who ran Caroline closest. Although the Vanderbilts could not be admitted to the Patriarchy because they were engaged in trade (railroads), they were immensely wealthy and, unlike the Belmonts, they were prepared to buy their way into the very highest society.

In 1883, at the height of Mrs Astor's reign, Alva Vanderbilt announced that she was to hold a fancy dress ball to mark the opening of her new, two-million-dollar castle on Fifth Avenue. She sent out twelve hundred invitations, carefully ignoring Caroline. This placed the queen in a difficult situation: everyone who was anyone would be at the Vanderbilt ball and if she did not attend the whole structure she had erected around herself would very likely collapse. Mrs Astor prompted one of her friends to mention the omission to Mrs Vanderbilt – presumably it was merely an oversight. Not at all, replied Alva. She did not actually *know* Mrs Astor, and one surely could not invite complete strangers to one's home. Caroline bristled, but then saw a way of saving face. She told a friend, 'We have no right to exclude those whom the growth of this great country has brought forward, provided they are not vulgar in speech and appearance. The time has come for the Vanderbilts.' Her calling card was left at the Vanderbilt mansion and an invitation to the ball was forthcoming. Caroline made herself the star of the show by appearing very late (in the costume of a Venetian

---

* August Belmont, the great financier and American consul of the Rothschilds, being Jewish, was automatically barred from Mrs Astor's court – she did not like Jews or Catholics, though in later years she was obliged to overlook her prejudices in certain cases so that she could ward off ambitious rivals with fewer scruples about who could be invited.

princess) and wearing *all* her jewelry, which shone far more brightly than the electrically lighted stars some of the young ladies wore on their foreheads. But the real victory was Mrs Vanderbilt's, and it foreshadowed a new era in New York society – an age in which money and the lavish spending of it became more important than breeding. Ironically the Astors, who for some time yet were to remain the richest of all, had become much too aristocratic to allow themselves to be drawn into that sort of competition.

It was in Newport that Mrs Astor's reign lasted longest. Even when the throwing around of 'new' money turned the New York scene into an anarchic bunfight, the little colonial harbour on Narragansett Bay remained a haven of good form and rigid status and Caroline continued to hold sway.

After playing its part in the Revolution as a base for the French navy, Newport had been a summer retreat for Southern planters, the bracing breezes providing a welcome antidote to the humidity of their native climes, and their example was eventually followed by wealthy Northerners who liked to sail, but it was not until the second half of the nineteenth century that the town became a great social centre. Caroline was a pioneer in this development: she did not particularly like Ferncliff and saw a 'cottage' on Rhode Island as the perfect compromise for summer living, since William could moor his yacht in the basin. (Of course, the John Jacob Astors had also bought a vacation home there, and anything the senior branch could do Caroline was determined to do better.) The house, Beechwood, had been built in 1851, one of several lining a cliff overlooking the Atlantic, but by the time William was persuaded to buy it thirty years later it had been completely reconstructed after a fire. The purchase price was fairly modest, $190,000, but if William thought he was getting a bargain he was wrong, for Caroline insisted on redecorating and furnishing all sixty-two rooms at a cost of two million dollars. Craftsmen were brought to Beechwood from all over the world and put to work making furniture and ornamentation from the most expensive materials. The Music Room, for example, was panelled in imported ebony adorned with gold leaf, and musical instruments were set into the woodwork. In the dining room, the thirty-five-foot table was surrounded by sixteen soft leather chairs with the initials W.A. embossed in gold on their backs.

One could hardly say, then, that money was not important at Newport – some of the grand balls given by Mrs Astor and her neighbours cost $200,000 apiece – but class counted for more. Ward McAllister once noted: 'If you were not of the inner circle and were a newcomer, it took the combined efforts of all your friends backing and pushing to procure an invitation for you. For years whole families sat on the stool of probation awaiting trial and acceptance, and many were rejected.' At Bailey's Beach, a sheltered cove on the south side of the island where the top people bathed, a gold-braided commissionaire refused entry to anyone either unknown to him or without a letter of introduction, and the Horse Shoe Piazza at The Casino was little more than an annexe to mansion morning rooms where refreshment was taken to the accompaniment of a string orchestra. Protocol and precedence were everything: on Bellevue Avenue, a long road that runs south from the harbour to the promontory known as Land's End and around which all the mansions are grouped, it was unforgivable for one's carriage to overtake that of a person of superior rank in the social hierarchy.

In such an atmosphere, Mrs Astor's resources and social skills kept her firmly in command. Her hauteur cowed even Mrs August Belmont and Mrs Stuyvesant Fish, Mrs Hermann Oelrichs and Mrs Ogden Goelet, and indeed their names are long forgotten while that of *the* Mrs Astor remains synonymous with luxury and style. Through the 1880s and into the 1890s her balls and dinners were the grandest: on one occasion she covered her dinner table to a depth of several inches with sand in which she buried diamonds, sapphires, rubies and emeralds as party favours for her guests, and by each place-setting was a small bucket and spade in sterling silver. There's class for you!

By and by, though, the vulgar profits of trade and commerce began to appear in Newport. In 1892 the Vanderbilts moved in next door to Beechwood when William K. of that ilk opened Richard Morris Hunt's reconstruction of the Petit Trianon under the name of Marble House. Three years later nine million of Cornelius Vanderbilt's railroad dollars bore fruit in The Breakers, a vast pile modelled on a sixteenth-century northern Italian palace and occupying the prime site of Ochre Point. As the century turned, everyone and his brother seemed to get in on the act: Mrs Oelrichs built Rosecliff, also next door to Beechwood, in the manner of the Grand Trianon, and the architect Horace Trumbauer designed The Elms (after the Chateau d'Asnières near Paris) for a Pennsylvania coal king, of all people. Beside these monumental creations Beechwood began to look like servants' quarters and Caroline was forced to concede that, in architectural terms at least, she had been bested by fortunes that were earned rather than inherited.

Back in New York, she played one last card in the attempt to save society from the iconoclasts. With John Jacob III dead, his son William Waldorf had decided not only to settle in England but also to turn the old homestead on Fifth Avenue into a hotel. Clearly the William Astors would have to move, and Caroline decided to give the 'newcomers' a run for their money. She engaged Richard Morris Hunt, the architect of palatial homes for the Vanderbilts and Belmonts among others, to build for her a 'Renaissance chateau' uptown on Fifth Avenue overlooking Central Park. The great white stone house at the corner of 65th Street, which cost some three million dollars to erect, to decorate and to furnish in period style, was divided by a removable partition so that Caroline could live in one half and her only son, John Jacob IV, and his family could occupy the other half. With the partition removed the Astors boasted the largest ballroom in New York, hung with paintings and bedecked with marble statuary. Here the great balls would continue for another decade and the faithful would wait as anxiously as ever for their invitations, but there was a world of difference between the 1880s and the 'Naughty Nineties' and Caroline Astor had already become part of history.

She was old now and alone. William had died of a heart attack in Paris in 1892, long before the new palace at 840 Fifth Avenue had even left the drawing board. 'The death of Mr William Astor has not robbed New York of a personality of great importance,' commented the bitchy *Town Topics*. 'His place in society was indicated by the activity of the lady who bore his name... Even his face and form were relatively unknown while every *gamin* could point out Mrs Astor...' But Caroline missed him, even if no one else did. She also missed Ward McAllister when he died in 1895, though he faded into the background before that under an outburst of public hilarity at his foolish book *Society As I Have Found It*, a masterpiece of unconscious self-parody. As his successor Caroline tried to 'bring on' an unpleasant social climber called Harry Lehr who lived high on the hog by providing amusement for the rich and using his contacts to obtain limitless credit. Lehr, however, soon defected to the entourage of the more exciting Mamie Fish, who cheerfully consented to the enlivening of her parties by such novelties as an elephant and a monkey in an evening suit. That was definitely not Mrs Astor's style, though even her standards slipped under the pressure of Lehr and the *jeunesse dorée*, to the extent that she was actually seen eating dinner in a public restaurant.

She had never been very closely in touch with reality (a situation that was becoming not unusual among the Astors), but in her later years she became even more detached. She allowed Nixola Greeley-Smith, of the New York *World*, to interview her but when the reporter returned to have her copy cleared Caroline sent out a maid with her apologies and a two-dollar 'tip'.

'Tell Mrs Astor,' said the grand-daughter of the great Horace Greely, 'that she not only forgets who I am, but she forgets who she is. Give her back the two dollars with my compliments and tell her that when John Jacob Astor was skinning rabbits my grandfather was getting out the *Tribune* and was one of the foremost citizens of New York.' That was the kind of thing all Astors preferred to forget.

The January occasions went on until 1905, but the last great event at 840 Fifth Avenue was a banquet in honour of Prince Louis of Battenberg, when Mrs Astor remembered her old rules and invited only seventy-nine guests, who did not include a Vanderbilt. The following year, the ball was cancelled because Caroline had fallen on the stairs and had to use a wheelchair. She never fully recovered and would wander the halls of her great empty house reliving the triumphs of the past and speaking of old friends and relatives as if they were still alive. Finally, broken in body and mind, she died at the age of seventy-seven on 30 October 1908.

The funeral at Trinity was attended by all the members of the Old Guard who had looked to her for leadership and guidance, and who perhaps owed much of their social position to her approval. 'I am not vain enough to think that New York cannot get along without me,' she had said, and of course she was right, but the city would never see her like again. All her energies had been devoted to covering up the deficiencies in her life with a gilded screen and it might be said that she contributed nothing of value to the world, yet she gave millions of Americans something to aspire to and, like the film stars and pop singers of today, she brightened drab lives with glamour and wonder. None of the high-society hostesses who succeeded her would have quite the same *cachet* because their even greater excesses tended to rob them of the dignity that Mrs Astor always preserved.

As for the family itself, it will become clear in the following pages why Caroline is remembered to this day as *the* Mrs Astor.

III

'We have to be more exclusive in New York,' Caroline Astor once said, 'because in America there is no authority in society. Each woman is for herself...' She, of course, maintained that she was not out for self-gratification, but was more interested in displaying her daughters to that section of society which in her judgment was capable, through breeding as well as money, of providing suitable husbands. If that had truly been her purpose, the endeavour would not have been particularly successful.

The eldest girl, Emily, was to have been the beneficiary of the first Astor-McAllister foray: she celebrated her eighteenth birthday just in time for the winter season of 1872–73. But when she anounced her intention of marrying two years later, the prospective bridegroom came from a family quite definitely not numbered among the Patriarchs. Even William balked at the idea of having James Van Alen as a son-in-law and as a result was challenged to a duel by the young man's father, a choleric cavalry colonel who was known in New York as an inveterate womanizer. The duel did not take place and the marriage did, but its durability was never really tested since Emily died in childbirth in 1881.

Helen, the second daughter, did marry well, but there is no

evidence that Caroline's social dominance had anything to do with it. The bridegroom was James Roosevelt Roosevelt (half-brother of Franklin D. Roosevelt), with whose family the Astors were already connected through Laura Delano, Caroline's sister-in-law. The couple moved to England, where the Roosevelts had a country house near Ascot, but Helen too was destined to die young – in 1893 at the age of thirty-eight.

It was the marriage of the third girl, Charlotte Augusta, that proved to be the greatest disaster. In spite of a magnificent debutante ball at 350 Fifth Avenue, Charlotte insisted on marrying one James Coleman Drayton, from Philadelphia, a man of little fortune and somewhat threadbare background (at least as far as Caroline was concerned). Worse was to come. In 1891 Charlotte, by then the mother of four children, fell passionately, madly in love with Hallett Alsop Borrowe, son of one of New York's leading insurance tycoons. In an effort to avoid scandal, the Astors sent Drayton and his errant wife to London, but Borrowe followed them and had secret assignations with Charlotte. Drayton found out and challenged Borrowe to a duel in Paris, at which point the whole affair burst into the public prints because one of the seconds Drayton had chosen for his duel sold the correspondence relating to the challenge to the New York *Sun*.

Somehow the actual duel could never be organized, but the matter simmered for long enough to keep the press interested, the public amused and the Astors acutely embarrassed. To add to the fun, Charlotte and her husband were involved in a court battle over custody of their children, and there were persistent reports that Drayton had received a pay-off from the Astors to keep his mouth shut – a bargain which, if it was ever struck, he clearly did not keep. Throughout, Charlotte maintained that her honour was intact and eventually, under pressure from her family, she convinced a judge of that fact, obtaining a divorce on the grounds of Drayton's 'cruel suspicions as to her marital fidelity'. Borrowe, meanwhile, was sentenced by his father to 'internal exile' in Newark, New Jersey, and 'as pretty a social disturbance as ever agitated New York society' gradually faded away. For a time Mrs Astor's balls were sparsely attended by people of the 'better sort' because she resolutely stood by her daughter, so Caroline must have been mightily relieved when

Charlotte retreated across the Atlantic again to marry a wealthy Scotsman.

Even the youngest daughter, Carrie, who made her debut at the very zenith of her mother's reign, married 'beneath herself', choosing the son of a Civil War profiteer, R.T. Wilson, whose claims to acceptability rested on a million dollars, the ownership of the late Boss Tweed's mansion on Fifth Avenue, and the marriage of his daughter to Ogden Goelet. The Astors tried to prevent the match by settling half a million dollars on Carrie and insisting that the prospective bridegroom receive the same settlement, but Wilson saw the value of such an investment and acquiesced. Putting on a brave face, Caroline made the wedding the social event of 1884, which even the bride's father was prevailed upon to attend.

Amid all these blighted hopes, however, there was one notable success, in social terms at least. Caroline's only son, John Jacob IV, having been paraded before the world at numerous Fifth Avenue occasions, chose from the throng of nubile young ladies a girl who was not only beautiful but also boasted a lineage that not even the Astors and the Schermerhorns could match, since it involved a pride of English kings dating back to Alfred the Great! This paragon was Ava Lowle Willing, from Philadelphia, feted as the belle of Newport in 1890 and pronounced bride of the year in 1891. On 17 February, the day of the wedding, the *New York Times* reported (being careful to cram all the salient points into the first paragraph, in the style of the 'new journalism'): 'New York practically took Philadelphia by storm today ... Not content with carrying off by the hand of its wealthiest marriageable son, John Jacob Astor, the greatest belle of the foremost family of the Quaker City, Miss Ava L. Willing, the wealth and fashion of New York came on, if not in immense numbers at least in such an influential way as to obliterate Philadelphia characteristics for the time being and give the fashionable heart of the city an air of gayety and animation entirely foreign to it.'

For Caroline Astor, in her eighteen-room suite at the Stratford Hotel, it was everything she could have wished. 'Joy unbounded with wealth surrounded' as one newspaper put it. If the couple were to prove fundamentally incompatible and the marriage – which, according to some Astor relatives, Ava was forced into by her parents – was rapidly to deteriorate into a bitter slanging match, that was just too bad. At least it had been an 'ideal wedding' in the eyes of the world.

In fact, neither partner, despite wealth and breeding (or perhaps because of it), was much of a catch. Ava's undoubted physical beauty was not matched by any loveliness of spirit: she was hard, selfish and vicious of tongue. As for John Jacob IV – the first of his name to be known generally as Jack – he was neither handsome nor animated and displayed in uncomfortable measure the male Astor inability to communicate and the tendency to withdraw into a strange inner world. Unfortunately these inherited traits were not matched by the traditional Astor strength of character, with Jack leaning towards his father's line of least resistance even more markedly than William had done. He, too, loved his yacht and the solitude of Ferncliff, neither of which appealed to his wife.

Brought up with a stern, gruff and remote (because usually absent) father, and a mother who both smothered and dominated him, John Jacob IV had little chance to mature either emotionally or intellectually. His education at St Paul's and Harvard owed more to convention than anything else and according to *Town Topics* he was known by some contemporaries as 'Jack Ass'. That scurrilous and scandalous publication greeted Jack's introduction to society in 1887 with the comment that he was 'one of the richest catches of the day and at the same time voted so much less brilliant than his father that it is very questionable whether, were he put to it, he could ever earn his bread by his brains'. The slur was both unfair and unfounded: Jack was not stupid; it was simply that his awkward, arrogant and somewhat adolescent manner made him appear gauche and foolish. After all, even his father's academic brilliance counted for little against the psychological handicaps wrought by his family background.

In fact, Jack could probably have made quite a good living for himself if required to do so, for he had a grasp of scientific and mechanical principles both intuitive and imaginative, as well as a definite practical bent, which led him to produce a number of inventions. If the devices he dreamed up met with a certain amount of scorn, it was partly because they were not likely to revolutionize civilized life or make a lot of money, and partly because there was something faintly ridiculous to the American mind of the late nineteenth century about the prospect of a multi-millionaire and leading citizen fiddling about with bits of machinery and strands of wire. Yet one invention, a pneumatic machine for improving the surface of dirt roads, won first prize in an exhibition at the Chicago World's Fair, and the Astor bicycle brake attracted an offer of $2,000 for the patent (Jack turned it down).

More imaginative was his idea for a rain-induction process using pumped warm air, even if nobody took it up, and Jack himself made use of his improved accumulator battery, which he installed on one of his yachts. His interest in marine matters prompted him to experiment with turbines – he had a laboratory built at Ferncliff – and he presented his designs to the world in 1902. He also had a way with internal combustion engines and developed a method of using peat as a fuel which was considered worthy of inclusion in the *Scientific American*.

But the apogee of his scientific thought, and the psychological basis of his interest in science, is to be found in words rather than machinery. In 1894 he published a novel entitled *A Journey in Other Worlds* in which he imagined what life would be like in the year 2000. His predictions were by no means unique, but they demonstrated his familiarity with current scientific knowledge. He wrote of electric automobiles and aircraft; of weapons so terrible that war became unthinkable; of magnetic railways and hydrofoils; and of television (which he called the 'kintograph'). The main story concerned a space-traveller, but there were subplots involving the now highly topical subject of energy conservation, a scheme to 'straighten' the earth's axis by pumping water from the North Pole to the South (which Astor suggested would produce eternal springtime), and the discovery of a force equal and opposite to gravity. Up in space, science became confused with Astor's conventional but sincere religious beliefs: the souls of the righteous departed were found on Saturn, where, to a background of weird music, 'pulsating hearts, luminous brains and centers of spiritual activity quiver with motion'. Indeed, Jack's faith in the future, as he explained in a preface to the book, was based on both God and the ingenuity of man. 'Next to religion,' he wrote, 'we have most to hope from science.'

The psychology is plain enough. Faced with a wife whose coldness and aggression were inexplicable to him, and unable to come to terms with the complexities of his own emotions, he retreated into a dreamworld where all problems – even the mysteries of the universe and the questions of life and death – could be explained by scientific rationalism. It was so much safer than the real world, which Jack had never been equipped to deal with, protected as he was by his father's wealth and his mother's fairytale existence.

There was about Jack a distinctly tragic quality, but nobody noticed it except perhaps his son Vincent, who revered his father's memory even though there had never been any relationship between them in the deeper sense of the word. Jack's contemporaries merely disliked him or envied him or laughed at him. Certainly he was capable of making a fool of himself, as he did in 1894 over the case of 'the Astor tramp', according to newspaper reports of the time.

The tramp in question, a man named John Garvey, appears to have been one of the many who took to the streets after the severe financial crisis of 1893–94. Wandering along Fifth Avenue one wintry night, Garvey paused a while in the bright lights and bustle of the Waldorf Hotel and noticed as he did so that a basement door of the neighbouring number 340 was ajar. His curiosity – and perhaps other instincts – aroused, the tramp approached the door, saw that it led to a comfortable room (in fact the quarters of the Astors' laundress, who happened to be away that evening), and went inside to sleep. Next morning he was found by a servant, but rather than simply throwing him out, Jack Astor had him arrested. Garvey went before a magistrate and was fined five dollars, but since he could not pay he was committed to prison.

The press was naturally interested in such a bizarre invasion of the Astor citadel and sought comment from Jack. 'It does not seem right to me,' the young master said, 'that a man can enter the house of any citizen and only be fined five dollars. My mother is frightfully alarmed over the matter and something must be done to punish this man so he will not repeat his offence. If he goes free there may be hundreds of others doing the same thing, and I cannot have that.'

These ill-judged remarks, betraying the right-wing Republican Astor's fear that under the Democratic Administration of Grover Cleveland the country was on the brink of anarchy, were sufficient to make John Garvey a *cause célèbre*. People muttered about heartless landlords and the newspapers wondered what sort of society it was that denied a homeless, harmless vagrant a bed for the night, especially at a time of economic depression and consequent hardship among the poor. Within a couple of days a charitable citizen came forward to pay Garvey's fine and release him from jail.

Jack Astor was furious. 'I am utterly at a loss to understand why anyone would want to pay the fellow's fine and let him get away,' he told reporters. 'I think it is a most outrageous act. The idea of a man's being able to enter a house at night and escape with the punishment of two days in prison! A great piece of injustice has certainly been done.' Unable to see the moral weakness of his position, he brought a private prosecution for attempted burglary and had Garvey jailed for a year, amid widespread public sympathy for the tramp. Thus do trivial incidents earn a place in history. Jack Astor had been head of the family for only two years (William Waldorf having defected to England in 1890), and already he was getting a bad press. Not only that, but he was making the Astors look hopelessly outmoded, a dangerous thing to do in the revolutionary spirit of the times. The awe in which the family had been held would rapidly disappear under Jack's stewardship of the fortune, to be replaced by sniggering iconoclasm or socially conscious indignation or, worse still, that species of idle curiosity which drives people into museums to stare at reconstructed dinosaurs.

Even his own class tended to laugh behind their hands at John Jacob because of his talent for making himself look rather ridiculous. His sailing misadventures, for instance, became a standing joke. He had inherited his father's second yacht, *Nourmahal* (named, appropriately enough in view of the use to which it had been put, for the temptress 'Light of the Haram' in Moore's *Lalla Rookh*), but it brought him less pleasure and more trouble than William had found at sea. After first hitting a reef in the Hudson, the boat went on to collide with a ferry in New York harbour and ram the Vanderbilt yacht *North Star* during an Americas Cup race off Newport, which led to a

$15,000 lawsuit. Undaunted, Jack re-rigged the *Nourmahal* as a schooner, increasing her speed to seventeen knots, and fitted her out luxuriously with electric lighting and a sixty-seat dining room. Bearing in mind the yacht's record, he added a forty-foot steam launch and six lifeboats, not to mention four rapid-firing cannon which were meant to repel Caribbean pirates (though none actually appeared). The new image made little difference. In 1904 the *Nourmahal* raised more smiles by running onto rocks in Brenton's Cove, Newport. Maybe there were omens in all this, for the sea was to be the death of Jack Astor.

On land he enthusiastically took up the new-fangled motor car, a pursuit that proved almost as hazardous as his sailing, but in spite of a number of dramatic spills he acquired the reputation of a competent and fearless driver and was invited to serve on a committee considering the provision of the first roads designed specifically for the automobile. He also, incidentally, foreshadowed the development of the motor lodge by giving to the New York Automobile Club an old house on land he had bought near Ferncliff, for use as a way station welcoming drivers en route from New York to Albany. It was, of course, rather more exclusive than the modern-day Howard Johnson's.

Yachting and motoring were manifestations of a schoolboyish sense of adventure which also prompted military ambitions in Jack, to the extent that he organized for himself a colonelcy on the militia staff of the state governor. For a while he was satisfied by the glamour of the uniform, then in 1898 came his chance of real glory with the outbreak of the Spanish–American War. Having bought the favour of the federal government by lending his yacht to the navy and presenting to the army a fully equipped and manned artillery battery (at a cost of $75,000), he became a lieutenant-colonel of the U.S. army, attached to the inspectorate of the chief of staff. He came under fire while watching the battle of San Juan Hill in Cuba, but the by now customary jinx caught up with him and his military career ended somewhat ignominiously when he was invalided out with a fever caught from sleeping on wet grass. It was enough for him, though: ever afterwards he was known as 'Colonel Astor', and proud of it.

That such an insignificant and ill-deserved 'honour' should

203

have been a source of pride speaks volumes about John Jacob IV, for there was little else in the way of achievement to which he could put his name. It could and should have been otherwise. Aged twenty-eight when his father died in 1892, Jack was the youngest Astor ever to have come into his fortune (though his son Vincent was to break that record), and notwithstanding the split in the family that inheritance remained considerable at some fifty million dollars, of which a mere fifty thousand went to Caroline, no more than five million was divided among William's daughters and their offspring,* and just $145,000 was given to charity – at one-third of one per cent of the total, the meanest of the Astor bequests. (The donations included a paltry $50,000 for the Astor Library, which served to erase the family name from that institution: it was merged into the New York Public Library three years after William's death.)

A young man controlling so much money as an exciting new century approached had the opportunity to do something spectacular, but John Jacob was not the person to meet that sort of challenge. The paradox of the man was that for all his interest in scientific discovery and his dreaming about the future, the soles of his elegant boots were planted firmly in the past. So conservative was he, so steeped in the Astor notion of holding on to what one had that he could not take the risk of putting his money where his dreams were, of trying to do something towards the creation of the new world he saw in his imagination.

As a landlord he took no action to improve the lot of the slum-dwellers upon whose rents he depended, though as public criticism grew more vociferous he did sell off a few of his very worst tenements – at a handsome profit. As a property developer he invested in the rapidly expanding market for commercial buildings, with early skyscrapers such as his Schermerhorn Building fetching rents of $75,000 a year and upwards, but he failed to capitalize on the real estate boom that followed the Spanish–American War because he slavishly continued the practice of the first John Jacob in granting long

* Charlotte Augusta's amorous adventures had cost her the $850,000 her father had intended to leave her, but after William's will was read Caroline persuaded Jack to give his sister the money.

leases which took no account of inflation. His only important projects were undertaken by way of competition with his cousin William Waldorf, and they were all hotels. When the emigrant Astor opened the Waldorf Hotel on the site of his old home on Fifth Avenue in 1893, Jack first threatened to build stables next door, but the enormous success of the Waldorf convinced him that there was money to be made in the business and he negotiated with William Waldorf to erect an adjacent hotel. Thus was born the great Waldorf-Astoria, boasting a thousand bedrooms and with salons and restaurants that became the focal point of New York high life. When William Waldorf opened his Netherland and Astor hotels, Jack countered with the St Regis and the Knickerbocker, the former catering for 'people to whom the thought of dispensing with home comforts, good service and cuisine, and the atmosphere of taste and refinement has ever been a hardship', while the more downmarket Knickerbocker promised 'Fifth Avenue luxuries at Broadway prices'.

Like his namesake of the previous generation, John Jacob dipped his toe into the swirling currents of Wall Street, but his investments in railroad stock, for instance, were dictated less by business sense than by the fact that his holdings gave him the opportunity to drive trains – which engineer was going to object when a director of the company wanted to take the controls? Other directorships interested him little and his voting rights were usually handed over to proxies or left with officials of the companies concerned to use as they wished. As with so many other aspects of his life, it was the idea that counted rather than the practice.

What his idea of marriage to Ava was it is hard to know. Some have suggested that he wanted her simply because she was more beautiful than William Waldorf's bride. Be that as it may, the marriage cannot have lived up to his expectations. The narcissistic Ava soon made clear her resentment at being tied to the ungainly and unprepossessing John Jacob, and her feelings about the conception and carrying of his son may be judged from the dislike she habitually displayed towards the hapless Vincent. She did not have another child for eleven years, and rumour had it that Jack was not the father of the girl, Alice, born in 1902.

Ava whirled from New York to Europe to Newport and

back again, surrounded by adoring young men, while Jack
played with his yacht and cars, tinkered with his inventions and
gained a reputation as a man who could not resist pawing any
woman within range. When they came into contact with each
other they fought like cat and dog, to the embarrassment of a
constant stream of guests. It was the sort of marriage that
becomes so bitter the partners seem to go out of their way to do
things hated by the other. Ava would play bridge while Jack
'shambled from room to room . . . in a vain search for someone
to talk to', according to Harry Lehr's wife, occasionally trying
to amuse himself with a pianola, which inevitably brought a
sharp rebuke from his wife. Of course, Ava was happy with
Jack's money and made full use of it, but there was nothing else
in their relationship and in 1909 a divorce was arranged on the
grounds of adultery by Jack, probably with the help of a
professional co-respondent.

The divorce became final in 1910, Ava emerging with a pay-
off of $787,000 to add to her marriage settlement of $1,738,000.
Within a year Jack was married again, to a girl young enough to
be his daughter whom he had met at Bar Harbor, Maine, a
summer resort as popular as Newport but less exclusive.
Madeleine Talmadge Force was neither particularly beautiful
nor particularly rich (her father was a moderately successful
businessman in Brooklyn), but she was pliable and gratifyingly
passionate, two qualities which Astor found irresistible after
Ava. He escorted Madeleine to a number of swell New York
affairs during the 1910 season, but his peers assumed he was
merely sowing wild oats and would pay her off when he tired of
her. To their horror, however, in September the following year
their assumption was proved wrong and the Colonel married
his Madeleine in the great ballroom at Beechwood (having been
obliged to offer a thousand-dollar fee before he could persuade
a clergyman to perform the ceremony).

'Now that we are happily married,' Jack said in a statement
to the press before leaving for a honeymoon at Ferncliff, 'I do
not care how difficult divorce and remarriage laws are made. I
sympathize heartily with the most straitlaced people in most of
their ideas, but I believe remarriage should be made possible
once, as marriage is the happiest condition for the individual
and the community.'

His first marriage had certainly not been the happiest condition for him as an individual and his second did not make the community happy. With one or two exceptions, Colonel and the new Mrs Astor were shunned when they returned to New York. So difficult did their situation become that they decided to have a second honeymoon immediately and sailed off to Egypt, hoping that their absence might make the hearts of their neighbours grow fonder. But for John Jacob the absence was to be permanent: on the last leg of their journey back to New York in the spring of 1912, they were aboard the liner *Titanic*, which struck an iceberg in the North Atlantic in the early hours of 15 April and sank with the loss of fifteen hundred lives.

There is an old story, so often quoted that it has entered into journalistic folklore, that Jack, standing at the bar after the ship struck, said: 'I asked for ice, but this is ridiculous.' It does not sound much like him – he was never famous for his sense of humour. More believable are the stories of his calmness in the face of death. Colonel Archibald Gracie, who was with Astor shortly before the end, said Jack helped Madeleine into a lifeboat then asked the officer in charge if he could accompany her. The request was refused and Astor argued that he merely wanted to look after his wife, who was five months pregnant, but the officer told him men could not take places in the boats until all the women had been accounted for. Astor turned away after saying goodbye to his wife and helped people into another boat, which proved to be the last.

Madeleine's recollection was of being woken by her husband in the middle of the night to be told that something had happened to the ship. He helped her to get dressed and they both put on lifejackets when they reached the deck. 'I got into the next to last boat,' Madeleine went on. 'Colonel Astor said to me, "The sea is calm. You'll be all right. You're in good hands. I'll see you in the morning." Then he kissed me affectionately and stood smiling down at me as the lifeboat was lowered. I noticed that the ship was settling as we rowed away, and I could make out the figure of Kitty, my favourite terrier, running about the deck. Then I saw the *Titanic* go down.' Astor apparently met his death when he was hit by debris tossed about the deck in the ship's final plunge. He was forty-eight years old.

'Had the Four Hundred or the Two Hundred and Fifty shown themselves less implacable,' said the family's former attorney, Joseph H. Choate, 'Astor would not now be lying at the bottom of the Atlantic . . . I think we may say, "Judge not, that ye be not judged." It is no light business to take into mortal hand the jurisdiction of the Almighty . . . If some sides of his character do not commend themselves to general esteem, we may surely let the veil of charity fall gently over all that.'

There was not much else to say about the late John Jacob Astor IV, except the words of the rector of St Thomas's church, Fifth Avenue; 'He died like a brave man.' But how had he lived?

6 *The Young Master*

I

The untimely death of Colonel Astor left the stewardship of the family fortune in the hands of a tall, awkward college boy, William Vincent Astor, aged twenty and nearing the end of his first year at Harvard. 'The richest young man in the world,' the newspapers christened him, with only mild and entirely excusable hyperbole. Upon reaching his majority in the autumn of 1912, Vincent – that was the name he preferred – gained personal control of virtually all the Astor wealth remaining in America, a total of some seventy million dollars. By the time he died he would have almost doubled the value of his father's legacy, but the American Astors would no longer be counted among the super-rich of the richest nation on earth, and the international magic of their name would be associated only with a dimly remembered past. This was not the result of any marked lack of business acumen on Vincent's part, but merely because of the kind of man he was.

In a sense, Vincent Astor reflected one of the major conflicts of modern Western society: the division between the right of an individual to amass, hold and inherit great wealth and the right of society, having contributed to the creation of that wealth, to expect benefits from it. Vincent's tragedy, if such it may be called, was that he represented both sides of the argument.

He was born on 15 November 1891 in the Fifth Avenue mansion from which his grandmother, the incomparable, imperial Caroline, still reigned over the part of New York society that really mattered, though her power was already past its zenith. The move uptown to 840 Fifth Avenue came when Vincent was three, and the story goes that on a visit to the excavations for the mock chateau his father had commissioned, Vincent burst into tears because he thought he was going to have to live in a hole in the ground.

In spite of the opulence, elegance and outbursts of formal gaiety for which those Fifth Avenue homes were famous, they provided a joyless background for a little boy. The coolness of his parents towards each other, and later their violent quarrelling, were really the least of his problems. Far worse was the fact that his father, by nature withdrawn and taciturn, found it difficult if not impossible to relate to Vincent with any warmth, while Ava could barely stand the sight of her son.

Never one to allow her own needs and demands to take second place, Ava liked to be surrounded by beautiful people as well as beautiful things, and Vincent was a bitter disappointment to her. Though far from being an ugly child, he was not built along classical lines and he grew to be lanky, loose-limbed and clumsy, constantly bumping into things or knocking something over. Ava's way of dealing with her distaste for and embarrassment at her son's lack of physical perfection was to ridicule and shame him in front of her friends and admirers. This heartless behaviour was to have a profound effect on Vincent's later relationships with women.

More immediately, Ava's cruel and unnatural punishment of her son simply for being himself provoked in him a deep and abiding hatred for her. His father's approach, on the other hand, produced distortions of a quite different kind. John Jacob IV was perfectly cast in the role of the remote, heavy-handed Victorian father and he believed that discipline and self-restraint should be the main element in the upbringing of an Astor heir. Accordingly, though surrounded by every comfort and with the possibility of obtaining every luxury, Vincent was raised in a stern and rather spartan manner. His behaviour was regulated by a series of strict rules formulated by his father, the penalty for disobedience of which was a beating with a strap or slipper, or being sent to bed without any dinner. Nor was Vincent allowed to take advantage of the legion of servants inhabiting the house: anything he wanted them to do for him had to be relayed through his parents. Another child, perhaps one with a soft and doting mother, might have rebelled against the restrictions placed on him, but not Vincent. Forced from an early age to conduct himself with solemn and dignified mien, he merely postponed his careless youth until he was older. At the same time, he developed an image of his father not far removed from the old-fashioned child's view of God – a distant, superior being controlling everything and demanding obedience as the price of his mysterious, unexpressed love.

As for affection, Vincent depended for that in his earliest years on a plump, maternal Irish nurse named Catherine Hennessey, of whom he became very fond in the time-honoured tradition of rich people's children expected to occupy only the fringes of their parents' lives. This surrogate mother was removed when Vincent was six and her place was taken by an altogether different character, a starchy German governess, though even she found a place in the heart of a boy denied real maternal protection and love. The governess was allowed to remain for only two years, however, at which time it was decided that male guidance was required and a tutor was retained to prepare Vincent for his departure to boarding school at the age of twelve.

The overwhelming impression that emerges of Vincent's childhood is not one of unhappiness or cruelty, but of solitariness and dull routine. He saw little of his parents, and playmates of his own age were few since candidates were expected to possess a family background in keeping with the status of the heir to the greatest fortune in America. Eventually there was his sister, Alice, born when Vincent was ten, but he hardly knew her until she was an adult: he went away to school when Alice was two and during his late teens the break-up of their parents' marriage took the girl away to England to live with Ava.

While under the care of his male tutor, Vincent's life was a model of regularity. He would take breakfast alone at seven-thirty each morning then work at his studies until noon, except in the winter when his lessons continued until one o'clock. After lunch he was permitted to amuse himself as best he could and, in spite of a delicate constitution that made him more than usually susceptible to childish ailments, he was an enthusiastic cyclist, roller-skater and horse rider. He would retire to bed immediately after dinner – always assuming he had committed no misdemeanours – and read until it was time to go to sleep, preferring adventure stories and counting the works of Stevenson, Kipling and Henty as chief among his favourites. It was far from being a fun-filled existence and was no doubt designed to produce yet another dour, sober, inarticulate Astor male, but its very monotony and isolation were developing in Vincent eccentricities that in later years would lead him to break the family mould.

And there were certain compensations, not the least of which was his freedom from the age of eleven to drive automobiles around the Ferncliff estate, reflecting his father's pioneer interest in motoring. What became a lifelong fascination with cars and speed began when Vincent was allowed to pilot the colonel's steam-driven Toledo in 1902 and shortly afterwards was taken on an exciting tour of Cuba and Jamaica in a two-cylinder Buick. The following year, John Jacob took Vincent along when he entered another steamer, a Locomobile, in a race at Newport, but this turned out to be less of a treat than it should have been, ending with the rather sickly twelve-year-old obliged to help his father to push the monstrous vehicle.

Vincent's health gave cause for concern throughout most of his childhood. He missed an entire year at his first prep school – Westminster, in Simsbury, Connecticut – because of sinus trouble and later underwent surgery for both appendicitis and a throat ailment. His delicate constitution prevented him from taking part in most sports, though his courage and Astor stubbornness did earn him a place in the tennis team at his senior prep school, which was St George's in Newport. Even poor health was not without some reward, however: on medical advice, he enjoyed a number of memorable winter holidays with his father in the crisp, snowy splendour of St Moritz.

His schooldays were unremarkable. Fellow 'preppies' at Westminster remembered him as something of a little Braggadochio either boasting of his lineage or singing the praises of his father's achievements and inventions. In other respects the worth of his family was not very noticeable. Vincent's allowance was a mere fifty cents a week and to maintain that paltry sum he had to ensure that his class marks were good and his behaviour unexceptionable. Even at Harvard University, which he entered in 1911, he was kept on a tight financial rein. His outgoings were expected to be no more than $2,000 a year, and included in that sum were the costs of his tuition and board. Although some undergraduates endowed him with a certain amount of notoriety in the newspaper gossip columns by spinning fabulous fictions about the supposed vastness of his wardrobe, Vincent was constantly in debt during his time at Harvard, not least because of the lavish entertaining that was considered to be incumbent upon a young man of his background. So short of funds was he that when a neat little second-hand motorcycle took his fancy he was forced to borrow forty dollars from a friend in order to buy it.

Of course, he was an Astor and he had to be taught respect for money. And in spite of the apparent recklessness of some of his later actions – reckless, that is, by traditional Astor standards – the early lessons were never forgotten. 'Each dollar,' he would intone, 'is a soldier that does your bidding.' He never felt resentment at his father's parsimony or other parental failings: to Vincent, everything the Colonel did was right and the disadvantages and disappointments of his own young life were accepted as the lot of one being trained to take command in due time of all those greenbacked soldiers. Added to which there was beneath his father's stiffness and reserve a discernible layer of affection and concern, in sharp contrast to the indifference that seemed to run right through his mother and became even more marked after the birth of Alice than it had been before. The relationship between father and son strengthened as that between father and mother gradually disintegrated. Though neither Jack nor Ava spent a great deal of time with their children, when they did feel able to provide parental company it was done separately, the Colonel taking Vincent on a cruise to the West Indies, for instance, while Ava and Alice travelled in Europe. After the divorce in 1909, it was Vincent who stood next to Jack in the receiving line for the last great ball at 840 Fifth Avenue – the father he worshipped was taking proper notice of him at last.

Things changed, of course, in the autumn of 1911 when John Jacob IV married a girl younger than his own son, but before Vincent's disapproval had time to harden into bitterness his father was dead and could be placed on a pedestal for ever.

In view of the awkwardness and emptiness of his family life, it may seem surprising that the young Vincent was not a sullen, introverted character but a high-spirited, friendly and likeable youth. His two great passions were cars and the sea and while the latter was temporarily stilled by his father's refusal to let him attend the United States Naval Academy at Annapolis, the former could be given free rein, often with unfortunate results. Though he loved driving, he was never very good at it: he was impatient, disinclined to think of his own or other people's safety and unable to judge how fast was too fast. Though the automobiles of the early 1900s look quaint and harmless now, they were as lethal as anything on a modern highway and both Vincent and the residents of Dutchess County and Newport had some narrow escapes.

In fact, Vincent was lucky ever to reach Harvard in 1911, for that summer he had received permission from his father to transform a modest tourer into a stripped-down racing machine and had challenged his friend Herman Oelrichs to race against him in a similar vehicle along a Rhode Island beach. The two young drivers reached eighty miles an hour, then Oelrichs had to jump for his life when his car burst into flames. Watching the spectacle, Vincent lost control of his racer on a bumpy patch of sand and roared into the sea, emerging wet, shaken but miraculously unhurt. On another occasion he ruffled the fine plumage of Newport's migratory millionaire class by unceremoniously removing the rear bumper of a car conveying Mrs Ogden Goelet, having failed to observe that the vehicle, which was in front of him, was making a turn. More seriously, driving too fast, as usual, near Tarrytown, New York, he ran a motorcyclist off the road then crashed into a tree, fortunately without any real harm to either himself or his victim. His record of convictions for speeding and other motoring offences was a long one, the usual penalties being fines and stern lectures from judges.

Appropriately enough, an automobile figured strongly in one of the more romantic episodes of Vincent's brief college career. In common with other young men about Harvard, Vincent spent a lot of time during the Christmas vacation seeing the hits of the New York theatre season. While engaged on this cultural odyssey in 1911, he fell under the spell of the beautiful and talented Ina Claire, who was starring in *The Quaker Girl* on Broadway, and he could not rest until he had secured a date with her. At first the actress gently rebuffed the impetuous undergraduate but his persistence eventually wore her down and she agreed to have supper with him one evening after the show. Vincent desperately wanted to impress Miss Claire with the image of a dashing man of the world and to achieve that, he felt, he needed a fast car. An urgent canvass of his friends yielded no one who was both willing and able to lend one (hardly surprising in view of Vincent's reputation as a driver) and since he did not own a car himself he was on the verge of despair when inspiration struck: he might have no automobile himself, but his father had thirty garaged at Ferncliff, and his father was away on holiday with his new bride. Vincent immediately took the train to Rhinebeck and surveyed the vehicular harem. There was nothing that could really be called sporty, but there was a little Stearns runabout that might be made into something. Gathering up a variety of tools, including an axe, Vincent set to work stripping off extraneous bodywork, removing the bumpers and, in a further flash of inspiration, cutting out the muffler so that the engine made an authentic throaty roar. The result was not exactly pretty but it was a fair imitation of a racing car, so with cap and goggles to complete the picture Vincent roared into the city to claim his fair lady and take her on an ear-splitting drive before treating her to supper.

Miss Claire must have been somewhat impressed – though she was probably more amused than anything else – for she allowed Vincent to take her out several times. It was no more than a mild flirtation, but it made Vincent a hero at Harvard, where the story of his conquest, no doubt greatly exaggerated, was a source of admiration and entertainment for quite some time.

The sequel to the affair, however, was tragic for Vincent, who was neither to enjoy his new reputation as a ladies' man for very long nor to face the consequences of having broken up his father's car. As we have seen, John Jacob IV never reached home and his son's careless youth came to an abrupt end.

As it happened, Vincent was in New York City on the morning of 15 April 1912, when news of the *Titanic* came through by radio. When he was told of the collision he was only mildly concerned, for after all the great ship was said to be unsinkable. But when he found the offices of the White Star Line, the ship's owners, besieged by distraught relatives of the passengers, he began to worry and he burst into tears as it was

215

announced that the rescue ship *Carpathia* had accounted for only 703 of the 2,200 people aboard the *Titanic*. Rushing to his father's office on West 26th Street, he rounded up the staff and with them spent the entire night telephoning newspapers and wire services in an attempt to discover whether the Colonel was among the survivors of the disaster. No information could be obtained, so at breakfast time on the 16th Vincent returned home for his first meal in twenty-four hours then, having bathed and changed, went back to the office. While the quest for news continued, he persuaded his father's business partners to donate $10,000 to a fund established for the benefit of needy families of the *Titanic*'s victims.

At five o'clock that afternoon, the names of the survivors were released: Madeleine Astor was on the list, John Jacob was not. Vincent collapsed and had to be taken home, but next morning he was at his father's desk again and on the telephone, clinging desperately and pathetically to the hope that the Colonel, a strong swimmer, had somehow survived. For more than a week he refused to believe that his father was dead, until finally there came a message from one of the ships on the scene, the *Mackay-Bennett*, that Colonel Astor's body had been recovered. The *Mackay-Bennett* reported that she was heading for Halifax, Nova Scotia, and Vincent was there to meet her when she docked about a week later. As he accompanied the body back home by train, he could take some comfort from the stories he had heard of his father's calmness and courage as the *Titanic* went down: the image of the hero remained untarnished.

The whole community turned out for the funeral at Rhinebeck on 3 May. Some of the most honoured names in the county formed the party of pallbearers and the Prince of Wales sent flowers. There was no eulogy, at the insistence of Vincent, but two days later, during the Sunday services at St Thomas's church on Fifth Avenue, the rector of that most fashionable parish delivered what he called his glorious epitaph to John Jacob IV: 'He died like a brave man.'

Of course, John Jacob IV also died a very rich man and for the first time the exact worth of an Astor became a matter of public record. Current rumour put the fortune at $175 million, but the official appraisal of the Colonel's estate showed it to be rather more than half that sum, $87,218,000, with by far the largest part, some sixty-three million dollars, remaining in real estate. Ferncliff was valued at about half a million dollars, 840 Fifth Avenue at just over six hundred thousand, not counting its art collection. There was more than half a million in cash deposited with the Astor Trust Company and a further quarter of a million dollars on deposit with Morgan, Grenfell.

It almost goes without saying that the will was awaited with great interest. Not only had the Astors' lack of generosity grown into something of a legend, but in this case there was also a very young, pregnant second wife to be taken into account. Jaws dropped when it was disclosed that, firstly, Madeleine had been persuaded to sell her widow's right in the estate for a pre-marriage settlement of a paltry $1,695,000 and, secondly, she had been granted the income from a five million dollar trust fund, plus the use of the homes on Fifth Avenue and at Newport, only on the condition that she did not remarry. This was seen as unbelievably harsh treatment of a girl with most of her life still ahead of her and although it did not seem to affect Madeleine herself very much, it was to be a source of deep resentment in her as yet unborn son, for whom the will provided a three million dollar trust fund.

If anything, John Jacob IV proved himself to be even less of a philanthropist than his forebears. The extent of his charitable bequests ran to modest sums for Astor trustees and some employees, and $30,000 for his old prep school, St Paul's. His only contribution to the public good was $3,274,000 in estate duty, a little more than three and a half per cent of his fortune, which in the midst of a swelling tide of radicalism was considered a derisory amount.

The remainder of the estate was Vincent's to do with as he wished when he became twenty-one. As well as being the youngest Astor heir, he had the distinction of being the first to be allowed complete mastery over his inheritance, John Jacob IV having ignored the family tradition of leaving half in trust. It was a mixed blessing as far as the recipient was concerned. On the one hand, Vincent was conscious of the great power that had been placed in his hands and aware that he was now in a position to indulge his every dream; on the other hand, he saw clearly his responsibilities as both the head of the Astor family in America and the steward of a vast fortune carefully nurtured over many years. At the same time, he was in a more difficult position than any previous Astor heir had been because of fundamental changes in the public mood. The banner of social justice had been raised and, though its followers were to make considerably more progress elsewhere, even in America the holders of great wealth were being challenged to prove their value to society at large. Inherited wealth was a particular target of idealistic and vociferous social reformers: in 1912 one radical in the United States Senate went so far as to propose that fortunes such as that which had recently passed to Vincent Astor should be subject to an estate duty of seventy-five per cent, and although the forces of entrenched privilege quickly combined to kill the proposal, it indicated that henceforth the rich were going to be on the defensive. Rich they might continue to be, but they were no longer to be permitted to remain idle and there was going to be a determined attempt to make them use the surpluses they clearly did not need for the good of the less exalted people who formed the soil in which the flower of wealth might flourish. In an emerging new scale of values, the established owners of land and property were to be regarded as less worthy than the aggressive entrepreneurs and merchant princes who were (and still are) perceived as benefiting the nation as a whole while lining their own pockets.

Vincent Astor, young, naive and romantic, saw before him the path to true happiness. He would set out not to make more money but merely to hold on to what he had, which would in any case provide him with a continuing surplus sufficient to indulge his budding social conscience and to set the Astor name, of which he was very proud, for the first time among the ranks of public benefactors. After his father's will was published, he told a reporter: 'It is my duty to show my gratitude now by taking an interest in great public movements and in every way to attempt to aid mankind.' Coming from an Astor, that sounded like heresy and Vincent was to discover that the road of the heretic does not necessarily lead into a golden sunset.

Still, he set forth with hope in his heart. Abandoning Harvard without much regret, he devoted himself to learning all there was to know about the real estate business in which so much of his inheritance resided. On hand to guide him were his father's trusted associates Nicholas Biddle, who had managed the estate office for many years, Douglas Robinson, William A. Dobbyn and James Roosevelt Roosevelt, Vincent's uncle by marriage and half-brother of Franklin Roosevelt. This quartet did its best to instruct the new player in the rather doleful but nevertheless highly profitable music of his ancestors and after seven months' tuition handed him the baton, not, it is to be imagined, without a certain amount of trepidation.

II

On his twenty-first birthday, Vincent spent the morning in the office on West 26th Street then in the afternoon drove to Rhinebeck and passed a pleasant hour or two sailing on the Hudson. In the evening he dined with his mother and sister, who had come from London to keep him company (Ava no doubt also to offer her own advice as to Vincent's future conduct), then strolled out to the garage to revel once more in the collection of automobiles he had inherited. That collection grew when, as one of his first acts upon coming into his fortune, he purchased two racing cars (one costing $6,000 and previously driven professionally) with which he was to alarm the road users of Dutchess County even more than he had done before.

The day after celebrating his majority, he was at his desk in the city by nine o'clock and already planning what amounted to a revolution in Astor business practice. The careful explanations of his father's associates, far from moulding Vincent to the traditional pattern, had convinced him, in the light of his own researches, that the operating principles of the Astor Estate were wrong. The notion of buying land in the right places and simply holding on to it until the demand for development forced up the price had worked extremely well in the early days of New York City's growth, but now it was virtually impossible to forecast in which direction the metropolis would spread next and consequently it was the developer rather than the landowner who was making most of the running in real estate. The day of continuous construction had arrived. Accordingly, within three months of assuming command of the Astor Estate,

Vincent announced that the company was going into the property development business. His colleagues were startled: the only buildings ever erected by Astors had been their own mansions and the luxury hotels that had afforded them so much prestige – the Astor House, the St Regis, the Knickerbocker and the great Waldorf-Astoria. But Vincent insisted that not only was construction likely to be very profitable, it would also help to remove from the Astor name the stain of the slumlord. After all these years, he believed, it was time the Astors were accorded a little goodwill.

After carefully assessing the various parts of Manhattan in which he owned land or property, Vincent chose Broadway as his first development site, erecting an apartment house between 89th Street and 90th at a cost of one and a half million dollars. Encouraged by the success of that venture, Vincent announced his intention of building an office block at the other end of Broadway, between Barclay and Vesey streets on the site of the old Astor House, which had been demolished in the course of subway development. This happened to be the block next to the recently completed Woolworth Tower, then the tallest sky-scraper in the world, and the real estate fraternity had visions of an even bigger edifice rising to overshadow the creation of this parvenu shopkeeper Frank Winfield Woolworth. Vincent, however, was not looking for that kind of prestige and erected a mere eight-storey block which was quickly rented, as he had guessed it would be. Word spread that the new hope of the house of Astor was something of an operator and property men began to wonder where his new policy would lead.

But Vincent's ambitions lay in other directions, too. In the spirit of his promise to do all he could to aid mankind, he paid a visit in February 1913 to the Governor of New York, William Sulzer, seeking advice as to how he and his money might be best employed on behalf of the public. Sulzer, who combined a healthy respect for wealth with an extravagantly romantic turn of mind (or at least of phrase) drew for his solemn young guest a metaphorical picture of a house with ten windows, each one offering a view over some field of useful endeavour. Vincent was impressed by the presentation but not particularly excited by the outlook through the windows, until Sulzer led him to the one that opened on to agriculture. 'That's my window,'

Vincent is reputed to have said, adding that he would give the state his farm at Rhinebeck for use as an experimental station whose research findings could be used to help the whole farming community. Overcome with enthusiasm, Sulzer promptly named Vincent as a delegate to an international agricultural conference that was to be held in Rome the following May. Vincent later decided not to attend the conference, but he retained his interest in farming, became a prize apple-grower, tested a new variety of oats, raised Angus beef cattle and was elected vice-president of the Dutchess County Agricultural Society.

None of this, though, completely fulfilled Vincent's desire to serve the people and during 1913 he began poking his head through a number of windows Governor Sulzer had not even thought of. He joined the National Civic Federation, a coalition of conservative businessmen and union leaders, and was appointed chairman of a committee set up to examine laws relating to food and drugs at both state and national level. He served as a director of the Public Schools Athletic League and made a point of attending all of the league's mass exhibitions, observing that in such activities lay a source not only of physical development but also of moral and social improvement. Like his father before him, he was a patron of the Police Honor Legion. He was made an honorary deputy sheriff of Dutchess County and a member of the Rhinebeck baseball club, to which he presented a playing field and grandstand. The Rhinebeck Fire Department offered him the chairmanship of a committee formed to raise funds for a motorized fire engine and he responded to the honour by paying for the engine himself. New York Hospital made him a governor, he joined the state naval militia and he served on housing committees in Manhattan and the Bronx. It seemed that almost any sphere of public service was worthy of his attention, even politics: he served as campaign treasurer for John Purroy Mitchell, the so-called Fusion candidate in the New York City mayoral election, and after Mitchell's victory joined the mayor's committee on unemployment. In Dutchess County, Vincent was one of the leaders of a campaign against vote-buying, and at a much less parochial level he lent his name to a civil rights campaign on behalf of Jews in Romania, declaring with impressive but dubious authority that, 'Romania's injustice to her Jewish subjects has long been a world scandal.' Perhaps he thought there really was something in a lurking suspicion that the Astors had Jewish ancestry.

Vincent also displayed a rather alarming tendency to put his money where his mouth was. He upset many among his own class by joining in one of the periodic rows over the allotment of playground space in Central Park with the observation that it was 'better to have dead grass in the park than sick children in the tenements', and followed this up by establishing a playground in Harlem on a plot of land with a market value of a million dollars. During the steamy New York summer, he invited hordes of slum children and their mothers to boat trips and beach parties. The soapbox radicals of Union Square sneered at such 'paternalism', but one passionate reformer saw the possibility of striking a blow for socialism in the very midst of the ruling class.

Upton Sinclair, finding fame with his novels exposing the underside of American working-class life and a founder with Jack London of the Intercollegiate Socialist Society, wrote to Vincent Astor early in 1914 in the following terms: 'It is a monstrous thing that in a country of such natural resources as our own millions should have to suffer the horrors of destitution. I cannot believe that a man who is young and has his life before him can be wholly indifferent to the conditions... The poor people see in the papers the pictures of your magnificent and luxurious home and they realize that it is out of the rents which they pay in one form or another that all this luxury comes...' Revolution was in the air, Sinclair insisted – 'listen to the rumble of the approaching storm'. The time had come for Astor to give up playing the public benefactor and to show his true mettle by declaring for the Socialist Party.

Naive Vincent may have been, but he was certainly smart enough to know that socialism was not the American way, and there were plenty of older, wiser friends to silence any doubts he might have had that capitalism was the way, the truth and the life. He wrote a well-rehearsed reply pointing to the 'fallacious and impracticable' nature of socialism and asserting that although 'I am not unmindful of the wrongs to be righted, and that it is the duty of every man who has the interest of his country at heart to do what he properly can to establish and maintain industrial and social righteousness ... I am fully convinced that the serious evils which have attended our industrial development can be and will be in time eradicated without overturning the fundamental basis upon which our government and social fabric is founded.'

To an establishment based upon revolution and yet terrified of it ever since, Vincent's letter was a well-aimed broadside at the advocates of reform at all costs. Conservative newspapers showered praise on Vincent's head and even the American Federation of Labor – never as fanatical as the British model – lined up behind him. The blow Sinclair had hoped to strike had rebounded and the writer was reduced to comforting himself by grumbling about the power of wealth in the ordering of public affairs.

Not all of Vincent's sallies into public affairs, however, were so successful or so warmly applauded. The spring of 1913 found him tramping the streets of a shabby neighbourhood on the West Side knocking on the doors of houses he owned and questioning the tenants. Sometimes the only answer he would get was the door slammed in his face, in which case he would doggedly pass on to the next house and repeat the interrogation. The newspapers naturally made inquiries into this bizarre behaviour and discovered that the young property magnate, supported by a team of private eyes, was personally checking into rumours that some of the houses he owned were being operated as brothels. Where the suspicions were confirmed, he either evicted the tenants, when such action was legally possible, or informed the police, who raided the offending premises. Vincent piously made it known that he could not bear to profit indirectly from vice, but for all his high-mindedness the instances of prostitution actually revealed were few, the number of outraged tenants was large in proportion, and the attendant publicity was extremely unwelcome. Like many other innocent would-be benefactor, Vincent was beginning to discover that suffering humanity tends to want to choose the ways in which it will be helped.

The newspaper headlines occasioned by Vincent's good works were as nothing compared to the attention focused on the more romantic side of his life. He was young, he was rich and he was single, and the coverage he got was of the kind we nowadays associate with film stars, pop idols and princes. There were feature articles about and photographs of his various homes, and the gossip writers 'announced' his engagement to literally scores of society maidens. In May 1913, when he presented new flags to the Police Honor Legion, he was mobbed by a large crowd of girls and women and had to be escorted in and out of the hall by a phalanx of policemen.

It was not that he was particularly handsome – indeed, probably the best way of describing him in one word is with the American term 'homely'. Six feet four in height, he was hollow-chested and had inherited his father's receding forehead and protruding upper lip, fashion dictating that he should not disguise the latter feature with a heavy moustache as the Colonel had done. His movements were abrupt and ungainly and he was cursed with inordinately large feet that splayed outwards, penguin-like, when he walked. On the other hand he could be a passionate lover, was kind, amiable (except first thing in the morning) and generous, and he was a good conversationalist, although his speech was rapid and somewhat indistinct and he developed the irritating habit of cupping his hand round his right ear to give the impression of not having heard something for which he was unprepared.

In spite of all the speculation – and no doubt to the chagrin of many a Manhattan matron – Vincent's choice of a bride was both surprising and safe. Helen Dinsmore Huntington had never been in the running according to the society gossips, but she enjoyed the advantage of having known Vincent all his life since her father's estate, Hopeland House, was very near Ferncliff. She was tall, sporty, intelligent, well educated, steady and dependable, unostentatious and of impeccable background, tracing her descent not only from one of the signers of the Declaration of Independence but also from the founder of the famous Adams Express Company. The engagement was announced on 8 November 1913 and the wedding took place on 30 April 1914, having been postponed because Vincent had failed to recover in time from an illness brought on by overwork. The spring weather was damp and dismal and the bridegroom was brought to the ceremony in a wheelchair, but the affair was everything it was expected to be, with breathtaking banks of flowers, an entire orchestra to provide the music and a dazzling parade of the New York elite. Afterwards the couple spent a month or two cruising on Vincent's yacht (the *Noma*, inherited from his father) then returned to New York to take up their position as – never mind who was in the White House – 'America's Number One Family'.

Not that Vincent and Helen were by any means leaders of society in the conventional sense, despite the fact that for the first ten years or so of their marriage they dwelt in the marble halls which had once been the meeting place of The Four Hundred. Indeed, the master of Caroline Astor's household, Thomas Hade, remained at his post for some time overseeing the regular domestic staff of twenty people. But the great days of 840 Fifth Avenue had passed beyond recall. Both Vincent and Helen deplored any vulgar parade of wealth and saw it as the responsibility of the very rich to use their position to promote the well-being of the community as a whole. As a result, much of their large-scale entertaining was born of charitable intent, like the 'Make Americans' banquets they hosted with the aim of finding some way to make it easier for immigrants to be assimilated into the life of the New World. Academics, social workers and high officials of the immigration service would sit in the vast dining room discussing questions such as why immigrants tended to huddle in ethnic groups and cling to the cultures and traditions of the countries they had abandoned, or whether the labour troubles and social disturbances of the day were the result of immigrants somehow failing to become fully committed Americans.

The tradition of the Astors' January ball was maintained for several years and, though it was rather less formal then it had been in the time of *the* Mrs Astor, it was no less splendid. There was some broadening of the guest list, however, which Ward McAllister would never have tolerated. Mingling with the descendants of the original Four Hundred were such undesirables as actors, politicians and even Roman Catholics. Worse still, one of the balls was organized as a charity affair, with the guests obliged to buy old crockery and then, urged on by Vincent, to smash it by throwing baseballs. The event was a great success, but Caroline would not have been amused.

On the whole, Vincent and Helen did not care for formality

and preferred to entertain privately. 'It is pretty hard now to get me to a formal function,' Helen was once quoted as saying, 'but it is infinitely harder to get my husband. In the evenings he wants to hear real talk and see real people.' Such people might include writers, journalists, political leaders and even boxers – Vincent loved to go to the fights.

More conventional was life at Beechwood in the summer, for Newport continued to be a redoubt for the old guard of New York society, with the Vanderbilts, Van Halens, Bruguieres and Goelets protecting their compounds against incursions from the wealthy but nevertheless unacceptable mercantile class. Mornings would be spent on Bailey's Beach; lunch would be taken at The Casino and followed by golf or tennis for the younger members of the clique; in the early evening there were bridge parties (which Vincent hated and always avoided) and later on liveried servants would wait on gatherings at one or other of the 'cottages'. Even more than the nouveau riche, boredom was the bugbear of Newport, and Vincent kept his yacht nearby in case he should feel the need to return to the real world of New York City or escape from the empty chatter and ceaseless socializing by heading off on a cruise.

The world of the old families and everyone else, however, began to change within a few months of the Astors' marriage. America was not immediately affected by the outbreak of the First World War, other than by the annoyance of the British naval blockade and harassment of neutral shipping, but nevertheless a strong body of conservative opinion supported Britain and her allies and accepted the possibility of eventual military involvement. After the sinking on 7 May 1915 of the Cunard liner *Lusitania* by a German U-boat, with the loss of American lives, those in the United States talking of 'preparedness' (including Vincent Astor) began to gather a majority of the public behind them. Vincent himself was engaged in building up the strength of the New York state naval militia, in which he then held the rank of ensign. A few years earlier he had become passionately interested in flying, having taken a trip in a German airship, and had in fact been offered command of an airforce by another aviation fanatic, ex-King Manuel of Portugal. The king had met Vincent on a transatlantic voyage and, since Astor was still fresh with the excitement of his first flight, the talk naturally turned to aircraft. King Manuel spoke enthusiastically of his own airforce and his plans to expand it through the purchase of a second plane: Vincent would be just the man to take command, the king suggested, with perhaps the title of Duke of Astor – come the counter-revolution, of course. Vincent was sceptical, as well he might have been, and he never did get the chance to command the Portuguese airforce because the exiled king's attempt to regain his throne was a failure. But Astor did assume command of one of the New York militia's first airborne battalions in 1915.

He had been taking flying lessons from W. Starling Burgess, whose aircraft factory at Marblehead, Massachusetts, he had visited and who had first taken him up in a 'string bag' biplane. At the end of his course of instruction, Astor bought a Burgess-Dunne seaplane, had it transported to Rhinebeck and swooped over the countryside at an airspeed of fifty miles an hour, using the Hudson River as his landing strip. Impressed, the naval militia, which already had one seaplane, made Vincent chairman of a committee to raise funds for a second aircraft, whereupon Astor did the decent thing and bought for the unit a Burgess-Dunne like his own. In the face of such generosity, it would have been churlish not to have offered him a command.

He was active on the water, too, pioneering the use of light, high-speed boats to hunt submarines. He gave a dramatic exhibition of the technique off Newport, overtaking and 'sinking' a submarine with a speedboat. And neither was he above doing his stint of less exhilarating shore duty, such as guarding Brooklyn Bridge against possible sabotage.

Inevitably, the Astor fortune was of some importance to the American backers of Britain and the allies. Vincent contributed a substantial sum to the first War Loan raised by the financier John Pierpont Morgan, Jr, which critics later claimed put pressure on President Woodrow Wilson to commit American troops to the European conflict. In 1917, when the United States entered the war, Vincent put two million dollars into the so-called Liberty Loan, turned over his yacht to the navy, put Ferncliff at the disposal of the government as a hospital and offered financial inducements to employees of the estate to volunteer for military service.

Much more important to him, though, was the realization

that at last he was able to achieve his boyhood ambition of going into the navy. His service record is somewhat confusing, but it seems that his first posting was as a junior officer aboard his own yacht, commanding a gun. Later he was sent as a port officer to Bordeaux, a desk job that had the advantage of allowing him to spend plenty of time with Helen, who was working in a Y.M.C.A. canteen nearby. He apparently did see some action when he was transferred to the coastal patrol vessel *Aphrodite* (as senior lieutenant, he was the ship's executive officer) and he may even have come under fire, although most of the German submarines that were encountered ran without a fight and were almost impossible, in the days before sonar equipment, to destroy or even detect when submerged. None the less, war was a thrilling experience for Vincent, as it had been for his father. Arriving home aboard a captured U-boat he declared: 'I can say that I have thoroughly enjoyed every minute of the service that I have been able to render my country.'

But now it was back to business, with an inheritance to protect against a background of sudden and seemingly erratic change. Unlike his predecessors, this Astor could not simply sit back and watch his money breed.

Vincent had already broken with tradition by becoming a property developer as opposed to merely a property owner and his building operations continued to the tune of about three million dollars a year – though not all his projects were attended by success. He spent almost a quarter of a million dollars on the construction of a magnificent public market on Broadway at 90th Street, but within twelve months of its completion he was obliged to sell it at a loss. It was a case of the do-gooder in him triumphing over the businessman. He was carried away by the vision of creating a significant improvement in what we now call the 'urban environment' and he spared no expense: the terrazzo was fashioned by craftsmen brought from Italy and a Californian artist was hired to paint some of the largest murals ever seen in America. Unfortunately, the spiritual qualities of the building were not appreciated enough to make it anything more than a nine days' wonder and the high hopes and high prices of the traders profited no one in the end. Perhaps it was simply ahead of its time. How different things might have been given the sort of tourist industry that underpins such modern 'olde worlde' projects as the new Covent Garden Market in London, or Fanueil Hall in Boston, or Gastown in Vancouver.

Such failures, however, were rare at this stage of Vincent's career. Most of his developments were well thought out, needed, and profitable. On the other hand, the buildings he already owned, the real estate he had inherited in 1912, produced less and less profit during the First World War and the years immediately following it, partly because of ever-increasing real estate taxes and partly because many of the buildings were in districts no longer considered desirable. It has been estimated that between 1914 and 1919 Vincent's taxable income – most of which, of course, still came from property – was cut in half, with a continuing decline projected.* It did not in the least worry Vincent that the name of Astor was no longer placed at the very top of America's millionaire class, but there certainly was cause for anxiety in the realization that unless he did something he would be hard pressed to hold on to what he had inherited. He could not count on growing fat, as his ancestors had done, on the rents his property brought in, so again he found himself departing from established family policy. In 1919, he began to dispose of some of the jewels of the Astor empire.

The site of the Paramount Theatre building was sold for $3,845,000; the Schermerhorn Building on Broadway went for one and a half million dollars; in Times Square, the Longacre Building fetched more than two and a half million; the great Waldorf-Astoria Hotel was demolished to make way for the Empire State Building, Vincent and the British Astors each receiving $7,560,000 from the sale. Indeed, Vincent pulled out altogether from the hotel business, suffering as it was from the lunacy of the Volstead Act of 1919, which began the fourteen years of Prohibition: the St Regis was sold and the Knickerbocker was converted into a high-rent office block.

* No official figures are available and most Astor documents appear to have been destroyed, accidentally or otherwise, but published estimates put the income at about three million dollars in 1914 and $1,367,000 in 1919. It actually dropped, again according to estimate, in 1920 to under $800,000 but four years later it was a more healthy $1,900,000, as reported to the Internal Revenue Service, whose figures were publicly available from that year.

This purge of white elephants even extended to Vincent's own home, sold for three and a half million dollars to the Jewish Temple Emanu-el. In 1926, after a final, nostalgic January ball, the ghost of *the* Mrs Astor was buried under the rubble of 840 Fifth Avenue and her grandson moved into a modest Georgian-style town house at 130 East 80th Street, built for what in Astor terms was no more than small change – a quarter of a million dollars. (Perhaps Caroline's spirit was somewhat mollified when the Astor Estate bought and demolished the Vanderbilt mansion that had struck her pride such a blow.) The shade of John Jacob IV, however, moved with his son. Vincent had his father's old bedroom recreated in the house on East 80th, complete with the bathroom and its fireplace.

The liquidation – realizing some forty million dollars over a little more than ten years, which represented a gain of five million over the book value of the properties sold – would no doubt have won the approval of John Jacob I, accomplished as it was on a rising market for real estate sales. Some of the founder's descendants, though, might have balked at the way Vincent set about redeploying his capital, since he chose to reinvest only part of it in property while the remainder went into a variety of stocks and shares, not to mention a motion picture. During the 1920s he joined the boards of American Express, the City and Suburban Homes Company, the Chase National Bank, Western Union Telegraph, the Fruit and Sugar Securities Company and four railroads – the Great Northern, the Illinois Central, the Dubuque and Sioux City, and the Chicago, St Louis and New Orleans. Two companies of which he was a director were particularly dear to his heart, International Mercantile Marine and the North Atlantic Steamship Corporation: 'Shipping', he once said, 'is about the only business that's still got romance in it.' Old John Jacob would no doubt have endorsed that view, too.

The movie in which Vincent invested was *Ben Hur*, the first film version of the Lew Wallace novel, made by MGM in 1926 with Ramon Novarro and Francis X. Bushman as the stars. The film was a sensation and grossed ten million dollars, giving Vincent a profit of $371,000 on a stake of just under a quarter of a million. That windfall did not go back into the business.

Never one to deny himself, Vincent put it towards the purchase of a new luxury yacht.

Stocks and movies, however, could never replace land and property as the foundation of the Astor fortune, and Vincent showed a good deal of shrewdness in carrying out his development policy. The tenements which had been the Astors' bread and butter for years were emptying, partly because many of those who filled them now sought homes in the rapidly growing suburbs and also because there was no longer an unlimited supply of immigrants to take their place.

The suburb, as one commentator put it, 'is not primarily a mechanism, nor is it in any sense a modification of something previously existing; it is a world peculiar to itself and – as with a theatre's drop scene – before and behind it there is nothing.'* That kind of shot-in-the-dark development Vincent was content to leave largely to others: his one major venture in suburban real estate was the acquisition of three hundred and twenty-two acres at Port Washington, on Long Island, where he built what in America is called a subdivision (in England it would be a select housing estate) with a private beach, a casino, tennis courts and bridle paths. He was much more at home in the modification business and he guessed correctly that in Manhattan there was a need for the developer who could take a rundown tenement and convert it into well-appointed accommodation for the people most likely to want and best able to afford the attractions city life had to offer.

One district ripe for a well-heeled invasion was that in which Vincent placed his new home, the East Eighties. This blighted area between First Avenue and the East River had fallen into decay as its inhabitants, encouraged by the easy transportation furnished by subway development, had moved outwards into newer and less crowded regions. The focal point of the neighbourhood was the Carl Schurz Park, and it was here that Vincent erected three high-rise blocks of luxury apartments. Other tenement buildings were gutted and transformed into small flats at rents of between $600 and $1,000 a year. As an indication of the general raising of the tone of the district, the deadeningly named Avenues A and B – the main north-south

* J.M. Richards in *The Castles on the Ground*, published by The Architectural Press, London, in 1946.

thoroughfares – were rechristened York Avenue and East End Avenue (later the East River Drive). The project was not without a certain irony for Astor: it was almost the exact spot from which, in the garden of his country home, John Jacob I had watched the ships passing through Hellgate.

Of course, being landlord to the professional classes was a very different proposition from owning tenements and Vincent prided himself on the care he took of his tenants. Difficulties over unreliable elevators or the collection of garbage received his personal attention, while the doormen of his buildings were handpicked to suit the needs and overall character of the occupants. This was another radical departure from the Astor way of doing things. Who among his predecessors would have given a thought to the quality of life of the people whose rent money maintained the Astor family in the style to which it had become accustomed? Indeed, it is doubtful whether any of them had the slightest idea of what a tenant might look like.

It was perfectly in keeping with Vincent's social conscience that he should make money out of those able to pay high rents rather than exploiting people to whom any form of expenditure was a burden. It was also good business. But he did not forget that the less well off also needed places to live. In the Bronx he invested nearly a million dollars in the creation of one of the area's first fire-proof apartment complexes, converting an entire block into low-rental units overlooking a landscaped square. So pleased was he with this development that he named it Astor Concourse. The stain of the slumlord was to be removed at all costs. When, in the early 1930s, the *New York Post* went gunning for Astor and other tenement owners after a number of catastrophic fires in the Lower East Side, Vincent immediately contacted the city housing authority with an offer to sell it fourteen tenements on the Third Street block of Avenue A (York Avenue) at their assessed valuation of $442,500, of which only about a quarter covered the actual buildings. It is in the nature of bureaucracies to move slowly and the housing authority was no exception, in spite of the fact that its plans for public housing had yet to show some practical result, so Vincent gave it a little push by moving the occupants out of the buildings and helping them to find other accommodation. Still there were delays as the housing authority tried to make up its mind, then Vincent grew impatient and told the housing commissioner to 'write his own ticket' – which proved, in round figures, to be rather less than half the assessed value of the site. Some other owners of slum property blanched when Vincent accepted the offer and work began on the housing authority's inaugural project, called, with unarguable logic, First Houses and still to be seen today. But Astor insisted it was not an act of philanthropy, citing the appalling condition of the buildings, several of which had to be demolished. The truth is, that sale was worth as much again to him in terms of prestige: they were the last tenements ever to be operated by the Astors.

Providing for the poor, too, was turning out to be sound business practice and Vincent Astor acquired the reputation of being the best businessman in the family since the Founder.

III

In learning the family business and successfully adapting its operations to rapidly changing times, Vincent Astor displayed a remarkable degree of maturity. No doubt his rather curious upbringing had its part to play in this, since it had required him to develop early a serious and responsible attitude towards life in general and money in particular, to be adult before his time. The repression of natural, childish exuberance, however, and the notable absence of fun in Vincent's young life carried a price which was to be paid by the man himself, by the women in his life and ultimately by the whole Astor family in America.

While the early death of John Jacob IV demanded that Vincent be in some respects even more serious-minded than before, at another level it gave him the opportunity to enjoy what had until then more or less been denied him – his boyhood. He inherited the money and the power to indulge his fantasies and, since his father was dead and he was estranged from his mother, there was no one to keep him in check. The result was that, to the end of his life, Vincent never quite grew up, remaining naively romantic, impatient, self-indulgent, temperamental, dependent, restless and in many other ways adolescent.

By far his greatest romantic, boyish attachment was to the sea. Tales of the rolling deep were among his favourite reading matter and for many years his yacht was the mainstay of his life, though not, as had been the case with his father and grand-father, because it provided an escape from unhappy domesti-city. With Vincent it was simply a matter of fulfilling his teenage dream of being a sailor.

He had inherited two yachts from his father, the *Noma* and the ill-omened *Nourmahal* which had caused John Jacob IV so much trouble. The former was donated to the war effort in 1917 and Vincent never got it back from the Navy (one reason why he was more than a little upset to be accused of war profiteering by the Senate commission on munitions). The *Nourmahal* was soon outgrown by Vincent's maritime ambitions and after the resounding success of his film venture in 1926 he decided to build a larger boat.

This new *Nourmahal*, paid for partly through the sale of the old one and partly by the profits from *Ben Hur*, was built at Kiel in Germany at a cost of one and three-quarter million dollars – seven times the price of Vincent's new home on East 80th Street. Her diesel engines gave her a cruising speed of sixteen knots and a range of twenty thousand miles, and into her length of two hundred and sixty-four feet was crammed all the latest in nautical equipment. Her accommodation was spacious, to say the least: eleven state rooms on three decks, several lounges and a walnut-panelled dining room with seating for eighteen people, a library clad in pine and, in case of emergency, a fully equipped operating theatre. There were even cabins for all the officers of the forty-two man crew. The yacht's operating costs ran to about $125,000 a year, and as far as Vincent was concerned she was worth every penny.

He did not captain the *Nourmahal* himself, despite his love and knowledge of the sea and ships (he knew the vital statistics of every vessel in *Janes Fighting Ships* and could give precise descriptions of everything the U.S. Navy had in the water). The skippering was done by a Swede named Captain Klang, while Vincent's role was more that of admiral and entertainments officer combined.

Two, three or more months each year were spent on full-scale cruises, usually in the Caribbean or the South Pacific. Vincent would invite a select company of friends and on some occasions he took along marine biologists to collect rare tropical fish which were presented to either the aquarium in New York or the one in Bermuda, where Vincent kept a holiday home for a number of years.

Other diversions provided for the cruise parties were less scientific. During a winter voyage in 1937, Vincent handed out picks and shovels to his guests and led them ashore on tiny, remote Charles Island, one of the Galapagos group, to hunt for a secret cave where he suspected the body of a supposed murder victim might have been hidden. Charles Island had become internationally famous during the early thirties following a succession of mysterious disappearances among an odd assortment of refugees from civilization who had taken up residence there. Having met some of these people in the course of his ocean wanderings, Vincent was naturally intrigued by the case and he decided to investigate personally when the island's most celebrated resident – a bizarre lady by the name of Mrs de Wagner, a self-styled baroness who pretended to be Empress of the Galapagos – was added to the list of missing persons. Mrs de Wagner had been murdered, Vincent decided, and her corpse had been concealed in a half-mile-long cavern which had been shown to him by one of the island community.

Thus it was that the cruise guests of 1937 found themselves trudging across Charles Island under a scorching sun with digging implements on their backs. Vincent assured them that his sense of direction was faultless, but as time went by and the party grew hotter and wearier, doubts began to be loudly expressed. Finally, after five hours of searching, there was an outbreak of mutiny and Vincent was compelled to lead his exhausted party back to the *Nourmahal*, the cave undiscovered and the mystery of Mrs de Wagner unsolved.

Another of Vincent's adventures ended somewhat ingloriously when South American troops turned up to prevent what might have become a blood bath. This time the object of the expedition was buried treasure and the scene was Coco Island, off the Pacific coast of Costa Rica, a haven for buccaneers in former times. Unfortunately, the Astor party fell foul of a rival band to whom treasure hunting meant more than a holiday diversion and there is no telling what would have happened if the Costa Rican government had not dispatched a detachment of soldiers to keep order. No doubt the Costa Ricans, who after all owned the island, had designs other than the protection of a handful of crazy Gringos, but in the event everyone left empty-handed.

Most of the *Nourmahal's* cruises were less eventful and rather more relaxed, the only excitement occurring when native canoes put out from some palm-fringed isle bearing gifts to these visitors from another world.

But if sailing was his first love, it was certainly not the only form of transport to unleash Vincent's boyish enthusiasm, as we have seen. Apart from cars and aeroplanes, he loved trains and at Ferncliff there was three-quarters of a mile of miniature railroad around which he would drive a powerful steam locomotive, three feet long and capable of pulling more than twenty people in its carriages, with Vincent sitting astride the engine. So keen was he on this innocent form of entertainment that he had a second railway track, eight hundred and fifty feet long, built at his vacation home in Bermuda.

Nor did Vincent ever outgrow an adolescent delight in practical jokes, though in perpetrating them he brought to bear experience, psychological insight and organizational ability that was entirely adult. He selected his victims with great care and, having analysed their personalities, knew just how far he could go without causing a nervous breakdown. A good example of this concerns a house guest at Rhinebeck who arrived with his newest prized possession in tow – a splendidly equipped motor caravan with fitted carpeting, its own library of leather-bound books and picnic crockery in bone china. The proud owner expatiated at boring length about the merits of his mobile home, until Vincent saw a way to put an end to the boasting. He arranged for the guest to be taken for a drive and while the man was gone Vincent and some of his servants surrounded the caravan with brush wood, soaked the wood in paraffin and set it alight. When the returning guest saw the flames and smoke he almost collapsed and it was not until the fire had been extinguished and he was able to carry out a minute inspection of the vehicle that he could be convinced the blaze had been a hoax.

A favourite dinnertime amusement of Vincent's was to employ an actor to pose as a waiter who would spill soup on a chosen guest and then insult him, driving the victim into a rage that was greatly enjoyed by the rest of the company. Another long-running gag hit the victims where it hurt most – in the wallet. This would take place during a cruise and required a certain amount of advance research on Vincent's part. The *Nourmahal* customarily received news bulletins and stock market reports by wireless and the essence of the joke was for Astor to plant a fake radio message indicating that the value of stocks to which he knew the target was heavily committed had fallen through the floor. Sometimes, when the 'mark' was obviously not a suicidal type, a series of ever gloomier messages would show him to be facing financial ruin, until his broker was miraculously reached by ship-to-shore telephone. For some people, those sought-after cruises were more of an endurance test than a pleasure trip.

Of coure, the effectiveness of a practical joker tends to diminish as his reputation spreads, but Vincent was more than equal to the challenge, reaching perhaps the acme of achievement in this field with his widely known newspaper trick. This prank required a lot of preparation: Vincent would compose a scurrilous account of an entirely fictitious scandal which featured one of his house guests, then he would have it printed as a newspaper page, complete with illustrations, and inserted in the Sunday paper delivered to the guest with his or her breakfast tray. After several repeats of this particular form of mental cruelty, Vincent realized that it might be in danger of losing its impact but he could not resist the temptation to prove that he could still outwit his friends. He selected a female member of a holiday party staying at Beechwood and put his plans into operation.

When the newspaper containing Vincent's addition was delivered, the woman refused to panic until she had checked the provenance of the offending article. She visited some of the Astors' Newport neighbours and was dismayed to find that the piece appeared in their newspapers, too, but she remained unconvinced and marched out to the nearest newsvendor – only to find that her 'story' was in the copy he showed her. It was not until much later that she discovered all the copies of the paper she had seen had been thoughtfully provided by Vincent in anticipation of her scepticism and determination.

There is no record of Vincent having lost good friends

through his pranks, no doubt partly because his sense of humour was infectious and also because he could make fun of himself as easily as he could laugh at others. One source of self-deprecation was his ungainly frame and inelegant mode of movement. His splayed-out feet prompted him to adopt the penguin as his mascot and as time went by the genus *Sphenis-cida* became something of an obsession with him. Whereas most people rich enough to use bespoke cigarettes had them adorned with their initials or family crest, Vincent had the figure of a penguin imprinted on his. His various homes and his yacht were littered with penguin bookends, penguin clocks, penguin doorstops and similar bric-à-brac, while his vast, custom-built, sixteen-cylinder Cadillac town car was instantly recognizable by the chromium penguin that sat on its radiator cap. As well as collecting fish on his cruises he also sought out specimens of the various penguins inhabiting the southern oceans and presented them to a number of zoos.

Other childlike fixations, though, contained not a hint of irony. For instance, Vincent was quite fascinated by his name and more particularly by his initials. He insisted that his friends address him as 'V.A.' and his cars always bore what are now known as vanity plates – VA1, VA2, VA3. He got a thrill from signing his full name, which he customarily did with an outsize fountain pen, and his property advertisements in the news-papers were usually headed, 'Vincent Astor Offers...' He never used his first name, William, which in itself is interesting because William is a traditional Astor name while Vincent (meaning 'conquering', of course) appears just this once in the family tree. It was as if this Astor had a sense that he was very different from those who had gone before and that after him, in America at least, the family tradition would not matter much anyway.

Further illustration of the part of Vincent's personality that never quite reached full maturity is provided by the adolescent mixture of wilfulness and dependence that often marked his behaviour. This, combined with sudden and inexplicable swings of mood, left confused impressions among those who knew him. To some he was a true friend, kind, generous and loyal, while others have characterized him as niggardly, capri-cious and vindictive. Certainly, as will become apparent, he was capable of hypocrisy of a high order when his own interests and desires were concerned, and his treatment of his half-brother and some other members of the family was very much less than creditable, yet he was always ready to dip into his pocket-book for a needy friend and his generosity to his widow was unparalleled in Astor history. Probably it all hung on which sub-section of his nature – the wilful or the dependent – was dominant at the time.

His dependence on servants at least, and especially his faithful valet, Jepson, was almost legendary. When Jepson was obliged to take a day off through illness, the story goes that Vincent spent hours searching for his clothes, and was not completely dressed until noon. That incident may be apocryphal, but several people have recalled another occasion on which Jepson's absence was noticed. It was a weekend party in the country and the accommodation was limited so the guests were asked not to bring their servants with them. At breakfast on the first morning, Vincent appeared in proper attire but without his shoes and when taxed about this he admitted that he had been unable to find the footwear he had arrived in and could not remove 'the damned shoe trees' from the other shoes he had brought.

This lack of domestic skills was a source of some embarrassment to Vincent and, as if to make up for it, he fell into the habit of patrolling his house on Sunday mornings filling the cigarette lighters and adjusting the wicks. He also tried to maintain a steady routine. When he was in New York his day customarily began at seven o'clock, when he took breakfast in his room and carefully scanned the morning papers. His waking temper was foul and no one in the house dared to approach him at least until he had breakfasted. He usually arrived at the office about nine and, if he did not spend the whole day there, he would work until lunchtime and after lunch would either attend a board meeting of one of the companies in which he was interested or pass a pleasant few hours at the exclusive Brook Club, on Fifth Avenue at 51st Street. He was actually, in his prime, a member of thirty-eight clubs, but the Brook was the only one in which he felt really at home and it was noted that he often wore the blue and yellow tie of the club.

Ideally, his evenings would be spent at home and they were

marked by a habit that was virtually unbreakable. At seven o'clock the radio was switched on so that Vincent could listen to the *Amos 'n' Andy* show – during the fifteen minutes the programme ran, telephone callers were informed that Mr Astor was not at home. Dinner followed promptly at seven-twenty. If there were the sort of guests Vincent liked, who would offer him 'real' conversation, the drinking and talking would go on until the early hours. Otherwise, Vincent generally went to bed about eleven, unless he indulged in a late-night chess game with his friend J. David Stern, the publisher of the *New York Post* (the fact that Stern always won never discouraged Vincent).

Astor's dependence on servants and on routine was matched by his dependence on tobacco: for most of his life he smoked fifty cigarettes a day, as well as cigars and, after dinner, a corncob pipe. He also depended on women, though there was only one – and Vincent did not find her until it was really too late – who truly understood the nature of his need.

To all intents and purposes, Ava Astor had abandoned her son long before her divorce from John Jacob IV, with the result that Vincent's upbringing had been seriously out of balance. He had had a father to whom he could look for an example, for discipline and for guidance of a sort, but his personality had been warped through lack of a mother to provide softness, undemanding love and indulgence. Thus in Vincent the element of the mother figure that most men unconsciously look for in a wife was, like so many other things about him, greatly exaggerated.

In many respects, Helen was a perfect wife for him – attractive, well bred, intelligent. Though a trifle distant in manner, she was disgusted by empty snobbery and shared Vincent's abhorrence of the crude parade of wealth. Like her husband, too, she felt that the days were over when the rich could tread their gilded path oblivious of pressures from below, and that the class system should be founded on degrees of public service, not simply on the acquisition of money. She was kind-hearted, not overly emotional, fairly undemanding, easy-going and utterly dependable. But there were two main points of departure between Helen and Vincent. The first was that their general interests were completely different: Helen was immersed in music and the arts, a talented pianist, while

Vincent cared for neither. The second barrier was the fact that while Helen did not actively object to Vincent's whims and fancies she did not indulge him by sharing in them – she merely put up with them. As time went by and the lives of Helen and Vincent followed ever more divergent courses, it was inevitable that outsiders should suspect yet another Astor divorce in the offing, particularly since there was not even a child to keep the couple together.

The first rumours began to circulate in 1922, the year Helen took a house in Paris 'for an indefinite period', as the *New York Times* put it. Helen was stoical about the gossip. 'If the newspapers are bound to divorce me, let them do it,' she said. 'I don't care.' Vincent was outraged. 'You can't make that denial any too hot for me,' he told inquiring journalists. 'Neither Mrs Astor nor myself nor any agent representing either of us has made any move toward a divorce or instituted any legal action in the United States and its dependencies on land, water or in the air.'

Yet the fact was that the couple were spending more and more time in the company of others. Vincent rarely accompanied his wife on her prolonged trips to Paris and London, while Helen hardly ever set foot on the *Nourmahal*. Having become a director of the New York Philharmonic and Symphony orchestras, and of the Metropolitan Opera Association and of the New York City Center for Music and Drama, not to mention her founding role in the Musicians' Emergency Fund, she claimed that she could not bear to spend so much time away from the city's cultural life as a yacht cruise would take up. Vincent, on the other hand, took to sleeping aboard the *Nourmahal* sometimes even when she was docked in New York and Helen was at home. It seemed that only a small push was required to produce a complete breakdown in the relationship, yet year after year it endured and year after year there were the same denials of the same speculation – 'pernicious', Vincent called it.

There were, perhaps, too many compensations in Vincent's life at that stage for him to realize what was lacking in his relationship with Helen: his real estate business was flourishing, despite the Wall Street Crash of 1929 and the subsequent Depression; the 1930s were the great days of his cruises, and also from the beginning of that decade he developed a consuming interest in politics and the national life. And the year 1935 marked the start of a grand obsession that was to eclipse all others, to fill a gap in his life, some said, that should have been occupied by a child. It was no doubt appropriate that the new object of his devotion was a building – the St Regis Hotel.

As has been noted, the St Regis was part of Vincent's great liquidation bonanza, which he completed shortly before the 1929 collapse, but he had retained a large mortgage on the property. The new owner, Benjamin N. Duke, had managed to keep the hotel afloat throughout the last years of Prohibition but the Depression was more than he could handle and in 1934 the St Regis went into receivership. Vincent foreclosed and spent half a million dollars turning the hotel into the sort of place he would have wished to stay in himself, convinced that was the way to make it pay. Oppressive respectability gave way to fashionable pastel colours, new restaurants and ballrooms were created and a crude but effective central air-conditioning system was installed, the first in any hotel anywhere. The leading establishments of Europe were closely studied in order to discover what had made them great and out of this came the idea that the St Regis would keep files on its guests so that when they returned their individual likes, dislikes and requirements would immediately be known.

Vincent, raising in his own way yet another monument to the father whose gold pocket-watch he still wore, was like a man possessed, involving himself in everything from the mechanical details of the air-conditioning to the floor shows and menus in the various dining rooms. His friends were earnestly questioned as to their preferences for the sort of mustard to be served with corned beef or the dimensions of a lamb chop, while every egg served in the hotel was delivered fresh from the Astor farm at Rhinebeck.

Such attention to detail quickly paid off: the St Regis began to show a profit, as well as becoming one of the centres of Manhattan social life. Vincent spent some part of almost every day there when he was in New York. He had his own table in the Oak Room where he generally lunched – most often on fish – though his business sense would not allow him to leave the table unused if he had an engagement and the head waiter would be told to let it go that day.

Within a couple of years, however, the St Regis was to witness the appearance of two rivals for its master's affections. One of them was a struggling magazine called *Newsweek*, which was destined to remain a pet for as long as the hotel did. The other was a pretty, vivacious young woman named Mary Benedict Cushing – her period of favour was to be somewhat shorter, but no less intense.

Vincent first met Miss Cushing, known to all as Minnie, at a dinner party in the home of James Roosevelt, who was married at the time to Minnie's sister. There was an almost immediate attraction between them, though Vincent, at forty-five, was some fourteen years older than Minnie, and out of this came an invitation for the young woman to join that winter's cruise on the *Nourmahal*. (It happened to be the year of the Coco Island adventure, which may indicate that Vincent was in particularly boyish spirits and therefore likely to find the animated, energetic Minnie a most suitable companion.)

Before long, the rumours that had dogged this Astor and his wife for fifteen years or more were to come true. In 1940, at Vincent's instigation, Helen went to Wyoming and stayed on a dude ranch to establish residence qualifications before filing for divorce on the vague grounds of mental cruelty. When the decree became final, Vincent and Minnie married secretly and slipped away for a honeymoon aboard the *Nourmahal*. All this was a flagrant breach of the moral code Vincent had set for himself: he had disapproved of his father's second marriage and in 1932 he had severed relations with his sister, Alice, after she had obtained a divorce. But like many rich men, Vincent appeared to believe, first, that whatever he wanted should be his for the asking and, second, that the principles he espoused for the world at large did not necessarily apply to him.

'The rich are different from us,' Scott Fitzgerald once said. 'Yes,' came the reply from Ernest Hemingway, 'they have more money.' It was Vincent's money, nothing more, that gave him the right to do as he pleased while criticizing other people for doing the same thing. He enjoyed the privileges of wealth and used its power, taking for granted that he had been placed above other mortals. A sign of this was the fact that in his *Who's*

Who entry he gave his occupation as 'Head of the Astor family in America'. Yet always at the back of his mind was the desire to be closer to the rest of mankind – an object he began to seek in various ways, but one which he achieved only in death, as we shall see in considering the descent of the Astors from the high plateau on which the first John Jacob had set them.

On the other side of the Atlantic, Vincent's cousins – the descendants of that William Waldorf Astor who had deserted America to seek refuge behind the class barriers of England – had in the meantime taken more positive steps towards bringing the richest family in the world into contact with common humanity: they had become the first Astors to embark on a life of public service. But before examining their roles in the rise and fall of the dynasty, we must see how and why they came to be in England at all and what effect the translation from American millionaires to British aristocrats had upon them.

PART III
This Sceptred Isle

7 A Home Fit for Gentlemen

John Jacob Astor turned his back on London and headed for America in 1783 because he believed that he would never be able to make headway against the closed ranks of England's hierarchical society. His great-grandson, William Waldorf Astor, abandoned New York in favour of England in 1890 because he found American society too open and longed for the respect and protection built into the English class system. The determinedly democratic attitude which had made possible the rise of the Astors from humble beginnings proved to be less suitable than the oligarchic principles of the Old World to maintain their dynastic status once their financial superiority had been established – at least, that was the view of William Waldorf Astor.

'As early as the days of Benjamin Franklin,' he wrote in 1899, 'there were not wanting thinkers who questioned the wisdom of submitting complex and delicate problems of society and statecraft to the decision of the multitude.' The founders of the Republic, he contended, had written the constitution in such a way as to make it appear 'aristocratic and un-American to be rich', while their successors had impoverished the very heroes of the Revolution by legislating against the concepts of primogeniture and inheritance. America, he had therefore concluded, was 'not a fit place for a gentleman to live'. And he was once quoted as saying: 'America is good enough for any man who has to make a livelihood, though why travelled people of independent means should remain there more than a week is not readily to be comprehended.'

But then Willie Astor was by no means a typical product of his time, his country or his family. To be sure, he had inherited the innate conservatism of William Backhouse and John Jacob III, as well as the pathological shyness and inability to

246

communicate that marked the Astor men who lived in the long shadow of the Founder. But at the same time he possessed ambition, imagination and energy worthy of the first John Jacob. This was an Astor who would not be content merely to sit and watch the money grow in the hothouse of New York real estate. He was like old John Jacob, too, in that he admired the traditions and practices of European life and would have wished that they could be recreated in the New World.

Willie was brought up very much in the manner of his father and grandfather, completing his academic studies in Germany and then browsing among the relics of ancient civilizations to draw what lessons he might. In his case, Italy was the scene of his reflections on times past and his stay there imbued him with a passion for the life and power-politics of the Renaissance aristocracy, particularly the activities of the Borgias. His interest was to bear fruit later in a completely unexpected way.

When he returned to New York, he took a law degree at Columbia and also became a leading member of the law school's sports and athletics clubs, himself founding a boxing group known as the Bull Pups. Tall and well built like his father, he was a keen sportsman who mastered not only boxing but also fencing and shooting. His mental energies, however, did not find a comparable outlet. There was nothing very exciting about the Astor Estate Office, nor was there likely to be, and an Astor of Willie's generation – brought up in luxury and privilege – would hardly consider soiling his hands with the sort of commercial activity that had made the Astors rich in the first place (indeed, the family's peasant past and John Jacob's early toil had become something of a social embarrassment). There remained politics: the Astors had always found it convenient and profitable to take an interest in state and national government, but they had remained aloof from the business of politics, feeling that it was all rather beneath them. Willie, however, knew that in England it was perfectly acceptable, even honourable, for a gentleman to embark on a political career, and he saw no reason why that should not be so in America. He was to discover to his cost that there was a world of difference between the public life of England and the bruising hurly-burly of American politics.

He was a Republican, of course, and as an Astor with plenty

of cash to pour into campaign chests, he had no difficulty in having himself nominated as the party's candidate for a safe seat in the New York State Assembly. Upon his election in 1877 he declared: 'I do not go in the interests of any class, but for the city's good.' Actually it was for the party's good and his own, for he assiduously followed the Republican line in the hope of progressing to the more important state Senate, to the Congress in Washington, and after that . . . well, an Astor as President, perhaps?

Two years later, right on schedule, his loyalty was rewarded by nomination to an equally safe senatorial district. Convinced that nothing could now stop him from winning national office, Senator Astor began to act from the single-minded self-interest that was to mark most of his life. For reasons no one else could quite understand, he introduced a bill to cut the fare on the New York elevated railway from ten to five cents (either he was trying to encourage commuting and therefore develop the Astor real estate in the Bronx, or he simply wanted to bankrupt the El, which the Astors had long opposed). After heated debate, the measure was crushingly rejected by the Senate. On a different tack, Astor voted against an attempt to regulate fares on the state's railroads – an important part of the Astor stock portfolio – but the incident that brought the first real criticism of Willie as a public man concerned his attempt to have the Croton Aqueduct moved from its site at Fifth Avenue and 42nd Street, something dear to the hearts of the Astors and their neighbours. He pushed the bill through the Senate but it failed to attain the required majority in the Assembly, whereupon Senator Astor was said to have made a list of those assembly-men who had voted against him and exacted his revenge by withholding his vote from legislation of theirs which required the unanimous approval of the Senate.

A year in the Albany upper house gave Astor the urge for still greater things and he told his Republican bosses that he would welcome a congressional district. They obliged with the Seventh, a working-class area with a high proportion of German immigrants who lived in Astor apartment blocks. The district normally voted Democrat, but a Republican had won in the previous election. 'My education and the fact that I am of German descent,' said Willie at his adoption meeting, 'has made me, I think, better acquainted with the character and aims of that nationality which forms so large a portion of the population of the Seventh District than ordinarily falls to the lot of a native-born citizen.'

He also had more money to spend on his campaign than the average native-born citizen, and a thousand 'canvassers' were hired to whip up support. But he was up against Tammany Hall on its own territory and although a Republican Administration under James Garfield was elected, Astor lost by 165 votes. He did not have long to wait for a second chance. Garfield fell foul of the New York Republican leaders over civil service appointments in the state and a bitter struggle ensued between Washington and Albany which split the party in the state. Astor, still a member of the Senate, supported the local bosses, Roscoe Conkling and Thomas C. Platt, when they resigned their seats in Washington and ran instead for the state legislature. The Republicans divided into 'Stalwart' and 'Halfbreed' factions, the former supporting state's rights, the latter endorsing presidential prerogative, and it was the Halfbreeds who eventually triumphed (though the object of their loyalty, Garfield, was assassinated in July 1881 by a deranged Stalwart). Willie Astor thus found himself out on a political limb, but although Conkling and Platt had failed to win seats in Albany they still controlled a large section of the New York party and, bearing in mind Astor's loyalty to them, they put him up for the United States Senate in the normally safe upper-class Fifteenth District.

This time, however, the split in the Republican Party converted the Fifteenth into a marginal constituency, and the choice of candidate only served to help the Democratic cause. Astor, said the *New York Post*, had shown a slavish adherence to the party machine that was 'inexcusable on the part of a man in politics not for the money in it but for an ambition to serve the public'. The *Sun* declared that 'apart from his money Mr Astor is one of the weakest aspirants who ever sought the suffrages of a New York constituency'. He had been tried in the legislature and 'proved himself the most partisan, the most narrow-minded, the most selfish of representatives'. Even the staunchly Republican *Times* was only lukewarm in its support, pointing to Astor's 'disregard of the wishes of his constituents' at the time of the Stalwart-Halfbreed battle in the legislature.

Sensing the opportunity for a coup, the Democrats ran a candidate who had very nearly as much money as Astor to play with and the election degenerated into a vulgar and cynical contest to determine who could buy most votes. The press was disgusted. 'The Republic has fallen upon evil times,' said one editorial, 'when it comes to be generally believed that no classes but unscrupulous rogues or hardly less unscrupulous millionaires dare aspire to office...'

This sort of rough and tumble was not at all what Astor had had in mind when he had decided on politics as a career. Here he was, an American aristocrat, being pilloried in the public prints and at the same time finding himself forced to shake hands with the denizens of saloons (he carefully kept his gloves on) in order to persuade them to vote for him. It was all too demeaning for a man of his sensibilities. To make matters worse, after all his efforts he lost the election and was further humiliated by a patronizing editorial in the *Times*: 'The moral is that the possessor of an honored name, of great wealth, of sound ability and of an unexceptionable character, may throw all these advantages away when at a critical moment in his political career he forgets what is due his constituents as well as to his own independence and self-respect.' Adding insult to injury, the *Times* seemed to see right through to the root of Astor's ambition when it remarked that his campaign, 'suggestive of the electioneering methods of an old-fashioned English borough', was out of place in a great American city.

To be rejected and dismissed in such a fashion was simply intolerable. The doubts about the fitness of America as a domicile for a person of quality began to crystallize in Astor's mind. If the vulgar horde did not want to be represented by its betters, then let it rot. He would seek elsewhere the respect he deserved. As it happened, President Chester Arthur, who had assumed office upon the assassination of Garfield, came to Willie's rescue with a plum foreign posting – the job of American Minister to Italy. Nothing could have been more calculated to appeal to Astor: he had official dignity and moved in the sophisticated, well-ordered world of diplomacy, where protocol and etiquette were all, and just to add savour he was in the land of his beloved Borgias.

It was a combination to stir Astor's imagination, and in 1884 he produced a novel of the Renaissance entitled *Valentino*, which Scribner's published the following year. Loosely based on the life of Cesare Borgia, the book was utterly without literary merit yet was treated kindly by the New York critics and enjoyed a brief vogue. After all, no Astor had ever before set pen to paper in a creative way and the literary world could claim a certain respectability from including such a prominent citizen among its number. Willie was encouraged to write a second novel, called *Sforza, A Story of Milan*, but even though the *Times* reviewer suggested it was not the fault of the author but of contemporary taste that the book should not be a success, *Sforza* had even less to recommend it than its predecessor and, of course, it lacked the novelty value of the first Astor book. Willie was no more destined to be a famous author than he was to be a successful politician – though he would later found a magazine partly for the satisfaction of seeing his literary thoughts in print.

In Italy, too, Astor became an avid art collector, buying a number of significant paintings. With classic Astor acquisitiveness he also bought the entire balustrade of the Villa Borghese, including the statues and fountain. But in 1885 the idyll came to an end along with the presidency of Chester Arthur. Willie arrived back in New York with nothing to do and little to look forward to. He was fundamentally out of sympathy with the mood of his native land, but like all the Astors he was able to survey the world from the pinnacle of his pocket-book and overlook those parts of it he found offensive, and for a time it seemed that he could come to terms with American life. Now that he was out of politics he had no reason to come into contact with the common people and he did find a certain amount of pleasure in the New York–Newport social round and his clubs: the Union, the Union League, Knickerbocker, Century, Lawyers and the new Tuxedo country club, which of course gave its name to the dinner-jacket that the club's founder, the tobacco tycoon Pierre Lorillard, introduced from England in 1886. It was a civilized and comfortable existence, though not a very exciting one, and it satisfied Willie until, early in 1890, he succeeded John Jacob III as head of the senior branch of the family.

With a fortune of one hundred and seventy million dollars, half of which was his to disburse as he wished, and an estimated annual income of six million dollars, he now had the power to live as he chose and to ignore criticism from whatever source. And with three generations of landed wealth behind him he was undoubtedly the leading aristocrat of America. To express his pride, establish his reputation as a real estate mogul and create a symbol of his superiority, he immediately let it be known that he would build on the site of his father's house the finest hotel the country had ever seen, to be named after himself, and that he would erect a lordly mansion uptown on Fifth Avenue, where he and his wife could take their places at the head of New York society. How much his actions were influenced by pique over the posturings of his Aunt Caroline is a matter for speculation, but there was certainly no love lost between the two Astor branches and it was in Willie's sensitive nature to be nettled by the fact that his parents had been content to remain aloof and smile privately as the pushy Caroline constructed her social power-base. They had felt secure enough to ignore such rivalry, but Willie was different. He would see to it that things would change: the senior branch would have its day. *The* Mrs Astor would no longer be Mrs William but Mrs William Waldorf.

Unfortunately for Willie's ambitions, his wife was neither by inclination nor constitutionally able to stand up to Caroline Astor. The former Mary Dahlgren Paul, whom Willie had met at Newport, was a Philadelphia beauty of impeccable lineage. She had large dark eyes, lustrous hair that reached her feet when she let it down and a fine-featured face that gave an impression of tenderness, modesty and diffidence. Mamie, as she was known, was perfectly comfortable in the goldfish-bowl of society, but at heart she was a homebody quite happy to take a back seat to her husband and children. This was not exactly what Willie required from a bride, but Mamie's sweetness and well-bred manner appealed to his romantic nature and he courted her assiduously during his first term in the state legislature. In 1878 their engagement was announced, much to the delight of both sets of parents, and they married in Philadelphia later that year. As if to prove her suitability, Mamie gave birth to an heir, William Waldorf Jr, in 1879, at the home John Jacob III had given the couple on East 33rd Street.

All seemed set fair. Mamie fitted well into the social circle Augusta, Willie's mother, had gathered round her and during the couple's time in Italy she became a great favourite at the court of King Umberto, where she was described as the most beautiful woman in the land. In ten years she produced five children, four of whom survived – Waldorf, Pauline, John Jacob V and Gwendolyn, though the latter died at the age of fourteen – and she was a devoted mother. Yet overall the marriage was not a happy one. Willie, with his egocentricity and extremely thin skin, was a difficult man to live with and Mamie's retiring nature did not stand up well to the demands he made upon her. Furthermore, Astor's political humiliation left him morose and disillusioned at a comparatively early age, which did nothing to improve his treatment of his wife. His obsession with punctuality, even when he was entertaining guests, and his eccentric notions of what constituted good form cannot have made life any easier for Mamie.

Yet no doubt Willie loved her in his own peculiar way – even if, as some contemporaries suggested, he was rather disappointed in her. He dedicated his second book to her and, after the deaths of his parents, he determined that Mamie should assume her rightful place as the Astors' leading lady, so that he could be proud of her as he had been in Italy. Mamie had already proved herself a capable and popular hostess in New York and Newport and at her country home on Long Island, but she did not see this as a way of life and, much to Willie's irritation, she was more interested in pleasing her guests than in making the affairs great spectacles to be admired by the rest of the upper crust. Thus it was as much to satisfy Willie's childish vanity as to establish Mamie's position that the summer following the death of John Jacob III was chosen to mark the triumphal accession of his son and daughter-in-law.

The couple installed themselves for the first time as master and mistress of Beaulieu, a rather more imposing if less famous residence than Caroline's Beechwood, but hardly had they done so when Willie discovered just how far his aunt's ambitions went and how entrenched she was. He learnt that Caroline's cards were imprinted simply with the name 'Mrs Astor', which to Willie's mind was the prerogative of his wife –

Caroline should have styled herself 'Mrs William Astor', as she had done before the death of Augusta. Perhaps, then, it was his influence that prompted the organizing committee of Newport's annual Casino Ball to list 'Mrs William Astor' among the patrons of that important event. Caroline was furious: she wrote to the committee saying that the addition of 'William' to her name was an insult and withdrawing her patronage. As a slap on the wrist to her impertinent nephew, who should have had more respect for his elders, she informed her friends that during the summer months any correspondence for her required no more identification than 'Mrs Astor, Newport.' Willie retaliated in kind, instructing the Newport postmaster that all mail addressed merely to 'Mrs Astor' should be delivered to Beaulieu and not Beechwood.

At this point the newspapers got wind of the family feud and before long the whole of America was enjoying this priceless farce. One journal reported that the broad-beamed Caroline had been denied her customary double pew in church by some rebellious members of Newport's gilded youth, which indicated that they supported Mamie's claim to precedence. The Sunday papers discussed the merits and extent of the rival ladies' jewelry collections and their two factions became known as 'the swells' (who supported Caroline) and 'the howling swells'. Unkindest of all was the notorious Colonel Mann of *Town Topics*, by far the most popular of the Society 'fan magazines'. Not only did he suggest that Mary Astor was better fitted to lead the glittering throng because she could waltz whereas Caroline could not, but he went on to indicate that Caroline was past it: 'With a pertinacity worthy of a better cause she has worn herself out in the endeavor not to be a part of Society and an aid to its advancement in worthy directions, but to reign over it and have her subjects stand in awe of her power. At sixty years of age she finds her position disputed. She is at war with nearly every woman in the Astor family and all that there is to repay her for the turmoil and ridicule that beset her is the acknowledgment by the Lord High Steward' – Mann was referring to Ward McAllister – 'that she really wears the crown.'

But even at the age of sixty Caroline had formidable staying power, and since in the nature of things the opinions of the older socialites carried greater weight than that of the young people who championed Mamie, *the* Mrs Astor remained just that. Not that Mamie minded very much – she was more concerned with baby Gwendolyn, born in 1889 – but William Waldorf was mortified. Humiliated by his insufferably pretentious aunt, he was also being made fun of by the multitude. He had had enough of these coarse, irreverent people who could not recognize quality and natural superiority when they saw it, who did not play by the rules of lineage and primogeniture. As the Newport summer began to fade, Willie unobtrusively made arrangements for his business affairs to be managed in his absence, and on 27 September 1890 he and his family took ship for England, where Willie confidently expected to be welcomed as the aristocrat he really was.

II

It is hard to guess the exact state of William Waldorf's mind as the shores of America receded behind him. Many people have assumed that his defection was a simple case of pique, a rather infantile reaction to his rejection by, as he saw it, both the lower and upper classes of his homeland. Others have concluded that he went to England for the express purpose of buying himself a peerage, the outward symbol of the natural superiority he had always felt. Certainly he was attracted by the condition of the upper classes in England. Despite the Industrial Revolution and the social changes accompanying it, such as the growth of an ambitious bourgeoisie, the British aristocracy clung firmly to its ancient privileges and practices, insulated by tradition as much as by wealth from the aspirations of the underclasses. 'Knowing one's place' was the central principle of social harmony and to a man as conservative, as steeped in the past as William Waldorf, the idea of a title that automatically conferred unquestionable rank would have been enormously appealing. Yet was that the whole story? William Waldorf's behaviour both immediately before and after he moved to England seems to suggest that his exile was actually a manifestation of some deeply rooted mental disturbance.

Announcing his intention of emigrating, Willie said that what had finally convinced him to go was the fact that his children had been threatened with kidnapping. No substantiation of that claim was forthcoming. Astor also lived in constant and unaccountable fear of assassination (though some said he had been warned by a drunken fortune-teller). He slept with two loaded revolvers on his night table and went to extraordinary lengths to protect his London office against intruders: there was only one street door in the building, the ground-floor windows were protected by thick iron bars, and on his desk Astor had a button which operated locks on every door inside the building. Moreover, his desire to keep away from hoi polloi assumed pathological proportions in England. He was dismayed to find that parts of the estate he bought by the Thames in Berkshire were traditional haunts for picnickers and boating parties, so he built a massive, shard-topped wall round his grounds, which kept out the public and earned him the nickname of 'Walled-off Astor'.

Even among his own kind, or rather the kind he seemed to want to join, his behaviour indicated a desire to remain isolated. House guests were required to conform in every detail to the rules of the establishment in a way more reminiscent of the archetypal seaside boarding house than of what purported to be a stately home. On one occasion, a lady who had told Willie she planned to spend the afternoon writing letters appeared in the garden shortly afterwards only to be told by a servant that, in effect, she had no business to be out strolling when she was meant to be writing letters – visitors were expected to keep to their programmes. Enraged, the woman announced her intention of leaving immediately and ordered the lackey to call the carriage. 'I'm sorry, Madam,' the man replied, 'but Mr Astor doesn't allow the carriage to be called at a time that has not been appointed.' The woman ended up walking with her bags to the nearest village, where she engaged a hansom to carry her to the railway station.

Still more astonishing was Willie's treatment of a man who attended a musical evening at the Astor town house. 'I have not had the pleasure of your acquaintance,' Willie told the embarrassed guest, 'and I must ask you to leave. I will insert a notice in the newspapers about this.' The visitor, who happened to be Captain Sir Berkeley Milne, R.N., a former commander of the Royal Yacht, retreated to his club and sent Astor a written apology, explaining that he had been brought to the soiree by Lady Oxford, with whom he had been dining and who had assured him that the host would not object. In spite of Milne's honourable action, the *Pall Mall Gazette* (which Astor owned) published the following announcement: 'We are desired to make known that the presence of Captain Sir Berkeley Milne of the Naval and Military Club, Piccadilly, at Mr Astor's concert last Thursday evening, was not invited.'

This was too much for the clubmen of St James's, who closed ranks and muttered about barring Astor from the Carlton Club, which he had been invited to join through the good offices of the Prince of Wales. The prince himself showed his displeasure at Astor's appalling behaviour by inviting Milne to share the royal box at the theatre the evening after the offending paragraph had appeared, and the *Saturday Review*, describing Willie as 'unfit to tie the latchet' of Milne's shoe, pronounced: 'We only regret that the gallant servant of Her Majesty so far forgot his dignity as to accept a second-hand invitation to the house of this purse-proud American whose dollars could not save him from the contempt of his countrymen. Mr Astor wishes his entertainments to be exclusive. His desire is likely to be granted in future beyond his expectations.'

Realizing the risk of ostracism he was running, Willie tried to make amends, but he could not bring himself actually to apologize. Instead the *Gazette*, announcing its regret at the publication of the paragraph referring to Milne, explained somewhat disingenuously that it had been 'due to a misunderstanding' which entirely absolved the captain from 'any individual discourtesy'. Grudging though it was, this retraction was enough to save Astor from disgrace, though it did nothing, of course, to add to his popularity.

It was not long before the Establishment had an opportunity to get its own back on Astor, who sued the *Daily Mail* claiming that he had been held up to public ridicule by an item concerning 'Mr Astor's strange dinner party' at which, in order to win a £500 bet, he seated forty people around a huge circular slice of redwood tree brought from California. Willie retained Sir Edward Clarke, a former Solicitor-General and, by an odd coincidence, the Conservative Member of Parliament for Plymouth, the seat Astor's eldest son, Waldorf, was to win in 1910 and which was to remain in the fiefdom of the Astors, through the outrageous Nancy, for many years. The *Mail* was represented by Sir Edward Carson, Q.C., who declared amid laughter in the court that 'some people are annoyed by these things and others are not'. Even the Lord Chief Justice, who heard the case, could not resist a dig at Astor over the Milne incident: 'I cannot fail to see that there is a growing fashion, perhaps copied from the press with which Mr Astor is better acquainted than we are, of publishing personal paragraphs which are annoying.'

The matter was settled by an apology, with no defamation admitted and no damages awarded. The *Mail*'s sister paper, the *Evening News*, remarked sarcastically that Astor's 'remembrance of the courteous, polished manner in which his native newspapers deal with him makes him apparently a highly censorious critic'.

Poor Willie. For all his sense of dignity and honour, something warped in his personality, some mental imbalance or psychological quirk impelled him to act in a manner which could not have been more calculated to make him look a fool if that had indeed been his intention. Most bizarre of all the reflections of his character was the celebrated death hoax, for which it is generally believed that Willie himself was responsible. It happened just two years after his departure from the United States. On 12 July 1892, almost every newspaper in New York reported that William Waldorf Astor had died of pneumonia, and obituary notices spoke of his 'learning, his talents, and the noble qualities of heart which were his most distinguishing characteristics ... his nature was kindly, his manner simple, unaffected, sincere...' (clearly they were written by people who did not know him). The news had apparently come by cable to the Astor Estate Office in New York and it had been released to the press by the Rev. Morgan Dix, the Rector of Trinity, among whose claims to fame was regular officiation at Astor funerals. The Associated Press wired a denial, but only the *Herald* chose not to believe the original announcement. Of course, in Mark Twain's words, the reports of Astor's death were exaggerated, and next day it was headlines again as the papers confirmed 'W.W. Astor Is Not Dead'. In London, meanwhile, Willie was said to be reading his flattering obituaries with great enjoyment – it was probably the only time the American press had been kind to him. The Astor offices in both New York and London went through the routine of an investigation, but although the staff in neither was very large no culprit was ever found. The assumption must be that the perpetrator of the hoax was William Waldorf himself, no doubt from some twisted reason of vanity, and perhaps the London wire service correspondents were not all that far from the truth when they sent stories suggesting that Willie was losing his mind.

Of course, he was not insane, not by a long way, but his erratic behaviour did betray a certain mental instability and one suspects that it was only his wealth and position that persuaded other people he was eccentric rather than slightly mad. Yet such peculiarities are not without cause, and in the case of William Waldorf it might well be that his psyche was disturbed by the unfavourable conditions of his childhood. He himself recalled that he had been raised in the sternest, most austere surroundings, threatened with hellfire almost daily as he indulged in the normal mischief of the small boy. What he would not have appreciated was the effect on an only child of being brought up in isolation not only from other children but also from his parents. For all her intelligence and charitable instincts, Augusta Astor did not relate well to her son – probably his energy and high spirits were considered too much for her fragile health to bear. Willie was left in the charge of nannies and governesses and tutors, without a mother's affection to make up for what amounted to the lack of a father, since John Jacob III was obviously a natural for the grim, shadowy role of the classic Victorian Papa and probably even hammed it up because of his Astorian introversion (itself an inherited trait which added to Willie's difficulties).

What, then, would be more natural, we may think with the benefit of hindsight, than that Willie should have grown up demanding attention wherever he could get it? A person ignored will either suffer severe loss of confidence or else devote all efforts towards demonstrating an intrinsic worth which appears to have been overlooked. Associated with this is often a measure of unconscious self-disgust, a feeling that because one has been ignored there must be nothing worth noticing. Perhaps it was something of the sort that led to Willie's anti-social behaviour, reinforced as it would have been by all the criticism heaped upon him as a representative of the landlord class and a would-be politician. On the other hand, the desperate need for attention would have remained strong, so that a conflict arose in Willie's mind which caused him to act irrationally, often against his own interests, and also tended to lessen his pleasure and sense of achievement when he did receive the recognition he craved. Small wonder that throughout his life he could never escape from nagging feelings of dissatisfaction, disappointment and disillusion.

The move to England, then, was the complex gesture of a complicated man. When he arrived, though, he set about establishing himself with businesslike efficiency. He rented Lansdowne House at $25,000 a year while he looked round for a suitable town residence and, unable to find a commercial building that suited him, he bought a house in Temple Gardens, overlooking the Thames, which he converted into the Astor Estate Office – in all it cost him one and a half million dollars. Marble, jasper, mahogany and cedar graced this Tudor-style building, which boasted a first-floor hall of medieval proportions and a staircase adorned with carved figures of the characters from Astor's novels. Later on he bought his own splendid mansion in Carlton House Terrace, running parallel to The Mall and a three-minute walk from Buckingham Palace. This he redecorated with a disregard for expense that would have done credit to Caroline Astor, though with rather more taste than his aunt generally displayed. Paderewski played and Nellie Melba sang at an inaugural reception which found princes, grand dukes and a host of noble British names around the forty-foot, flower-bedecked dining table.

As he became acclimatized to this rarefied atmosphere, however, Astor noted that his titled companions cared less for their town residences, which were for the most part dour and gloomy, than for their 'country places'. It was among the fields and woods, parks and lakes that the heart of the British aristocracy was to be found. Whatever the attractions of the London season, the blue-bloods were never happier than when they could withdraw to their feudal acres, the very soil from which they sprang. As a man reared in the real estate business,

Astor could sympathize with this attachment to land, and he also realized that if he was ever to join the coronet-and-ermine club he must have a country seat. Money being no object, he selected Cliveden, one of the loveliest of English estates, and persuaded the Duke of Westminster to sell it for a consideration reported to be one and a quarter million dollars. As its name implies, Cliveden occupies a prime site on a cliff overlooking the Thames near Maidenhead. The house itself is not outstanding. It was built in 1850 for the Duke of Sutherland by Sir Charles Barry, who is best remembered for the Houses of Parliament, and the design was inspired by an Italian villa (which of course was enough to commend it to ex-Minister Astor). The proportions of the building have often been criticized – the central section is altogether too massive for the wings, giving the whole a rather top-heavy appearance, and the windows are perhaps too narrow and too numerous – and the chief feature of distinction is the vast terrace with its ornate basement entrance, the remnant of a previous house which burned down in the 1840s. But there is no argument about the magnificence of Cliveden's situation and the superb gardens, which include a flowerbed set in the shape of a sword to commemorate a duel in 1668 between Cliveden's first owner, the Duke of Buckingham, and the Earl of Shrewsbury, with whose wife the duke had eloped. (The fight, in which the earl was killed, did not actually take place at Cliveden.)

Willie Astor is said to have spent six million dollars on refurbishing Cliveden to his taste. The Italian influence was emphasized by the addition, below the terrace, of the complete Villa Borghese balustrade and its enormous fountain, which Astor had bought in Rome, and ancient Roman sarcophagi were placed in various parts of the grounds. Inside the house, Italian craftsmen laid a mosaic floor in the great hall and painted on the ceiling of the dining room a classical-style fresco depicting the gods at a feast. Roman statuary and wine jars were positioned in the hall, along with other antiquities. Elsewhere were to be found wainscoting from a hunting lodge owned by Madame de Pompadour and a series of tapestries which, though bought by Astor in Paris, had in fact hung in the original Cliveden house destroyed by fire in 1795.

The year 1893 marked another important purchase for Astor:

he bought the *Pall Mall Gazette*, an evening newspaper founded in 1865 and edited in their day by some of the greatest journalists of the nineteenth century – Frederick Greenwood, John Morley and W.T. Stead. By the time Astor got it, the *Pall Mall* had gone through a number of changes in emphasis – Conservative, Radical, Liberal – and he decided to return it to its Tory roots (after all, it was the Conservative establishment he had to influence if he wanted his peerage, quite apart from the fact that his sympathies leaned naturally towards that side of the political arena). This was unacceptable to many of the staff, who left to found a rival *Westminster Gazette*, but Astor was both shrewd and fortunate in his choice of replacements, not least of the new editor, Harry Cust, heir to Lord Brownlow, Member of Parliament and man of letters. Under Cust's direction the *Pall Mall* became a showcase for some of the best new writers of the day – Rudyard Kipling, H.G. Wells, Alice Meynell – while Astor's bottomless purse was used to begin the ambitious, free-spending development of journalism which, in the next century, would lead to the golden age of Fleet Street.

If money was no problem as far as the editor of the *Pall Mall* was concerned, Willie's own literary ambition was, and Cust had to be light on his feet to sidestep the publisher's attempts to have his work printed. Finally, to remove the pressure completely, he suggested that his proprietor's prose was better suited to a literary magazine – so Astor started one, the monthly *Pall Mall Magazine*, which of course accepted the owner's romantic short stories and articles. Finding how easy and satisfying it was to be a successful publisher provided one had the money, Willie also started a women's weekly called the *Pall Mall Budget*: it seemed he had at last found a niche for himself, and an occupation entirely suitable for a gentleman.

In America, meanwhile, the capital base of Astor's fortune continued to expand. A sharp financial crisis in 1893 hardly touched real estate, and the subsequent economic recovery, combined with steadily growing numbers of immigrants, further inflated property values. Willie also had plans of his own for New York, though whether these were the result of business considerations or something else is not clear. His promise to build a hotel next door to the home of Uncle William and Aunt Caroline was taken as a symptom of spite, but like so much else about this Astor the motivation was more complex than it appeared. No doubt there was an element of revenging himself on those who, he felt, had prevented him from assuming his proper place in the Astor firmament. Yet perhaps more important was a desire to make his name known throughout America as a byword for style, quality, superiority – hence the title of his hotel, the Waldorf (and his insistence that cousin Jack's addition should be called the Astoria rather than the Schermerhorn, as had been intended). Then, too, Willie was emulating the first John Jacob, whose Astor House had not only been a commercial venture but had also embodied a monumental quality – and it is probably no exaggeration to say that the Waldorf, particularly after it became the Waldorf-Astoria, did more than even Caroline to establish the Astor name as an international symbol for luxury, a synonym for 'the best'.

That the Waldorf was the best of its time is beyond doubt: it set the standard for every luxury hotel that followed it, and at the same time it altered the social habits of New York, contributing to the decline of the great hostess in the Caroline Astor mould (thus eventually to the decline of the great house) and creating the background for the so-called cafe society that was to emerge from what Mark Twain dubbed 'the Gilded Age'. Each of the public rooms was furnished in period style – one of the restaurants was appropriately fitted out with the furnishings from the dining room of John Jacob III – and orchestras seemed to play in almost every corner. The glass-walled Palm Room had special ventilation so that gentlemen could smoke after dinner without their delicate ladies having to withdraw, and it was joined to the great Empire Room by a corridor that became known as Peacock Alley because of the constant parade of elegance that trod its magnificent carpet. Of course, the building was illuminated electrically, but there were candles in every room lest the new and somewhat unreliable lighting should fail.

Under the management of George C. Boldt, the proprietor of the fashionable Bellevue Hotel in Philadelphia, and Oscar Tschirsky – who entered social history as the great chef 'Oscar of the Waldorf', though he was in fact the maitre d'hotel – the service offered and the food were unlike anything seen in

America before. Room service extended even to the provision of breakfast in bed, an innovation from Europe that some straitlaced Yankees found decadent; the most favoured guests were greeted with gifts of wine and cigars and every lady had flowers to brighten her room; staff were deployed at strategic points on every floor so that there should be no delay between call and response (and the men were required to be clean-shaven, a daring injunction in a hirsute age, because Boldt thought it made them look smarter). As for the *specialités de la maison*, the Waldorf Salad containing walnuts and apple slices was to become a familiar item on menus all over the world.

Willie's monumental hotel, which he visited only once in his life, opened in March 1893 with a reception for fifteen hundred people, accompanied by the New York Symphony Orchestra, and immediately enjoyed a success exceeding even the dreams of its owner. A number of rooms reserved for permanent residents were quickly taken up, the salons were hired for dinners and balls that would previously have taken place in Fifth Avenue mansions, Wall Street gathered during out-of-office hours in the Astor Restaurant or the Men's Cafe to make deals and play poker. The bedrooms were filled not only by European royalty and statesmen from as far away as China but also by visitors from the great American interior, wealthy bourgeois come to be treated like aristocrats – and to pay through the nose for it, of course. George Boldt, once described as a sort of Ward McAllister of the hotel business, had certain standards which he imposed on staff and guests alike, understanding that people would pay almost any price for what they believed was exclusivity and that a great hotel must not appear to be there for the purpose of making money. When a guest complained, for instance, that his bill was too high, Boldt tore it up, telling the offender not to pay . . . and never to come back. Such is the vanity of mankind that few will say with Groucho Marx, 'I don't want to join a club that will have me as a member.'

With the Waldorf Hotel, then, and his *Pall Mall* stable of publications in London, Willie Astor seemed to have done himself a power of good through his self-imposed exile. He had proved himself to be a shrewd businessman in ways that had nothing to do with rent-rolls, leases and mortgages and, as well as manipulating the social life of New York in a manner that would have been impossible if he had stayed to be the resident senior member of the dynasty, he exerted influence on the political and literary life of Britain. Yet none of this brought to his name the honour he so desperately sought, that he believed was his by right. His quixotic ambition was to be what, in truth, he never could be: a nobleman in the full medieval sense of the word. He still had a long way to go in search of his impossible dream, and the unsympathetic destiny against which he fought was by no means defeated yet.

III

'In England,' *Harper's Weekly* commented in 1893, 'they take their millionaires more seriously than we do and are much readier to give them a chance and fit them out with a suitable rank and proper employment.'

Actually, England had done nothing of the sort for the subject of the *Harper's* article, William Waldorf Astor. Any progress he had made along the road towards a suitable rank had been achieved entirely by his own efforts and indeed, as the citizen of a foreign country, there was no prospect of his being granted a British title. He had not even applied for British citizenship in 1893, which seems to indicate that he hesitated before finally and irrevocably renouncing his native land. One reason for this delay may have been the attitude of his wife. Mamie, though she felt relief at being removed from the silly yet worrisome competition to be *the* Mrs Astor, soon longed to be among her own people again. At first London was exciting, and even if she was at heart much more domestically inclined than the great ladies she found in her salon and at her dining table, Mamie could nevertheless count herself a social success, capturing the goodwill of no lesser personage than the redoubtable Duchess of Buccleugh, Queen Victoria's Mistress of the Robes, who so far forgot her contempt for 'our transatlantic cousins' as to introduce Mrs Astor to Court circles. One may imagine Willie's pride over that.

But the move from Lansdowne House to Carlton House Terrace and the purchase of Cliveden signified a more permanent aspect to what she may have originally assumed was no more than a whim on her husband's part. Mamie began to be homesick and to envy those visiting relatives who were still speaking to her side of the family when they returned to America after staying in London. 'She was miserable,' said a cousin's daughter who stayed at Carlton House Terrace.

Perhaps Mamie asked Willie not to take the decisive step, or maybe he held back out of consideration for her homesickness. There must be some significance to the fact that her premature death in December 1894 appeared to stiffen her husband's resolve. He became a naturalized Briton in 1899, having completed the five-year period of residence from the date of application required by the Naturalization Act of 1870.

At the same time as becoming a British subject, Astor published in the *Pall Mall Magazine* a complex genealogical chart which purported to show that he really did have blue blood in his veins, a further nudge towards the desired ennoblement. The Jean Jacques d'Astorg who had unaccountably turned up in Walldorf in the late seventeenth century and sired the Astor family there was the starting point for a painstaking historical investigation that led by a somewhat circuitous route through the French nobility to the Spanish Counts of Astorga, particularly that Pedro who had been granted his crest by the Queen of Castille and had died during a Crusade in 1100.

The contemporary Count of Astorga found the connexion ridiculous, according to *Town Topics*, which quoted him as saying that the Astor table was 'an appalling mixture of facts, some of them actually turned upside down'. A prominent American genealogist hired by the *Sun* to check the veracity of Astor's claims suggested that Willie had been deliberately misled by his researcher, no doubt on account of the fee expected, and that a date had been falsified in order to make the French connexion. Far from being heretical Protestants, like Jean Jacques d'Astorg, the French aristocrats of that name had been staunch Roman Catholics and honoured servants of Louis XIV. The Astors, the *Sun*'s man remarked, might equally claim descent from Isaac Astorg, a Jewish doctor who had lived in Carcassone in the late thirteenth century – that red herring was to endow the Astors with an unpleasant odour in some anti-semitic quarters, and even today some people ask: 'The Astors? Weren't they Jewish originally?'

But while the American press sneered at Willie Astor's intimations of nobility, it and its readers were goaded to fury by his change of nationality. *Cosmopolitan* magazine called him 'a blot on the escutcheon' of the family; *Life* caricatured him aboard H.M.S.S. *Britannia* with a 'life preserver' at his side and the caption 'WILLIAM WALDORF ASTOR, Englishman'; *Town Topics* accused him of 'amazing caddishness and snobbishness . . . the richest man that America ever owned and that disowned America'; he was burnt in effigy in Times Square with the placard 'Astor the Traitor'.

Willie responded in characteristic style. When he heard that the flag of the American frigate *Chesapeake*, which had won glory if not victory in the War of 1812, was up for sale, he bought it under the noses of American bidders and presented it to the Royal United Services Museum. To his rejected homeland this was adding injury to insult. 'Everywhere,' roared the New York *World*, 'one hears the opinion expressed that it is a deliberately malicious affront.' Another paper spoke of Astor's obvious hatred for 'the country that gave him birth and which has supplied him with the millions in money through which alone he has been able to secure recognition in England'. And what would his new countrymen think of him now? According to the *North American Review*, 'The powers that be . . . understand quite well that to confer a peerage on this gentleman would, perhaps, do more after this episode to weaken their cherished entente cordiale with America than any other small mistake they might make.'

But the powers that were had no intention of conferring a peerage on Mr Astor. As a matter of fact, Senator Henry Cabot Lodge, who was in London at the time of the *Chesapeake* flag affair, told President Teddy Roosevelt that Arthur Balfour, the man who within a couple of years would as Prime Minister have the power to dispense honours, held the same opinion as most Americans and 'resented Astor's conduct about the flag'. Furthermore, even if the government had felt disposed to bestow recognition on Astor, it would have been nothing more than a knighthood or a baronetcy, since it was generally assumed that peerages could not be given to non-native citizens – and 'Sir William Waldorf Astor' was not at all what the gentleman had in mind, although in desperation he would later begin to style himself 'The Honourable'.

Willie was at least able to further his cause a little, though, as the nineteenth century drew to its close. Britain went to war in South Africa and Astor donated about $100,000 to the imperial coffers, including $25,000 for an artillery battery (another parallel with Cousin Jack: the Astors must have had a penchant for big guns). And that was only the beginning of the largess he showered upon his new country. Over the next few years, Oxford, Cambridge and London universities received more than a quarter of a million dollars among them, while charities and hospitals collected some $275,000 from 'that most generous American gentleman', to use Lord Curzon's phrase. This was wholly out of character for an Astor, but then Willie, as we have seen, was far from being typical of the breed – and he had a definite purpose in view for his philanthropy.

So certain was he of ultimate success in his campaign that in 1903 he purchased a baronial domain, the thirteenth-century Hever Castle in Kent. Hever was everything the ardent medievalist could desire, though by then run down and being used as a farm. There Henry VIII paid fatal court to Anne Boleyn, and to keep the castle Anne's father lied against her in the court that condemned her to death – though the fickle Henry later gave Hever to his fourth wife, Anne of Cleves. Despite its dilapidation, Astor was entranced by the history of the place and he spent something like ten million dollars on adapting it to match his dreams of what the modern nobleman's ancient castle should be. Thirty acres of land were drained and the River Eden diverted to form a boating lake; a mock Tudor village was built around the castle to accommodate guests; the drawbridge was restored for daily use; Italian gardens with the inevitable fountains were created; a deer park, a model farm and a generating plant were provided.

The decorations, of course, had to be in keeping with the castle's antiquity, and Astor's inventory makes astonishing reading. The Holbein portraits of Henry VIII and Anne Boleyn were accompanied by Titian's study of Philip II of Spain, Clouet's likeness of Edward VI and Cranach's representation of Martin Luther. The golden helmet of Spain's last Moorish ruler was joined by the armour of the French kings Francis I and

Henry II. Martin Luther's Bible shared a home with Cardinal Richlieu's sedan chair, Anne Boleyn's bedposts and headboard, Queen Elizabeth's clothes brushes and slippers, and King Henry VIII's personal lock. The whole thing had an air about it that foreshadowed Disneyland, and the English who cared about such things did not like it much – there was a local joke to the effect that Anne Boleyn's ghost, said to have haunted Hever, moved out in disgust. And, it almost goes without saying, Astor added to his unpopularity by building a twelve-foot-high wall all round his kingdom.

But still he lacked the cherished title to match his lands and wealth, and to reward his munificence towards his adopted country. The passing of Queen Victoria had offered hope, as King Edward VII, with whom Astor claimed at least acquaintance, had ascended the Throne, yet by 1903 there was no sign of honour, and neither would there be when the reign came to its end in 1910. That year, Astor added to his press holdings and therefore his influence by purchasing the venerable Sunday newspaper *The Observer*. Apparently it was not so much the paper itself he was interested in as its editor, J.L. Garvin, whom he had wanted to edit the *Pall Mall Gazette*, fallen into the doldrums following the departure of Harry Cust after a disagreement with the proprietor. The independently minded Garvin had no wish to leave *The Observer* and could not be bought, so the equally obdurate Astor simply made Lord Northcliffe an offer he could not refuse and acquired the editor along with his paper. As it turned out, not even the skills of the great Garvin could save the *Pall Mall* and Willie finally got rid of it. *The Observer*, on the other hand, was to remain under Astor control for many years, with Garvin editing it until 1942.

In the short term, though, the platform of the Conservative *Observer* did no more for Willie's title ambitions than the *Pall Mall* had done. For one thing, the Liberals had won office in 1905 and showed no inclination to relinquish it, while the House of Lords was full to bursting point with Tory peers who were making life difficult for the government. The story goes that in 1911, at a fancy dress ball held at Claridge's to celebrate Empire Day, William Waldorf arrived in mock robes of state and a coronet, to the amusement and applause of the assembled dignitaries. This extremely broad hint was not taken. By chance, 1911 was the year the Liberal government chose for its assault on the powers of the House of Lords through the Parliament Bill, and the creation of peers became a political threat to coerce the Upper House into consenting to its own emasculation. (And even if the threat had been carried out, the peers thus created would not have been hardline Tories like Astor.) No, it took the Great War to bring Willie to his destiny, and then, ironically, it may have owed as much to the fact that he was an American as to his generosity, or so some newspapers thought in reporting the creation of the first Baron Astor of Hever.

Yet Astor's financial contribution to the British war effort could not be ignored. In 1914 he gave $100,000 to the Red Cross, $175,000 to the various public funds that were set up and $125,000 to the subscription benefiting officers' dependants. During the disastrous year of 1915, when it became clear that winning the war was going to be a long and bloody process, a further $100,000 was donated to the Red Cross. Half a million dollars in all: his place in the New Year's Honours List of 1916 seemed, in those jingoistic days, to have been well earned, though there were some who carped.

'There is a widespread conviction that the grant of honours in exchange for money, though the transactions are disguised, amounts to corruption ... which, if it is allowed to continue, will bring democracy into putrefaction.' That from the dear old *Spectator*, which would see little good in anything a Liberal government did, even though in this case it benefited a Tory. The review *New Witness*, meanwhile, wondered whether Astor's elevation would serve to encourage support for the war from the United States, and suggested that it would not: 'The only effect ... will be to provoke Americans to renewed anger against the Astor family.' The dissenting voices were few, however, and even among Americans reaction was muted for they had a new young Astor, Vincent, to idolize. The iconoclastic historian Charles Austin Beard set the tone when he remarked in a magazine article that William Waldorf was merely joining 'a host of English cotton-spinners, soap magnates, tobacconists, journalists and successful brokers' in the House of Lords. The only trace of real bitterness came from an Astor collateral, John Chanler Chaloner, who suggested in a wicked little verse that Willie might choose a butcher's cleaver for his coat of arms. Astor did, as it happens, acknowledge his heritage by choosing for his badge the figures of a fur trapper and an Indian – but the main symbol was the hawk of Pedro d'Astorga.

Here at last, then, was his chance to indulge in gentlemanly politics, but he did not take it. Content to feel like a proper castle owner, he attended the House of Lords just once when he was introduced, then once more in 1917 when he was moved up to the second rank of the peerage as Viscount Astor. The reasons for this promotion have never been clear, though there were suspicions at the time of undue influence or under-the-counter dealing, and a writer in the *Daily News* demanded an explanation: 'He has contributed, I believe, generously to some of the war funds, but what rich man has not? If only to guard against ill-natured rumours, a clear statement on the subject seems desirable.' According to Nancy Astor, Willie's daughter-in-law, it was merely to give the old man something to do, a way of encouraging him to play an active part in the Lords. If that was the case, it was a failure. The taste of public life Milord Astor had experienced in America had been more than enough to put him off, and the only effect of his viscountcy was to make him withdraw even further. Having tired first of Cliveden and then of Hever, and being prevented by the war from visiting the villa he had bought some time before in Sorrento, he settled in a mansion in Brighton and spent some more of his fortune on creating his own Italian landscape there (behind a substantial fence, of course).

He was sixty-nine now and he passed the time in eating prodigiously and, like many others of his generation, watching the world he had known fall to pieces. It wasn't only the war, but the hornets' nest of socialism it seemed to have stirred up. Lloyd George, he believed, was an 'extreme radical' and in 1918 Astor foresaw that 'the new House of Commons is likely to be a curious medley of labour, socialists and women. The next House, a year or two hence, is likely to be much more revolutionary.' As for America, the labour movement was the main threat: 'For the coming year, or longer, I think it useless to attempt any development of the estate in New York. Useless to compete with strikes and the demands of labor.'

There were to be some developments, though, but only unwelcome ones of a technical nature to avoid the growing demands of taxation, the first time such a problem had troubled an Astor, and one at that who was least suited by nature to deal with it. During the war the income tax in England went up to six shillings in the pound, and in Astor's case the supertax on unearned incomes raised his contribution to the Exchequer to almost half his annual returns, while he also fell victim to the various attempts of the American government to introduce its own income tax in the face of complaints that such a measure was unconstitutional. Willie was obliged to sell some of his real estate – tenements in particular – in order to maintain his capital base and reduce the tax burden. What remained, however, was also under pressure from the mounting criticism of inherited wealth and it became necessary to take action to avoid estate duty that seemed to be punitive. By the summer of 1919 all Willie's remaining New York property had been transferred in trust to his two sons, Waldorf and John Jacob V.

Whatever short term gains this produced, however, were to be lost in the rising clamour for the redistribution of wealth, the heirs being forced to sell their birthright, the very rock on which the dynasty was founded, as a way out of the double-taxation trap Willie's emigration had set for them. There was undoubted irony – some might say poetic justice – in the fact that the country William Waldorf had seen as the last bastion of privilege should travel much farther down the socialist road than America has ever done. The first Viscount Astor, it seems, was a man who never quite got it right: unlike his illustrious ancestor, whom he resembled at least in energy and imagination, he swam against the tide of history rather than letting it carry him forward, and in so doing made his contribution to the decline of the house of Astor, though the family he left behind in Britain was to bloom in a most unexpected way.

Willie's last years, as I have said, were spent more or less in seclusion at Brighton, yet although one might feel a twinge of pity for this lonely, misunderstood and possibly misguided man, there is nothing to suggest that he was actually unhappy in his isolation. His interest in good food and wine, always strong, developed into something of a passion and there is evidence to suggest that other fleshly pleasures were at least considered, for at the age of seventy he was talking of marrying again. Who the intended bride might have been is a mystery, but it has recently come to light that Willie indulged in at least one romantic attachment after the death of his wife and he indicated to the lady in question that if she succumbed to his blandishments she would not be the first. The known object of his affections was Lady Sackville, wife of the third baron and mother of Victoria Sackville-West, and the discovery of some letters from Willie to her show that beneath his cold exterior the blood could still run hot. In one passage, he urges her to visit him in his eyrie on the Embankment, guaranteeing absolute discretion and pointing out that his butler has seen many things about which his lips are sealed. (That elaborate precaution against intruders may well have served more than one purpose.) Lady Sackville seems to have led him on then drawn back when his ardour became dangerous, and the amour apparently ended when Lord Sackville put his foot down. Considering the nature of the circles he moved in, it is interesting to speculate where else Willie's roving eye might have come to rest.

That eye closed forever on 18 October 1919, and there was about his death that element of comic pathos that seemed to have followed him all his life. After a good dinner of roast mutton and macaroni, washed down with a fine Beaune, Lord Astor retired to the lavatory never to emerge alive. It was a somewhat inglorious demise for a man so convinced of his nobility: the press announcement said he had been found dead in bed.

The death excited little comment, but it was significant nevertheless, for in passing on his title to his eldest son, Waldorf, the viscount created an opening for the woman who was to become the most famous member of the dynasty, Nancy Astor.

8 *Whose Nancy?*

I

'Since America exported Lady Astor to England, there's an entire absence of political comedy,' Harold Laski wrote to Bertrand Russell from Harvard in December 1919. In that sense, America's loss was Britain's gain. Nancy Astor, Christian Scientist, would-be social reformer, mistress of Cliveden and the first woman Member of Parliament to take her seat at Westminster, was to provide an entertaining political sideshow for twenty-five years. Her achievements as a Conservative M.P. were negligible – indeed there is every reason to suppose that she regarded the House of Commons as merely a stage for her theatrical personality – but she exerted tremendous influence on certain leading figures of her day and, particularly in that period of political stagnation and mediocrity between the two world wars, her flamboyant personality stood out like a shining beacon among the grey men who tried vainly to run the country. Unlike her political compeers – after Lloyd George a generally unprepossessing lot – she had talent in abundance. What she actually did with that talent is quite another matter. The curse of the Astors, the dead hand of old John Jacob and his millions that lay heavily upon almost everything his descendants tried to do as individuals, fell too upon Nancy, the Astors' leading lady of her generation. With her energy and wit, her art of being original, she could have had much to contribute to public life. The fortune gave her the start she might otherwise not have had, but the certainties of wealth and social superiority blinded her to the potential of her political position, reducing her to a lightweight and sometimes ridiculous figure.

Yet, as one of her children was to say, Nancy's name was and remains 'as much a household word as later became – though for different reasons – Mrs Roosevelt, Greta Garbo and

Marilyn Monroe'. The secret of her fame was manifold: her tyrannical nature, her unshakable conviction that she was right, her almost complete lack of regard for people who opposed her, her power over certain types of man. Central to these aspects of her character were her religion and the influence of her father. 'He had a quick temper and was a bit capricious,' she said of him once, a description that fitted her perfectly. And, like him, Nancy had a desire, almost an obsession, to astonish people.

She was born Nancy Witcher Langhorne in Danville, Virginia, on 19 May 1879,* the eighth of eleven children of Colonel Chiswell Dabney Langhorne and the former Nancy Witcher Keene. Both her parents were of good family – the Langhornes, for instance, owned plantations and cotton mills in Lynchburg, Virginia – but in the postwar South of the 1870s and 1880s this meant nothing in material terms. 'Chillie' Langhorne, having joined the Confederate army at the age of seventeen, returned to civilian life four years later with 'nothing but a wife, a ragged seat to my pants and a barrel of whiskey'. In the social sense, however, class was all: the defeated Southerners, suffering all kinds of privation during the harsh years of the Reconstruction, maintained the illusion of their old, leisurely way of life and social structure, and since the former aristocrats of the plantations were now in the main as poor as the people who had worked for them, background and not money was the mark of distinction.

Chillie Langhorne made a living and supported his rapidly increasing family as best he could on his earnings as a tobacco auctioneer and his winnings from poker, at which he was extraordinarily skilful. Then he decided to try a different sort of gamble, seeing that the railroad business was a growth area in the slowly recovering Southern economy. He knew nothing about railroad construction, but covered his ignorance by adopting an archetypal Southern attitude: 'Only Yankees and niggers work,' he would say. 'I'm not such a damn fool. I get other people to do the work for me.' Beneath this nonchalant pose, however, he worked extremely hard at acquiring knowledge of railroad engineering and putting it into practice, so that in 1885 he and his family were able to leave destitute Danville and move to shabby but still elegant Richmond, the former

* The same birthdate as her husband-to-be, Waldorf Astor.

275

capital of the Confederacy, where they settled in what was for the times rather grand style on Main Street.

Gamblers' luck, though, is a notoriously uncertain commodity, and Langhorne's soon ran out. The family was forced to retreat to the more lowly Third Street and Chillie sought employment where he could as an auctioneer once more. Then good fortune appeared again in the form of an ex-colonel from the Union army who had encountered Chillie during the war and who happened to possess valuable railroad concessions granted by the federal government for the Richmond area. The old comrades' act – even though the two men had been on opposing sides – worked for Langhorne and he soon found himself hiring engineers to lay new tracks. What Vanderbilt was doing in the North and West, Langhorne did in his own more modest way in the South, and it was not long before he had the money to match his natural position.

It is worth remembering that throughout the period of these varied fortunes the Langhornes, because of their 'natural' superiority, remained in comparatively comfortable circumstances. Poverty is a relative term: for instance, even the humble house on Third Street was staffed by servants. Yet the memory of those years was to remain with Nancy for the rest of her life, causing occasional anxieties about money even when she had more than ordinary people could imagine, and leading to her reformist political stance as a Member of Parliament. She felt she could identify with poverty and hardship, though her own dimly remembered experiences were a world and an age away from the conditions in which the poor of Britain lived after the First World War. And as the only Astor to make a real, if somewhat eccentric, mark in national politics, she still failed to see that the wealth from which people like the Astors benefited was rooted in the very misery which she and her fellow reformers sought to alleviate. Perception of the plight of other people is always filtered through the distorting mirror of one's own condition and however good the intention it is a rare reformer indeed who realizes that sacrificing some of his or her own privileges is the first step towards social justice. Given her background and advantages, it was inevitable that Nancy Astor the politician should be patronizing and 'paternalistic' in her approach. But of course in that she differed little from most of the public figures of her day, who sought to treat the symptoms rather than attempting to cure the disease.

In 1886 or thereabouts, with the railroad business booming and Colonel Langhorne receiving a large and regular income, the family was able to settle in fashionable West Grace Street in Richmond, where the eight surviving children had the benefit of a large garden and the freedom of what even today are quiet avenues. Then in 1892 the now wealthy Chillie bought a country estate called Mirador, west of Charlottesville, almost in the shadow of the romantic Blue Ridge Mountains. The house was a classical redbrick Virginian mansion, built in the early nineteenth century but – like so much else in the South – owing a good deal to the eighteenth. With these elegant surroundings the Langhornes returned to their roots, living like the old plantation aristocracy and indulging the Southern passions for horse-riding and hospitality, in both of which activities Nancy took a leading part.

The house in Richmond was retained, since her father needed to be in the city for business, and Nancy lived there with him during term time when she attended 'dame' school. Not that much stress was laid on her education: in the South of Chillie Langhorne, learning was for boys while all girls were fit for was a good marriage. To this end, Nancy at seventeen was sent to New York, where her married sister Irene lived. (Irene's husband was the famous graphic artist Charles Dana Gibson, and Irene, the most beautiful of the Langhorne sisters, was the prototype for the 'Gibson Girl'.) There Nancy attended Miss Brown's Academy for Young Ladies, a fashionable finishing school which taught the daughters of the rich little more than how to be clothes-horses. Nancy loathed the brittle, empty-headed and self-centred young ladies among whom she found herself, but she did learn one thing that was to help her in later life – the appeal of being outrageous. To the prissy misses who were her classmates, she was a peasant who spoke in an appalling Southern drawl and knew nothing of sophisticated life, to which Nancy responded by accentuating those qualities that they found most awful. 'I set out deliberately to shock them all,' she later recalled. She dressed in the worst taste, lengthened her vowels even farther, peppered her conversation with racy Southern slang, and let it be known that her father was a drunkard and her mother supported the family by taking in laundry. 'They came to look on me as an exciting if not very desirable character.'

If well brought up young ladies found the pose exciting, imagine how much more attractive it was to the young men of the East Coast polo-playing set to whom Nancy was introduced by Irene and her husband: there was nothing more likely to appeal to them than a spirited, good looking girl who could be 'one of the boys' and knew how to break a horse. How titillating the young Nancy must have been to those brash sportsmen when she did things like seizing two chairs at a society ball and commanding her escort: 'If anybody takes these while we're dancing, punch him in the nose.' But such behaviour, while effective in gaining attention, also betrayed a certain lack of maturity and Nancy appears to have had no real idea of what to do when men responded to her teasing, tomboyish charm. Her sense of shock when she discovered at the age of eighteen what it was that the men who flocked round her really wanted may be said to have influenced her relations with the male sex for the rest of her life.

The unwelcome revelation came as the result of a meeting at Newport with a dashing Bostonian polo-player named Robert Gould Shaw. This young Brahmin seems to have made up his mind at once that he would marry Nancy and carry her off to the North Shore, home of Boston's old landed aristocracy, where she would fit in perfectly with the horsey set that frequented (and still does frequent, for that matter) the exclusive Myopia Hunt Club. For her part, Nancy was immensely flattered by the courting of such a 'spectacular' – her word – man, the more so because her conquest naturally became the subject of widespread and perhaps rather envious gossip among her new friends. It was all such fun, but then Shaw asked her to marry him and Nancy agreed almost without thinking (her capacity for reflection, by all accounts, was never very highly developed). According to her own recollections, which she wrote down in 1951 and which are not always accurate, she later broke off the engagement because of a nagging suspicion that she did not love Bob, but was pushed into the marriage by both her own family and Shaw's. She gave the impression that she was in a sense hoodwinked, that the man she thought she was getting was not what she actually got. For instance, she accused the Shaws of concealing from her the fact that their son was an alcoholic. Yet Nancy herself was not at all the good sport she pretended to be, as her husband was soon to discover.

The wedding took place at Mirador in October 1897 and the couple went to Hot Springs for their honeymoon. What exactly happened on their wedding night has never been revealed, but the experience was enough to send Nancy rushing back home the following day. Perhaps Shaw got drunk, or possibly it was simply that he did not treat his young bride with kindness. On the other hand, it might not have been his fault at all – the revulsion against sexual intercourse which rose up in Nancy could have stemmed from purely psychological difficulties. (It may be significant, for example, that her mother always said she had never wanted children.) Later on she managed to achieve some sort of acceptance of the animal lusts of men, but it is interesting to note that in her mature years she tended to attract the kind of admirers with whom she could flirt in the sure knowledge that they were never likely to make any kind of sexual demand.

At Mirador after the disastrous honeymoon, her family were kind but firm and one can imagine them offering advice of the 'pull yourself together' variety. She was young, she had never really been away from the family before, but she must realize that she was a woman now and she had wifely duties to fulfil. In a few days she returned to her husband and, though miserable, tried to make the best of things. The marriage, however, never lost its nightmarish quality: as well as being a heavy drinker, Bob had inherited from his mother a degree of mental instability which manifested itself in wild behaviour and violent outbursts of temper. Nancy left him on a number of occasions, once being found by a friend of her family on Washington railway station where she had run out of money during an attempt to get back to Mirador.

She had, of course, become pregnant immediately upon her marriage, and her son Bobbie was born in 1898. Nancy recalled that the baby mitigated her misery for a time but this was not sufficient to allow the establishment of a point of contact between her and her husband. Chillie Langhorne, who rather liked his rakish son-in-law (presumably he fitted in with a particular concept of maleness), did his best to save the marriage, even buying the couple a country home in Virginia where they lived in relative peace for some months, but all efforts failed and Nancy left her husband for the last time in 1901. 'Your beautiful daughter is back home again, unwanted, unsought and part widowed for life,' she told Chillie. It was a comment very revealing of her self-image. Though attractive she was not exactly beautiful (certainly not in comparison to her sister Irene, the Gibson Girl), but she always wanted people to think her so and she most definitely had a strong desire to be wanted and sought after. There lies the key to much of the rest of her life.

Having abandoned her unfortunate marriage, Nancy faced the problem of how to end it officially. She was advised to seek a divorce, but in the course of growing-up she had acquired a rather fundamentalist, even child-like religious faith that would admit of no compromise, so the idea of 'whom God hath joined together let no man put asunder' was firmly fixed in her mind. Even when Frederick Neve, the archdeacon who had crystallized her ideas of Christian goodness, counselled divorce, Nancy refused to consider it, and in 1902 signed a deed of separation, though even that required a good deal of persuasion.

But if she was content to remain in a sort of half-wedded limbo, Bob Shaw was not. Late in 1902 his parents arrived at Mirador with the news that he had gone through a form of marriage with another woman and would face imprisonment for bigamy if Nancy did not immediately divorce him. They suggested that an action for incompatibility would serve the purpose and avoid any scandal, but Nancy would not hear of that: if she was to compromise her religious principles, then the truth must be told. The Shaws and the Langhornes gritted their teeth and Nancy sued for divorce on grounds of adultery – there was a satisfying biblical ring about that. Lawyers dealt with everything very discreetly and the parties were not even in court on 3 February 1903 when the decree was granted. In fact, on that very day Shaw was getting married legally.

To revive Nancy's spirits after her marital disaster her parents decided that she should have a holiday in Europe, and immediately after the divorce her mother took her and a friend named Alice Babcock across the Atlantic. They went to Paris first, but it was England that really appealed to Nancy – arriving there made her feel as if she were coming home, she recalled. By a curious coincidence one of the first people she met there was Ava Astor, by that time so tired of her marriage to John Jacob IV that she had taken to wintering alone in London. Glad to have compatriots for company, Ava invited the girls to stay with her, which they did for a month, while Mrs Langhorne returned home to look after Nancy's son. It would be a neat conclusion to report that during this visit Nancy first set eyes on her future husband, but it was not so: contact between the John Jacobs and the William Waldorfs was anything but a normal occurrence. Indeed it was several years and a number of suitors later that Waldorf Astor, the man who was to offer Nancy the chance of fame, appeared on the scene.

Nancy returned to Mirador in the spring and settled comfortably into the life she had known before her marriage. She attracted an ardent new admirer in the shape of a young Ulsterman, Angus McDonnell, the second son of the Earl of Antrim, who in common with many second sons of the peerage had chosen voluntary exile in the attempt to make his fortune. He had gone into the railroad business and, while he was working at Manassas, Virginia, became a regular visitor at the Langhornes' home, hoping – vainly as it turned out – that the warm friendship Nancy offered him would develop into love. From his point of view the problem was that the whole family took him to its heart; he ended up with a permanent berth in the room of Nancy's brother, Buck, and it was perhaps inevitable that Nancy should come to look upon him as another brother, rather than the lover he so desperately wanted to be. 'For the next few years,' McDonnell wrote later, 'my feelings for Nannie influenced me more than anything else.' That situation was to become familiar to a number of other men, even after Nancy's marriage to Waldorf Astor.

The visit to London had broadened Nancy's horizons and though she enjoyed being back at Mirador she kept in mind the possibility of building a new life for herself in England. The sudden death of her mother, at the age of fifty-five, in the summer of 1903, however, set back any plans she might have had. Deeply shocked, Nancy felt unable to do anything but remain at home and try in some measure to fill her mother's place. For a year she stayed, keeping house in rather haphazard fashion and more often than not clashing with her father, whose ego was at least as well developed as her own. Then Chillie, in his rough good-humoured way, rescued things by suggesting that Nancy might like to go back to England for the winter season of 1904. At first Nancy hesitated, but when Chillie convinced her that it was what her mother would have wished, she decided to go. In October 1904 she set sail for London, taking with her Bobbie and his nurse and accompanied by her sister Phyllis – whose marriage was in decline – and her two children. After staying a while at Fleming's Hotel in Half Moon Street, the two women rented a house called Highfield, near Market Harborough, in the heart of the Leicestershire hunting country. Here Nancy was in her element, riding to hounds with all her Virginian dash and courage and having much the same effect on the men around her as she had provoked among the East Coast polo-players back home.

Now, though, she was older and wiser and the hot-blooded horsemen who lusted after this high-spirited, attractive and flirtatious divorcee were smartly rebuffed. She went to church regularly, coolly refused to join in the copious consumption of alcohol and made it clear that she was not available for surreptitious sex. She did, however, fall in love, romantically and physically. The object of her affections was Lord Revelstoke, the dandyish but extremely successful head of the Baring banking business. He was then thirty-four and balding, but to Nancy he seemed like Apollo. The relationship that grew between these two is enigmatic, since only Revelstoke's letters have survived, but it seems clear from those letters and from the recollections of contemporaries that Nancy was very much the dominant partner. Despite his financial brilliance and worldly sophistication, Lord Revelstoke displayed a certain schoolboyish earnestness and naivety when it came to women, and to Nancy in particular. On her side one may detect an element of getting her own back on the male sex, her treatment of the besotted Revelstoke being in a sense 'revenge' for the wrongs she felt she had suffered at the hands of Robert Shaw.

Accepting Nancy's own assertion that she was deeply in love

with Revelstoke, the passion did not last very long. Her version is that she was misled (shades of Robert Shaw again!), that she believed Revelstoke had no romantic attachments, whereas she subsequently learnt that he had been having an affair for years with Lady Desborough, the famous country-house hostess, collector of young men and mother of the two brilliant Grenfell boys, Julian and Gerald, both killed in the 1914–18 war. Revelstoke's protestations that his love for Nancy exceeded anything he had felt for anyone else were of no avail. Nancy blamed Lady Desborough (though her name was never actually mentioned) for seducing Revelstoke away from her, concluding in self-justification that he was not the right man anyway, being a frightful snob whom Chillie Langhorne had 'seen through' at once when he visited his daughter during her first Christmas at Market Harborough. All this seems a bit unfair to his lordship, whose letters indicate that he worshipped the ground Nancy walked on, but with hindsight one might say he had a lucky escape – he was so vulnerable that she would probably have made his life a misery if she had married him.

After touring France with Phyllis in the spring of 1905 Nancy returned to America, where the faithful Angus McDonnell awaited her. He was even less successful than Revelstoke had been in pursuing his love, particularly when he abandoned the role of the moonstruck swain and began to make his own way in the world (with the aid, it must be said, of Chillie's financial backing). If he had thought Nancy would be proud of his achievements he could not have been more wrong: the fact that he could get on so well without her seemed to irritate her, touchy as she was over her real or imagined wound at the hands of Lord Revelstoke. In any case, she seems to have settled on winning a British husband, for she wrote to Herbert Asquith, with whom she had become friendly, to ask his advice as to which of the men who had courted her in London and Leicestershire she should consider marrying. Asquith found himself at a loss to answer, but even if he had done so his counsel would have been wasted, for chance was about to take a hand.

It happened as Nancy sailed back to London with her father in December 1905: among her fellow passengers was Waldorf Astor. It has been suggested that the reason why that particular sailing was selected was that Chillie knew Astor would be aboard, but be that as it may, Waldorf met Nancy and was captivated by her vital charm and ready wit. Being American by birth, he was not nervous of her natural ebullience, as some of her English suitors had been, and since he was heir to one of the richest men in the world he felt he had no cause to worry how Nancy would be received by society if he were to marry her.

At first Nancy was fascinated by the aura of almost unimaginable wealth that surrounded Waldorf. 'What I like about rich people,' she told her sister, 'is their money.' He was also handsome, polished and self-possessed, and as she got to know him better she realized, too, that he was intelligent and quietly determined, not at all a man who would fawn on her as McDonnell and Revelstoke did. Furthermore, there was about him a sense of responsibility, an awareness of the world beyond the velvet lining of his fortune, which corresponded with her own firm if somewhat idiosyncratic ideals of Christian duty.

The now sad figure of the blighted Revelstoke was still in the picture and he continued to plead his cause, to the extent that when Nancy telegraphed her father in the spring of 1906 with the news that she was engaged to be married, Chillie quickly and anxiously inquired who the bridegroom was to be, no doubt having a sigh of relief when he discovered it was Waldorf. (Lord Revelstoke, 'low and wretched' at the news, never married, which says something about Nancy's suspicions of him.) What the opinion of William Waldorf Astor was is unknown – not only was he a man who found extreme difficulty in expressing his feelings, but he had also been struck down by gout at the time – though considering his views on Americans a certain disappointment may be inferred. Nancy remained in awe, almost fear, of him until he condescended to visit his son and daughter-in-law after the birth of their first child.

Parental feelings aside, there were serious obstacles in the way of marriage between Nancy and Waldorf. Divorce in England at the time, though far from unheard of, was much more difficult and stigmatized than in America, and the established church so frowned upon it that the remarriage of a divorced person by an Anglican clergyman was forbidden. How the ceremony would be accomplished with the proper solemnity was the talk of London society after the engagement had been announced, and in some quarters it was forecast that even if a clergyman could be persuaded to officiate there would be angry crowds outside the church. Friends offered their castle in Leicestershire, but the local curate – no doubt at the risk of his living – refused to countenance the wedding. Finally Nancy called on the Bishop of London and, after explaining all the circumstances surrounding her divorce from Shaw, received his permission to marry in any of the churches under his jurisdiction. Even so the ceremony took place almost surreptitiously at All Souls, Langham Place, on 3 May 1906.

Neither Chillie nor William Waldorf was present at the wedding but the latter, who had been charmed by Nancy during a brief visit to his sick bed, signified his blessing by presenting his son with Cliveden. The golden age of the English Astors was about to begin.

II

The Astor Nancy had married was, for the most part, quite unlike any of those who had gone before him. True, Waldorf bore a marked physical resemblance to his father and also exhibited the familiar Astor shyness, but there the similarities ended. One could see in his brown eyes a warmth and compassion which is completely lacking in the portraits of his ancestors, and his personality included a concern for his fellow men with which – in contrast to his cousin Vincent, for example – he was entirely comfortable, seeing no conflict between his desire to improve the lot of mankind and his own privileged position. He makes an interesting case study in the psychologists' debate over whether genetics or environment plays the greater part in character formation. He had the same blood as William Backhouse and John Jacob III and William Waldorf, all of whom displayed in their varying ways the Astorian characteristics we have noted, yet his behaviour and attitudes seemed to be derived from completely different roots. One might detect here the influence of his mother, who by all accounts lacked the air of grand detachment to be found in most Astor wives, but probably more significant was the fact that Waldorf had grown up in an environment far removed from anything previous Astors had known.

Not for him the basic American education followed by a couple of years studying and travelling in Europe and points east. He left America at the age of three or four when his father was posted to Rome, so that the culture he absorbed first was European, and then at the age of nine he was sent to board at a preparatory school in England. The regimen of such institutions in the late nineteenth century was built on classical studies, the acceptance of established order and the concepts of 'being a man' and 'playing the game', the latter applying not only to sports but also to general behaviour. In the best traditions of such schools Waldorf was both a keen student and a hero on the football field and cricket pitch, which meant that when he went on to Eton he fitted perfectly into the mould of the conventional English young gentleman. He became Treasurer of the Eton Society, editor of the *Chronicle*, house captain, winner of the Prince Consort's French Prize and Captain of Boats.

But Eton meant more to him than such transitory successes: it was there that he learnt to accept the social responsibility which by British custom was attached to his class. This sense of *noblesse oblige* has had a long history in Britain and, though by today's standards it appears paternalistic and even insulting to the people on the receiving end, there is no doubt that in its time and in its purest form, it did make a contribution to the stability of the nation. So long as the symbiotic relationship between the rulers and the ruled was accepted by both sides and seen to be of benefit to each, it was easier to be rich in England than in America. When Vincent Astor came into his fortune in New York, he found himself at a loss as to a method of reconciling his wealth and position with his embryonic social conscience, and never did quite achieve harmony between the two: his money was a barrier between him and the rest of the world. In England, perhaps because money was less esteemed for its own sake, Waldorf Astor had no such difficulty. His wealth was a positive advantage to his ambitions for improving the lot of his fellow men – there was no conflict between a natural desire to maintain the privileges of the rich and at the same time to play a worthy part in the lives of the under-classes. Indeed, it is not without a certain irony that although he was ultimately to be eclipsed as a public figure by his wife, he

286

understood the symbiotic aspect of the British class structure far better than Nancy ever managed to do. But then he had had the benefit of an English education, with its attendant insight into the workings of the system.

From Eton Waldorf progressed naturally to Oxford, where at New College he pursued the fashionable course for rich young men, all play and no work, and was lucky to walk away with a fourth-class degree. Much of his time was taken up by sport and even though he was forced to renounce rowing because of heart trouble, he represented the university at fencing and polo, as well as being master of the draghounds. He came down in 1902 with no very clear idea of what he might do with his life, just a vague feeling that he wanted to undertake something useful and worthwhile, and for some time he devoted his attention to the development of a stable of thoroughbred horses which was to make him a leading figure in flat racing circles. Apart from that, he enjoyed the leisured existence of the English gentleman of his day, but in 1905 even his hunting, shooting and Swiss winter sports had to end when angina was diagnosed and his doctors also noticed a susceptibility to tuberculosis, from which his sister Gwendolyn had died in 1902. Waldorf was never to be entirely fit again, and often would be completely incapacitated for several months at a time: in such circumstances he might well have grown to be as remote as his father, given the Astor shyness and stiffness of manner he had inherited, but his meeting with Nancy Langhorne Shaw was to save him from that fate.

Nancy and Waldorf were the perfect complementary couple. He was sober, thoughtful, modest, methodical, acutely conscious of manners and the limits of good behaviour. She was intuitive, lively, skilled at repartee, imperious, dedicated to having a good time and to making people notice her. Without Waldorf's wisdom and restraining influence, it is likely that Nancy's life would have continued as unsatisfactorily as it had begun with her marriage to Robert Shaw. Without Nancy's gaiety and energy, it is doubtful whether Waldorf would have done anything more than breed horses, dabble in farming and donate money to worthy causes. They found in each other assets lacking in themselves which they could use in their different ways to give substance to an existence that otherwise would have been empty and meaningless. Overall it was Nancy who got the best of the bargain, though as we shall see it took her a long time to realize it.

The first year of marriage was, of course, exciting and hectic. After a honeymoon in Switzerland and Italy, the couple went to take up residence at Cliveden, and Nancy immediately set about ripping out many of the classical features lovingly and expensively imported by William Waldorf – 'The Astors have no taste,' she had exclaimed on seeing the interior of the house for the first time. Work had barely begun, however, when the new master and mistress left to visit Nancy's family in Virginia, where Waldorf's Astorian soul must have been shocked by the unconventional manners and overwhelming hospitality of his hosts. On their return to England in the autumn of 1906 they bought an elegant, eighteenth-century London home on the eastern side of St James's Square, and towards the end of the year Nancy became pregnant.

They were settled now, a separate unit independent of the backgrounds which had moulded them, secure in their social position. (Some of the stuffier seigneurs and their ladies looked askance at them, considering them pushy foreigners who could not be transformed into English gentry merely by the stroke of a Home Office pen, but an early visit to Cliveden by King Edward VII and Mrs Keppel provided an unchallengeable endorsement.) Yet there remained the question of how these two young Astors were to employ their restless energies, how they could make a mark upon the world, how they might satisfy a shared desire to 'do good'. As a young girl Nancy had helped her local Episcopalian archdeacon with missionary work among the rural poor folk of western Virginia and she was never to forget the sense of goodness and achievement to be found in helping others. Waldorf, for his part, felt that his father had ignored his obligations as a rich landowner and wanted in some practical way to atone for this neglect. The couple discussed such matters between themselves and with their friends and it was finally decided – on Nancy's initiative, according to her own recollection – that Waldorf should crystallize his vague urge towards public service into a political career. He was by nature a liberal – and in some respects a radical one, as he was later to show – but he felt that the

Conservative policies were likely to be better for the country, so it was to the Tory party that his request for a candidacy went, supported by Arthur Balfour and Lord Curzon (both of whom were firmly under Nancy's spell).

There was an immediate offer in 1907 of a safe parliamentary seat, but it is a measure of Waldorf's character that he just as quickly rejected it, preferring to acquire political skills and the knowledge of how to use them at the hustings rather than taking an easy ride to the House of Commons where his lack of experience would have meant that he had no purpose other than making up the numbers in the division lobbies.

It was a year before the challenge Waldorf wanted presented itself. In July 1908 he was adopted by the Plymouth Conservative Association as prospective parliamentary candidate, mainly, it may be gathered, on the strength of his ability to meet election expenses, the fame of his name, and the deficiencies of his fellow-candidate, the elderly Sir Henry Mortimer Durand (Plymouth being one of those even then anachronistic constituencies that returned two Members of Parliament). Indeed, with the Liberal Party in the ascendant nationally, there seemed little prospect of Plymouth voting for a Tory even if he was a millionaire with liberal tendencies, but a fight was what Waldorf had sought and he prepared for it with a will, enthusiastically supported by Nancy, who saw this as the beginning of a new adventure. Despite the dim prospects for election, the couple bought a house in Plymouth – 3 Elliot Terrace, on the Hoe – and set about getting to know what they seem to have been convinced would eventually become Waldorf's constituency. In a sense this was a sign of their 'unBritishness': there was no requirement (and still is none) for a parliamentary candidate to have particular associations with the constituency he was chosen to represent, whereas in America it was and is considered essential that a congressman should be closely identified with his district – even when William Waldorf Astor ran for office in a working-class area of New York it was one in which he owned property and the electorate was made up largely of German immigrants. Thus Waldorf, by actually buying a home in Plymouth, instantly set himself apart from the general run of British politicians, and his determination to be part of the life of his constituency was to make it an Astor preserve for thirty-five years.

Waldorf was rather fortunate in having more than a year in which to establish himself in Plymouth before being called upon directly to confront the predominantly working-class electorate. Early in 1910, the Liberal Prime Minister, Herbert Asquith, went to the country on the issue of the so-called 'People's Budget' presented by David Lloyd George and vetoed by the House of Lords. As a Tory, Astor was required to defend the power of the Lords, which did not entirely conform to his democratic ideals, but as Nancy canvassed from door to door she let it be known that her husband was really a Liberal at heart and stood for the Conservatives only because their programme as a whole appealed to him more than that of the Government, which was perceived even by some of its supporters as being soft in its response to German imperialism and uncertain over the Irish Question. Waldorf's obvious sincerity and concern for the people he sought to represent swayed large numbers of previous Liberal voters, helped by Nancy's energetic doorstepping (she claimed to have visited thirty thousand homes, though that figure probably benefited from hyperbole), and the Tories gradually began to think that they could win. Two factors were against Astor, however: the political ineptitude of his fellow candidate – which Nancy said was exploited by the Liberals – and his own uncertain health, which collapsed as the campaign reached its climax, forcing his absence from Plymouth for all but three days of the crucial final period before the poll. When the returns were declared, Waldorf had lost by five hundred votes out of the fifteen thousand cast, but the increase in Tory support was such that even defeat was a cause for celebration. At Cliveden the staff unhitched the horses from the carriage of the homecoming campaigners and manhandled it up the long drive to the house. Everyone assumed that on such a showing victory would be Waldorf's next time.

It was only eleven months before the next time came round. The House of Lords remaining obdurate, Asquith consulted the voters again in December 1910 and – with a new running-mate – Waldorf and Nancy returned to the fray. Any shyness Nancy had originally felt about asking people to vote for her husband had completely disappeared by now. She thoroughly enjoyed canvassing and the electors seemed to enjoy her down-to-earth style with its jokes and sharp repartee. The support the Astors had attracted the previous January had transformed Plymouth from a Liberal stronghold into a marginal seat, and this time Astor won it, despite the overwhelming support for the Liberals in the country as a whole. Plymouth celebrated with a torchlight procession and for the two young Astors – they were still only thirty-one years old – it was one of the most exciting days of their lives.

In the House of Commons, Waldorf's ambitions did not run to thoughts of ministerial office. He saw himself as a wielder of influence rather than power, and his ability to exert that influence was greatly enhanced when his father made him acting chairman of the newly acquired *Observer*. In 1912, Waldorf told Garvin, the editor of the paper, that he was more interested in getting things done than in jockeying for political favours – he saw himself, at this stage anyway, as a reformer rather than a careerist. It was for this reason that he became associated with Philip Kerr and the other members of the so-called Kindergarten of young men who had developed a common view of Britain and her empire while serving on the staff of Lord Milner in South Africa during the period following the Boer War, when the Union was being forged. After the introduction of the new South African constitution in 1909, these young men considered that their work in the country was finished and they returned to Britain with the aim of pressing for the creation of a new 'federated' structure for the Commonwealth on the South African model. To this end, Kerr and his friends – who included Lionel Curtis, Robert Brand, Lionel Hichens and John Dove – founded a magazine called *Round Table*: 'a quarterly review of the politics of the British Empire'. Under Kerr's editorship, the first issue of the *Round Table* appeared in November 1910, just a month before Waldorf's entry into Parliament.

Astor had known Robert Brand at Oxford and their acquaintance was renewed upon Brand's return from South Africa. Nancy, meanwhile, had met Kerr, a rather strange ascetic and idealistic man who had become enchanted by her. With these two came Curtis (who had become a Fellow of All Souls) and later Geoffrey Dawson, former editor of the

Johannesburg Star, who was to be closely and fatefully involved with the Astor family as a future editor of *The Times*. Personal relations with the group were to be further cemented by Brand's marriage to Phyllis Langhorne, Nancy's sister, but there was also a communion of thought between these men and the Astors: they were more interested in the philosophical and intellectual aspects of politics than in a particular party line, and although Waldorf was nominally a Conservative they found his liberal views sympathetic. The Astors, for their part, saw virtue in the *Round Table* vision of a sort of federation of English-speaking peoples, which was presumably intended to dominate the world.

Kerr and his colleagues took to holding some of what they called their 'moots' at St James's Square and at Cliveden, and Waldorf was stimulated by the wide-ranging discussions and even arguments – for the participants were by no means all of one mind – concerning the issues of the day. Nancy found it all a bit over her head and tended not to take part in the debates, but she learnt a great deal from the opinions of what were regarded as brilliant young men and was excited by the thought that something important – as it seemed at the time – was happening under her roof. 'Their coming,' she once said of the former Kindergarten members, 'changed all our life.'

Meantime, Waldorf allied himself with progressive elements in Parliament, too, joining a group of relatively inexperienced Conservative backbenchers who were trying to drag the party into the twentieth century against the Victorian attitudes of the hoary old die-hards of the right wing. Inspired by the leadership of the great F.E. Smith, this group formed itself into the Unionist Social Reform Committee, which set about the task of bringing Tory policy up to date by undertaking far-reaching investigations into social questions and suggesting solutions on the basis of evidence from people with first-hand knowledge of the problems. This was radical stuff in 1911, much criticized, and although the always variable degree of cohesion among the members of the committee finally collapsed as a result of divisions over Irish Home Rule (which Waldorf opposed), their attitudes did influence Conservative thinking and at least some of them – notably Edward Wood (who became Lord Halifax) and Stanley Baldwin – would in their later careers help to steer the party into a more democratic age. In the company of such men, who knows to what heights Waldorf Astor might have risen?

But Waldorf was even more radical than most of his colleagues on the committee and during his first year in Parliament shocked the party managers by voting with the Liberal Government and aiding the passage of Lloyd George's revolutionary Health and Unemployment Insurance Bill, which laid the foundation for the modern welfare state. That small act of rebellion – though it was carried out on humanitarian grounds rather than with an eye to his personal future – proved to be of considerable help to Astor's career. Shortly afterwards Lloyd George appeared among the guests at a Cliveden weekend, and in due course Waldorf was invited to become chairman of the State Medical Research Committee, set up under the national insurance act, which had special concern for the treatment and prevention of tuberculosis. The death of his sister and his own precarious health gave Waldorf a particular interest in T.B. and he was soon in the forefront of the campaign against tubercular milk. (His son Michael recalled a train journey to Scotland on which the Astors were accompanied by a cow from Cliveden so that there should be no risk of their children having to drink infected milk.) Lloyd George marked down Waldorf Astor as a man with whom he could work.

To us it might seem paradoxical that Waldorf, with his liberal-democratic inclinations, should sit in Parliament for the party that represented resistance to change and the retention of privilege. Yet in his mind there was no contradiction: he certainly wanted to do something for the benefit of society, but at the same time he was a member of the rich and privileged class and he was well aware that his own interests were likely to be better served by the Conservatives than by the Liberal Party and its populist policies. Politically speaking there was nothing anomalous in his position for although party strife was, if anything, fiercer than it is today, polarization was less evident, in addition to which there was a high degree of factionalism within both the main parties. It is therefore less strange than it might seem to find Waldorf supporting the Liberal Party on national insurance while opposing it over Home Rule for

Ireland on the grounds that the policy would harm the British economy and English farmers in particular.

To his credit it should be said that there was nothing cynical or opportunist about Waldorf's political thought. Though hatred of Socialism was one thing – perhaps the only one – he shared with his father, he nevertheless maintained close and regular contacts with leaders of the Labour movement and established a special friendship with J.H. Thomas, assistant secretary of one of the railway unions, who entered Parliament as a Labour M.P. in the same year as Waldorf won Plymouth.* All shades of political opinion were represented at Cliveden house parties – even Winston Churchill, whom both the Astors but especially Nancy disliked and mistrusted, was to be seen among the guests. Nancy was to have some memorable exchanges with Churchill during her own political career, but one of the most famous took place long before she entered Parliament, when the Astors were staying at Blenheim Palace, home of Churchill's cousin, the Duke of Marlborough. Nancy and Winston reacted to each other with antipathy that was almost chemical and when they came down to breakfast one morning after an entire weekend of arguing, Nancy looked at Churchill across the table and said: 'Winston, if I was married to you I'd put poison in your coffee.' To which Churchill replied: 'Nancy, if I was married to you I'd drink it.' It may be that in some ways their personalities were too similar.

The political hothouse in which the Astors lived boded well for Waldorf's parliamentary career, but as with many others it was the outbreak of the First World War that gave him his first important chance. Rejected by the army because of his bad heart (and envious of his brother John, who as an officer in the Life Guards went to France with the British Expeditionary Force), Waldorf at first insisted on undertaking some form of military service and badgered the authorities into making him a major in the army inspectorate. His task was to tour cook-houses and quartermasters' stores and suggest ways of reducing waste: it was, despite appearances, not the most comfortable job

* Jimmy Thomas became general secretary of the National Union of Railwaymen in 1917. He was later a member of the Labour and National Governments (1924–36), with responsibilities for the colonies and dominions and ministerial rank.

in the world, since in the jingoistic fever of 1914 a young and seemingly healthy man who was not with the B.E.F. was likely to be regarded with scorn – and the fact that Waldorf was both rich and an M.P. gave rise to suspicion in some quarters that he had bought himself a safe billet. In the circumstances it took some courage for Waldorf to put on a uniform at all. But his real contribution to the war effort was to be in the civilian rather than the military sphere.

He was much concerned with Plymouth, of course, because of its importance as a naval base, and he was horrified to discover, on a visit shortly after the declaration of war, that the Y.M.C.A. canteens for the military were nothing more than tents. He spent £1,000 on building and equipping a proper mess hut at Crown Hill Barracks and, when it proved to be a success, provided six more. Nancy, meanwhile, worked in the various improvised hospitals that received the first great flood of wounded. She encouraged the men to take up knitting and embroidery to keep themselves occupied during their recovery and prevent their minds from dwelling on the horrors they had so recently experienced – and if any of them were shy about doing 'women's work', it may be imagined that Mrs Astor's forthright manner soon overcame resistance.

The Astors had, in fact, offered Cliveden to the government as a military hospital but had been told that it was not required (actually the War Office had, quite understandably, judged the huge rambling place unsuitable for conversion but had been too tactful to inform the eager owners of this). Appalled by the makeshift wards into which the rapidly growing numbers of unfortunate men were being put, Waldorf tried again in November 1914, this time approaching the Canadian Army, whose medical officers were astute enough to see the potential of the vast covered tennis court and bowling alley, which was about a mile from the main house. Here a hospital was established by February 1915, with room for more than a hundred patients and its staff settled in the neighbouring Dower House. By war's end the accommodation had been extended to take six hundred men and the main house, stripped of its able-bodied male staff and with its flower gardens given over to vegetable plots, was a convalescent home.

Nancy was in her element here and later claimed to have

helped to make her hospital 'the best in the kingdom' and the happiest. She moved among the men jollying and sometimes bullying them back to health, and she was quick to put the British case to the wounded German prisoners who found their way to Cliveden. Of course, not all the men in the nation's happiest hospital could be saved, and by 1918 there were forty graves in the Cliveden grounds, beneath a memorial statue for which Nancy's head was used as a model. Nancy kept up her work in Plymouth, too, and several anecdotes tell how she badgered broken men until they regained their will to live. Later in the war the Astors' home in St James's Square was also delivered up to military use, serving as a hostel for American officers and known by them as 'the Waldorf-Astoria'.

In the midst of all this, Waldorf remained busy in Parliament. Not only was he by now chairman of the Unionist Social Reform Committee (though this was by no means the power-house it had been under F.E. Smith), but he was also running the Medical Research Committee, which Lord Milner, helped by Astor and his colleagues, was to develop into the Ministry of Health. To these were added new duties in 1916 when Lloyd George succeeded Asquith as Prime Minister in the Coalition Government and invited Waldorf to be his parliamentary private secretary. This gave Waldorf automatic membership of perhaps the most influential group in the country, the Cabinet Intelligence Unit created by Lloyd George as a presidential-style secretariat and nicknamed the 'Garden Suburb' because its early operations were directed from huts in the garden of Number 10 Downing Street. It is not without significance that the leading 'Suburbanite' was Philip Kerr, and it is also noteworthy that Kerr and Astor were two of only four members of the Cabinet Intelligence Branch who remained throughout all the changes made in his 'staff' by the impulsive and capricious Lloyd George.

Waldorf's political career now seemed destined to reach the heights and he began to harbour ambitions of eventual ministerial office in the Coalition – Minister of Health, perhaps, in view of all his committee work in that field. But it was not to be. Despite his intelligence and his innate sense of what was good for the people, Astor was not really a political animal: he was too modest and self-effacing. When the plums were handed out at the end of the war, none came his way.

In 1918 he won a second election in Plymouth – now divided into three single-member constituencies of which Waldorf's was the Sutton Division – with a majority of almost twelve thousand over his nearest rival, the Co-operative Party candidate, but he remained at the level of parliamentary secretary, at the Ministry of Food, then the Local Government Board and finally at the new Ministry of Health he had helped to establish. His star had waned, partly because the political situation had changed and partly because he was prepared to sacrifice his own career at the altar of his wife's political ambitions. From now on, he would have to participate from the sidelines.

Nancy blamed old William Waldorf for her husband's blighted hopes. If Willie had not gone all out for a peerage, she claimed, Waldorf might have remained in the Commons and done great things: as it was, he was forced to enter the House of Lords as the second Viscount Astor in 1919 and forgo his parliamentary dreams. This explanation betrays an imperfect understanding of the British system, which Waldorf must have shared since he appeared to abandon all hope of holding high office after his friend Jimmy Thomas failed to secure Commons approval for a Bill to allow peers to renounce their titles. In truth, there was and is nothing in constitutional practice to prevent a peer from holding high office – Lord Curzon was a contemporary case in point, and there are many other examples up to the present day. Waldorf Astor might not have wanted his peerage – indeed, it led to a rift with his father which ended only with the death of the old man – but it was not the reason for his lack of advancement in public life. If anything, Nancy was more to blame for that.

III

'Lady Astor,' wrote the Princess of Pless (the former Daisy Cornwallis-West) in 1928, 'is very sharp and witty and has that unusual combination – to be found only, I think, in Americans – a cynical mind and a sentimental heart.' It was a combination that would guarantee success, of a sort, in politics for Nancy Astor, though it must be doubted whether she would ever have been given a start had it not been for the modesty and good nature of her husband, or indeed whether she could ever have won a parliamentary seat other than Plymouth Sutton.

Not that a political career was something that she seemed to have longed for, but it is clear that she would not have been as happy to take a back seat to Waldorf as he was to stand in her shadow: she needed a purpose in life, a means of both warding off boredom – her greatest enemy – and bringing her the attention, even the notoriety, she craved. The early years of her marriage to Waldorf had certainly not been lacking in either interest or the attention of the world, but by 1911, with her husband making a name for himself in Parliament and becoming an honorary member of the Milner Kindergarten (from both of which Nancy was to a large extent excluded), she had begun to fret over the supporting role in which she seemed to have been cast, the star part having gone to Waldorf. Her second child, Phyllis (always known as Wissie), had been born in 1909 and her third, David, was due early in 1912, and it has been suggested that it was the pregnancy which, in 1911, gave rise to a mysterious illness that was to make Nancy a semi-invalid for the better part of three years. The cause of the malady, however, is perhaps more likely to have been psychosomatic, arising from the fact that she felt bored and rather left out. From girlhood she had been highly strung – she was not given a coming-out ball because her parents thought it would be too much for her – and had been prey to periods of unexplained illness which were almost certainly nervous in character: now she frequently took to her bed because, according to her son Michael, she could see no new worlds to conquer, felt uncertain of herself in the intellectually exalted company Waldorf had gathered round him, and was frustrated at the thought of devoting the rest of her life to being nothing more than a glamorous hostess.

Michael, in fact, suggests that his mother's malaise was evident in her diaries as early as 1907, the year after her marriage, and attributes it on the one hand to Nancy's constitutional inability to come to terms with the conventions of English life and on the other hand to inner tensions arising from the lack of any guiding principle such as appeared to motivate her husband and his Kindergarten friends. In marrying Waldorf Astor, Michael says, Nancy had bitten off more

Viscount William Waldorf Astor, who died Oct. 18, 1919, gave $46,000,000 to his two sons two months before. On this they paid $10,800,000 taxes in 1922 to the Treasury which claimed the transfer had been made in anticipation of death. When they lately sought to recover this, plus nearly $10,000,000 interest, a Federal Jury decided against them.

William Waldorf Astor, founder of the family's English branch. Disgusted by America's 'vulgarity', he moved to London and eventually became a peer.

Cliveden, the great house overlooking the Thames which was bought by William Waldorf and turned into something resembling an Italian palace. It became famous as the centre of 'the Cliveden Set', with Nancy Astor as its chatelaine.

Hever Castle in Kent. William Waldorf had the River Eden diverted to create a lake and built a mock Tudor village in the grounds.

Waldorf Astor, the Second Viscount and husband of Nancy. He believed his political career was ruined by his peerage but encouraged his wife to become the first woman to take her seat in Parliament.

John Jacob Astor V, second son of William Waldorf. As the owner of *The Times,* he became a peer in his own right.

Nancy Astor — the famous portrait by John Singer Sargent, painted in 1907.

A rarely seen photograph of David Astor in the 1940s. He became editor of *The Observer,* owned by his father.

Hever Day: every year between the wars, John Jacob Astor V and his wife, Violet, entertained the staff of *The Times* and their families at Hever Castle.

Nancy Astor with her son Bill and seven-year-old grandson William on her eightieth birthday in 1959. Bill was later to become embroiled in the Profumo scandal.

Michael Astor, third son of Waldorf and Nancy. He was a non-conformist who dabbled in painting and writing.

David Astor, grandson of Waldorf and Nancy. Today's Astors work for their living.

than she could chew: she was unprepared, both psychologically and intellectually, for the rarefied atmosphere of upper-class England once entry into it ceased to be a challenge and an adventure. Her limited education had endowed her mind with the spirit of inquiry but had not been extensive enough to train her in the habit of original and constructive thought. On the emotional side, her simple religious faith was, if anything, a complicating factor because her childlike notions of Christian goodness and self-sacrifice could not cope with the immense wealth and barriers of privilege that surrounded her: though the cynical side of her character enjoyed the material luxuries and the advantages of elitism, the sentimental part was troubled by a sense of guilt and distaste towards worldly success. Perhaps her desire for a large family, which seems to contradict her tendency towards sexual frigidity, had its roots in the thought that motherhood might fill the worrying void in her life and resolve some of her internal conflicts, but even there she came up against convention, which dictated that the children of the upper classes should grow up apart from their parents, in the care of nannies, governesses, servants and other surrogates.

So for a long time Nancy languished, suffering from an illness that apparently defied diagnosis, often keeping to her suite of rooms where, as the Cliveden butler, Edwin Lee, recalled, she would try to cheer herself up by giving dinner parties for small groups of close friends. She would sit up in bed while her guests clustered round a small table at the foot and the meal – always a full dinner, as would have been served in the dining room – was brought up from the kitchen on trays.

Spas, rest cures (often taken at Rest Harrow, a less than appealing villa Waldorf had built on Sandwich Bay in Kent, or at the Astors' shooting box in Scotland, which Nancy rather disliked) and various prescriptions were tried, but none brought any improvement in the patient's condition. That Nancy herself was aware of the possible nature of her illness is evident. For a time, in the search for some simple framework or discipline that might give shape to her life, she flirted with the principles of New Thought, a rather curious system of therapeutics much in vogue at the time in America, which sought to alleviate life's difficulties by suggesting that whatever one wanted could be gained if only one thought about it hard enough. Not surprisingly, Nancy found that the theory did not work; her doctors, meanwhile, discovered that she had what was described vaguely as an 'internal abscess' and performed surgery in February 1914. The operation was not a success in either medical or psychological terms and Nancy was told a second one would be necessary. Lying on the balcony at Rest Harrow, where she had gone to convalesce, Nancy, in deep despair, brooded on her situation and, by her own recollection, came to the conclusion that sickness and misery could not be part of God's plan for the human race, that there must be some spiritual answer to her condition. The agent of enlightenment proved to be her sister, Phyllis, who arrived from America and, in discussing Nancy's troubled thoughts, outlined the principles of Christian Science, which holds that sickness is a state of error which can be overcome by prayer and mental discipline leading to the true knowledge of Christ. Nancy was fascinated and demanded to know more. Phyllis was acquainted with a Christian Science 'practitioner', or faith-healer, from America called Maud Bull and arranged for her to visit Cliveden. Nancy was converted in a day, having read the first chapter of *Science and Health with Key to the Scriptures*, the book by Mary Baker Eddy which sets out the creed of Christian Science. 'It was like a new beginning for me,' Nancy would say later. 'My life really was made over ... I was no longer frightened of anything.'

Soon after her conversion (which must have been the quickest of Mrs Bull's career) she underwent the second operation ordered by her doctor – though in the first flush of her new faith she did her best to cancel the surgery and only succumbed when Waldorf put his foot down – but this time her recovery was swift and complete and, as she said, 'from then on I had done with doctors'. Even those who did not share Nancy's beliefs have testified that she was never ill again, apart from the odd head cold, a boil and a mild attack of shingles. Nor did she appear to suffer from that sickness of spirit which had probably been, more than anything else, responsible for her physical symptoms. Christian Science was her panacea because it gave her something solid to cling to, an easily assimilated set of concepts that she did not have to think through for herself in the way that the more conventional forms of Christianity require. Whatever the merits or otherwise of Christian Science in particular, it was admirably suited to Nancy's physical needs (it was ill-health, after all, that led Mrs Eddy to found her church) and it provided direction for her lively, questing but untutored intellect. Indeed, in her case it was particularly appropriate with its rejection of man's animal nature and material form, claiming that 'Spirit is God, and man is His image and likeness. Therefore man is not material; he is spiritual.' The animal and the material had been problematical for Nancy Astor.

At any rate, her conversion to this spiritual state and the renewal of her energies came just in time. Four months after her enthusiastic espousal of Christian Science, Europe was engaged in the bloodiest war of its history and all her resources were required for the work she was called upon to undertake. Furthermore, though she was to lose no close relatives in the war, her son Bobbie was on active service and some of her dearest friends or their sons were killed: in her previous state the nervous strain might well have been too much for her to bear, but her new-found faith was her guide and her strength and she was able to accept the sacrifices with equanimity. 'After two years in that war,' she wrote later, 'we did not look at the casualty lists any more. There was nothing to look for. All our friends had gone.'

Of course, the tenets of Christian Science did not sit well with Nancy's commitment to wartime hospital work, but the apostles of Mrs Eddy had an answer for that, too: rather than squaring up to the moral dilemmas presented by the bloodshed, the Christian Scientist was to maintain a strictly personal stance and refrain from passing judgment on other people. How that principle might apply to a soldier on the battlefield, with very real bullets that inflicted very real wounds, was never altogether clear (presumably Christian Scientists should, by rights, have been conscientious objectors), but at least it left the way open for Nancy to care for the wounded without compromising her belief – and in fact she boasted of the power of mental pressure in aiding the recovery of some of her charges.

The war over, Nancy needed a new outlet for her energies and found it quickly enough in campaigning for Waldorf in the

1918 election, the first in which women were able to vote, thus giving Nancy's efforts added impetus. What she would have done subsequently, had it not been for Waldorf's involuntary elevation to the House of Lords a year later, cannot even be guessed at, but of course she was never put to the test of finding something to occupy herself. The *Evening Standard* pointed to the road ahead on the very day the first Viscount Astor died when it reported a rumour that the wife of the former Conservative Member for Plymouth Sutton was to stand in his stead at the by-election caused by his assumption of his inherited title. The Astors always insisted that such an arrangement had never been discussed, yet Waldorf was well aware that his father's ennoblement would one day – sooner rather than later, for the old man was getting on in years – mean the end of his own career in the House of Commons and must surely have given some thought to ways of protecting the investment of time, effort and money he had put into his constituency. Of course, in the beginning there was no prospect of Nancy being able to succeed him, since it was not until 1918 that women had the right to vote and to stand for Parliament, but once the possibility did exist it would have been strange indeed if it had not been considered, given Nancy's experience at the hustings on behalf of her husband. It must have occurred to someone, at least, for the *Standard* to have been so quick off the mark.

Throughout a week of intense press speculation following the first suggestion of Nancy's candidacy, Waldorf turned away all inquiries with the reply that the matter was under consideration and that the choice lay with his wife, but the *Pall Mall Gazette*, which was naturally believed to be most likely to know, indicated that the new Lady Astor would probably not fight the by-election, giving rise to speculation that the mantle would pass to John Astor, Waldorf's younger brother, who was known to be in search of a seat. On 24 October, however, the Plymouth Sutton Conservative Association formally invited Nancy to be their candidate (to the dismay of some old-fashioned Unionists in the local party) and Nancy telegraphed her acceptance two days later.

'Peer's Wife Enters,' said the *Daily Herald*, adding characteristically: 'To Fight the Workers at Plymouth'. Representing the workers was William Gay, the Labour candidate Waldorf had soundly beaten the previous year, but although Nancy inherited a substantial majority on which to base her hopes it soon became clear that she would not have things all her own way. The disgruntled Plymouth Unionist wing of the Conservative Party, who wanted no truck with either women in Parliament or the Lloyd George Coalition of which Waldorf had been such a prominent member, put up their own candidate, the Liberals of the old school (Asquith supporters), who also had no time for Lloyd George, trundled out their thrice-defeated man, Isaac Foot, a local lawyer who sensed that this time he might have a chance, with the prospect of the Tory vote splitting between Nancy and the Independent Unionist, Alderman Lionel Jacobs.

Waldorf, however, who was not above indulging in a political slanging-match, for all his high principles, remained supremely confident of his wife's victory. The Liberals, he said, supporters of the Asquithian 'Wait and See' policy which had almost led to disaster in the early part of the war, had selected a candidate 'who is accustomed to getting beaten'. He almost received a writ for slander from the Labour man, whom he described as 'a young man who, I am told, has not been a great success as a manager in the Co-op'. He went on to attack Gay's pacifist views, calling him a 'well-meaning sort of extremist belonging to the Bolshevist wing of the Labour Party' and claiming that 'if he and his friends had had their way we should have lost the war'. What upset Mr Gay was the allegation that the Co-operative Society had not been pleased with his abilities as a manager.

Yet there was the problem of Nancy's sex: in the 1918 election none of the serious women candidates had secured a seat – the only winner had been the eccentric Countess Markiewicz, and she had been shocked and appalled by her victory, having stood more out of mischief than anything else.* Nancy quickly set about counteracting the antipathy towards the idea of women in the House of Commons. 'I am not a sex

* Countess Markiewicz (Constance Gore-Booth), representing Sinn Fein, was elected the first women M.P. in Britain in 1918. A fervent Irish nationalist, sentenced to death and then reprieved for her part in the Easter Rising of 1916, she refused to swear the parliamentary Oath of Allegiance and therefore could not take her seat in the Commons.

candidate,' she declared. And: 'I have heard it said that a woman who has got children shouldn't go into the House of Commons. She ought to be home looking after her children. That is true, but I feel someone ought to be looking after the more unfortunate children. My children are among the fortunate ones, and it is that that steels me to go to the House of Commons to fight the fight, not only of the men but of the women and children of England.' Women were voters, too, now and this was the sort of stuff that would appeal to them. Furthermore, there was a certain novelty value about a female candidate. 'If you want an M.P. who will be a repetition of the six hundred other M.P.s, don't vote for me,' Nancy told her adoption meeting on 3 November 1919. 'If you want a lawyer or if you want a pacifist, don't elect me. If you can't get a fighting man, take a fighting woman... If you want a party hack, don't elect me...'

Clearly she intended to base her campaign on personality rather than policy, and with support for the Labour Party noticeably increasing that was perhaps the only way she could have won. Whatever political points she had to make were supplied by Waldorf – who acted as researcher, adviser, campaign manager and speechwriter – and, as a Coalition Conservative, she was supported by an endorsement from Lloyd George (though Philip Kerr actually drafted the document): 'Your sympathies were genuinely with the people long before you had any notion of becoming a candidate yourself, and even before women's suffrage became an accepted fact.' Nevertheless the Coalition and the Prime Minister would only be supported in return, Nancy declared, when she thought they were right. The people of Plymouth were to vote not for party but for Nancy Astor. 'Although I am one of the most serious minded women in England, I have got the sort of mirth of the British Tommy. I can laugh when I am going "over the top". I do not believe in sexes or classes. It is the heart that really matters... You will not expect long reasoned speeches from me, I hope, because if you expect 'em you won't get 'em. It is not what I call my style.'

Of course, the other candidates could not match this breezy, unconventional approach. The Independent Unionist quickly withdrew from the fray and the others – particularly the Labour man, who by the very nature of his politics was crushingly earnest – had their parties to consider and therefore lacked Nancy's freedom to present only themselves to the electorate. Nancy could skip merrily away from contentious issues or questions about what she would actually do in Parliament; her rivals had political programmes to contend with.

Even her wealth and social position she was able to turn to advantage, quipping that, 'I have more, far more than I ought to have, but if some members of the [Labour Party] possessed what I do they would not be asking for your votes today.' She travelled round the constituency in her coach, dressed immaculately, haranguing almost any group she could find in her shrill, piercing voice with its Virginian inflection and tendency to drop the 'g' on words that ended in 'ing'. So extraordinary a sight was she that people could not resist listening and joining in – and once they got that far she held them. The ordinary folk were not used to great personages joking with them, trading insults with them and generally behaving in a quite uninhibited fashion. When one man shouted obscenities at Nancy she appealed to the crowd: 'I want every woman in this street to see that this man doesn't vote for me. I don't want the vote of a man who uses language like that to a woman when he is sober.' And to a woman who tried to catch her out by asking a question about the divorce laws she retorted: 'Madam, I am sorry to hear you are in trouble.'

More astonishing still to her audiences was the fact that she teased them. 'And now, my dears,' she concluded on one occasion, 'I'm going back to one of my beautiful palaces to sit down in my tiara and do nothing, and when I roll out in my car I will splash you all with mud and look the other way.' It was less of an election campaign than an entertainment, and the newspapers were in no doubt that the people would be happy to pay for the show with their votes. 'Lady Astor is laughing her way into Parliament,' commented the *Evening Standard*, though *The Times* accused her of 'treating the whole affair as a huge joke'.

A joke it was not: Nancy was determined to win and set about doing so in the only way she knew how. She played the advantage of novelty for all it was worth and worked hard to create the impression in the minds of her audiences that she was a nob who could come down to their level, whereas in fact her words and actions, when considered coldly, were patronizing in the extreme and displayed a contempt always felt by certain sections of the upper classes for their social inferiors. William Waldorf, with his distaste for the sweatier aspects of democracy, would have been proud of her, recognizing that unlike him she had the ability to capitalize on her superiority. To her the voters of Plymouth were like children who could be cajoled or bullied into doing what she wanted them to do.

But if her campaign was no joke, neither did it have much to do with politics. Nancy set herself up as an honest politician, one who could be frank and open with the electorate, but if contemporary accounts of her electioneering are accurate, she said virtually nothing about where she stood politically or what she intended to do for her constituents if she secured their votes. That she was sincere in wanting to be a representative of the people is beyond doubt (why else would she have done it, since she already enjoyed a status far above that of any mere M.P. and she had no creed or dogma to which she was passionately attached?), but all it really meant to her was a vague, sentimental and somewhat quixotic idea of righting wrongs and doing good. The one definite political stance urged upon her by Philip Kerr – that of total prohibition of the sale of alcohol, such as had recently been enacted in America – she rejected because she knew that, in spite of support for the measure in certain well-meaning quarters, it would lose her votes in Plymouth. Just what the 14,495 burghers who elected her thought they were voting for may only be imagined (Mr Gay got 9,292 votes and Mr Foot 4,139). One cannot escape the conclusion that for Nancy it was the winning that was important and beyond that she had no very definite aim in view other than using up her energies, filling her life with interest and amusement and attracting all the attention she could wish for. As she had established herself at her New York City finishing school by shocking and amusing her classmates, so she made herself seem important as a politician, turned herself into a phenomenon, by teasing first the voters and then her fellow Members of Parliament.

By the end of the first week of her election campaign in Plymouth, the crowds were calling her 'Our Nancy'. That was distasteful to her, but it was also a misconception: it was they who were hers. Everyone always had to dance to the tune that Nancy Astor chose.

9 *Charmed Circle*

While Nancy Astor was flashing like some unexpected and unpredictable comet through the firmament of English public life, her brother-in-law was also seeking to make his mark on the affairs of the nation. Less brilliant than Waldorf and certainly much less flamboyant than Nancy, with whom he was never on the best of terms, John Jacob Astor V was not likely to set the world on fire. His approach was closer to that of his American forebears, whose reticence and dislike of publicity he had inherited: it was his money that talked.

Born in 1886, in America of course, John Jacob had arrived in England at an even more impressionable age than Waldorf and became even more the model English gentleman than his elder brother. Like Waldorf he was educated at Eton and New College, Oxford, but then their paths diverged as John took a commission in the Life Guards. In 1911 he was posted to India as an aide-de-camp to the Viceroy and remained there three years, acquiring a reputation as a fearless tiger hunter and leaving behind him rather exotic commemoration of the Astor name in a Kashmiri town and a tributary of the Indus river. When the First World War began, John's was one of the first regiments to be sent to the aid of Belgium, and within three months Captain Astor was seriously wounded at Ypres when a shell exploded near him, breaking his arm and peppering his body with shrapnel. Invalided home, John became close to Lady Violet Mercer-Nairne, the young widow of a brother officer killed at Ypres, and in 1916 they were married. The match was warmly welcomed by old William Waldorf, since Violet was the daughter of Lord Minto and therefore in genealogical terms much more suitable than his elder son's choice of an American divorcee. After his wedding, Captain Astor returned to active service and was wounded again at

Cambrai, during the last German offensive of the war: again it was shellfire that hit him, but this time his right leg was so severely damaged that it had to be amputated.

John left the Life Guards with the rank of major, which he carried proudly – and with good reason – for the rest of his life. Like many officers returning to Lloyd George's promised 'homes fit for heroes' he had a mind to go into politics, desiring so to order the world that the horrors he had experienced would never come to pass again. He was also a very rich man and a landowner – on his father's death in 1919 he had inherited Hever Castle, the magnificent London home in Carlton House Terrace, a half-share in a fifty million dollar trust and at least five million dollars of his own in American stocks and bonds. With such wealth and such a war record behind him, it was not difficult to find accommodation in a safe Conservative parliamentary seat and in 1920 he became the prospective candidate for Dover, which had the added advantage of being near his country home.

The war, however, had removed many of the old certainties from British politics; the broad consensus which had sustained the Conservative and Liberal parties for half a century or more no longer existed. Further, a growing body of opinion in the country was becoming tired of the 'adventurism' of Lloyd George and deeply suspicious of his populist approach. The dynamism which had originally inspired the nation was now beginning to be perceived as a destructive force: many people were tired of continual alarums and excursions; they wanted a quiet life, and Lloyd George was not the man to give them that. John, whose shyness made election campaigning a nightmare for him, found himself opposed by a Tory right-winger standing against the 'socialistic' and free-spending policies of the Coalition, which John, like Waldorf and Nancy, supported at the time, as did the mainstream of the Conservative Party. His rival, Colonel Sir Thomas Polson, was backed by both *The Times* and the *Daily Mail*, which had grown tired of the Prime Minister they had once supported and daily attacked the 'squandermania' of Lloyd George's policies. The Dover election came to be perceived as a test of the Coalition's popularity; as it turned out, it was not popular in Dover and Astor lost the election by more than three thousand votes. Lloyd George's days as a national leader were numbered, but Major Astor lived to fight again, taking advantage of the country's yearning for 'tranquillity'.

If John had learnt one thing during the campaign it was the value of having the press, or at least very influential sections of it, behind him, and before the next election was called he was able to ensure that the right kind of support would be forthcoming in the future. In the autumn of 1922, shortly before the resignation of Lloyd George and the dissolution of the Coalition, Lord Northcliffe, the megalomaniac proprietor of *The Times* and the *Daily Mail* died and John Astor was given the chance to emulate his brother by acquiring a newspaper. Northcliffe's brother, Lord Rothermere, took control of the mass-circulation *Mail*, but the position of *The Times* was more complicated.

Northcliffe had bought the paper in 1908 from John Walter, a descendant of its founder, and his will gave Walter first option to buy after Northcliffe's death. Under the control of North-cliffe the circulation of *The Times* had increased from 40,000 to 165,000, but only at the cost of lowering its cover price from threepence to a penny, which did nothing for its financial viability. Northcliffe's main reason for holding on to it was the furtherance of his own political ambitions and its international reputation and authority had suffered badly during his dictatorial and eccentric rule, particularly the virtual insanity in his last months, when the situation in its offices at Printing House Square was chaotic. John Walter wished to maintain a family presence within the paper and also to restore it to its former position of pre-eminence, but he lacked the money to buy it, so he approached John Astor, suggesting that a million pounds (roughly five million dollars at the time) would secure control and that he himself would be happy with just a small percentage of the equity.

Astor agreed to put up the money – after all, this was the paper which had helped to engineer his defeat at Dover, where he was to be a candidate once more – but in order to prevent Rothermere from capitalizing on the fact that such a rich man was bidding, his name was to be kept out of the negotiations. Walter was simply to approach Rothermere with his offer, citing funds from a secret backer.

At this point, Astor legend enters into the story, seeming to show that the shrewd Rothermere was outwitted. There is, however, more than one interpretation of the way things went. What is certain is that Rothermere let it be known in the corridors of Printing House Square that he would bid for *The Times* himself. Geoffrey Dawson, associate of the Kindergarten and friend of Waldorf and Nancy, himself a Northcliffe editor of *The Times* who had been forced out early in 1919 during one of the proprietor's manic phases, noted in his diary that the possibility of Rothermere's purchase of the paper was being openly discussed among *Times* management and editorial executives towards the end of September 1922. Having suffered for more than a decade from the vagaries of Northcliffe, the *Times* men were not about to welcome his brother as proprietor and they passed on all they heard to Walter and to Bobby Grant, the American banker who was acting for Astor. The consortium, it seemed, would have to outbid Rothermere, but in order to do so, Walter needed to know how much the rival bid would be.

The story goes that Sir Campbell Stuart, the managing director of *The Times*, who supported the Walter/Astor attempt to buy the paper, was invited to dinner by a friend of Rothermere's, apparently for the purpose of discovering what the bid would be. During the evening, Stuart overheard a telephone conversation between his host and an unidentified person (assumed to be Rothermere). The caller asked how much Walter was offering for *The Times* and then revealed that the press lord's bid would be something more than one and a quarter million pounds. Stuart immediately reported to Walter, and as a result the Astor bid went to £1,350,000, which was accepted by the Northcliffe estate, frustrating, it would seem, the great Rothermere.

However, there is, as I have said, another side to the affair. First, Rothermere was Northcliffe's executor and therefore was in a position to determine how the terms of his brother's will were carried out. In the circumstances, he would have been closely involved in the negotiations for the sale of the paper and would not, as the legend suggests, have been reduced to using intermediaries to discover what Walter's bid would be. Second, Northcliffe's will gave Walter the right to buy the paper *at its market value*, so there was in fact no question of any sort of auction: all Walter had to do was raise the money the paper was judged to be worth, and it became his. And finally, a close associate of Rothermere has reported that there was never any question of his buying *The Times*, which was as much a liability as the *Mail*, with its two million circulation, was an asset.

On balance, then, it appears to have been the wily Rothermere who did the outwitting, forcing Astor to pay more than he really needed to with the device of the staged telephone call. Indeed, it is not impossible that Rothermere knew who the 'secret backer' was, or at least had a pretty good idea, given that the Astors already owned *The Observer* and that the financial consultant was an American banker. Nor is it without significance that Campbell Stuart was involved: he was forced to resign as managing director after Astor and Walter brought back Geoffrey Dawson to edit the paper, one of the conditions of Dawson's acceptance being that the powers of the managing director over the editorial conduct of the paper – supreme in Northcliffe's time – should be removed. Stuart was keen to portray himself as a disinterested party anxious only to secure the future of *The Times*, and indeed remained on its board of directors after the take-over. It was obviously to his credit that he should be thought to have 'saved' the paper from another Northcliffe.

It was 23 October when Astor gained control of *The Times* (he had ninety per cent of the shares against Walter's ten per cent) and it was 15 November when Dover and the rest of the nation voted, with the Conservative Party now united under Bonar Law and eschewing its former coalition with the Lloyd George wing of the Liberal Party. In this new situation, the right-wing diehard was swept aside and Astor was elected on the official Conservative programme, which above all else promised 'tranquillity'. The new Member of Parliament and owner of *The Times* took the same view. In a statement of policy for his paper he declared: 'The function of a paper like *The Times* is not to enter into rivalry with the Government of the day or to usurp for the benefit of its readers a party's prerogative of formulating political programmes. It will lean as far as possible to the support of the Government of the day and especially so when the Government is the spokesman of the nation in international affairs. Be it Tory, Liberal or Labour the Government in office will in so far as *The Times* is concerned be entitled to all that rightfully belongs to the Government of Great Britain. At a period of scarcely restricted democratic rule, it is all important that this organ, at any rate, should be universally acknowledged to express the thoughts and feelings of the ordinary citizen of the country.' In other words, the paper was to be as conventional and uninspired as the men who now took over the running of the country. It was a time when Britain buried its head in the sand, and *The Times*, its owner and his brother and sister-in-law helped to dig the hole.

Three days before the State Opening of the new Parliament, Astor and Dawson met to discuss the latter's terms for returning to *The Times*. These were, in effect, that there was to be no interference by the proprietor in editorial policy. Astor was 'very nice' about it, by Dawson's account, and by the first week of December the appointment of the new editor could be announced, though it was not until New Year's Day 1923 that *The Times* itself formally indicated Dawson's return. Glad to be back at the centre of events, and this time without a Northcliffe to cramp his style, Dawson began to promulgate the Establishment line as faithfully as any archbishop, and indeed the diaries of this rather vain and pompous little man show that he was almost mystically attached to the editor's chair. In 1928, for example, he rejected an offer to take up the presidency of Magdalen College, Oxford, partly on the grounds that there were not enough young men at *The Times* to carry it on – though he used the offer as an opportunity to assure himself that Astor would not welcome the chance of replacing him with someone younger.

As agreed, Astor did not interfere in the editorial policy of the paper, confining his activities to the management side. He appears to have been equally reticent in his political career. When the new Prime Minister, Stanley Baldwin, called a general election in the winter of 1923 (Bonar Law had resigned on health grounds and died shortly afterwards) Astor was not even in Britain for the campaign, preferring to visit Egypt instead. When he did return home it was to take his seat in the Commons – even though Labour had won overall – but he made the mistake of voting without first having been formally sworn in, which in constitutional practice automatically voided his election. So the man who disliked campaigning and hated publicity was obliged to present himself to the voters again, though since he was unopposed the result was a foregone conclusion. Not that it did him much good, for the collapse of the first, short-lived Labour Government sent everyone back to the hustings in October 1924: fortunately for John, the Conservatives won a solid majority and he was not called upon to campaign again until 1929. (Whether Stanley Baldwin's second administration was as lucky for the country is another matter entirely.)

In Parliament, J.J., as he styled himself, was no more effective than Nancy Astor and considerably less visible. Indeed it is hard to see why he wanted to be there at all, unless it was simply to do his bit to preserve the status quo in the face of a groundswell of socialist thinking. He did not appear to seek ministerial office, though he was no less striking than many of those who did, and he championed no reformist causes, as Waldorf had done. The contribution to political life for which his name is best remembered is the winning of the parliamentary squash championship in both 1926 and 1927, which was in truth no mean achievement for a man with one leg. On the other hand, like the pathologically shy John Jacob III in America he was something of a power broker because of his ownership of *The Times* (though it was Dawson who liked to take the credit for influencing Prime Ministers). Together with Waldorf and Nancy he was at the centre of a tight little circle of 'new' Tories, reconstructed Liberals, former Kinder – Robert Brand, for example, was on the *Times* board – and others who exerted perhaps the most powerful, and some would say damaging, influence on British attitudes and policies between the wars. Of the three principals, J.J. was the only one who escaped censure when the British Establishment finally had to face up to the realities of the world, because he was the one who said least.

The basis of this wilful refusal to see things for what they were was a naive belief in the innate goodness of man and a tolerant, almost paternal view of the world's sins and troubles which was undoubtedly fashioned by a comfortable way of life in which whatever was desired could be obtained without much difficulty. To put it another way, those who subscribed to this philosophy, if such it can be called, were generally the rich and privileged (and, of course, because of their positions, best able to influence others). They had seen poverty, misery, disease and decay, but they did not really understand any of these things; they believed enlightened capitalism – whatever that might be – was the answer to all ills while socialism held all the terrors of the pit; they even seemed to think that happiness and harmony could be achieved by legislation. At first, such beliefs seemed plausible and attractive and good, but they ultimately became a form of extremism (when the world did not conform to the model so constructed) and selfishness that was actually dangerous and potentially destructive.

America, less sensitive to and guilty about the disparity between rich and poor, began to wonder just what its native sons and daughters were up to when Lord Astor expounded to New Yorkers in 1921 a policy that struck them as pure socialism. Defending Lloyd George's welfare and housing programmes (soon to bring down the Welsh Wizard, in fact), Waldorf said they were 'insurance against revolution'. Europe, he maintained, was on the edge of a volcano and nobody knew how thin the crust of civilization might be. Unless the capitalist system could be improved, it would be replaced by force, he implied.

'It is bad business to allow the continuance of conditions which kill or cripple unnecessarily. It is well known that bad housing does have these results . . . It is bad business to tolerate slums. Equally it is bad business for capital to have strikes, seething discontent and revolution . . . Our housing policy is, in one sense, uneconomic. It will cost the taxpayers money, but it is cheaper than revolutions and the money invested will bear a high rate of interest later in the improved physique, increased morality and reduced mortality.'

Of course, that is not socialism, nothing like it. What Astor was saying was that the ruling class should remain just that but should hand out goodies to the workers to make them healthy and happy . . . and quiet. Nancy spelled it out during her 1923 campaign in Plymouth when she declared that she was 'out to fight the Socialists to the last ditch and leave them there. I am not doing that out of hatred of the Socialist Party, but for the great majority of the working men and women of the country.' To her the working men and women were like children to be guided and rewarded in return for good behaviour: they were not grown-ups like the Astors and their kind and the last thing they could cope with was the responsibility for their own lives that socialism promised them, which in any case would upset what Waldorf called 'the national balance sheet'.

To be fair, such views were sincerely held – that is, the Astors and their friends genuinely believed that they were a force for good in the community – and they certainly represented a striking advance on the old-style Toryism which held that if a man was poor it was either his own fault or the will of God. Nor is there any reason to suppose, on the evidence of the present century, that doctrinaire socialism is of any more real benefit to the man in the street than good-natured paternalism. The flaw was that Waldorf and Nancy and John and very many of the politicians with whom they associated seemed to believe that fundamental change could be so achieved as to leave things fundamentally the same. Being accustomed to the best of everything in their own lives, they assumed it was possible to create the best of all worlds for everybody. It did not occur to them that what the national balance sheet really meant was that in order to improve the lot of those less well endowed they themselves would have to relinquish some of the things they took for granted. As we shall see, that is precisely what they were obliged to do.

In 1924, however, the fall of the first Labour Government after only a few months in office ensured that the liberal Toryism of the Astors and their circle would survive for some time to come. Nancy and John were returned to Parliament in the Conservative landslide of October that year, with Dawson of *The Times* publishing a leading article on Baldwin's 'amazing good fortune' in being given a second chance so soon – which was assumed, of course, to be lucky for the country, too – and going on to instruct one of his leader-writers to stress the need for continuity and stability. He spoke for the Astors and their class, for there was nothing they desired more than stability and continuity, in other words the maintenance of the status quo. Change must come, they conceded, but let it come slowly and let it not upset the established order from which they so signally benefited.

As far as the two branches of the Astor family were concerned, though, the gilt-edged alliance was united by ends rather than means. John and Vi, who were both retiring by nature and preferred the peace and quiet of Hever even to their own London home, seldom visited Cliveden or took part in the galactic gatherings at St James's Square. Politically speaking, gentleman John was deeply suspicious of Waldorf's espousal of what were perceived as radical causes and he thoroughly deplored Nancy's tactics both inside and outside Parliament. Her slanging matches with the Plymouth voters were to him humiliating spectacles and he was seen to writhe in embarrassment at her undisciplined behaviour during Commons debates. On the other hand, Dover for him was as much a 'pocket borough' as Plymouth Sutton was for his sister-in-law, with election expenses being met out of his own pocket (as was the salary of the local Conservative agent), regular donations to local charities and good causes, and a carefully established tradition of 'treats' for the inhabitants. 'There can be few divisions', it was reported, 'where political organization is maintained so actively from year to year. The Unionist associations throughout the constituency meet regularly, and Major Astor, who always pays great individual attention to the division, conducts an autumn campaign each year.'

In effect, J.J. was a latter-day lord of the manor, representing Dover in Parliament for more than twenty years less because of the party he stood for than because of the man he was. It was often said of him that he would give his undivided attention to whatever he was interested in, and his electors responded with enthusiasm. Even in 1929, when 'Tory democracy' was at a low ebb, he was returned with a majority of eleven thousand, and by 1931 it had soared to almost twenty thousand. Even though his constituency encompassed almost the whole of the Kent coalfield, with its strong trade unionism and support for the Labour Party, a reporter noticed that 'it is illustrative of Major Astor's popularity that his meetings in mining centres have been most orderly and well conducted. He has been heard with respect, and questions have come at their rightful place, the close of his speech.' (Another contrast there with Nancy's style, which was to cover up her inadequate command of policy by simply arguing with the crowds.)

He described his philosophy as 'enlightened conservatism' and dismissed as dangerous illusions the claims of socialism to be able to provide a better life for working people. 'There is no short cut to a heaven on earth,' he told his constituents in 1929, 'and if anyone told me that there was, and that he had a scheme for obtaining it, I would regard that scheme with the utmost suspicion, and would ask what it was going to cost the country.' Self-help and standing on one's own feet were the way forward.

That he really believed what he said cannot be in doubt. 'Heaven helps those who help themselves,' was his message to British industry in a speech in February 1926, and a couple of months later, when the General Strike began, he demonstrated exactly what he meant. Both Geoffrey Dawson and the general manager of *The Times* were abroad when trade unionists withdrew their labour in May 1926, so Astor himself took charge of contingency planning for what was to be a rather thrilling test of Tory democracy, at least as far as the middle and upper classes were concerned. Before it became clear whether the press would be affected by the strike in the same way as industry and transport, the paper's pensioners were mobilized as stand-by staff and six multigraph machines were installed at Printing House Square. When the printers did walk out in the early hours of 4 May *The Times* was ready – so much so that Major Astor sportingly sent some of the strikers home in cars he had hired for the people who were to ensure continued publication of the paper.

The following night forty-eight thousand copies of a single-page paper were produced on the multigraphs and *The Times* thus became the only national newspaper to be available on 5 May, the first full day of the strike. This gallant effort was warmly received. As the paper itself reported later: '*The Times* became the very centre of fashion. A strong contingent of the Chairman's friends in the House of Commons came down at once, and continued to come night after night. Members of half the clubs in London offered their services. Undergraduates began to appear from the universities. The list of volunteer motor-drivers included directors not only of *The Times* itself but of great banks and public companies. A Governor-elect put

in some strenuous shifts as a packer in the intervals of packing
his own boxes for the Antipodes.'

Lady Violet also acted as a packer and the duchesses of
Sutherland and Westminster were among those who drove
lorries to distribute the makeshift paper. An attempt at arson,
when petrol was poured through a machine-room window and
set alight, only strengthened the resolve of Astor and his blue-
blooded volunteers. Plans were made to produce something
more like the regular copies of the paper and skilled non-union
workers were imported from various parts of the country to set
type and operate the presses. On 6 May there appeared a
miniature edition of the familiar *Times*, just four pages but
including the famous classified advertisements. Seventy-eight
thousand copies were printed the first night, but by the end of
the week more than 150,000 were rolling off the presses, and on
the official final day of the strike, 12 May, almost 350,000 were
distributed, and not only in London. The amateur drivers –
protected by patrols of 'shock troops' who sometimes came to
blows with pickets trying to stop the distribution – carried *The
Times* throughout the capital and the Home Counties and also
as far afield as Liverpool, Manchester and the Midlands.

When the strike was over, the *New Statesman* spoke for
many people as it offered 'our gratitude and our congratulations
to *The Times* for the struggle which it made . . . and for the way
in which it selected the comparatively small amount of news it
was able to print, and maintained its best traditions of
truthfulness and impartiality'. Geoffrey Dawson, who had
returned to London on 7 May, regarded the exercise as 'one of
the most singular and successful experiences of Printing House
Square' and there was an unmistakable hint of self-satisfaction
in his leading article of 13 May celebrating 'The Nation's
Victory', for it had also been a famous victory on the part of
The Times. 'It is a governing consideration,' Astor had written
in 1923, shortly after gaining control of the paper, 'that *The
Times*, above all else, ought to deserve the confidence of the
public.' It had certainly earned it on that occasion.

Astor himself was also deserving of confidence and respect,
though he was never the public figure that his sister-in-law
became. 'The shyest of men (to the point of inaudibility),' it
was once said of him, 'he could also be one of the firmest. Kind,

considerate, imaginatively thoughtful, dedicated to the public good, he was above all a man that everyone instinctively and rightly trusted... No man can have been more thorough; no one can have done good with a greater absence of fuss.' Nancy's career, however strong her ambition to serve the people, was largely motivated by her own theatrical personality and need to be noticed, perhaps even worshipped. John, on the other hand, was moved more than anything else by a desire to do the right thing. 'He was a rich man; he regarded his wealth as a trust', and his ownership of *The Times* was to him 'a high and serious responsibility'. He fulfilled public duties with difficulty, owing to his shyness, but with an overweening sense of helping other people, of – in what now seems like a ludicrously old-fashioned phrase – 'doing his bit'.

Ownership of such an august publication automatically made him an important figure in newspaper circles throughout the world and he worked hard on behalf of the Empire Press Union, whose president he became in 1929 and which was concerned, in Astor's own words, 'not merely with the question of facilitating press communications, but with such matters as the development of Empire resources and trade and with Empire migration'. The importance of his position in the Union was emphasized by a long article in the Ottawa *Evening Citizen* in 1937: 'He has attended press conferences all over the Empire. Each year his palatial home in Carlton House Terrace, London, is thrown open for the annual conference of the Union and for a reception to the members. He presides regularly at the meetings of the Empire Press Union and no matter relating to the work of the overseas correspondents in London is too trivial for his attention.'

To his employees on *The Times*, Astor was an almost godlike figure. 'He had a fine nature – honest, direct, simple, and all of us on *The Times* are very much in his debt,' said an associate editor after Astor's death. 'He was a great man... He brought out the best in you in every way... Northcliffe was an emperor, a Napoleon; and John Astor came along as a constitutional monarch... He saw that an editor must be an editor in his own right and so he accepted a code that defined an editor's responsibilities and independence and that code ... has been quoted and copied throughout the Commonwealth and abroad.'

Another *Times* man recalled: 'In 1922, when the then Major Astor became chairman and chief proprietor of *The Times*, the paper had been living either distressfully or dangerously for some twenty years. He gave it a long period of stability and security – one of the longest in its uniquely eventful history. Lord Astor had a paternal feeling for his staff. Paternalism is now out of fashion. It may or may not be the right way of running a business and today it is perhaps scarcely a possible one. Be that as it may, Lord Astor did it superbly well. The reason was that he liked doing it: he liked people. To have his gardens at Hever filled with a milling mass of *The Times* staff and their wives, with his old regimental band thumping away in the background, was to him not a duty but an agreeable way of giving pleasure to many . . . Everybody recognized his sincerity and reciprocated.'

Those Hever weekends were an important feature of life on *The Times* for twenty years, until the Second World War put an end to them. Here is a report of one such event, taken from *The Times* of 15 June 1925:

The staffs of *The Times* Publishing Company and *The Times* Book Club were entertained on Saturday by Major Astor, M.P. and Lady Violet Astor at their home, Hever Castle, Kent. This was the third successive year in which their hospitality has been extended in this form, and the number of their guests has increased on each occasion, so that on Saturday over 3,000 people, including not only direct employees, but their relations and friends, were present.

This huge party travelled in six special trains from Victoria to Hever, and a shorter journey along the narrow country roads from Hever Station to the Castle grounds was made in motor omnibuses and coaches. Luncheon was served in great marquees which were used later for the service of tea, and light refreshments were available at a big buffet tent for those who needed ices and cooling drinks during the hot afternoon. There was also a creche tent for the accommodation of babies who could not be left at home. Yet all these preparations had been made carefully so that the tents were not visible from the most lovely parts of the grounds where the visitors spent the sunny hours of the afternoon. The lawns, gardens, and mazes, the lake, shady walks, and the Castle itself, deep in a wood-fringed saucer of land, seemed remote from the rest of the world, and in these beautiful surroundings a wholly enjoyable time was spent...

There was tennis, swimming, rowing, a conducted tour of the castle and 'a treasure hunt, which led over a long and intricate trail, through a fearsome smugglers' cave, to the prize... Throughout the day music was played by the band of the Green Howards, and after tea there was dancing on the lawn of the Italian Garden.' The grateful staff presented their hosts with a golden replica of *The Times* masthead and Astor accepted the gift 'as a token that, whatever might befall that is beyond the control of any of us, our personal friendship will endure'. That friendship, he added, 'is far deeper and closer than any mere business association. We are all members of a great industry and as such we have certain conditions imposed upon us, but I like to think that within that industry we of *The Times* have our own real family life.'

Looking back many years after the last of the Hever gatherings, a *Times* man recalled them as 'a wonderful thing for us – we could meet Churchill, Harold Macmillan, Eden and the Commonwealth prime ministers in the easiest of circumstances'. John Astor, he said, 'really was the most friendly and warmhearted man you could wish to meet'.

In politics, too, John's 'complete fairness and sense of what was right' guided his actions. Though a Tory by nature and a sincere believer that the paternalistic Conservative philosophy was the best thing for the country he was no mere party hack. In his first successful election campaign, in 1922, he told the people of Dover: 'If you return me to Parliament I shall generally support the government of which Mr Bonar Law is now the head; but I reserve to myself the right to vote against the government in any case where I think their proposals are not in the best interests of the nation.' In practice, however, he rarely found himself at odds with a Conservative administration, since the 'progressive' wing of the party, which reflected his own views, remained for the most part firmly in control during the years between the wars.

One of his great political themes was the Empire and the vitality that the developing nations of the British 'family' could bring to the old country. After a long visit to Australia for an Empire Press Union conference in 1925, he noted that 'a voyage round the great countries of our Empire would help to quicken the pulse' of British industry. The Australians, he said, found it hard to understand 'the difficulties and anxieties of an industrialism like ours' and showed 'some good-humoured impatience with us for our slowness in accepting ideals that have commended themselves to great numbers of Australians ... I was more than amused to discover that, though there is a universal respect for Great Britain as the long-armed defender of the Empire, some of our most genuine admirers in this respect are not a little puzzled to know how so economically unenlightened a country has contrived to do it.' The future for British trade, he believed, lay in 'imperial expansion', both in the flow of 'unlimited raw materials' from the Dominions and the export of British goods to them (not to mention the export of British workers, which would have the effect of rapidly shortening the dole queues at home).

In essence, John Jacob Astor V was an old fashioned idealist. His was a world of simple problems with simple solutions, of honesty and straightforwardness, of tolerance and harmony, of gradual and measured change, of 'playing the game'. Alas for him, the other players were not prepared to accept the same rules. By the end of his first decade as Member of Parliament and owner of *The Times*, forces were at work that would ultimately sweep away all the comfortable certainties upon which the English Astors depended. And ironically, John and Nancy and Waldorf would be partly responsible.

II

While John Astor, in the words of a contemporary, 'sought to avoid publicity wherever he could', his sister-in-law Nancy suffered from no such diffidence. From the very beginning her parliamentary career was a remarkable exercise in self-assertion, self-indulgence and self-promotion – though, of course, she would have hotly denied all that, believing herself to be not only the representative of her constituents but also of the entire female sex. In fact what she represented was only herself and, in part, the views of a few close friends who were responsible for her political 'education'. But at least she was good for a laugh.

Her very introduction to the House of Commons had its moments of high comedy. As both the first woman to take her seat and the wife of Viscount Astor, and therefore a personage of considerable importance, she was introduced by Lloyd George and Balfour, who in the time-honoured manner were to escort her to the Speaker's table where she would sign the register. The short walk from the Bar of the House to where the Speaker sat was normally undertaken in silence – but not on this occasion. Soberly dressed in black, with white collar and gloves, Nancy was chatting to Balfour when the Speaker signalled the party to approach him, so that the sign was seen only by Lloyd George, who set off without his companions and had to be called back, which sent the Honourable Members into fits of laughter. Even when the trio did begin the walk together, the men stepped out too smartly for Nancy, who pulled them back alongside her by their arms, then insisted on talking to them until the point was reached where they were required, by custom, to bow to the Speaker. In confusion and embarrassment, Lloyd George neglected to perform the traditional act, which brought an audible rebuke from Nancy: 'George, you forgot to bow.' More laughter in the House, and a shout from the Labour leader, Will Crooks: 'George, you'll be losing your job.' Finally the Speaker's table was reached and the two sponsors were able to withdraw, not without some relief, it is to be imagined. Thinking that the formalities were now over, Nancy began to chat amiably to the Speaker, James Lowther (later Viscount Ullswater), who had often been a dinner guest at Cliveden and St James's Square, and with Bonar Law, who sat nearby. So engrossed in conversation was she – by Lloyd George's account – that she forgot to sign the register and this time had to be called back herself before taking her seat in the second row below the gangway.

After this diversion, a debate began, but Nancy was in no mood to sit and listen to boring speeches. As the notorious Horatio Bottomley (who went to jail not long afterwards after being found guilty of a gigantic fraud) held forth on a motion he had introduced, Nancy wandered about the chamber talking to friends and making herself known. One of the M.P.s she encountered was an Irishman named Devlin, who had been speaking at the moment of her arrival at the Commons and had delayed her introduction. 'I want to tell Mr Devlin what I think of him for keeping me waiting at the bar,' said Nancy jokingly. 'Don't do it again.' Later she realized Devlin, who did not know her, might have taken her rebuke seriously, so she invited him to dinner at St James's Square.

'They call it the best club in Europe,' Nancy said of her first day in the House, 'but it didn't seem like the best club to me. I can't think of anything worse than being among six hundred men none of whom really wanted you there.' Privately, though, she admitted that she had been received with 'the dauntless decency of the English', even though her arrival did occasion another of the famous exchanges with Winston Churchill. Admitting that some M.P.s believed they could discourage women from following Nancy's example if they rigorously excluded her from their after-hours meetings, Churchill said a woman entering the Commons had the same effect on him as one entering his bathroom when he had nothing with which to defend himself except a sponge. To which Nancy replied that he was not handsome enough to have worries of that nature.

In any case, Nancy was not the sort to allow herself to be ignored and in due course came the day – 24 February 1920 – when she was to make her first speech in Parliament. The subject she chose was a difficult one, but dear to her heart – the sale of alcohol. She had seen enough heavy drinking during her Virginian childhood and her first marriage to be well aware of the evils of alcohol abuse and she was to be a lifelong campaigner in the cause of temperance, in which she was supported by both Waldorf and Philip Kerr. (It will be recalled that Kerr had suggested that she fought her first Plymouth campaign as a prohibitionist, capitalizing on the introduction of Prohibition in America in 1919, but Nancy had wisely decided against this – probably having been talked out of it by her shrewd political secretary of the time, Miss 'Bunny' Benningfield, who was both a Christian Scientist and a pragmatic politician.) Once in Parliament, however, Nancy could give fairly free rein to what were termed in those days 'pussyfoot' views on alcohol, and in 1920 she decided to stand up and oppose a move to relax the restrictions on the sale of drink which had been introduced during the Great War.

The motion to abolish the Liquor Control Board was proposed by Sir John Rees, who, having seen Nancy's name on the list of those speaking against him, concluded with: 'I know what is coming to me from the next speaker. Not only shall I accept the chastisement with resignation, but I shall be ready to kiss the rod.' This was a challenge to Nancy's much-vaunted gift for repartee. When she stood up she looked Sir John straight in the eye and said: 'I shall consider the Honourable Member's offer . . . after his conversion.' Her speech was not perhaps the best argued that the Commons had ever heard, but it was charged with emotion on behalf of the women and children who might have suffered both physically and financially if the sale of alcohol had not been controlled. 'I do not want you to look upon your lady Member as a fanatic or a lunatic. I am simply trying to speak for hundreds of women and children throughout the country who cannot speak for themselves . . . I could talk for five hours on the benefit to women the Board has been.' But she gave herself away when she said: 'Do not think I am urging prohibition. I am not so stupid as that, though I admit I hope England will come to it one day and I am not afraid to say so.' That certainly did brand her in the minds of many people as a fanatic.

In the event the Liquor Control Board stayed, though the credit for that, despite the claims of some American writers, was hardly all Nancy's since the Government itself opposed the motion to abolish it on the grounds that it wished to amend rather than remove restrictions on the sale of alcohol, which was subsequently done. Nevertheless, Nancy's speech was widely reported and warmly received by the press. 'Lady Astor is always on the side of the angels,' commented one observer, 'even though the angels have no votes and some people think they are rather extreme in their views.'

Speeches, however, were not Nancy's forte in the House of Commons. Treating the debates rather like her election meetings in Plymouth, she seemed to regard M.P.s who disagreed with her as hecklers and frequently heckled them back. On one occasion, according to a report in the *Morning Post*, she interrupted no fewer than fifteen speeches, and broke off in the

middle of her own to shout comments at other Members.
'When she did not directly interrupt to explain, comment,
deny, expostulate, she interjected,' said the *Post*. 'She popped
up excitedly. She subsided suddenly. She opened her mouth.
She shut her mouth. She turned to this side and that. She
shrugged her shoulders. She said "tch, tch". She tapped an
irritated toe tattoo.' Not, mark you, that debates in the House
of Commons are usually conducted in an atmosphere of
reverent silence from the listeners: it was simply that Nancy's
forms of interruption were rather more original than the
Honourable Members had been used to. The Speaker was
sometimes obliged to reprimand her: 'I must ask the Honourable Member to bear in mind that in this House it is not in order
to say "You, you" across the floor of the House.' Nancy
retorted that addressing her remarks through the Speaker took
too long when she had a lot of things to say. But she always had
a lot of things to say. The journalist Hannen Swaffer once
remarked: 'I am, among other things a film critic. I have often
attacked American talkies. Nancy is one of the worst American
talkies I know.'

Yet, as Lloyd George told Nancy, her voice was her fortune
and her ability to hold an audience was far more important than
what she actually said. Important for what purpose is not quite
clear, but the purpose it served was to make her famous very
quickly. Her jocular and outspoken style made her much in
demand as a public speaker; she was modelled in wax for
Madame Tussaud's; she was a heroine in the press on both sides
of the Atlantic – the Americans were thrilled at the sight of one
of their own apparently making mincemeat of the stodgy old
British Parliament. She made enemies too, though, and one of
them was the unscrupulous Horatio Bottomley, an unashamed
populist who saw the publicity Nancy was getting as a threat to
his own position. Within a month of her entry into the House
of Commons Bottomley was attacking her in his weekly paper,
John Bull, and when the House rose for the Christmas recess of
1919 he was presented with more ammunition by a paragraph in
The Saturday Review, which was also apparently no friend to
Lady Astor: 'That astonishing book *Who's Who* for 1920 has
reached us ... we were arrested by the biography of Plymouth's heroine, the dashing, peerless peeress, Nancy Witcher,

who is described as "the widow" of Mr Robert Gould Shaw at the time of her marriage with Mr Astor. We are loth to think that Nancy fibs: but is this a correct statement?'

Bottomley filed away that paragraph and ordered his journalists to look into the circumstances of Nancy's first marriage. The information was easily obtainable, but Bottomley did not use it immediately; he waited for a telling moment, and found it in the spring of 1920 when Parliament debated the recommendations of a royal commission on reform of the divorce laws. There was a widespread view at the time that the legal attitude towards divorce was archaic, adultery being the only grounds on which an action was permissible. It was proposed that the law should be changed to allow petitions on the grounds of desertion (after three years), cruelty, habitual drunkenness, incurable insanity and life imprisonment, and it was assumed that Nancy Astor would support a Bill to this effect since she had set herself up as a champion of women and the measure seemed to offer the chance of freedom to women who were tied to husbands capable of ruining their lives. Nancy, however, surprised even her friends by joining the old-guard Tories who successfully opposed the Bill as an assault upon the moral fibre of the nation.

'I am not convinced that making divorce very easy really makes marriages more happy or makes happy marriages more possible,' she said. 'In the Christian world it is the spiritual aspect of marriage that the law attempts to protect, and it is the spiritual element that makes marriages happy ... we women particularly know it. The spiritual idea of marriage, though started in the East, has been more highly developed in the West, and it is that that has elevated the Western women a little above their Eastern sisters. That is the difference between the East and the West. We must do nothing which will weaken it.'

It was an unpardonably silly speech (apart from its unpleasant overtones of racism) for a woman to make, particularly one who had herself benefited from more liberal divorce laws, and it was rightly condemned not only by very many women but also by intelligent, liberally minded men. Some said she was just a wealthy woman who had no idea of what real life was like; some women sent her letters saying it was presumptuous of her to pretend that she could speak for her entire sex; a conference of Labour women denounced her in an official motion. And Horatio Bottomley saw his opportunity. *John Bull* placards all over London proclaimed 'Lady Astor's Divorce' and on 8 May the paper carried that headline and added: 'A Hypocrite of the First Water. The Poor and The Rich'. The accompanying article, in the midst of a general attack on Nancy's parliamentary performance, gave the facts of her divorce from Robert Shaw, reproduced some gossip from the New York press to the effect that there had been collusion over the action, and noted that in *Who's Who*, Burke's *Peerage* and other reference books Waldorf Astor's entry recorded that he had married 'Nancy Witcher, the widow of the late Robert Gould Shaw', a man who was not only not dead but was a leading member of New York society.

This was damaging material, and there was not much Nancy could do about it. There had been no collusion in the divorce case, but the Astors could not sue for libel on the basis of the implications in the article because the facts were essentially true and there was no denying the false entries in the reference books. Bottomley was roundly condemned for his tactics and the Commons gave Nancy an ovation as an expression of sympathy for the victim of such a smear, but many felt that the apparent covering up of the divorce ill suited one who made so much of being frank and outspoken, particularly when she had just helped to kill an attempt to offer other women benefits similar to the one she had enjoyed.

For more than a month Nancy fretted while Philip Kerr – who, in being converted to Christian Science, had become her spiritual mentor – implored her to take comfort from her religion. At last she decided that she could not allow Bottomley's attack to remain unanswered, and at the annual meeting of her party association in Plymouth she announced: 'I have waited for this meeting to deal with charges which, if true, would affect my position as your representative. You would have been entitled to ask whether the charges were true. I assume that you have not done so because you trusted me and may have guessed the motive behind them. If you assumed that there was no justification for the attack, you were right. But however unpleasant it is to deal with the period of great unhappiness I went through seventeen years ago, I prefer to tell you all about it.' She went on to explain how the divorce had come about, and was given a unanimous vote of confidence by her constituency party – a vote that seemed to be justified two years later when Horatio Bottomley was jailed for seven years because of his fraudulent Victory Bonds scheme.

But Nancy had been lucky. Bottomley had simply over-played his hand. If he had concentrated on the hypocrisy of Nancy's anti-divorce speech when seen in the light of her own fortunate experience he might have capitalized on the resentment felt by supporters of the reform and thus might have done greater harm to the woman he regarded as his enemy. As it was, his smear tactics served to evoke public sympathy for a woman so cruelly abused and blinded people to the underlying scandal of the situation. It might be thought that the escape was not one Nancy really deserved, having helped to set back divorce reform for at least fifteen years and joined herself with the forces of reaction she so heartily denounced on other occasions (i.e. when they opposed her). And she never was called upon to explain just why Waldorf had seen fit to falsify his *Who's Who* entry.

If the incident proves anything, it is on the one hand the force of Nancy's personality and on the other that her political career had rather more to do with her own psyche than with the aspirations of the people she represented. In one respect at least she was as much a populist as Bottomley, cynically following her own course while claiming to speak for the masses. And this was not the only occasion on which it was to bear bitter fruit, though the second time helped to change the course of history.

To be fair, however, Nancy Astor did champion some worthy causes in Parliament and if more of them were lost than were won it was mainly because the forces of reaction dug in their heels just as much, for instance, over shorter hours for shopgirls as over easier divorce. She helped to save the policewomen who were threatened with abolition once the perceived need for them during the Great War had disappeared and she argued for equality for women in the Civil Service, though it took another war for that to become a fact. Encouraged by Waldorf, she supported innumerable measures aimed at social reform, especially if they were of particular value or interest to women, and she also defended the Royal

Navy and the ship-repair industry, on which her constituency depended. She was by no means an originator, but it was sometimes her dogged persistence that made the difference in the passing of a Bill and there can be no doubt that she enlivened most of the debates in which she took part, even if it was only as an interrupter with comments such as, 'Members are not losing their idealism – they never had any.'

Outside Parliament she was a tireless addresser of public meetings and if she seemed sometimes not to know what she was talking about the audiences did not mind. As Lloyd George had said, they came not to hear what she said but just to hear her. She had three secretaries to make notes and help in the preparation of her speeches, but often she would simply abandon her notes or else put aside a speech because she felt it did not suit the mood of the occasion. The effect could be disarming. In 1921 she told a London audience: 'I am not highly educated; I am not brilliantly clever. I have just got a little knowledge. Sometimes I wish I could understand things better. I wish I could understand the Budget.' That a great lady could say such things impressed a public less sophisticated than it is today and reached a wider audience than was gathered before her because the press knew she generally provided good copy. The 1920s and 1930s formed an age of escapism, first from the horror of war and then from the misery of recession and unemployment, and Nancy had the ability to take people away from the drab realities of the world. Perhaps that was her real contribution to public life. 'I made myself disagreeable,' she once said, 'but in a very cheerful way.' And to the Plymouth voters she declared: 'I do not know if I have become a force in the House of Commons as much as a nuisance. Perhaps you regret sending me. But I'll sit until you get somebody better.'

Such was her international fame that in 1922 she was given the opportunity to take her act on to a wider stage when she was invited to address the League of Women Voters at its Pan-American conference in Baltimore. Having heard so much about her, the whole of America was waiting to see her and the visit became something like a royal tour, with receptions in places as far apart as New York, Washington and Chicago, a meeting with the president and, most touching of all, a triumphal return to Danville, Virginia. As usual she had much to say about everything, from the fashion for bobbed hair to the League of Nations, and she said it with her customary verve and lack of tact, which occasioned a few attacks in the newspapers (notably those owned by the anti-British William Randolph Hearst). Overall, though, the tour was an enormous success and by its end Nancy Astor had become probably the most famous and talked-about woman in the world.

'Lady Astor,' said one of the New York papers, 'has left a grateful memory. We did not take her very seriously up to the time of her arrival a few weeks ago; that is to say, we did not look upon her as a really great person. But she took us seriously and in discussing us and our affairs, always within the limits of good taste and courtesy, she revealed those qualities which have made her Great Britain's foremost woman. Her gifts are remarkable; her faculty for saying the right thing at the right time amounts to genius.'

The Astors returned to England to fight an election in the autumn of 1922 following the withdrawal of the Conservatives from the Lloyd George coalition. It proved to be a hard contest for Nancy, especially because she had a Conservative opponent, a man sponsored by brewery interests which did not, of course, think much of Nancy's views on the sale of alcohol. This aroused confusion in the minds of the voters, already puzzled by the sudden dumping of the great Lloyd George, who had been the hero in 1919, but Nancy relied again on the tactic that had won support in the previous election. 'If you want someone who is going to denounce Mr Lloyd George, Lord Balfour, or Mr Austen Chamberlain, then don't waste your time with me,' she announced. Her local party, unfortunately, relied on smear tactics against her so-called Imperial Conservative opponent, which brought a libel action upon its head, but it was the Labour candidate who proved to be the greatest threat, increasing his party's vote by fifteen hundred or more. Nonetheless Nancy Astor returned to Parliament with a reduced majority that was still a healthy three thousand, and perhaps with the memory of the recent campaign in mind – the brewers' candidate having taken votes away from her – she decided to tackle the liquor trade once more. She had kept rather quiet on the subject during the election, confining her comments to maintaining that she was not advocating American-style prohibition in Britain, and the Private Members' Bill she introduced in the spring of 1923 was equally muted: it sought merely to ban the sale of alcohol to persons under the age of eighteen and, since this seemed to many people a perfectly sensible measure, it attracted the sponsorship of the government.

There were two obstacles to the passage of her Bill (actually it was really Waldorf's Bill, since he had drafted it and rounded up government support). One was the Tory right-wingers, and Nancy attempted, rather ham-fistedly, to settle their hash at a Conservative meeting when she spoke of some members of her party 'who belong to the days of Noah. Not only have they not come out of the Ark, but to hear them talk one would say that they had never looked out of it... People who live in two houses do not realize what it is like to live in two rooms. That's what is wrong with the Conservative Party.' She had chosen the wrong forum for such remarks and it took the arrival on the platform of the Prime Minister, Bonar Law, to quell the 'disorder, uproar and pandemonium' that her speech engendered. She felt she had done a good job, however, by saying straight out what she thought. The second obstacle to her Bill, though, was much more difficult to deal with because it came in the form of a man who was in theory her greatest ally.

He was a Labour-leaning Independent by the name of Edwin Scrymgeour and he had apparently accomplished the impossible by defeating Winston Churchill at Dundee, fighting on the platform of total prohibition of the sale of alcohol. A mild and amiable man, he pronounced himself the Lord's anointed 'to wipe out drink in the kingdom', citing his election victory against such odds as evidence of divine intervention (what else, indeed, could explain it?). And as luck would have it, he had introduced a prohibition Bill at the same time as Nancy had put forward her more modest measure as a small step towards what both she and Scrymgeour apparently desired. The danger, as far as Nancy was concerned, was that her attempt to introduce a small but important reform would be linked with the cause of a man whom many M.P.s regarded as mentally unbalanced.

In the event, the filibustering tactics of the right-wing proved to be more threatening than the ridicule attached to any connexion between Nancy and Scrymgeour. The Die-Hard who took it upon himself to talk out Nancy's Bill was Sir Frederick Banbury, Member for the City of London, a man noted for opposing change of any kind and a past master in the art of prolonging a debate past the four o'clock time limit beyond which Private Members' Bills were automatically disqualified. Nancy had seen him in action before, both on her side in the matter of the Liquor Control Board and against her on the subject of reduced working hours in the retail trade. At the third reading of the Bill in June 1923, Banbury was in fine form and by the time he had finished speaking on the legislation that preceded Nancy's on the Order Paper it was a quarter to four, which left only fifteen minutes for the liquor Bill to be debated and voted upon. The provisions had already been carefully amended (not entirely to Nancy's satisfaction) during the committee stage and their proposer felt that perhaps a quarter of an hour would be enough – at least Banbury was sitting down. Then the worst happened: the Speaker called on Sir Frederick to propose an amendment to the Bill and he rose to address the House. Nancy grabbed the tails of his frock coat, shouting, 'I'll hold on. You shan't get up.' Banbury smiled and said, 'You're not strong enough', then calmly proceeded with his speech until the Speaker called 'Order,' indicating that consideration of the Bill was at an end. 'You old villain,' Nancy said, shaking her fist at her persecutor. 'I'll get you next time.'

She did, too. Because her Bill had government sponsorship it did not disappear but came up again on 13 July. Banbury was not in such good voice on that day and in any case the debate began at half-past eleven in the morning, which meant that his filibuster would have had to have been a marathon to be successful. Despite an intervention by Scrymgeour, whose own Bill had been heavily defeated, and who called Nancy a traitor to the cause of prohibition, the Intoxicating Liquor (Sale to Persons under Eighteen) Bill was approved by 257 votes to 10 and, after being piloted through the House of Lords by Waldorf, passed into law.

Despite its eminent common sense, the new liquor law was tremendously unpopular outside Parliament because many people believed that as a native of the country which had introduced complete prohibition Nancy wanted nothing short of that in Britain too. No doubt she would have been pleased to see it, but she realized that it was not a possibility at that time. This did not stop people thinking about it, though, particularly when there appeared to be a certain change of attitude between Nancy's speeches during an election and those in the House of Commons. Her position was not helped, either, by the publication in 1923 of her only book, *My Two Countries*, which was an account of her visit to America with extracts from some of her speeches there. It was an unexceptionable work, no doubt intended to polish her public image and perhaps to underline her belief that Britain and America were natural allies and should work together on foreign policy, but it did have the effect of fuelling resentment among those who saw Lady Astor as a brash, opinionated American determined to impose her 'alien' will on the British people through one of their most cherished institutions. The *New Statesman* published a slashing review of the book which suggested that the 'lofty sentiment' of Nancy's speeches was not matched by her personal behaviour and which ended with a repetition of the *John Bull* story about her divorce: '. . . having divorced her husband on the vaguest grounds she spoke . . . eloquently against relaxing the harshness of our divorce laws'.

That the *Statesman* was out to 'get' Nancy is beyond doubt, for in its following issue it published an 'apology' from the book reviewer which served only to emphasize the difference between Nancy's words and actions in the matter of divorce. Waldorf asked his lawyer to write to the paper, which published the letter with an editorial comment setting out its charges yet again. It seemed that the editor was determined to provoke a libel suit, which would probably have done irreparable harm to Nancy's parliamentary career, but the Astors were too shrewd to become involved in anything like that and after further correspondence published in the *Statesman* – including a letter from a reader who had investigated the legal aspects of the divorce case and found them quite correct – the matter was allowed to drop.

The episode shows that Nancy's enemies, and there were as many of them as there were friends (though not so well placed in the main), were always watchful. Her unrestrained behaviour and lack of clear thought were to give them plenty more ammunition and, as the 1920s passed and the grim 1930s began, she was to become perhaps more notorious than famous. Her flippancy and clowning ill suited the menacing events that led up to the Second World War and there would be those who claimed that her more serious views – or rather the opinions of the little circle that surrounded her, chiefly of Philip Kerr – did much to foster the conditions out of which that war grew.

All in all, the Intoxicating Liquor (Sale to Persons under Eighteen) Act, small step for mankind though it was, must mark the zenith of Nancy's political career.

III

Not much more than a year after her hard election battle of 1922 Nancy was back at the hustings, and in circumstances perhaps even more difficult. She made much of her position on social questions – housing, widows' pensions, public health, education and prison reform (all of which were subjects in which she took a lead from Waldorf's liberal views) – but the opinions she expressed were too radical for some Conservatives, particularly since she seemed to have fallen into the habit of criticizing her own party for its stick-in-the-mud policies. At the same time she continued to attract suspicion over the question of alcohol. People found it hard to believe that she supported prohibition but was not prepared to push for it. She had, after all, steered one restriction through Parliament, and while few would have argued with it, there was a nagging feeling that this might be just the first step towards emulating the Americans. To her opponents she was vulnerable, as on the divorce question, to the charge of hypocrisy: why was it that so little was heard of her prohibitionist leanings at election time, whereas in other circumstances she was prepared to fulminate against the evils of drink?

Nevertheless, on polling day, 7 December 1923, Plymouth Sutton returned her to Parliament once more, though the Labour vote against her rose and her majority was well below three thousand. She took comfort from the fact that, besides herself, seven women were elected to the House of Commons and indeed one of them, the Labour M.P. Margaret Bondfield, would shortly be serving in the government as parliamentary secretary to the Ministry of Labour. ('I am bitterly disappointed that the Labour Party has not given Cabinet rank to a woman,' Nancy complained.) Furthermore, the advent of the first Labour government made life somewhat easier for Nancy herself, because Opposition suited her and at least she could not be accused of undermining the position of her own party, as was the case when the Tories were in power.

Yet she continued to be, in her own term 'a nuisance', never troubling to learn the rules of parliamentary procedure and frequently in conflict with officers of the House over the way she asked questions, her interruptions and sharp personal asides, and her habit of making propaganda points on behalf of her own prejudices whenever she could. There was nothing anyone could do to keep her down. Apart from being an elected representative, she was an immensely influential woman, friend of royalty (she played golf with the Prince of Wales – graciously allowing him to win, it seems – and lent her house at Sandwich to King Carl Gustav of Sweden as a honeymoon retreat), and hostess to the nobility, wife of one powerful newspaper owner and sister-in-law of another. She had all the advantages on her side, allied with a certain kind of charm and an ability to make people laugh. She could do more or less as she pleased, secure in the knowledge that no criticism could bring her down and that the people of her constituency would go on voting for her so long as she played up to them and kept them happy. For their part, the voters – or at least more than enough of them – were content to accept her bounty. In 1924, for example, the Astors paid £10,000 for the building of houses to be rented to working people: if Plymouth's benefactors wanted to play politics, why shouldn't they? As Nancy said: 'If you vote for me, you will be getting tuppence for a penny, because you will be getting me and my husband as your representative. No other candidate can offer you as much. I belong to the tried old firm of Astor & Co.' She made the speeches and drew the crowds; Waldorf paid the bills (or, as some would have it, bought the votes).

But while Plymouth continued to do well out of the Astors and its unpredictable M.P. continued to attract as much interest and attention as ever, the political climate was becoming colder and more gloomy and Nancy came increasingly to be regarded as nothing more than light relief. She could still cause a stir in the House with an ill-judged comment or an exchange of abuse, but the fact that she blithely carried on in her old undisciplined way and never really interested herself in the weighty political questions that were emerging meant that she forfeited any chance of being taken seriously. She may have made history as the first woman to take her seat in Parliament, but she did nothing to further the cause of her sex there: that task was left to others more thoughtful and more committed.

Indeed, the House as a whole demonstrated what it thought of her contribution when Members objected to the hanging of the famous Sims painting of Nancy's introduction. Waldorf had commissioned the painting and Lloyd George and Balfour, among others, had consented to sit for it. When it was completed in 1924, Waldorf presented it to the Commons, having been advised by the Commissioner of Works that it would be an acceptable gift, and it was hung by the staircase leading to the lobby of the committee rooms. But whatever the Commissioner and the ministers he consulted may have thought, many backbench M.P.s objected strongly and the picture had to be hidden by a dust sheet while the general opinion as to its suitability was canvassed. Feeling against it ran so high that the painting was finally removed. (It was hung in the Bedford College for Women and later sent on loan to the University of Virginia.) A chagrined Nancy commented: 'They missed the whole point. It was not a picture of Lady Astor; it was never intended to be a picture of Lady Astor. It is a picture of an historical event.' Possibly M.P.s thought that history had chosen a not entirely suitable candidate as its agent.

It is noteworthy, too, that Nancy Astor was not the token woman selected by Stanley Baldwin for a government post when the Conservatives were returned to power on a tide of fear about Labour's intentions in 1924. Since the previous government had elevated a woman to its ranks and since women were becoming much more important as voters, Baldwin felt that he had better follow Ramsay MacDonald's example, and the Duchess of Atholl became parliamentary secretary to the Board of Education. Nancy, who had benefited hugely from the swing to the Tories and doubled her majority, would have been a more obvious choice in one way, since she was still extremely popular, attracted a steady measure of press attention and was naturally the most experienced woman in the House, but of course on other grounds she was impossible. Her lack of political purpose and parliamentary sobriety, coupled with her penchant for rounding on anyone, of whatever party, who disagreed with her, would have made her appointment a dangerous one, and Baldwin wisely steered clear. Nancy, in her sporting way, welcomed the duchess's appointment and it was suggested by her friends that she herself would not have accepted such a minor post because it was merely a sop to women, but a man who knew her well for many years has suggested that she was hurt by being passed over in such a manner. For some months afterwards, in fact, she was very quiet, absorbing herself in charity work, entertaining and domestic life and rarely appearing in the columns of the newspapers.

Not without significance, too, is the fact that from then on Nancy's electoral fortunes mirrored the standing of the Conservatives as a whole. When the Labour Party was voted back into power in 1929, she came close to losing her seat; the Tory landslide of 1931 left her with a majority of more than ten thousand; when Baldwin routed the MacDonald faction of the Labour Party in 1935 – the last election before the war and the last Nancy was to fight – she was elected by a comfortable margin of more than six thousand votes. It is difficult to escape the conclusion that, as the electorate polarized, people voted not so much for Nancy Astor as for her party: in political terms she was becoming recognizably what she had in reality always been – an eccentric, interesting and entertaining irrelevance. Personally she was hard-working, generous, committed to good works (she raised £20,000, for instance, to fund the growth of the nursery school movement) and sincere in her wish to help other people, but as a parliamentarian and politician she did not really count.

Calling her 'The Pollyanna of Politics', Harold Laski wrote in 1930 that, 'It would be difficult to argue that Lady Astor has made any mark in the House... Her speeches are generally amiable, but do not display any familiarity with the things of which she speaks.' Her heart was in the right place, no doubt, but her attitude was that of 'noblesse oblige; compassion for the poor; a half regret that they do not work harder; a determination that they shall not drown their sorrows in drink; a yearning for a proper understanding between capital and labour, whatever that means; a feeling that with a little kindness we can conquer the world'. Even allowing for Laski's position as one of the leading socialist theoreticians in the inter-war period, there is a good deal of truth in what he said, though the many apologists for Lady Astor over the years have been at pains to discredit his attack on her. Was it not Nancy herself who once suggested that the Labour Party leaders were unfit to run the business of the country because they did not run businesses of their own? She it was, too, who commented when laying the foundation stone of a nursery school in a working-class area: 'Truly the children who come here are more fortunate than the children of the West End, who have to bear the horrible monotony of being dragged through the parks from two to five o'clock by their nurses.' Even as a joke such a remark carries some seed of Laski's charge that 'she is the perfect instrument of the aristocracy for persuading the people they have nothing to complain of'.

In her own mind, of course, Nancy was far from being a political lightweight. By 1930 she had been in Parliament for ten years and during that time she had become an international celebrity, treated for the most part by press and public as if she were some senior statesman with the capacity to influence world events. Inevitably, all this attention and gratifying coverage of what she had to say began to suggest to her that she really did have a part to play on the global stage, perhaps the greatest starring role of her life. As far back as 1922, under the influence of Philip Kerr, she had tried to 'sell' the League of Nations to suspicious Americans. 'You need not call it the League of Nations,' she declared. 'You can call it anything you like. You can give it a new name every day. But for God's sake give it a chance.' The idea of countries cooperating in a spirit of tolerance and harmony to maintain world peace was central to the cosy, humanitarian philosophy of the Astors and their circle, and it appeared to be a moderate stance to which few thinking people could object. But in the 1930s, the years of what Winston Churchill called the gathering storm, the theory that it was wisest to cooperate with any regime, whatever its political colour, for the sake of peace, started to assume the characteristics of extremism, particularly when it became the central plank of the government's foreign policy. It was an example of political naivety, but as the dictators of Europe struck ever more bellicose attitudes, the pursuit of peace at any price appeared to be more like a conspiracy.

Concern about what the Astors and their political friends were really up to first surfaced in serious form in 1931, when Lady Astor, the fearless critic of socialism, visited Soviet Russia. It was not Nancy herself who received the invitation from the Soviet government but her great friend George Bernard Shaw (she was a determined 'lionizer'; it was once said that there could not be a celebrity who had not passed through her dining room). Shaw's socialist views were, of course, well known in Russia and he was regarded as a useful publicist for the communist cause. Indeed it was a significant propaganda coup for Stalin's regime to invite Shaw: the Russian people would be impressed to find such a famous man among them – his 'socialistic' plays were very popular in Moscow – and his visit would help, or so it was hoped, to make the Soviet system seem more respectable in the eyes of the rest of the world.

Shaw's wife, Charlotte, was not fit enough to accompany him so he suggested to the Russian ambassador that he should take a party of friends with him. No doubt the Russians expected him to bring colleagues from the Fabian Society and they readily agreed. Shaw, however, chose Waldorf and Nancy Astor, their son David (who was then aged nineteen), Philip Kerr (who had recently succeeded to the title of Marquess of Lothian), and a Christian Science friend named Charles Tennant. The Russians must have been a little taken aback when they learnt the composition of Shaw's party, but such an illustrious figure could not be denied – and then it surely dawned on them that the propaganda would be immeasurably increased through visitors who were not fellow-travellers but people from the opposite side of the political spectrum. For their part, the Astors were thrilled and, such was their unworldliness, completely blind to the sort of embarrassment likely to arise from their being entertained by the hated Bolsheviks in the company of Shaw, who claimed, 'I was a socialist before Lenin was born.'

The party left London on 18 July, travelling first to Berlin and then by train to the Russian frontier. On the journey they were introduced to Maxim Litvinoff, the Soviet minister of foreign affairs, who just happened (it was said) to be on the same train. Litvinoff, who spoke English, went out of his way to be friendly to the distinguished guests and by the time they reached the Soviet border they were on very good terms. It was no doubt important to create the right impression before Shaw and his friends saw Russia for themselves. At the frontier post, Nancy saw something that should have given her pause – a female forced labour gang working with shovels on the railway line. But her hosts informed her that these were happy workers who had volunteered to do men's work and were well paid for their efforts, and Nancy talked to them of the feminist cause. The Soviets were determined that their visitors should see the benefits of a people's democracy.

Shaw was welcomed everywhere like a hero, while Nancy was hardly noticed, which must have been a new and perhaps frustrating experience for her. They did the official tourist rounds: the Kremlin, Lenin's tomb, the Museum of the Revolution. When they were shown the remnants of the jewels which had adorned the crown of the Tsar Nancy remarked that she had more jewelry herself – it was only later that she realized that there had been many more gems before the Revolution. There were also visits to factories, farms and other showplaces of workers' control of the means of production. One group of workers complained that the capitalist press told lies about slave labour in Russia, to which Shaw replied puckishly: 'I wish forced labour would be established in England, then two million English unemployed would find work.' It was a remark that was likely to be misinterpreted when relayed back to the capitalist press, as were the polite comments offered by the Astors.

The high point of the tour was a meeting with Stalin himself. The party spent about an hour with him, talking mostly about matters of no significance, and the Astors told the dictator that Winston Churchill, for whose abilities Stalin apparently had high regard and who was the leading anti-Soviet voice in Britain, would probably lose his seat at the next election, or if he did not he would be kept out of the Cabinet; in any case, they said, Churchill would never be Prime Minister, as Stalin seemed to think. There may or may not have been some tension – accounts vary – when Nancy asked Stalin why the regime found it necessary to kill so many of its own citizens. According to Waldorf's diary the dictator replied that he hoped the drastic treatment of political prisoners would soon stop.

The visit lasted nine days. When it ended, the embarrassment and the criticism began. It was mainly Shaw who was to blame, for the Astors said little about their experiences (and Waldorf in particular, as his diary of the tour shows, had seen through the propaganda exercise the Russians had undertaken). The playwright, however, by now past his intellectual peak, made one ill-judged statement after another. 'I am a confirmed communist,' he told the *Chicago Tribune*. 'I was one before Lenin and am now even more so after seeing Russia. Stalin is an honest and able man. There is no starvation in Russia. Workmen there are happier than in other countries.' Back in Britain, he went even further. 'The success of the Russian five-year plan is the only hope of the world,' he declared at a Labour seminar. 'Capital punishment is absolutely abolished under the Soviets ... though there is some shooting for political offences.' The newspapers had a field day with him, and some of the criticism rubbed off on the Astors, especially Nancy, who was of course much more in the public eye than Waldorf. The fact that Nancy saw fit to say virtually nothing about what she had seen actually told against her, in view of the complimentary remarks she had made to Russian reporters while in the Soviet Union.

The most savage attack on the visit came, naturally, from Churchill, writing in the *Sunday Pictorial* shortly after the party's return home. Shaw and the Astors, he said, 'like to have everything both ways ... Shaw is at once a wealthy and acquisitive capitalist and a sincere communist. His spiritual home is Russia, but he lives comfortably in England. He couples the possession of a mild, amiable and humane disposition with the advocacy and even glorification of the vilest political crimes and cruelties... Similar, though different, contradictions are to be observed in Lady Astor. She reigns in the old world and the new, at once a leader of smart society and of advanced feminist democracy. She combines a kindly heart with a sharp and wagging tongue. She accepts communist hospitality and flattery and remains Conservative Member for Plymouth.' The public, he added, 'tired of criticizing, can only gape'.

Possibly his last jibe was correct. Nancy's name had become such a byword for eccentric behaviour that very little she did surprised people any more. It is the fate of the jester not to be taken seriously, though in this case it was as well for her parliamentary career that she was not. In any case, the economic collapse of 1931 concentrated people's minds far more than Lady Astor's activities.

It was much later in the 1930s, and in connexion with a cause that could hardly be more different from Soviet communism, that deep and widespread resentment of the Astors' political circle appeared. It was not Russia which was most feared then, but the Germany of Adolf Hitler, and the Astors came to be suspected of conniving in the rise of the Nazis' Reich. They were completely innocent of the charge (though there is plenty of evidence to suggest that certain sections of the British upper classes admired Hitler's early achievements even if they disapproved of his methods), but they certainly were guilty of the blindest naivety and, while their defenders rightly maintain that they did not stand behind the British government pulling the strings, there is no doubt that the views of the Astors, of Lord Lothian, of Geoffrey Dawson, Garvin of *The Observer* and a number of others within the Astor circle did influence both government policy and public opinion and did help to discredit the warnings of men like Winston Churchill and Anthony Eden. It has been claimed that what came to be known as 'the Cliveden Set' never really existed, but while the idea of a conspiracy or 'invisible government' or 'second Foreign Office' does not stand up to close examination, there is no doubt that a Cliveden Set did exist in the sense that the phrase represents a set of assumptions and presumptions to which the Astors and their friends were among the most important subscribers. As early as 1932 Anthony Eden was warning of 'the tendency to pay too much attention to the mechanics of peace and too little to its fundamentals', and this is precisely what the Astors' group did.

Since it was Nancy at whom most of the 'Cliveden Set' opprobrium was directed, it is instructive to examine what her

opinions were. The significant influence here was Philip
Lothian: having been involved in the drafting of the Versailles
treaty which sought to punish Germany for the First World
War, he later came to the conclusion that its terms had been
much too harsh and it was that fact which had led to its
aggressive stance in the 1930s. Since, as a zealous convert to
Christian Science, he seems to have become the fount of all
wisdom in Nancy's eyes, she accepted his view absolutely. She
wrote: 'I have desired to restore a sense of security in Europe
by treating Germany as an equal. I have worked for the reversal
of the policy of goading her people and rulers into restlessness
by trying to keep them in a state of inferiority.' But that was a
political explanation for something that was in fact more
emotional – a fear and hatred of war, and not only for its own
sake but also because of what it would do to Britain and her
Empire. While men like Eden and Churchill correctly foresaw
that the only way to stop Hitler was to fight him, people like
Lothian correctly predicted that a second major war would
spell the end of Britain's role as a world power, which
depended so heavily upon the Empire. Furthermore, wars
made people restless: the world had never been the same since
the conflict of 1914–18; how much worse might the upheaval
be next time? Peace was the only way to retain such of the old
certainties as had survived the Great War. And, as Waldorf
pointed out, there were unmistakable stirrings in the East,
where the growing power of Japan threatened British and
American interests. Germans and Italians might be ruled by
dictators, but at least they were white. This under-the-surface
belief in the supremacy of the white races, which was of course
not at all unusual for the times, was also responsible for a lack
of interest when Mussolini claimed Abyssinia as part of the new
Roman Empire. War in Europe must be avoided at all costs.

There were two main planks in the 'peace' platform – the
League of Nations and disarmament. In 1933, shortly after
Hitler came to power in Berlin, Nancy's name appeared at the
end of a collective letter to the newspapers calling for air
disarmament, even though people who had actually attended
the disarmament conference that was going on in Geneva were
already forecasting (privately, it must be said) that it would end
in failure. The conference did fail at the end of 1933 when the

Germans withdrew, Hitler demanding rearmament (which was in fact already under way) while the other powers dithered over how they might disarm. As for the League of Nations, which Hitler denounced as a device for keeping those nations defeated in 1918 in permanent subjection, the member states were so bitterly divided that it could not act at all, yet as late as 1937 Nancy was still saying that the League was the best means of controlling Hitler. The worthy idea of 'peace in our time' was now turning into the disgraceful doctrine of appeasement.

It was in 1936 that the first shot was fired at Lady Astor's allegedly pro-German opinions. The weekly *Time and Tide*, which backed Churchill's line on most things, named Nancy in an article that spoke of important people who were impressed by 'the surface tidiness of the fascist regimes in central Europe' and who supported a policy of tolerance and understanding towards Germany. 'To some of them,' the paper said, 'Hitler, the dreamer, the visionary of the mystic face, a non-smoker, a non-drinker, the anti-Bolshevik, is becoming almost a Führer, almost, we should say, the Führer.' (In the spring of that year, Hitler had sent his troops to reoccupy the demilitarized zone of the Rhineland and Mussolini had claimed Abyssinia: the peace-keepers said the Germans could hardly be blamed for moving into their own backyard and caused sanctions introduced by Britain against Italy to be withdrawn.) Nancy replied to the attack in *Time and Tide* by saying she was not pro-fascist but she was in favour of peace and if that meant treating with understanding and tolerance the 'reasonable' demands of Germany, then so be it. This was by no means enough to allay suspicion, however, among those who found the British government's policy towards Hitler inexplicable, and the following year 'the Cliveden Set' was exposed or invented, according to one's point of view (and Nancy's son Michael said he was never quite sure of what was the truth).

The conspiracy theory was first put forward in 1937 by Claud Cockburn, a left-wing journalist of great skill and wide experience and at that time editor of a home-produced paper called *The Week*, whose influence far outweighed its tiny circulation but which sometimes failed to distinguish between what was real news and what was misinterpreted in the light of its own considerable prejudices. By this time, Stanley Baldwin had retired as Prime Minister and been replaced by an ardent appeaser, Neville Chamberlain. Lord Halifax, who was regarded with suspicion in left-wing circles, had visited Hitler 'in secret' allegedly to offer him concessions.

'Subscribers to *The Week*,' wrote Claud Cockburn, 'are familiar with pro-Nazi intrigues centring on Cliveden and Printing House Square' and he went on to speak of an intrigue involving 'Lord Lothian, the Astors, Mr Barrington Ward of *The Times* and its editor Mr Geoffrey Dawson at the heart of it'. The actual phrase 'Cliveden Set' appeared as the headline on a similar article a month or so later, and as soon as the 'conspiracy' had been graced by a title, news of it spread rapidly.

First the *Manchester Guardian* picked up the story and then the *News Chronicle*. The Astor connexion meant that details soon crossed the Atlantic, and the *New York Times* headlined its report, 'Friends of Hitler Strong in Britain – Fear of Communism Impels Many Men of Wealth and of the Middle Class'. The story said: 'The so-called "Cliveden Set" are widely regarded as the most influential of Germany's sympathizers in England... The strongholds of German influence are the aristocracy and the City of London, both of which are traditional sources of the Conservative Party's leadership and power... British aristocracy by its very nature is more hostile to communism than fascism. When men like Londonderry or Viscount Rothermere or Lord Astor have political nightmares the ogre of their imagination is Russia, not.Germany. Menace to their wealth, their social position, as they see it, is the creed of communism, and, in their minds, whatever endangers themselves endangers England.' This seemed to have the ring of truth about it, but another reporter went further into the conspiracy theory, suggesting that 'the best work for the pro-Germans was done by Lady Astor herself in her frequent parties. Hither came Lord Halifax, now Foreign Minister; here came the Marquess of Lothian, a former Liberal, now one of the leaders of the be-nice-to-Germany school. Prime Minister Chamberlain and his wife were weekend guests.' And the *Washington Post*, six months before the shameful Munich agreement, forecast the sell-out of Czechoslovakia: 'Astor Country Home Becoming "Real" Center of Britain's Foreign

Policy... The British government has given its blessing to Hitler's impending annexation of German-speaking Czechoslovakia, it was learned here today from sources close to Cliveden.'

The impression was further reinforced by the editorials of the Astor-owned *Observer* and *Times*. In the former, Garvin railed against 'worthy lunatics, windy apostles of crazy crusades' and 'a frantic medley of Left Front excitements and Tory Die-Hard delusions' advocating rearmament and the end of attempts to appease Hitler. *The Times* advised that, 'The peace-minded can best serve peace for the moment by ceasing to agitate themselves and others with morbid fancies about corrupt understandings, trampled Austrians and bartered Czechs', and when the Sudentenland crisis was at its height counselled that: 'It might be worthwhile for the Czechoslovak government to consider whether they should exclude altogether the project, which has found favour in some quarters, of making Czechoslovakia a more homogeneous state by the secession of that fringe of alien populations who are contiguous to the nation with which they are united by race. In any case the wishes of the population concerned would seem to be a decisively important element in any solution that can hope to be regarded as permanent, and the advantages to Czechoslovakia of becoming a homogeneous state might conceivably outweigh the obvious disadvantages of losing the Sudeten German districts of the borderland.' The British government denounced that leading article as a misrepresentation of the British position, but it proved to be precisely the policy that Chamberlain followed.

Geoffrey Dawson, indeed, added weight to the Cliveden conspiracy theory. He relied on Lord Lothian for most of his information about Germany, kept in constant touch with Lord Halifax and admitted in a letter that 'I do my utmost, night after night, to keep out of the paper anything that might hurt the susceptibilities' of the Nazi regime. He was a regular visitor to both Cliveden and St James's Square and, of course, his proprietor was none other than Major J.J. Astor, who was keeping very quiet about the line his paper was taking.

Cartoons began to appear in the British press depicting Nancy Astor and her friends dancing to the Nazis' tune and doing the goose-step at Cliveden, which became known as the

Schloss while *The Times* earned the title of the *Clivedener Neueste Nachrichten*. Cockburn wrote that 'the financial power of the Anglo-American set is as extensive as their social ramifications and is greater than their direct political influence... It is regarded as certain that sooner or later Britain's "other Foreign Office" at Cliveden will be brought very powerfully to bear on the Prime Minister.' Meanwhile, Lord Halifax's visit to Hitler had been 'as the representative rather of Cliveden and Printing House Square than of more official quarters...'

Sometimes Nancy tried to laugh off the idea of the Cliveden Set, as when she clowned with Dawson outside St James's Square saying they had been 'caught in the act' by the press, to whom Dawson gave his name as 'Ribbentrop'. But that the charges affected her deeply may be seen from a letter she wrote to the *Daily Herald* early in 1938. 'I have received so many letters ... asking whether there is a group which meets at Cliveden and which exercises a sinister influence on politics,' she wrote, 'and also asking whether I am a fascist or have fascist leanings, that I should be grateful if you would give me space to correct certain absolute untruths... In politics no one objects to hard blows and strong criticism but in a democracy it is essential that the public should be able to base their judgment on facts and not on fiction. A few years ago I used to be called a communist and accused of pro-Soviet leanings because I visited Russia with Mr Bernard Shaw and because I supported those who wanted a trade pact with Russia. But I was not then a communist any more than I am now a fascist. I believe in democracy and in parliamentary government and am opposed to all forms of dictatorship, whether fascist, Nazi or communist.

'It is true that as an individual I have supported those who are trying to correct by negotiations the mistake of the Peace Treaties or to remove some of the grievances of other countries whatever their forms of internal government, and that I favour the attempts to establish a better atmosphere between Britain and France on one side and Germany and Italy on the other... In supporting non-intervention in Spain I realize that this is an unsatisfactory policy but I believe any alternative would increase foreign intervention on both sides and would extend the civil war in Spain into European war.'

Then came the nub of the letter: 'There is no group which weekends at Cliveden in the interests of fascism or anything else. For many years my husband and I have entertained men and women of all political creeds (including Bolshevik), of all nationalities, of all religious faiths, of all social interests. As regards the imaginary Cliveden Set, some who are said to belong to it have never been to Cliveden, others not for years... The story is a myth...'

Myth it might have been, but it served to describe attitudes, thoughts, convictions that were only too real. True, the Astors were not the only purveyors of the idea that Hitler could be bought off, but their voices and those of their newspapers and their friends were loud, carrying even to the Chancellery in Berlin where Hitler listened to them as he laid his plans on the basis that Britain would not stand in his way.

Nancy's reply to the attacks in 1938 quietened things down for a while, but the Munich agreement later that year revived suspicions of the Cliveden Set and in April 1939 Bernard Shaw was moved to reply in the American magazine *Liberty*. Having dismissed the idea of a Cliveden conspiracy, Shaw went on to say that Lady Astor 'has no political philosophy and dashes at any piece of kindly social work that presents itself, whether it is an instalment on socialism or a relic of feudalism', while her husband 'spends his substance lavishly on public welfare in Plymouth and his life doing public work and getting no credit for it'. Accurate enough, to be sure, and if they had both concentrated their lives in the spheres of social work, or indeed even of domestic politics, there could have been little criticism of them other than from those who resented their old-fashioned paternalism. But, in Nancy's case particularly, her fame after she became a Member of Parliament went to her head and, as far as foreign policy was concerned, caused her to go in over her head. Under-educated and, in many respects, inexperienced and unworldly, she began to make pronouncements on subjects she did not really grasp. She would have served better if she had confined herself to things she knew. But the charmed circle in which she lived believed it could recreate the world in its own image, and the dream was just too tempting.

At least when the war did come Nancy had the grace to admit

that she had been wrong and she threw all her energies into the work of defence, especially in Plymouth, as well as urging the government to make good the damage which appeasement had wrought. In the spring of 1940 she was among those who felt that new blood was needed to mobilize the nation for the coming struggle. 'People are beginning to feel', she told M.P.s, 'that Mr Chamberlain is not the wisest selector of men. Duds must be got rid of, even if they are one's dearest friends. And if there is a sweep, it should be a clean sweep and not musical chairs' (a characteristic mixture of metaphors).

Waldorf had become Lord Mayor of Plymouth, which meant that Nancy was Lady Mayoress as well as M.P. and since Plymouth was an important naval base it was clear that the Germans would attack it in strength. They did, early in 1941. The Astors were bombed in their house on the Hoe but still managed to give dances there to keep up the morale of the citizenry under the repeated air attacks. They helped to organize evacuations and housing for people whose own homes had been destroyed, and Nancy teased and joked with her constituents just as she had done during her election campaigns. 'Their houses are down but their spirits are up,' said Winston Churchill when he visited the city, as Prime Minister, in May 1941. As in the First World War, Cliveden was given over to the Canadian army as a hospital, so Nancy was constantly travelling between Westminster, where she continued to attend the House of Commons, Cliveden and Plymouth.

The war over, there had to be a general election, since Parliament had been sitting continuously for almost ten years. Nancy had represented Plymouth for twenty-five years and the constituency party was keen to have her continue to do so. Waldorf had other ideas, however. They were both sixty-six years old and his health was deteriorating; more to the point, he had lost his taste for national politics, which in any case were deemed certain to change beyond recognition as a result of the war. Indeed, Waldorf was by no means certain that Nancy would be elected in 1945 as the people reached out for change. He told her to stand down. 'I don't want to go,' she said, 'and I wouldn't if it were not the wish of my husband.' She knew that without him supporting her she could not survive the political hurly-burly that would inevitably follow the war, could not perhaps even endure an election campaign that was bound to be hard.

'I leave the House of Commons with the deepest regret,' she said on the day of the dissolution, 15 June 1945. 'I don't think any other assembly in the world could have been more tolerant of a foreign-born woman, as I was, who fought against so many things they believed in . . . I am heartbroken . . . I shall miss the House, but the House won't miss me. It never misses anybody.'

If her actual achievements in Parliament had been minimal, at least she had reached the history books as the first woman to sit in the House of Commons. Now she had very little to look forward to as she tried to come to terms with a new age, an age which proved to hold little in the way of promise for Astors on both sides of the Atlantic. The name which had once meant unparalleled wealth and unassailable social position would, during the next few years, become an echo of the past, a curiosity.

PART IV

In the Company of Strangers

10 *All That Is Solid Melts into Air*

The political activity and publishing ventures that maintained and enlarged the fame of the Astors in England were also attractive to their cousin Vincent in New York. Vincent being Vincent, however, his approach was very different from that adopted by Waldorf and Nancy and John Jacob V: unlike them, he lacked the confidence to seek elective office and at the same time he was, of course, very much more a prisoner of the old Astor ethos, which kept politics at arm's length. He never managed to reconcile the guardianship of the family fortune with his unformed but insistent desire to do something positive and practical for his fellow men and, although of all the Astors he was the one most prepared to be a benefactor to mankind, it was only in death that he found the courage to make the grand gesture. As a result, he may be seen by history as a mere dabbler in political and social affairs during his lifetime, which is a little unfair, considering the responsibilities and restraints placed upon him at an early age by the death of his father.

It was entirely in keeping with Vincent's character that he should be an enthusiastic New Dealer in spite of the fact that President Franklin D. Roosevelt's far-reaching social pro-grammes depended on heavier taxation for the rich. Roosevelt, indeed, a Dutchess County neighbour from Astor's boyhood and a distant relative through Laura Astor's marriage to Franklin Delano, was an important influence on Vincent's political thinking as well as a firm friend, even when his policies went further than Vincent would have liked. Coming from similar backgrounds, the two men understood each other and shared a sense of mission, though Roosevelt's was obviously much stronger and more certain than Vincent's. Astor had, of course, grown up as a Republican and he contributed to the campaign funds of both Warren Harding in 1920 and Calvin

Coolidge in 1924. During the Coolidge era, however, Vincent came into contact with some of the leading lights in the Democratic Party, including William H. Wooding who was later to be Treasury Secretary, and was persuaded to switch allegiance. In 1928 he helped to finance Al Smith's presidential campaign against Herbert Hoover and in the same year backed Roosevelt all the way to the governor's mansion in Albany. By the time F.D.R. gained the presidency in 1932, Vincent was a member of the small group of close friends who supported Roosevelt's policies with hearts, minds and pocket-books.

Before his inauguration, Roosevelt took a cruise on the *Nourmahal* to recover from the rigours of the campaign. He was in a wheelchair, of course, having suffered a crippling attack of polio in 1921, and Vincent had ordered a special ramp to be built on his yacht so that the President-elect did not have to leave his chair to go aboard. One port of call on this cruise was Miami, where Roosevelt had agreed to address a Democratic rally at Bayfront Park. A motorcade took the presidential party from the *Nourmahal* to the rally and Vincent travelled two cars behind Roosevelt. At the park, F.D.R. was helped onto the top of the rear seat in his convertible so that he could make his speech and Vincent had a sudden premonition of doom: 'Why,' he said to his neighbour in the car, 'anyone in the crowd could stand back and shoot Roosevelt.' At that precise moment a mentally disturbed bricklayer named Giuseppe Zangara was taking aim with a revolver. By the time Zangara fired, Roosevelt had slid down into his seat, having finished his speech, but one bullet killed the Mayor of Chicago and four bystanders were wounded. One of the injured was brought to Vincent's car while Zangara was spreadeagled across its trunk with a policeman holding him down. Later, when the wounded man had been delivered to hospital and the assassin to jail, Vincent took the shaken Roosevelt back to his yacht to spend a quiet night.

It was on that trip that Astor met another man who was to exert a profound influence on him and who in fact was to be perhaps the closest friend of his life. Raymond Moley, an important member of the Roosevelt coterie, was everything Vincent was not – intellectual, urbane and utterly devoted to his principles. Though Moley's support for Roosevelt waned in the face of the compromises necessary to weld together an Administration and push the New Deal through the Congress, he remained close to Vincent and was directly responsible for Astor's plunge into publishing. For some time Vincent had been considering buying a newspaper and in the early 1930s he was approached by two other would-be publishers, Averill Harriman and his sister, Mary Rumsey, with an offer to join forces in an attempt to buy the *Washington Post*. Vincent was wary, since he did not like Harriman, but was persuaded by the news that Raymond Moley had agreed to edit whichever publication the trio might buy. The bid for the *Post* failed and, with no other prospects immediately in view, Astor and the Harrimans decided to found their own publication. Together with Moley they put their idea to Roosevelt and he immediately gave them a dollar as the first subscriber: it was to be a glossy news weekly to compete with the ten-year-old *Time* magazine and the newly published *Newsweek*.

The Harrimans invested $125,000 each and Vincent matched them with a quarter of a million. The first issue of *Today* magazine appeared in October 1933, but if its first subscriber had expected it to be a mirror for his policies he was wrong. Moley, originally appointed Assistant Secretary of State by Roosevelt, quit the Cabinet and became one of the most outspoken critics of the Administration and although Vincent became the major proprietor when Mary Rumsey was killed in a riding accident in 1934, it was Moley's editorial view that prevailed in the magazine. 'People say that I broke up Vincent's friendship with Roosevelt,' Moley once said, 'but it's not true. They remained friends until Roosevelt's death, although they disagreed on most things. Whatever their differences, Vincent voted for Roosevelt all four times, although I voted against him three times.' Vincent also remained friendly with Moley throughout his life: the editor was one of the few people, if not the only one, whom Astor could stand early in the day – they would usually talk on the telephone about the editorials in the morning papers while Vincent was having his breakfast.

As for Roosevelt, he inspired deep and abiding hatred among the members of Vincent's class who were being forced to pay for what they saw as an unduly inflated federal government which interfered too much in both the lives of its citizens and the operation of cherished free enterprise: those who begin life in a position of advantage tend to believe in the virtues of individual effort. Yet the man's conviction, optimism and enthusiasm were infectious and his charm was overwhelming, and Vincent was spellbound despite his reservations about the extent of the 'nanny state' that Roosevelt seemed bent on creating. Indeed during the famous 'first hundred days' of F.D.R.'s first term Astor was intoxicated by the heady brew of legislation that flowed from the White House through the awestruck Capitol – the creation of the Civilian Conservation Corps and the Tennessee Valley Authority; the beginning of vast programmes of public works; the introduction of farm subsidies; the abandonment of the Gold Standard; and the passage of the National Recovery Act, in which Averill Harriman was to play such a prominent part. As the President's confidant on all these measures, Vincent felt for the first time that he was making a contribution to the life of the nation. He even accepted the post of finance chairman of the so-called Recovery Party, which was Roosevelt's mechanism for consolidating the Democratic vote in the New York mayoral election of 1933.

Throughout the period of his first Administration, Roosevelt continued to spend holidays aboard the *Nourmahal*, passing most of his time fishing when he was not organizing boisterous games or masterminding 'initiation ceremonies' for the benefit of Father Neptune. Vincent was honoured by the presence of such an illustrious guest and went to the lengths of installing the very latest in wireless equipment so that the President could remain in constant touch with Washington, but F.D.R.'s ebullience could be demanding of a host and Vincent was only able to relax on the Sabbath which, after presiding at morning service, Roosevelt kept as a day of rest. Astor was also keenly aware of his responsibilities to the nation and always flatly refused when the President tried to persuade him to ignore weather forecasts and press on to good fishing grounds. And though in private the two were on 'Franklin' and 'V.A.' terms, Vincent always called Roosevelt 'Mr President' in the presence of other people and invariably stood up when he entered a room.

The friendship naturally caused a good deal of comment and

the number of cruises Roosevelt took on the *Nourmahal* was seen by some as a sort of barometer of his popularity among the moneyed and conservative classes. As opposition to the New Deal grew and the Supreme Court began to pounce on some of the President's measures to counter the effects of the Depression, it was noted that the editorial voice of *Today* was becoming increasingly shrill and early in 1936 a commentator remarked that 'it will be interesting this spring to see whether President Roosevelt takes his next fishing trip on the *Nourmahal*'. In the event he did not, and the story was told of a conversation between him and Astor the previous year, when Vincent had invited him.

'Oh, don't put that big thing in commission just for me,' Roosevelt had said.

'Mr President, the *Nourmahal* is in commission all the year round,' Vincent had replied.

Roosevelt had whistled in surprise and then laughed, commenting: 'I guess we'll have to raise the taxes on the rich again.'

Vincent was never as close to Roosevelt after this: it may be that he did recoil somewhat from the extent to which the President was attempting to change the American way of life and overturn long-established notions, and it may also be that, with a second term in his pocket and the mass of the people behind him, F.D.R. thought it prudent to shed his patrician image – he always was a skilful publicist. Nevertheless, Vincent's admiration did not wane and by 1937 even Raymond Moley was blaming the Administration's supposed excesses on the President's advisers rather than the man himself. 'The country might be better governed from a White House trailer, far from the vexations of Washington,' he commented, reviewing Roosevelt's visit to the Bonneville Dam in Oregon that September. 'Get the picture. The President is 3,000 miles from Washington... A Cabinet that, for four years, has dumped every minor problem into the President's lap is momentarily compelled to rely upon its own discretion. A group of zealots who dogged the President's heels in Washington, always pressing him to make more and more inflammatory declarations of a class warfare, is far away. If ever the President is himself, it is under such circumstances... There is a story to the effect that the President's young literary and legal aides prepared elaborate memoranda for a "fighting" speech about reactionary lawyers, utility octopi, economic royalists and the like – memoranda which he consigned to oblivion ...at Bonneville Dam, Mr Roosevelt delivered an utterance completely his own, out of a heart warmed by a friendly countryside...'

By that time Moley was writing in *Newsweek*, which had become Vincent's second most precious possession after the St Regis Hotel. *Today* had not done particularly well under Moley's editorship and *Newsweek* had fallen into deep financial trouble, so Vincent had merged them, poaching the great Malcolm Muir from McGraw-Hill to edit the new weekly. Muir had resisted at first, believing that Vincent merely wanted another plaything, but once again Moley had been the deciding factor, persuading Muir that Astor's interest in *Newsweek* was sincere (Moley himself was to be a contributing editor). In the years to come Vincent was to prove his sincerity many times over: it took the magazine almost a decade just to break even, and during that time Astor pumped five million dollars into it. He was chairman of the board and on press days would often be found in the magazine's New York offices reading galley proofs, taking a particular interest in any stories about shipping, on which he considered himself an expert.

With the St Regis and *Newsweek* as two great loves in his life, it was about this time that Vincent found a third – Minnie Cushing. Though she was neither the first nor the last of his wives, she is said by many people to have been the one he loved most, and it is rumoured that when she left him he threatened to shoot himself. Yet at the same time he retained a sort of proprietary interest in Helen, even though she remarried not long after their divorce. It was perhaps as a link with his youth that he valued her, since he was estranged from his mother (by this time, settled in England, Ava had become Lady Ribblesdale) and in 1938 broke off relations with his sister, Alice, when she divorced Serge Obolensky and married an Austrian named Raimund von Hofmannsthal. Helen's new husband, a real estate man named Lytle Hull, had an estate very near Ferncliff, and Vincent never broke the habit of dropping in on Helen to discuss whatever he was doing and find out how she was getting on. Helen remained the archetypal Hudson Valley chatelaine while the new Mrs Astor became closely involved with the running of the St Regis, some of whose suites she had redecorated in bright colours and chintzes. According to the journalist Walter Winchell, Minnie was so closely identified with the management of the hotel that the touchy Duchess of Windsor complained to her personally when a table reserved for her was let go. 'My good woman,' Minnie said witheringly, 'why don't you act your age?'

Within a year or so of marriage, however, Vincent and Minnie were separated by the Second World War. Vincent had remained in the naval reserve and was recalled to active duty with his peacetime rank of captain, of which he was inordinately proud. While Vincent was involved in shepherding convoys back and forth across the Atlantic, taking military supplies to Britain and bringing back wounded servicemen, Minnie organized recreation and parties for sailors on leave in New York. As in the First World War, Astor had given his yacht to the navy (having thoughtfully fitted gun emplacements as far back as 1928) and that marked the end of his seafaring days as a civilian: after the victory he did not even ask for the *Nourmahal* to be returned, contenting himself with an aeroplane instead, though he never got from it the pleasure he had once found in his boat and to the end of his life he liked to be addressed as 'Captain Astor' (another echo of his father, who had of course been generally referred to as 'Colonel Astor').

Indeed it might be said that in the years following the war that made America the most powerful nation on earth, there was very little that gave pleasure to Vincent Astor. He became ever gloomier and more irascible. Most of what had been the prime Astor real estate had been sold, including the old Estate Office on West 26th Street, and what remained was pretty run down; even his beloved Ferncliff was no longer as he remembered it, the big house having been demolished at the insistence of Minnie, who had the former sports complex remodelled as the living quarters. Vincent must have wondered what he had done with his life and his fortune: he had been an imperfect guardian of his inheritance, in Astor terms at least, and yet in sacrificing the more solid parts of his patrimony he had not achieved any of the dreams that had inspired him in his youth. True, he had the St Regis and *Newsweek*, but his business advisers were always telling him that the hotel was a poor investment and the magazine, though it continued to fascinate him and occupied a good deal of his time, was not the outlet for his good intentions that he had assumed it would be.

Furthermore his riches, with which he had never been entirely comfortable, now became an actual burden. In his earlier years he had been quirky in his personal expenditure, often showing surprising meanness in one who could be so generous and at other times spending money pointlessly on a whim, yet his business dealings had usually been sound and he had been prepared to take risks, most of which had paid off. In the 1950s, however, he became obsessed with the idea of protecting his capital in the face of the postwar inflationary trends. It was clear by then that the Astor fortune was no longer the greatest in America, even though Vincent had followed the pattern of his predecessors in doubling his inheritance, to something more than a hundred and twenty-seven million dollars. According to a survey by the business magazine *Fortune* in the mid-fifties, the oil magnate Jean Paul Getty led the field with between seven hundred and a thousand million dollars, followed by H.L. Hunt (also an oil man), the Rockefellers and the Mellons. Vincent's name appeared in the fourth division, behind the likes of Howard Hughes, the DuPonts and the Kennedys. Not that Vincent was in the least interested in how rich others were, but what concerned him was holding on to what he had: it was the age of the producer, and not since the days of John Jacob I and the fur trade had Astor wealth been based on production.

A dispute arose between Vincent and his advisers as to how to protect his position. Vincent wanted income – as one of his business associates put it, his idea of beating inflation was earning twice as much as he needed. The men who actually guided the Astor Estate, led by Alan W. Betts, saw the best prospects in long term capital gains, particularly at a time when the highest rate of tax on income was ninety-one per cent while that on capital gains was only twenty-five per cent. After much persuasion, Vincent agreed to invest in capital-producing stocks, but he watched them like a hawk, always suspicious that they were not as sound as real estate, even though they easily outperformed the Dow-Jones Index. 'He had a real thing about stocks,' Alan Betts remembered, 'He was scared to death of them.' If, as he read the *Wall Street Journal* over breakfast, he noticed that one of his common stock holdings was dropping, he would immediately telephone the office to complain. The other thing that bothered him was consolidation. When Betts first undertook a full-scale assessment of the Astor holdings, he discovered that fifty million dollars was spread over more than three thousand tax-exempt bonds in parcels of no more than $25,000 – that was Vincent's idea of limiting risks to capital. Betts had an uphill struggle to talk him into a wholesale conversion to common stock, which in four years added nineteen million dollars to their value ... and Vincent never was completely convinced of the rightness of the move. In fact, his third wife, Brooke, who comes into the story a little later, seems to suggest that worry about the state of his investments may have contributed to the poor health of his last years, a claim we shall examine in due course.

The New York real estate business was very different from what it had been when Vincent had come into his fortune, and his once-enlightened ideas of landlordism and development began to look distinctly old-fashioned by the 1950s. Encouraged by Betts, he began to divest himself of the properties that remained, many of which were returning no more than one per cent (for instance, one prize white elephant was a shoe shop of which the upper storeys had been condemned), but at the same time he could not shake off the experience of generations which had clung to real estate as a shelter against all storms and he seemed to retain a longing for the Astor name to dominate the property scene once more. Whether the grand scheme for Astor Plaza in Manhattan was his own or whether – as his widow, Brooke, maintains – he was talked into it against his better judgment, he announced in 1955 plans for a forty-six-floor luxury office building on the block bounded by Park Avenue, 53rd Street, Lexington Avenue and 54th. It was to herald a new era in Astor real estate, an investment in the future of New York – at a cost of seventy-five million dollars – to match the investments of his ancestors.

Unfortunately, it was not to be, and before long even Vincent's advisers were referring to the project as 'Disaster Plaza' (though not in his hearing, of course). Everything that could have gone wrong did so, almost from the first day. The site was an Astor one, but owned by the estate of William Waldorf. Having bought a long lease on it, Vincent applied to his English cousins for a mortgage to finance the construction of the office block but they (or more likely their managers) refused him: blood might be thicker than water, but in this case it was business that was flowing through the veins, and it was not customary in New York to grant mortgages on land destined for commercial use. Vincent did the rounds of the banks, but they were also shy, expressing doubts about some of his prospective business tenants. He went through agonies of anxiety, confiding to his wife that he must have had a hole in his head to have invested in a hole in the ground. The economic slump of 1957 finished him as far as Astor Plaza was concerned and he sold his lease to First National City Bank, which erected its own building. The hole in the ground had cost him three million dollars, much to the disgust of his managers, who thought that if he had waited for the inevitable upturn in the economy he could have cleared a profit of twelve million – the trouble was, one of them said, that the project was bigger than the man.

In a sense, that comment was correct. Always a vulnerable personality, Vincent had grown worse with age, becoming even more withdrawn than before and subject to constant worry about both his business affairs and his health. Given this parlous condition, the death in 1956 of his sister Alice, with whom he had become reconciled as his last link with the Astor past, was a bitter blow indeed.

II

The relationship between Vincent and Alice Astor was a serial story of good and bad patches. She was eleven years the junior and her brother was away at school most of the time while she was growing from a mysterious interloper into an identifiable sibling; by the time she was old enough for Vincent really to establish a relationship with her, her parents had divorced and she had been whisked off to England by her capricious and pleasure-seeking mother. No surrogate father appeared on the scene for almost ten years, only a confusing succession of her

363

mother's male friends, and during that time her real father died and she was shipped back and forth across the Atlantic almost like luggage as Ava trod the international social circuit. Even when Ava took Lord Ribblesdale as her second husband, the seventeen-year-old Alice seems to have been rather more of an encumbrance to the newly weds than a bonus. Her childhood and adolescence, then, must have been lonely and insecure, consisting chiefly of a search for attention and affection that was generally denied her – and in a way that was to be the story of her entire life.

Indeed, Alice fits perfectly the role of the poor little rich girl, for at the age of ten she became an heiress on the night the *Titanic* went down, with five million dollars in a trust fund earning each year interest that in itself would have been more than enough for a number of less materially fortunate people to live on. Like Vincent she was to discover that money, though it might help to blunt life's barbs, does not in itself bring happiness and is not always a source of security. Everything she wanted was within arm's reach, but she could not buy her way out of boredom and disillusion.

But while Vincent quaked in the presence of his mother and sought to avoid it, Alice – perhaps through familiarity – was proof against Ava's domineering nature and caustic tongue. Her psychologically deprived childhood had released in her a kind of inner strength, which showed itself mainly as wilfulness, and an unquenchable optimism: in the face of these, Ava was powerless and so was Vincent when he sought to impose upon his sister the discipline of 'the head of the Astor family in America'. Alice would go her own way against all opposition and would do it charmingly. Because of that she would become probably the most genuinely wasted and tragic member of the dynasty.

Though not quite the crowd-stopper that her mother had been, Alice was a pretty girl, rather tall and raven-haired, with eyes that signalled deep passions and an attractive pout to her lips. In addition, she was intelligent and talented – one of her contemporaries thought she could have been a writer – and deeply interested in literature, music, art and mystical religions. In later life she was to be a valuable patron and friend to dancers, painters and writers, though she never undertook creative activity herself, probably because she never had the self-discipline to commit herself for any length of time.

Of course, in her mother's eyes Alice's physical and mental attributes (not to mention her five million dollar inheritance) added up to wonderful marriage prospects: possibly a title, such as Ava herself had acquired, and certainly an inexhaustible bank account. Ava balked, therefore, when in 1922 Alice fell for a man who was not just titled but also royal, but who had no money to speak of. He was Prince Serge Obolensky, descendant of a thousand-year line of Russian royalty deposed by the Revolution. He was handsome, charming, urbane, fascinating – everything that the fairytale prince should be – and his connexions were impeccable, reaching, of course, even into the English Court. In fact, so striking was he that Nancy Astor, when she first met him in 1931, could not resist one of her iconoclastic quips: she had just returned from her visit to Soviet Russia and on seeing Obolensky remarked, 'What a wonderful job they've done over there in such a short time.' He was, on the other hand, penniless by Astor standards and, at the time Alice met him, he also happened to be married. Ava regarded him as thoroughly unsuitable as a prospective husband for her daughter and did her best to strangle the romance at birth.

Alice, though, found useful allies in brother Vincent, with whom she was getting on quite well at that period, and his wife Helen. Vincent was deeply impressed by Serge, no doubt because he was everything Vincent could never be, and Helen was romantic enough to sense his magic. While Ava schemed to get her daughter married off to someone more appropriate, Helen would entertain Serge and Alice at her house in Paris and they could meet, too, under Vincent's roof at Ferncliff. Ava was not to be beaten so easily, however. She paraded her daughter before a host of eligible young men in Britain, Europe and America – they included a Spanish sherry tycoon and, in an attempt to reduce support for Obolensky, Helen Astor's brother. But Alice remained unshakable. As soon as she reached the age of twenty-one, when she was beyond her mother's control both legally and financially, she became engaged to her prince and began the frustrating wait for his divorce to be finalized. They were eventually married on 24

July 1924, and three times over at that. At the first, civil ceremony, Prince Paul of Serbia was a witness; the second wedding was an Anglican service, at which Waldorf Astor gave the bride away; the third tying of the knot was in an Orthodox church and was attended by Prince and Princess Nicholas of Greece, John Jacob Astor V and his sister Pauline, who had married Lieutenant Colonel Herbert Spender-Clay. Ava, gracious in defeat, gave a sumptuous wedding reception for the young couple.

Alice and Serge spent their honeymoon in Deauville then set off for Canada, intending to purchase a substantial wheat farm, but Alice was put off by the vastness and emptiness of the country so they retreated to Ferncliff, where the new bride indulged her taste for a mean game of golf and she and Serge became sought-after guests among the Hudson Valley squirearchy and the high society of Jazz Age New York. Canada having been ruled out, they decided to make London their main home and bought a splendid house in Regent's Park from Admiral of the Fleet Lord Beatty, the hero of Jutland. For some reason Beatty immediately regretted the sale and attempted to buy back the house, Hanover Lodge, for more than the selling price. Alice was all for accepting the former owner's offer and handing the profit to Serge as a gift, but the prince felt that his pride was involved and refused. Hanover Lodge thus became the site of another Astor social club in London, the haunt of Continental royalty, the faster set of the British aristocracy and, given Alice's intellectual interests, many well-known writers and artists.

The couple's first child, baptized Ivan, was born in the summer of 1925, not long after they had moved into Hanover Lodge. Though given to self-indulgence, Alice proved to be a conscientious and caring mother, but of course Ivan was not allowed to interfere too much with his parents' lives, which quickly settled into a pattern of pleasure-seeking. According to the reminiscences of Serge, the annual round consisted of the French Riviera in the spring, New York and Newport in the summer, autumn at Rhinebeck, the Christmas season in London followed by winter sports at St Moritz, then on to Paris to get in the mood for the South of France again. The greatest difficulty Alice ever faced was what to wear for the succession of parties that their wanderings involved; often she would change several times before she was satisfied with an outfit for a particular function, her repeated sessions in front of the mirror invariably making her late. Her unpunctuality was a source of embarrassment to her unfailingly good-mannered husband, and several cures were tried. The provision of an extensive, mirrored vanity case in the family Rolls-Royce made no difference, and neither did the setting of the clocks at home forty minutes fast, since Alice knew they were wrong and therefore ignored them.

For the girl who had everything, nothing was quite enough to stave off boredom, and within a couple of years, by Serge's account, Alice even began to find married life boring, despite the constant travelling and activity. She tried to enliven things by pressing spectacular gifts upon her husband, but he was too proud and too fastidious to accept them and persuaded her to spend the money instead on a fund for helping penurious Russian émigrés (what could be more boring than that?). Vincent, though he deplored his sister's spendthrift ways and lack of discipline, offered some relief from ennui by giving Alice a ninety-nine acre corner of the Ferncliff estate, on which she built a pleasant stone house. Typically, she and Serge moved in and arranged a housewarming party without the thirty-room mansion having the benefit of some of the necessities of comfortable living, and these had to be acquired quickly – and at great cost, naturally – before their house guests arrived.

Their indulgent way of life served to increase the normal human tendency towards selfishness in both Alice – who had always been spoilt – and Serge. They were accustomed to getting what they wanted and anything that stood in the way was simply ignored or circumvented. It was not long before each began to apply this attitude to the other: if Alice, for example, wanted to do something on which Serge was not keen, she just went ahead and did it, leaving him to amuse himself some other way. When Serge was invited to the South of France at a time which did not suit Alice, he went alone, leaving her to catch up with him later. They began to quarrel: over Alice's insistence on inviting an unmarried male friend on a golfing holiday; over Serge's partiality to a nurse who looked after Ivan and over the attention he paid to some of the women who clamoured to dance with him at balls.

After five years Alice had had enough and, though Serge always protested his undying love for her (and really meant it, his son Ivan said), she asked for a divorce. Serge was bitterly upset and Vincent, who was still some years away from setting aside his principles regarding the sanctity of marriage, was appalled. For three years the partnership remained in limbo as Vincent and other relatives sought to effect a reconciliation. The question of Ivan's money, or lack of it, was raised, and to demonstrate his independence Obolensky moved out of Hanover Lodge and went to New York, where Vincent employed him first in the Astor Estate Office and then as manager of the Maisonette Russe restaurant in the St Regis. In due course, Alice followed her husband and for a while it looked as if they might stay married – so much so that when Alice finally went to Nevada to sue for divorce she was pregnant, a daughter, Sylvia, being born while the proceedings were under way.

The case itself was disputatious but not particularly acrimonious, the chief matter of controversy being the custody of Ivan. Helped by Vincent's own lawyer (the provision of whom did nothing to improve relations between brother and sister), Obolensky won and the boy thereafter spent only the summers with his mother in England. Alice, in a repeat of her own mother's divorce, was granted custody of Sylvia. Vincent more or less severed all contact with his sister, pointedly making something of a boon companion out of Serge, who frequently accompanied him on cruises in the *Nourmahal*.

Alice's concern for her son was more real than Ava's had been for Vincent. She remarried as soon as her divorce from Serge became final and planned to slip quietly away from America with her new husband, an Austrian writer named Raimund von Hofmannsthal (son of Hugo, Richard Strauss's librettist). But on the day the newlyweds were to sail for Europe, Ivan, who was then aged seven, suddenly became seriously ill and Alice flew to his side, remaining there until he recovered. Unfortunately, her example of maternal devotion rebounded on her, since news of her secret second marriage was leaked to the press, which indulged in some very unpleasant gossip. The ill-natured comment might as well have been an omen, for although the marriage gave Alice a second daughter, Romana, it soon ended in divorce.

In the wake of Alice's second divorce came the Second World War and with it a third husband. Unlike Ava, who returned to America through the good offices of the White House, Alice stayed in London and busied herself with war work, driving an ambulance during the London Blitz, organizing a mobile canteen for anti-aircraft gunners, working in an electronics factory and maintaining morale among her friends by keeping up her famous dinner parties. It was while she was bringing food to the gunners that she met Philip Harding, a journalist in peacetime, whom she married in 1940. Again this marriage produced a daughter, Emily, but it did not survive the war. Alice's search for who knows what seemed to be becoming desperate.

By now Alice was on very good terms with Serge again. They had seen each other in London during the war and after it Alice decided to settle in New York, which made Obolensky think that perhaps she might go back to him. Instead she married a well-connected architect named David Pleydell-Bouverie, but he was no more successful at making her happy than any of her previous husbands, and he did not last as long as some of them, though at least he had the distinction of being the last.

Finally alone, Alice took up residence in her house at Ferncliff and, to some extent, restored relations with Vincent, who of course had been divorced and remarried himself. Disappointed in matrimony, she turned instead to writers and dancers for company, numbering among her friends Tennessee Williams, Gore Vidal, Frederick Ashton, Edith and Osbert Sitwell, and especially Aldous Huxley. Before the war she had financed the first visit to America of the Sadlers Wells Company, which she had supported from its creation, and she now offered financial backing to the New York City Ballet. At the same time, however, her restless soul wandered into ever stranger byways in pursuit of peace and contentment, and there are those who say that in her declining years Alice became a little mad.

Long before, in 1922, to be precise, she had been one of the first people to enter the newly opened tomb of Tutankhamun (her mother having been a friend of Lord Carnarvon, one of its discoverers) and she had emerged from it with a remarkable necklace which had clearly been important to the Egyptian royal house. This ancient and priceless trinket, in which hundreds of golden rams' heads were set among gemstones, and the extraordinary circumstances in which she had obtained it, defying the curse of King Tut, always seemed to exercise a sort of mystical power over Alice – an effect of which even Serge appears to have been rather afraid. She had long been fascinated by ancient religions and when she wore the necklace it seemed that she could almost transport herself back thousands of years to the world of Tutankhamun and Ikhnaton and the fabulous Queen Nefertiti; to the rites of sun-worship and the death cults of the Pharaohs. It seems to have been only after the end of her fourth marriage, however, that her interest in such matters became an obsession, and she began to believe that she was the reincarnation of an Egyptian princess whose spirit cried out because she had been forced to renounce the life-giving religion of the sun, as preached by Ikhnaton, in favour of older and darker beliefs.

During her times of solitude at Ferncliff in the late 1940s and early 1950s, Alice began to delve ever deeper into the mysteries of ancient Egypt. She learnt to read hieroglyphics and pored over cryptic messages from the distant past. She made herself a copper 'horn' like those worn by the high priests who interpreted the will of the Egyptian gods. She began to experiment with telepathy, spiritualism and extrasensory perception and, with the encouragement of Huxley, she considered the potentialities of hallucinogenic drugs such as mescaline and 'magic mushrooms'.

Whether she actually became deranged is an open question, and an important one since it bears upon the rumours that surrounded her death, but what is clear is that her judgment did become clouded. One of her most trusted servants at Ferncliff has suggested that she fell victim to countless cranks, quacks, fake mediums and quasi-mystics to whom she paid over large sums of money. Alice herself reported that she frequently had a dream in which an ornate sarcophagus appeared in her room and opened to reveal a beautiful girl dressed in rags but wearing the ram's head emblems of royal birth. The girl would begin to rise from her coffin, but as she did so a ghostly hand would thrust her back again... Small wonder that some of her friends were worried about her.

In other ways, though, she was a perfectly normal, healthy, middle-aged woman, still beautiful and lively and as always notable for her generosity and charm. Indeed, despite a certain indefinable sadness about her face and the disappointments of a life which had seemed to contain a cloud behind every silver lining, she gave every appearance of being in good spirits. Which made the suddenness of her death, at the age of fifty-four, all the more suspicious.

It happened during the summer of 1956. Alice had visited friends during the afternoon and had then driven into the city to have dinner with her lawyer. The next morning she was dead, found lying in her bathroom by her maid. There was evidence that she had taken pills of some kind; she had taken alcohol; at her bedside was a copy of the ancient Egyptian *Book of the Dead*. As these items were imperfectly added up, the word spread that Alice Astor had committed suicide. But why? Well, there was this crazy obsession of hers with Egyptian death cults, and hadn't she been in love with some medium or mystic or somesuch who had refused to get a divorce for her? The whispers reverberated along the Hudson Valley, much to the distress of Vincent, who, shocked at the news and by no means in the best of health himself, already felt guilty enough that he had failed to give Alice the attention a sister deserved and had allowed irrational prejudice to keep them apart.

Matters came to a head when two men appeared at Vincent's door seeming to demand payment in return for suppressing an autopsy report which showed that Alice had killed herself. Dejected and ill as he was, Vincent was not the man to let it go at that. He took it upon himself to order a post mortem examination that would provide the truth. Its findings were that Alice's body did contain traces of alcohol and a drug, but only one drink and a fairly harmless sedative; the cause of death was indisputably a heart attack.

The truth, though, was not much comfort to Vincent. He was reminded of his own mortality, if he needed reminding, and when he was gone, what would be left of Astordom?

III

When Alice died, Vincent Astor was well into the third year of his third marriage. He and Minnie had gradually drifted apart after the war, she finding it ever more difficult to cope with his moods and he increasingly reacting against the showbusiness personalities she liked to entertain, such as Moss Hart and Rex Harrison. Minnie apparently began asking for a divorce in 1952, but it did not happen until the following year, when she immediately married the artist James Whitney Fosburgh. By that time Vincent had met and fallen in love with Brooke Russell Marshall, the features editor of *House and Garden*. The twice-married Brooke – Vincent usually called her 'Pookie' – was trying to pull her life together after the death of her second husband and another walk down the aisle was the last thing on her mind, but she was to discover that refusing an Astor was no easy matter.

Actually Vincent had known Brooke for many years – his sister-in-law (when he was married to Helen) had been the first wife of Brooke's second husband – but it was not until they found themselves at the same Park Avenue dinner party early in 1953 that Astor began to pursue her. At the time it was still customary for the ladies to withdraw after dinner – at any rate, in the sort of circles in question – and Brooke was somewhat surprised when Vincent followed them, buttonholing her in the living room and insisting on offering his apologies for not having written to her when her husband, Buddy, died. This formality having been accomplished, he remained talking to Brooke until Minnie approached and said it was time for them to go. If, as Vincent maintained, Minnie had already asked for a divorce at this time, she may have been seeking to take advantage of her husband's apparent interest in another woman, for she quickly offered Brooke a lift home in the Astor limousine.

Brooke, whose autobiography was published in America a year or two ago, says she was nonplussed when, during the drive to her apartment, Minnie invited her to spend the upcoming Memorial Day holiday weekend at Ferncliff, and Vincent enthusiastically endorsed the invitation. Brooke prevaricated and was further surprised the following day when Vincent telephoned her to invite himself for tea and immediately afterwards Minnie rang to press the Memorial Day plan. All this attention from people she hardly knew made Brooke feel uneasy, but when Vincent came to tea he was perfectly pleasant – though he did go a little over the top by offering to donate money to charity in memory of Brooke's late husband – and she decided that she might as well go up to Ferncliff for the holiday, reasoning that the Astors had probably taken her up simply because she was to some extent a new face.

On the Saturday of Memorial Day weekend, at the end of May, a limousine was sent to convey Brooke to Ferncliff, where she found her hosts in the middle of a game of croquet (a particular passion of Vincent's later years) on the indoor tennis court. Play was suspended while Vincent and Minnie showed the new guest to her room, an occurrence which surprised some friends Brooke found among the gathering, since Vincent would normally not hear of anything inter- fering with his croquet. At lunch, the Astors competed for Brooke's attention, Vincent insisting that she could accompany him on a drive while Minnie tried to persuade her to play canasta. Brooke excused herself by announcing her intention to go for a walk in the woods, and went off to muse on this curious behaviour. The surprises were by no means over yet, though.

On her way back to the tea house – which had been built on the site of the original mansion – Brooke ran into Vincent, who ushered her into his Mercedes and drove off round the estate. They had not gone far when he stopped the car and confessed to Brooke that Minnie wanted to leave him and had asked for a divorce: he had refused, but would change his mind if Brooke would agree to marry him.

Brooke, a sane and mature woman (she was in her late forties at the time) was shocked and bewildered by this proposal out of the blue. She protested that Vincent hardly knew her, but he replied that he knew a great deal about her and that if she would marry him he swore to make her happy and gain her love. In spite of herself Brooke was thrilled by his ardour and the drama of the occasion. She said she would think over Vincent's proposal, whereupon he kissed her and took her on a drive along the Hudson, entertaining her with stories of the rich and often eccentric folk whose estates they passed.

The remainder of the weekend passed without incident, though Brooke found herself constantly wondering whether Minnie realized what Vincent was up to. In the light of hindsight, it seems very likely that Minnie did know, and since she apparently had her own plans for remarriage she must have been almost as excited as Brooke was.

No sooner had Brooke reached her apartment back in New York on the Sunday afternoon than Vincent was on the phone making arrangements to come and see her. For the next few weeks he literally hounded her, telephoning several times a day, and, though she tried to keep him at arm's length, she found herself flattered and pleased by this boyish pursuit. In her book she confesses that she had been feeling lonely and missing the company of a husband: she needed someone to share her life, a man to give her strength and also to make her laugh, to take her out of herself. She began to respond to all this romantic attention. Of course, Vincent's temper and unpredictable moods were well known among their mutual friends, and some warned Brooke that he was merely acting on a whim and would drop her as soon as he had won her, so she remained on her guard while at the same time enjoying the dramatic and dreamlike qualities of the developing relationship. It was like being in a play, she said later.

They say absence makes the heart grow fonder, and the clincher for Brooke was a two-month trip Vincent made to Japan that summer. Before leaving, in the first week of July, he insisted that he still wanted to marry her and would not take no for an answer. While he was away, he wrote her five or more letters every day and it seems to have been these as much as anything else that won Brooke's heart. They were gay, schoolboyish letters, sometimes featuring an old crone of Vincent's invention who, he said, was Brooke's chaperone guarding her against him and secretly in love with him herself. Brooke responded in kind and, as she said, the two of them really came to know each other through their letters.

Brooke began to feel that, in spite of what she had heard about Vincent, he really could make her happy and she could really love him. She sought advice from her mother, who counselled her to go ahead, but she still had some doubts and it was not until the beginning of September, when she was staying with friends in Bar Harbor, that she finally took the plunge. Vincent was well and truly divorced from Minnie by then and sent a cable to Brooke begging her to say she would marry him soon. Encouraged by her friends she cabled back 'Yes'.

They were married quietly in Bar Harbor on 8 October 1953 and immediately left on a honeymoon that lasted all of an hour and a half. Vincent flew his new bride to Rhinebeck in his amphibious plane.

At first the couple lived mainly in the St Regis because Vincent wanted to refurbish his apartment, which took up the whole top floor of a block he owned on East End Avenue. He needed to be in New York during the week because he spent some part of every day at the *Newsweek* offices, which were also the centre of his real estate operations. Ferncliff was for summer weekends and in the winter there was a house in Arizona, on the golf course of the Biltmore Hotel in Phoenix with magnificent views towards the famous Camelback Mountain. Vincent had built the small adobe house there – there was a miniature of it in the garden bearing a sign 'Astor House Annexe: Birds Welcome' – because he believed the dry air was good for him, though by Brooke's account the dust bothered him terribly, particularly since he was still a heavy smoker. Many of the English Astors – Bill, Michael, Jakie and Gavin – spent holidays with Brooke and Vincent in Arizona.

The idyll had its darker side, though. Vincent was intensely jealous of Brooke's friends, especially those associated with her late husband. He developed a phobia about the telephone and asked Brooke not to phone her friends when he was at home: since that was most of the time, she lost touch with a good number. But instead of resenting his quirks, as his other wives had done to varying degrees, Brooke decided to humour him and try to keep him cheerful. She would happily sit up with him to watch some awful old movie on the Late Show; she would play interminable games of backgammon and dominoes without complaint; she would spend hours playing the piano and singing for him. She believed he needed a woman prepared to devote her life to him and she was almost certainly right: friends have said Brooke was the best thing that ever happened to Vincent.

It must have become immeasurably more difficult for her as

her husband grew older and business worries began to gnaw at him, particularly at the height of the Astor Plaza project. He would worry night and day about his affairs, often scribbling figures on small pieces of paper which he would pull out of his pockets when he complained about how much money he was losing every day. Brooke disagrees with the former managers of the Astor Estate that the plaza project was too big for Vincent. The trouble was, she says, that he was reluctant to embark on it in the first place, and when everything went wrong he was consumed by regrets. Eventually she grew concerned over his health and, on her own initiative, went to the estate office and told the executives they had better get out of Astor Plaza and another problematical development in Cleveland otherwise they would be the death of Vincent.

Indeed his health was failing rapidly, but it is impossible to say whether it was affected by his business worries or whether it was sickness that brought on the fears in the first place. Brooke has suggested that there was an element of hypochondria in Vincent's make-up and he had a rather pathetic faith in doctors, one of whom told him quite categorically that smoking could do him no harm and only changed her views when he developed a serious circulatory disease which caused one of his feet to turn black and made it difficult for him to walk throughout the rest of his life. According to Brooke, that particular woman doctor merely indulged Vincent and told him what he wanted to hear because she was in love with him.

Some of those who knew him said he was moody and bad tempered because of his drinking, which also influenced his business judgment, but in fact his declining health forced him to curb his intake of alcohol quite severely, and it is likely that his irascibility was simply the result of not feeling well.

Yet Brooke still managed to keep him relatively cheerful and fairly active. They travelled constantly between New York and Ferncliff, Arizona and Bar Harbor and in 1958 even managed a visit to England. It was that trip, though, that foreshadowed the end. They were staying at the Connaught in London and, though Vincent had given up smoking, his cough became so bad that a doctor brought an X-ray machine to the hotel to examine his lungs, on which a disturbing shadow was found. Vincent promised to undergo a thorough check-up back in

New York, but on the journey home he developed severe pains in his legs and a high fever which troubled him continually for the next two months.

By the end of January, however, Vincent was feeling much better and planned his usual February to April vacation in Arizona. They were due to leave New York on 4 February, and the previous day Vincent was feeling so much like his old self that he took Brooke to lunch at the St Regis. Malcolm Muir, the editor of *Newsweek*, had invited them to dinner that evening to listen to recordings of the magazine's coverage which had been prepared for blind people: since their departure for Arizona was to be early in the morning Vincent cried off but sent Brooke on her own because he wanted to know what the recordings were like. She returned late in the evening to find Vincent sitting up in bed and gasping for breath, so she immediately called his doctor. Within a few minutes of the doctor's arrival, Vincent seemed to be convulsed with pain and fell back on his pillows – dead at the age of sixty-seven.

His death marked the end of an era, the end of the Astors as a major force in American life. Always suspicious of his half-brother Jack, he had no one to whom he could pass on the fortune. He had tried to adopt Alice's son, Ivan, but not surprisingly the boy's parents had objected. After Alice's death he talked of adopting her daughter Emily, but that too came to nothing. Despite the fact that Jack shared the same father as himself, Vincent took the view that the Astor line came to an end with him and – though in so many ways he had been untypical of the dynasty – he clung to the belief which had been handed down from the first John Jacob, that the fortune must not be dissipated. So he did the only thing he could do in the circumstances: he left half of it to charity and almost all the remainder in trust.

From his early days as guardian of the fortune he had been interested in good works – his way, as he put it, of 'showing his gratitude' for the wealth and luxury into which he had been born. In his last years, charity became very important to him and in 1948 he created the Vincent Astor Foundation 'for the alleviation of human misery', which gave grants to such enterprises as hospitals and children's homes. Cynics sneered that he was merely trying to prevent himself from being tapped for donations or that the foundation was a tax dodge. They were proved wrong when Vincent's will was published. Sixty-five million dollars, half of his estate, was bequeathed to the Vincent Astor Foundation. Brooke got two million dollars outright and a life interest in the remaining half of the estate, which on her death she was free to dispose of as she wished. Apart from a few minor bequests, the rest of the family was ignored. Vincent Astor went down in the history of the dynasty as the man who gave the money away.

He had once said: 'If you label a man as a scientist he is instantly accepted by the public mind as a more than ordinarily useful person. If you label a man as a lawyer or give him any professional tag, the public mind associates him with worthwhile achievement. But if you say of a man that he is merely rich, he is immediately docketed as a wealthy wastrel, and whatever he attempts to do to show that he is a sincere well-wisher of his fellow men is either discounted or misinterpreted on account of his wealth.'

When he died, there was no room for misinterpretation.

11 *Strange Inheritance*

I

In Britain as in America, the Second World War marked the final stage in the decline of the Astors from the financial and social pre-eminence they had been accustomed to enjoying. In the case of Vincent, it was his childlessness more than anything else that determined the course of events – he had no heir to pick up the mantle and came to view himself as the last of the line, despite the presence of his half-brother Jack (John Jacob VI). The British Astors, on the other hand, had heirs aplenty: the causes of their gradual but inevitable withdrawal into private, almost workaday life, were largely economic. Taxes on wealth, on property and on inheritance narrowed the range of options previously enjoyed by the rich and the children of Nancy and Waldorf, John and Violet, soon came to terms with the fact that they would have to earn their keep.

Cliveden, that great symbol of Astordom in England, had been turned over to the nation in 1942, with the proviso that the family be permitted to live there. Waldorf set up an endowment for the upkeep of the house. Hever was to remain in the family for a further forty years, but eventually that, too, would have to go, as would *The Times* and *The Observer* in their turn. The name Astor would continue to excite interest, to conjure up the realized fantasies of the past, but the way of life followed by those who bore the name would be very different from that of their forebears.

Nancy had retired from Parliament – reluctantly and with a bitterness towards Waldorf that was to last for the rest of his life – in 1945 and John Jacob V had been defeated in his Dover constituency, one of the victims of the Labour landslide that helped to change the face and the attitudes of Britain. 'I'm an extinct volcano,' Nancy said. The press and the public continued to follow her activities with fascination, but as she grew older she ceased to be an appealing eccentric and became instead a domineering, shrewish and sometimes insufferably rude *grande dame*. A man who knew her well in her later years said he felt she could have toned down her act as the outrageous female and should have behaved with a dignity befitting her advanced years, but her demand for attention never diminished and she did not mind whom she upset or ignored in satisfying it. Encouraged by Shaw, she even suggested that she should be made a peeress in her own right, but since the overtures came after Winston Churchill had made his way back to Downing Street the idea was a non-starter. Unable to plague either the House of Commons or the House of Lords, she became a nuisance to her children instead, particularly after the death of Waldorf in 1952 which meant the end of her reign as mistress of Cliveden, the house passing into the stewardship of her eldest son, Bill.

For brother-in-law John, however, who had always lived in quieter fashion, the social and economic transitions of the postwar years appeared to be less difficult. Still the honoured figurehead of *The Times*, chairman of the Press Club for twenty-eight years and the first chairman of the Press Council, set up after the Second World War to adjudicate complaints against the conduct of newspapers, he also continued his activities in the field of charity, donating £400,000 in 1955 towards the rebuilding of the Middlesex Hospital Medical School in London, and adding a further £50,000 two years later. He was president of the Dover Club, a justice of the peace, a deputy lieutenant for the county of Kent and a lieutenant for the City of London. The onset of rheumatoid arthritis in the mid-1950s restricted his interests somewhat, but in 1956 his public works were rewarded with the offer of a barony. He hesitated, characteristically anxious that his acceptance of a peerage would somehow compromise the integrity and independence of his newspaper, but in the end he assumed the title which had first been granted to his father, Baron Astor of Hever.

At a dinner given by the staff of *The Times* to mark the chairman's seventieth birthday, his colleague of thirty-four years, John Walter, noted: 'There is or was an idea which I think must have originated in Printing House Square many years ago, that the position of chief proprietor of *The Times* was above and beyond the reach of any official recognition or Court favour; in fact, that the occupant of that position was per se immune from the danger of any such offer. I believe the idea still persists. I mention that because we know very well that our chairman, as chief proprietor of *The Times*, could have joined that distinguished group of press lords in the Upper House long ago if his ambitions had lain in that direction. It is a pleasant thought to all of us this evening that, having a natural respect for *The Times* and its traditions and also for himself, he has preferred to await a more fitting opportunity to enter that august chamber.

'That opportunity has now come. It is with all the greater pleasure and satisfaction that we unite this evening in congratulating our chairman on the peerage conferred on him by Her Majesty for public services. Some of those services are known to us, but many are not, because our chairman has a predilection for anonymity where good works are concerned. But knowing him as we do, we are sure of this much: that all those causes, national or other, in which he has taken a personal interest have benefited largely, not only by his generous benefactions but by the unstinted time and trouble he has devoted to them.'

Reflecting on his birthday, Astor said that 'from a comparatively short experience seventy seems to be a nice age. You can look back quite a bit. You can enjoy the present so long as you adapt yourself to circumstances. You can look forward – one hopes.'

Adapting to circumstances proved to be harder than he expected. Within six years of that celebratory dinner, Astor announced that he was being forced to leave England. 'The 1962 Finance Act,' he said in a statement, 'contains a clause which imposes a new liability for English estate duty on real property abroad owned by people who live in this country. It is said that undue advantage has been taken of the previous exemption by individuals who have invested their capital overseas with the sole purpose of avoiding English estate duty and that the law has had to be changed to prevent this happening in the future.'

His position, he added, was that he was entitled to the life interest in an American trust created specifically by his father for the benefit of his grandchildren. The trust comprised valuable real estate holdings in the United States built up by his forebears, 'starting with my great-grandfather one hundred and fifty years ago', but no part of the capital represented by that property had ever been in Britain. 'The trust is administered by American trustees. I have never had any power to touch the capital and the income which I receive from it, after payment of taxes in the United States and of course in this country, I have hitherto spent wholly in England.' But the new Finance Act meant that the trust would become liable upon his death to estate duties of eighty per cent: 'If this were to happen it would be very difficult for those concerned to meet the death duties both on the United States trust fund and on my property in England, and it would certainly mean that Hever Castle would have to be sold.' At the same time, he was barred by American law from relinquishing his interest in the trust. There was only one way out.

'My wife and I intend to make our home abroad in future, even though this must involve giving up properties, interests and activities in England, and much else besides.' Otherwise, 'my death will mean that almost the whole of the American property will disappear in death duties and my family will be involved in serious financial consequences... Because of the nature and history of the family holdings in America, I feel myself bound to do what I can to prevent this from happening.' Old John Jacob Astor's perspicacity all those years before had turned out to be a burden on some of his descendants. William Waldorf, his namesake son, his second son and even his grandson had battled for years against the ogre of double taxation, and now it had come to this.

On 27 October 1962, the three hundred villagers of Hever crowded into the village school to say goodbye to their lord of the manor. 'I never expected to have to do this at my time of life,' Astor said, his voice charged with emotion. 'I think it's terrible.' He announced that his eldest son, Gavin, would take over the castle and his youngest son, John, would buy the house in Carlton House Terrace 'for a consideration'. The villagers presented him with a bound volume of their signatures as he told them that he did not know what arrangements could be made for him to visit England from his new home in the South of France. 'I have to dispose of my English properties and establish myself as a permanent resident in France. When I have done that, my solicitors may say that brief visits are possible.'

A month later, John and Violet, accompanied by their butler, their chef and two beloved Manchester terriers, went into voluntary exile. 'My wife and I are feeling very sad,' Astor said. 'We are going to miss this country so much.' They drove to London Airport in their black Rolls-Royce, with its LAH 100 numberplate, through the dense traffic on the Great West Road. At the check-in they seemed lost as they fumbled for their tickets and had their baggage weighed. A friend who saw them go said Astor could never have been mistaken for anything but an Englishman in his brown tweed suit, suede shoes, 'British warm' overcoat and trilby hat – yet the country for which he had fought and of which he was so proud had forced him to leave. The communist *Daily Worker* took a different view. Lord Astor, it said, was leaving the country in the interests of his heirs: 'You may think that they are already enjoying comfortable incomes and abilities and opportunities to increase them. But then you would fail to recognize the sacredness of property. So great is it that it persuades even the chief proprietor of *The Times* to leave his country. Doubtless he will leave it secure in the faith that *The Times* will remain a pillar of private property, and all that it stands for, until the last.' But the Conservative *Daily Telegraph* leaped to Astor's defence: 'What Lord Astor of Hever is doing in changing his domicile is "striking" on behalf of a good many other English families who have held real property abroad for some generations, or who have invested money overseas with serious intent rather than the possibility of escaping the tax the day after tomorrow.' Perhaps, in the end, Lord Astor was no more than a victim of the class war.

While John remained chief proprietor of *The Times*, he had relinquished the post of chairman in 1959, handing over to his son, Gavin. But four years almost to the day after John's flight abroad *The Times* had a new owner, linked to *The Sunday Times* as part of the huge Thomson press empire. Inherited wealth was no longer enough to guarantee the survival of a newspaper: the backing of big business became essential. The new owner, Lord Thomson of Fleet, said: 'I am delighted that my old friend Lord Astor of Hever, who has done so much for *The Times*, has given his warm blessing to the new arrangement, and that his son, Gavin, has agreed to be life president.' But having enjoyed forty years of stability, *The Times* was embarking upon a new and risky phase of its long history, which would lead to closure for a year and the arrival of yet another owner in little more than a decade.

'Astor's period of ownership was a sort of golden age for *The Times*,' says a man who retired recently from the paper after serving it for half a century. 'Oh, the management was paternalistic, all right, but in those days nobody minded.'

John, meanwhile, had settled in a villa at Pegomas, near Grasse, in the Midi. He had chosen France so that his English friends could visit him easily and he was soon able to surround himself with familiar furniture and belongings, but he never recovered from the blow of his forced departure. 'To be forced to go abroad to die was a most cruel irony,' *The Times* itself commented, particularly because the money Astor saved was used to found a charitable trust for the purpose of helping medicine and education in Britain. When he did die, in July 1971 at the age of eighty-five (having survived his wife by six years), there were many people who felt inclined to say that this was the noblest Astor of them all.

Less noble, perhaps, but certainly more noticeable, even in old age, was Nancy. She never quite became accustomed to the idea that she was no longer the chatelaine of Cliveden and, though she had first a flat and later a house in London, she often descended on her former home and took charge, completely overlooking whichever of her son Bill's three successive wives happened to be the nominal ladyship at the time. The writer and art expert Maurice Collis, who wrote a biography of Nancy a few years before her death, included in his diary the details of a Cliveden party in 1955 at which the King of Sweden was a house-guest and the hostess was Bill Astor's second wife, newly returned from honeymoon and facing her first big test. After dinner, Nancy commandeered the most important guests, perched on a divan and loudly calling back those who had the temerity to drift away or attempt to pay attention to the new Viscountess.

Something else Nancy never really got over was the loss of

her political career, and she would argue politics with anyone she could trap. She also, in the early years of her retirement at least, loved to appear on public platforms and would make speeches whenever she got the chance. After Waldorf's death, she sought solace in travel and went to America, mainly to visit her family. During the course of her stay she met Senator Joe MacCarthy, who was just making a name for himself as a fearless hunter of closet communists whom he saw in every walk of American life, but MacCarthy made the mistake of meeting Nancy with a glass in his hand. 'What's that you're drinking?' she asked. 'Whisky,' said MacCarthy. 'I wish it was poison,' came the retort, which led to at least one demand that she should be arrested. Immediately after leaving America Nancy went to Rhodesia, where she is said to have greeted the Governor as 'one slave-holder to another', and she was back in Virginia for Christmas.

In 1959, when she celebrated her eightieth birthday, she was honoured with the Freedom of Plymouth, and though she was pleased to accept it she could not resist pointing out to a friend that she felt it was almost too late and that if she had been male she would have received the honour long before.

Much of her time during her last years was spent with her daughter Wissie, who had married the Earl of Ancaster and lived in a beautiful country home in Oxfordshire. She had difficulty in getting on with her male children, and with none more so than her firstborn, Bobbie Shaw, who caused her much grief right up to the end of her life. Bobbie had been a handsome boy, but a wayward one, with a form of instability that associated him in his mother's mind with the difficulties and heartache she had experienced during her marriage to his father. For his part, Bobbie clung to her during his childhood, worshipped her in a way that some have said was far from normal, but as he grew older he rebelled at every opportunity against her possessiveness and dictatorial manner, sometimes reducing her to outbursts of tears.

In early manhood, Bobbie bent to the will of his stepfather and joined the army (Waldorf, no doubt thinking of his own lack of fitness, insisted that all his sons undertake military service). He became a subaltern in the Royal Horse Guards but unfortunately, in reaction against the passionate teetotalism of his mother, he also took to drinking heavily. Bobbie served throughout the First World War, but in 1929 he was found drunk on duty and compelled to resign his commission in order to avoid court-martial. Both Nancy and Waldorf were understanding and treated him kindly, yet this seemed only to increase his resentment and after his resignation from the army his life settled down into reckless wantonness. His mother seems to have allowed him to go his own way, preferring not to notice what he was up to, although they frequently quarrelled. Then, shortly before Nancy and Waldorf were due to leave on their visit to the Soviet Union in 1931, came the bombshell: Bobbie was arrested on a charge of homosexuality.

The law covering homosexual offences remained at that time as harsh as it had been a century before and the police had no alternative but to prosecute. Bearing in mind the position of Bobbie's family, however, the officer in charge of the case told Waldorf that the issue of a warrant would be delayed for several days, and if during that time the young man suddenly discovered a pressing reason for leaving the country, well ... such matters could always be arranged. But whether out of pride or from a desire to wound his mother, the young man positively refused to run and the police, having gone this far, were left with no choice. A warrant for his arrest was issued.

It was almost certain that Bobbie would be sent to jail if found guilty, but worse than that was the publicity which would attach itself to the son of so famous a woman if the news of his arrest was broadcast. Of course, *The Times* and *The Observer* were safe, but there remained the popular press. Luckily, Garvin, the *Observer* editor, was an intimate friend of Lord Beaverbrook, owner of the *Daily Express* and the most powerful newspaper proprietor in the country, and a gentleman's agreement was quickly reached. Nancy agonized over whether she could carry on with the tour of Russia in the circumstances, but it was pointed out that since the trip had been so widely reported and commented upon any postponement would merely serve to excite suspicion and make things worse for Bobbie. So the Astors went, and while they were away Bobbie was quietly tried, found guilty and sent to jail for four months.

Back from the Soviet Union and because of that the victim of press harassment herself, Nancy kept in touch with her imprisoned son as best she could, anxiously awaiting news brought to her by a prison visitor and sometimes writing to him or visiting him herself. At last he was released, and Nancy took him to stay at the house in Sandwich for a time so they could be alone together and he could make an effort to rebuild his life. Waldorf was supportive as usual and other friends tried to help; George Bernard Shaw suggested a trip to South Africa, but Nancy and Bobbie did not go. For the latter it was probably too late anyway – he had lost control of his life and he was never completely to regain it.

Bobbie lived quietly in Kent, undergoing psychological treatment from time to time, but when the Second World War came he tried to enlist in the Scots Greys because he thought that regiment still had horses, which he loved (he had twice cracked his skull riding in steeplechases). Discovering that he was mistaken, and in any event not fit enough to be accepted in a fighting unit, he returned home and joined a barrage balloon company. During the Battle of Britain in 1940 he was wounded in a Luftwaffe raid, when a bomb fell on the public house where he happened to be drinking. After quite a long spell in hospital, he became an ambulance driver in London, where he completed his war service.

The fact that both mother and son were growing older did nothing to make their relationship any easier. They continued to fight and hurt each other, and Nancy continued to cry over her ill-starred boy. What appears to have been a climax for both of them occurred in March 1964: Bobbie tried to kill himself with sleeping pills and for three days, as he lay in hospital, it was feared that the suicide attempt would ultimately succeed. The family argued over whether Nancy should be told and it was finally agreed that she should, though the facts were concealed from her – the story was that Bobbie had suffered a stroke. Nancy went to visit her son, and when she returned from the hospital everyone who saw her noticed that a vital spark seemed to have been extinguished. She had evidently guessed the truth of Bobbie's condition. Two weeks later she herself suffered a stroke and in a month she was dead.

II

Some of the personal difficulties experienced by Bobbie Shaw, particularly in his relations with his mother, were also to be the lot of his step-brother William Waldorf Astor (usually known as Bill), the firstborn of Waldorf and Nancy. As Bill's younger brother, David, put it: 'For various family reasons, my elder brother's upbringing was more stilted than that of the rest of us. A lack of warmth in his earliest years seemed to produce an awkwardness in his human relationships which he strove all his life to overcome.' He was born in 1907 and, as a small boy, suffered from the effects of the long depression that afflicted his mother before her conversion to Christian Science. He suffered, too, from being naturally quiet and self-effacing and could not stand up to his mother's bullying ways. At Eton, for example, he had coxed the school rowing eight at Henley Regatta and had the bad luck to be in the losing boat: Nancy insisted that defeat was Bill's punishment for failing to do his Bible lesson that morning. Because of his diffidence and dislike of argument, she was to continue to harass and bully him for the rest of her life. Bill found it difficult, too, to get on with his brothers and sister. As the heir to the viscountcy, he felt himself somewhat apart from them and they, being of more high-spirited and rebellious nature than their eldest brother, did not make things easier.

But unlike his step-brother, Bill Astor did not withdraw into selfishness and eventually hopelessness. After leaving New College, Oxford, he devoted himself to a programme of public and charitable works which took him from the industrial areas of Britain, on behalf of the National Council for Social Service, to the Far East. In 1935, as was perhaps inevitable given the interests of his parents, he stood for Parliament as candidate for East Fulham. Nancy campaigned on his behalf (a mixed blessing in view of her outrageous style) and he managed to turn a Labour majority into a margin of a thousand votes in his favour. His work as private secretary to Lord Lytton with the United Nations Commission on Manchuria in 1932 had given him valuable political and administrative experience and he was quickly promoted to government office. In 1936 he became parliamentary private secretary to Sir Samuel Hoare, who was then First Lord of the Admiralty, and when Hoare moved to the Home Office, Astor went with him.

When the war came, Bill was commissioned in the Royal Naval Volunteer Reserve and posted to the Middle East as an Intelligence officer. After serving for three years in Palestine and Syria, he was transferred to the Naval Intelligence section of the Admiralty in London, which enabled him to become an active member of the House of Commons again.

In 1945, Bill became involved in a government scheme offering (if that is the right word) political education to German prisoners of war. The six-week courses were held at Wilton Park, Beaconsfield, where, in Bill's words, 'while it had the exterior rigours of a PoW camp, the atmosphere inside was academic – the principal and tutors even wore gowns'. The Labour Party had taken a particular interest in the courses and Bill had been invited to express the Conservative point of view so that the prisoners should not feel they were being indoctrinated. Bill enjoyed the experience. 'The audience was intelligent, receptive and quick to see jokes, even in English,' he wrote at the time. 'I suggested that if our aircraft industry had been nationalized before the war I would probably now be in the audience and they would be lecturing me, a point they took uproariously... The only difference I could observe from a British audience was that the questions, instead of being put semi-audibly to the speaker, were bawled out in a parade voice – a great convenience to all concerned.' The prisoners seemed to enjoy it just as much: when they returned to Germany many of them formed 'Wilton Park Circles'.

Less successful was his attempt to return to Parliament. Standing at Fulham again, he became a victim of the 1945 Labour landslide. He was adopted as Conservative candidate for Wycombe, Buckinghamshire, in 1950 but was again defeated. When he did return to the House, as M.P. for Wycombe, the following year it was to be a short visit: his father died in 1952 and Bill became the third Viscount Astor.

He did not, however, also succeed to the ownership of *The Observer*. As David Astor explained: 'The transfer by my father of the ownership of *The Observer* to a trust ... meant to my brother a major disappointment, as he had always expected to inherit it.' David, who had worked as a journalist, had become Waldorf's editor-designate in 1942 (though he could not take up the post at that time, obviously, because of his war service) and Bill had to be content with a directorship. Though he remained active in that role, he had to seek other outlets for his energies and abilities, not to mention the natural generosity which was one of his chief characteristics, according to those who knew him well.

One of Bill's chief interests in the field of public affairs was the international movement to aid refugees which grew up in the wake of the Second World War. He was a leading member of the executive committee of the British organizing body for World Refugee Year in 1959–60 and afterwards became chairman of the standing conference of British Organizations for Aid to Refugees, a post he held until his death. His was no mere armchair involvement, however. In 1957 he was awarded the Grand Cross of Merit of the Knights of Malta for his active participation in helping refugees from Hungary after that country's revolt against Soviet domination in 1956. He himself told the story of how, on Christmas Eve, 1956, he joined volunteers who paddled a rubber dinghy over the Andau Canal to bring refugees from Hungary to the safety of Austria. 'The dinghy could take three people at a time,' he said. 'We waited for signs of the refugees from the Hungarian side – they would flash lights and show torches to indicate where they were... The weather was icy cold all the time. It was an extraordinary experience because we used to get women, children and old people, even babies with frostbite.'

He remained in Austria for two weeks at the height of the crisis, working with the Knights of Malta and a British organization, which were the only groups allowed by the Austrian authorities to work on the frontier. 'I drove along the whole frontier from Czechoslovakia to Yugoslavia and visited all the different posts... The patrols used to go on all night. The refugees as they came over would be taken to Austrian farms near the frontier where they got rum and hot food before they were taken by lorry to centres farther back. I took over with me a Land-Rover and my chauffeur, an ex-Commando... It was chaotic. People could get across by night comparatively easily because during the period of "peaceful co-existence" the barbed wire had been taken down and the landmines removed, but to confuse the refugees the Hungarians put up Austrian flags at false frontier posts to make them think that they were on the Austrian side.' After this active service, Bill toured America on behalf of the Knights of Malta raising money for the resettlement of the refugees. He collected about $100,000 (worth £375,000 at that time).

Away from his more official activities, Bill had been keen on horses since university days (he got a half-Blue for polo and steeplechasing at Oxford) and he enthusiastically took over the Cliveden Stud founded by his father. Among its outstanding horses during the next few years were Ambiguity, which won the Oaks; Hornbeam, narrowly beaten in the St Leger; and, perhaps the most famous of all, Grey of Falloden. (There was much regret in British racing circles when the stud was sold after Bill's death, most of the horses going to America.) He was also interested in art, and for some years guaranteed an income to the painter Stanley Spencer.

Bill's marital history was as chequered as that of any Astor, though less sensational than some. His first wife was Sarah Norton, whom he married in 1945 after a brief courtship against the background of the victory celebrations and an engagement announced the day after his father's horse Court Martial had won the Two Thousand Guineas at Newmarket. Bill had been released from the Royal Naval Volunteer Reserve to contest East Fulham again in the general election of that year and Sarah gave up her wartime job at the Admiralty to help her fiancé with constituency work. They were married on 14 June, with the wedding reception held at Admiralty House, but their honeymoon lasted no more than a weekend because on Monday the 17th Bill had to attend his adoption meeting in Fulham, and throughout the following week he was booked to address campaign rallies in the constituency.

As it turned out, Bill's election campaign was unsuccessful and so was his marriage. He was thirty-eight, his bride twenty-six and she apparently preferred younger men for, by Bill's account, she fell in love with an Oxford undergraduate at about the time Bill's heir, also called William Waldorf, was born in 1951. Bill seems to have known nothing of Sarah's secret passion for another two years, for it came as a complete shock to him when in 1953 she announced that although she was not the man's mistress she wanted to marry him. Bitterly upset, Bill got a divorce.

His second marriage was even more shortlived. On 26 April 1955, in a Church of Scotland ceremony at St Columba's, Pont Street, in London, he married Philippa Hunloke, granddaughter of the Duke of Devonshire, but within little more than a year the marriage had collapsed. A friend noted that the couple seemed very much in love at first and Philippa gave birth to a daughter, Emily, but it soon became apparent that something was wrong and shortly before Christmas 1956 Philippa went home to her mother. Four years later there was a polite divorce on the grounds of desertion.

The third marriage was undoubtedly the happiest, though it was to be placed under greater strain than either of the others. Bill was fifty-three when it took place in October 1960 and his wife just twenty-eight: she was Bronwen Pugh, a judge's daughter who had made quite a name for herself as a model and an announcer on BBC television. Tall, green-eyed and auburn-haired, Bronwen had been voted 'woman of the year' in 1959 and at the time of her marriage was the principal model for the Paris designer Pierre Balmain – 'my beautiful wife', Bill called her. The wedding took place quietly at Hampstead Register Office, near the home of the bride's parents, and was followed by a blessing in the chapel at Cliveden and a reception for fifty guests. Nancy Astor, despite having said at the time of Bill's second marriage break-up that he should not get a divorce because then he would only marry a third 'damn fool', was the star of the wedding reception, regaling the guests with a selection of funny stories and anecdotes.

Bronwen was to give Bill two more children, Janet and Pauline, and she was to see him through the worst scandal in which the name of Astor ever appeared – indeed, one of the greatest scandals of the twentieth century. It has gone down in history as the Profumo Affair; it ruined a promising political career, almost brought down a government and, according to those who knew him well, it might have helped to shorten Bill Astor's life.

The central figure in the sex-and-spies drama was Stephen Ward, osteopath, artist and, as he was later to claim, an agent of British Intelligence; he was also an habitué of the seedier byways of London society – and a friend of Bill Astor. Bill it was, in fact, who indirectly caused the fateful meeting between a girl named Christine Keeler and the War Minister John Profumo, who was to give his name to the scandal. Astor met Ward in 1950 when he needed osteopathic treatment after a hunting accident and frequently attended his consulting rooms for some time afterwards. In 1952 he lent Ward more than £1,000 to help him to become established in a London practice and continued to advance him various sums, as well as guaranteeing an overdraft of £1,500. Ward made repayment in the form of his professional services. It was in 1956 that Bill made perhaps the greatest mistake of his life when he allowed Stephen Ward to rent a cottage on the Cliveden estate. In the words of the official report on the Profumo case, 'The cottage was down by the river while the big house is on top of the hill. To get from the cottage to the house it is a quarter to half a mile's steep walk, or one mile by road. Stephen Ward used to come up at weekends and give osteopathic treatment to Lord Astor and to those of his guests who desired it. The account, including payment for the guests, was charged to Lord Astor.' Ward often entertained his own guests at the cottage, but they remained out of the way when he visited the big house and did not generally mix with the Astors and their friends ... until one day in June 1961.

Among the Astors' house guests during that warm summer weekend were John Profumo, a rising Conservative politician, and his wife, the actress Valerie Hobson, while Stephen Ward was entertaining a bevy of beautiful girls, including Christine Keeler. Ward had Astor's permission to use the swimming pool at Cliveden and on that particular weekend had chosen to do so, along with the girls, of course. It was there that Profumo noticed what were later described as 'the undoubted physical attractions' of Christine Keeler. He could hardly have failed to do so in the circumstances. It was shortly after dark on the Saturday evening, and the Ward party was at the pool. While she was in the water, Keeler took off her swimming costume, threw it onto the bank and indulged in what is now referred to as 'skinny-dipping'. Not long afterwards, Bill, Bronwen, Profumo and his wife and several other guests from the big house strolled down to the pool. 'Christine Keeler rushed to get her swimming costume. Stephen Ward threw it on one side so that she could not get it at once and Christine seized a towel to hide herself.' Astor and Profumo, walking ahead of their wives, watched the incident and laughed, but the latter apparently liked very much what he had seen of Miss Keeler.

On the Sunday, Astor, Profumo and some others returned to the pool where the girls were again bathing. Also present was Captain Eugene Ivanov, naval attaché at the Soviet Embassy in London, who was staying at Ward's cottage. Profumo took some photographs and was pictured himself with some of the girls: the photographs were to haunt him later, particularly the ones in which Captain Ivanov appeared.

As the official report said: 'It is apparent that during this weekend Mr Profumo was much attracted to Christine Keeler and determined to see her again if he could. This was, of course, very easy, through Stephen Ward. In the next few weeks Mr Profumo made assignations with Christine Keeler. He visited her at Stephen Ward's house and had sexual intercourse with
• her there...' It was an indiscretion that would cost him his career, and his fall was seriously to harm Bill Astor.

What Astor and Profumo always maintained afterwards was that they did not know Stephen Ward was a man living a double and perhaps even a treble life. Astor did know that Ward was a communist sympathizer, for he often spoke of visiting the Soviet Union, saying that as an amateur artist – and a pretty skilful one, it is said – he wanted to draw some of the leaders in the Kremlin. Not only that, but he often peddled his communist leanings to his patients, and indeed he sought advice from Astor as to how he should approach the Foreign Office with a proposal that he act as an intermediary between the British government and the Soviet Embassy. (Ward later claimed he was a double-agent for British Intelligence; this was discounted at the time but rumours persist and the facts have not so far been clearly stated.)

But he also leaned towards things other than communism, most of them of a sexual nature. He had an insatiable appetite for women and he also ran a stable of prostitutes, of whom Christine Keeler was one. His technique was to sleep with a girl, persuade her to become a prostitute and then live off her earnings. At his flat he often held orgies involving the use of two-way mirrors, and he could also provide girls and equipment for the satisfaction of wealthy clients who appreciated flagellation and similar practices. Whether he knew it or not, Jack Profumo was on very dangerous ground, and so was Bill Astor.

The early 1960s was a time of spy mania, with revelation following revelation and a growing suspicion in the public mind that the country was full of traitors. The Security Service naturally took an interest in the pro-Russian activities of Stephen Ward, the more so because his friend Captain Ivanov was not merely a naval attaché but also an officer of Soviet Intelligence. During their investigations, British counter-espionage agents naturally came upon the relationship between Ward, Keeler and Jack Profumo. Since Profumo was War Minister and Ivanov was apparently a Soviet spy, and they both appeared to have links with Keeler and her friends, the security risk was obvious. The head of the Security Service had a meeting with the secretary of the Cabinet, and as a result Profumo was warned, very discreetly, of course, in the British manner, that he would do well to drop some of the company he was keeping. (According to the official report by Lord Denning, the Security Service did not know at the time that Profumo was having an affair with Keeler: if that was true, it was being incredibly inefficient.) At the same time, British Intelligence targeted Captain Ivanov as a man who might be 'persuaded' to defect – he might, after all, be vulnerable to blackmail because of his association with the Ward set, whose activities were well known in both Westminster and Fleet Street circles, though the pedigree of some of Ward's non-medical clients was such that no mention of them appeared in the newspapers. When the possibility of 'turning' Ivanov was mentioned to Profumo, he wisely backed away from any involvement, but to the end Stephen Ward maintained that he himself was an instrument of British Intelligence to achieve just that objective. It will be some time before the truth emerges, if ever.

In the end, though, it was not the spying aspects of the case that caused the most excitement, but its sexual overtones. An outburst of violence among the pimps and prostitutes with whom Ward and Keeler associated brought the police down on them, and during the course of inquiries into a shooting incident involving Keeler, detectives got wind of some of the highly placed names involved with Stephen Ward's ring of call-girls. When it became clear that there would be criminal proceedings, Christine Keeler announced that she had sold 'her story' to the *Sunday Pictorial*: Stephen Ward panicked and tried to buy her off, but since he was perennially short of money he asked Bill Astor for a loan, saying he would shortly have to meet 'legal expenses'. Astor gave him the money, telling him: 'Pay me back when you can, or you can work some of it off in treatment, should I have any sprains, bruises or hunting accidents.' As it happened, Keeler refused the bribe, so Ward used Astor's money to pay his rent and clear some debts, and at the same time made arrangements to sell his own story to the *Sunday Pictorial*, which preferred it to Keeler's. Christine promptly made a deal with the *News of the World*.

What followed was determined to a large extent by all this selling of stories to the newspapers. In order to push up the price, Keeler and some of her prostitute friends began to invent details and mention names that would immediately attract public attention. In the resulting melee of truth, half-truth, innuendo and falsehood, it remains to this day impossible to say with absolute certainty just who was among Ward's clients and who was not. But Bill Astor was one of those actually named by a prostitute named Mandy Rice-Davies, another girl who had lived with Ward, as Keeler had done, and who said that while at Ward's flat she had had sexual relations with Bill, something which he strongly denied. Furthermore, she claimed that Ward had asked her to marry him, saying that if they were short of money 'we have always got Bill to help us'.

By now the Prime Minister, Harold Macmillan, had ordered Lord Denning to carry out an inquiry into what became known as the Profumo Affair. It is a matter of history that Profumo lied to the House of Commons when he said his relationship with Keeler was an innocent one, and it was that lie, rather than any question of a connexion with Captain Ivanov, that brought him down. But at least Profumo's resignation ended the matter as far as he was concerned. The murky waters swirling around Bill Astor were not so easy to disperse.

Stephen Ward was brought to trial in June 1963, charged with living on the earnings of prostitution, procuring, conspiring with others to keep a brothel and counselling and procuring an abortion. Astor's name came up on the very first day of the trial, and was barely out of the headlines until it ended. Bill had a lawyer observing the proceedings, but the advice given to him was to say nothing. Even that was to tell against him later. A visitor to Cliveden during those anxious days noted: 'Bill will be lucky if he emerges unscathed.' Even Bronwen did not escape. The French newspaper *Paris Soir*, publishing a series of pictures of women whom Ward had helped to win rich husbands, included a shot of Bronwen, though the implication was quite untrue.

Despite the fact that Cliveden was besieged by reporters, some of whom hovered overhead in helicopters, Astor tried as best he could to maintain his normal way of life. At a dinner party on 6 July 1963 at Cliveden he appeared dejected, complaining that it was very difficult to prove that there was no truth in the stories that were being told about him in court, that his innocent actions had been just that, despite the interpretations that were being put on them. The hardest thing, he said, was to suffer the scandal without the opportunity of replying, yet he believed the right course was to maintain his dignity and not to become involved in 'a public slanging match'. For Bronwen – who was utterly contemptuous of the allegations being made against her husband – one of the worst aspects of the affair was the way in which old friends had suddenly deserted Bill, though she was able to raise a smile at the facetious comments of those who stood by him, complaining that in all the years they had known him he had never invited them to an orgy.

The trial ended on 31 July, but that was by no means the end of the whole matter. Ward, found guilty, had taken an overdose of Nembutal before the jury returned their verdict and he died eight hours later. The previous day he had told a reporter that his trial had been an act of 'political revenge', that he had been deserted by the members of the Establishment who had been his friends, that 'someone had to be sacrificed, and that was me'. The press and public, so eager to rake among the sordid details of Ward's life and then to crucify him, felt a twinge of guilt at his death and began to ask why none of his so-called friends had testified on his behalf. This new reaction was exemplified by a writer in the *Daily Express*: 'On the eve of the Stephen Ward inquest, everyone is still asking why Lord Astor did not – as the popular phrase goes – "come forward" in defence of his friend. That, I think, is unjust to Lord Astor. The truly puzzling question – which has gone unasked in all the excitement and tragedy of the last seven days – is why the viscount was given any choice in the matter at all. Why was he not brought into court as a witness for the prosecution? . . . The prosecution said there was no evidence to show why Lord Astor's celebrated cheque [the £500 Ward had asked for] was paid to Ward. If the Crown really wanted to know why, you would think that the first person to ask was the man who signed it.' The writer concluded that Lord Astor's evidence was judged unnecessary to the prosecution's case and that was all there was to it, but he added unctuously and at the same time suggestively, 'I am certain that there was nothing sinister about it.' Others were less guarded. A wreath of six hundred roses for Stephen Ward's funeral bore the legend: 'To Stephen Ward, a victim of British hypocrisy.'

Astor's view was simple: there was no reason for him to appear in court because there was nothing he could have said; he had known Ward for a number of years but had never taken the slightest interest in his private life, and even though Ward had spent a good deal of time at Cliveden his cottage had been so far from the main house that whatever activities he might have indulged in there had gone completely unnoticed. Yet after Ward's suicide he had issued a statement saying that, 'Stephen Ward possessed remarkable gifts of healing which he exercised conscientiously and generously. Those who were so fortunate as to have been treated by him will remember him with great gratitude. His readiness to help anyone in pain is the memory many will treasure.' But if that was what he thought, why had he not appeared at Ward's trial as a character witness? Many people felt that the evidence against Ward was hardly convincing, and it was clear that some of the prostitutes who gave evidence were deliberately inventing stories in order to maintain the interest of the newspapers that wanted to buy their stories. What if Stephen Ward was, to some extent at least, a victim of an Establishment which, as ever, did not want to see its dirty linen washed in public?

The Denning Report was published on 26 September 1963, but it was by no means an entirely satisfactory conclusion to the Profumo Affair. No one emerged from it with much credit, but on the other hand its terms of reference were limited and none of the hundred and sixty witnesses had given evidence under oath. Denning himself admitted: 'My inquiry is not a suitable body to determine guilt or innocence. I have not the means at my disposal.' He restricted his inquiries mainly to the security aspects of the affair and the lid was firmly put back on the out-of-hours amusements of those in high society who took advantage of what Stephen Ward and his girls had to offer. 'It might be thought – indeed it has been thought,' said Denning in his summation, 'that these rumours are a symptom of a decline in the integrity of public life in this country. I do not believe this to be true.' Perhaps he meant that hypocrisy had always been a feature of public life.

At all events, the Denning Report cleared Astor of any wrongdoing or indeed involvement in the sordid world it went some way towards describing. 'I was completely absolved,' said Bill. At the same time, as Bronwen pointed out to a friend, the Profumo Affair had ruined her husband as far as any public responsibility was concerned: an embarrassed government was not likely to commission him to head an inquiry or represent it in some capacity. All Bill had left was his family life and his charitable work. (To add insult to injury, Bronwen confided, a representative for Mandy Rice-Davies had actually approached Bill and offered him money to collaborate on a book Mandy was writing – 'Can you imagine it?')

It was only later, and privately, that Astor revealed that he had paid for Stephen Ward's defence, believing that the case against him would be thrown out for lack of evidence. When it became clear that Ward was likely to be found guilty, Astor sought 'the best legal opinion' and was assured that he would be acquitted on appeal. Indeed, he had been on the point of writing to Ward to reassure him that all would be well when news of Ward's suicide came. Whatever the morality of Ward's life and relationships, Bill felt certain that he had not actually made a business out of running prostitutes, mainly because he had no business sense (he was always short of money) and was far too casual in his approach to life: he had been a sad and ultimately tragic figure rather than an evil one.

If the Profumo Affair cost Stephen Ward his life, there are those among Astor's friends who believe that it hastened Bill's death, too. His health had been uncertain for some time and the strain of the public humiliation and vilification caused it to deteriorate. 'He was', said his younger brother David, 'profoundly wounded and in poor health' after 1963. He tried to put the troubles out of his mind by becoming even more heavily involved in 'the service of those in distress, which had begun long before', but 'he did not have an easy course: for instance, a letter of his advocating the coordination of voluntary bodies concerned with victims of mass disasters, such as earthquakes, was refused publication by respectable papers...' Finally, on 7 March 1966, Bill died of a heart attack while on holiday in the Bahamas. He was fifty-eight. Bronwen said afterwards that the shock of the Ward case had exacerbated the high blood pressure to which Bill had been prey for years, but one of his friends went further. John Smith, Conservative M.P. for the Cities of London and Westminster, said Astor had died 'of a broken heart... He was an extremely charitable man, not only with money, but with his time and service... He always gave people the benefit of the doubt... It is deplorable that such a man was killed by lack of charity in others... He minded dreadfully and it killed him.'

Viscount Astor's estate totalled something more than a million pounds in England and about two million dollars (£714,000 then) in America. It was a far cry from the Astor wills of the past.

III

If, by the 1950s, the social and political influence of the Astors in Britain was well into a terminal decline, in America it had virtually disappeared. Vincent's heir apparent, John Jacob Astor VI (Jack), son of Colonel Astor and his second wife Madeleine, had withdrawn, after a lifetime apparently spent in providing spicy copy for gossip columnists, into an existence so private as to be almost reclusive. Since the fortune in which he always believed he should have shared had gone mostly to charitable causes, there did not seem to be much else for him to do.

Jack first hit the headlines when he was barely three years old. Under the will of John Jacob IV, Madeleine had received only a five million dollar trust fund (having been previously bought off for a marriage settlement of $1,695,000, generous by Astor standards) and Jack himself had been given the income from a three million dollar trust fund until he was twenty-one, which gave him a mere $140,000 a year, of which twenty-five thousand was allotted to his upkeep. In 1915, Madeleine went to court to ask for more money. Over three years, she told the judge, medical bills had totalled $6,323, lawyers' fees had consumed $4,007, and almost $6,000 had gone on clothing, toys and other necessities. Overall, she claimed, her son needed $86,000 a year to be spent on him in order that he should be kept in the manner his father would have wished. Why, a simple ermine baby wrap had cost her $185 and a matching robe and muff $230. A little mink coverlet had set her back $580 – there simply wasn't enough money to go round and she was having to dip into her own income from the marriage settlement and trust fund. The newspapers guffawed over this tale of wanton extravagance, and the judge was not impressed by the petitioner's poverty: he directed that the amount dedicated to Jack's childhood needs should be reduced to twenty thousand dollars.

All the same, there was unfriendly comment to the effect that Vincent should have disbursed some of his father's fortune in Jack's direction. The child was, after all, as much an Astor as Vincent, and there was little doubt that John Jacob IV, had he lived, would have made more generous provision in his will. Vincent was impervious to such criticism. He had strongly disapproved of his father's choice of second wife, and his disapproval marked his attitude towards Jack for the rest of his life: it was as if he believed that Jack should never have been born and almost tried to pretend that he hadn't been. Madeleine, having considered at one stage challenging John Jacob's will, soon lost interest in such matters, for she married a banker named William L. Dick and renounced her own trust fund, but Jack would grow up nursing resentment at having been, as he saw it, treated like a second-class Astor.

Actually, in one way Jack would have been a less anxious recipient of the fortune than Vincent, for he was made to be a playboy. He had no interest in schooling or, as a young man, in the idea of earning a living. He once took a job with

International Mercantile Marine, but soon gave it up, complaining that, 'I didn't get through until five o'clock. It would be six o'clock before I got home and I would have to get up very early the next morning.' His main interest in life seemed to be fast cars, and when he did finally get his hands on his three million dollars in 1933 he immediately bought ten automobiles.

'We all thought Jack a rather pathetic figure,' says one of his prep school contemporaries. 'He was lonely and withdrawn, and I seem to remember he suffered terribly from constipation.' The sufferings of his later life, however, were mainly to do with women, of whom he has always admitted to being extraordinarily fond.

He had just come into his fortune when he announced his intention of marrying an eighteen-year-old named Eileen Gillespie, whose family were prominent members of the social set that still haunted Newport in the thirties. (With his inheritance, Jack had recently bought a 'cottage' in Newport which needed fourteen servants to run it and an outdoor staff of six: because of Vincent's intervention, he had failed to secure the fabled Belmont mansion, Marble House.) Jack presented Eileen with an engagement ring once owned by Empress Eugenie of France, which had been in the Astor family for years, and talked of making a marriage settlement of one and a half million dollars. His lawyers, and even Eileen's father, talked him out of the latter, and the figure was set at half a million dollars. Not that it mattered, for the marriage never took place. Jack and Eileen quarrelled constantly, often in public, and once in the entrance hall of a fashionable hotel. At last, amid great bitterness, they parted for ever and Jack went on a cruise round the world. He did not remain long in misery, announcing upon his return to New York that he intended to marry Ellen Tuck French, one of the girls chosen to be bridesmaids at the aborted wedding to Eileen. First, however, the Gillespies insisted on a written apology to their daughter, otherwise they would not return the fabulous engagement ring: Jack had no choice but to comply.

The combination of wealth and romance – after all, three million dollars was not exactly peanuts – was irresistible to the newspapers, and hundreds of reporters and photographers descended on Newport for Jack's marriage to 'Tucky' French on 1 July 1934. Even the sober *New York Times* gave the affair front-page coverage plus almost a full page inside the paper, while the *Herald Tribune* gave over its entire magazine section to the glamorous young couple. Among the guests was Ernst 'Putzi' Hanfstaengl, friend and aide to Adolf Hitler, invited by the bride's father, Francis Ormond French, who was soon to become society's bête noire as a result of a scandalous bankruptcy case and his attempts to make money by writing books about what went on among the upper crust at Newport.

The extent of this reportage, coupled with the publicity Jack received when he took his job with International Mercantile Marine and the even greater coverage of his premature retirement eighteen months later, helped to establish Jack as newspaper-fodder. He came to represent the idle rich, and within a few years he served as a symbol for the irresponsible as well.

'Tucky' gave him a son, named William Backhouse Astor, but the marriage was not destined to last long and in 1943 the couple were divorced, Jack settling a large amount – generally rumoured to be a million dollars – on his former wife. Three years later he married again, and laid the foundation for his real troubles. His new bride, Gertrude Gretsch, gave birth to a daughter, Mary Jacqueline, who was to be the comfort of Jack's later years, but again the marriage was not of the durable kind and soon turned into a separation. Jack was to have cause to wish it had stayed that way, but in 1954 he fell head over heels in love with a pretty twenty-five-year-old named Dolores Fullman, a tall, blue-eyed blonde with what Jack later described as 'the Kim Novak look'. Never one to do things slowly, he immediately obtained a Mexican divorce from Gertrude and married Dolly Fullman on 6 August 1954, just three weeks after their first meeting.

It did not take Jack long to discover his mistake. Not only did Dolly reveal that she had been married before, but he also learnt that he was still married to Gertrude: she had not consented to the Mexican suit and the divorce was therefore invalid. It seemed Jack had committed bigamy ... now neither of his wives wanted him, but each wanted some of his money.

Dolly left him after six weeks and sued for alimony; Gertrude sued for her upkeep and that of her daughter on the grounds that the Mexican divorce was invalid and Jack was therefore still married to her – she also slapped a writ of attachment on the property he owned in New York. Dolly obtained the services of an excellent lawyer who quickly demolished Jack's case that since he was not legally married to Dolly she had no call upon his property. The judge who heard the case, however, decided that Dolly was a fortune-hunter and awarded her only seventy-five dollars a week in alimony, plus legal costs of $12,500. Dolly appealed to the state supreme court in Florida, where the action took place, and got $250 a week, plus more legal fees: she was definitely married to Jack, the court decided.

In New York, meanwhile, Gertrude's attachment order had been set aside but the supreme court there decided that she, not Dolly, was Jack's legal wife and gave her $2,500 a month in alimony, $1,000 a month in child support, and $7,000 in legal fees (she had asked for $4,000 and a whacking $50,000 in costs). In effect, then, Jack was legally married to two women, without the benefit of either but with the responsibility for supporting both. It was an incredible situation and, as his own legal fees piled up, he asked the New York supreme court to resolve it. The court could only conclude that he *was* in fact married to both women, though the marriages were valid only in certain states, and it awarded Dolly another settlement in respect of her New York legal costs. By now desperate, Jack went back to the Florida court and asked for an annulment of his marriage to Dolly on the grounds that he was still Gertrude's husband under New York state law: that cut no ice with the Floridians and they turned him down, as did the Supreme Court of the United States when he appealed to it.

At length, Gertrude helped Jack out by getting the kind of divorce that is recognized in every state of the Union, which left him with only one wife to worry about, and that situation has never been completely settled – indeed the parties seem to have given up trying. It means that Jack can never marry again, which he may think is fortunate in the circumstances.

But Jack's legal difficulties have not stopped with his marriages. When Vincent Astor died, he was so shocked at the treatment of himself and his son from his half-brother's will that he set about challenging it. His case was that Vincent had both been mentally incompetent at the time of drawing up the will and had been unduly influenced by the executors. Hearings went on for several months, but in the end Jack saw that he was getting nowhere and settled for a quarter of a million dollars in cash offered by Vincent's widow, Brooke. 'There have been three important Astors,' Jack said at the time. 'John Jacob the first, who made the fortune; William Backhouse Astor, who doubled it; and Vincent Astor, who gave it away.' Having sold his house in Newport long before, Jack retreated to Miami and concentrated on keeping himself to himself, collecting pictures and reading. He maintained a flat in New York and travelled extensively, but at the time of writing he rarely leaves Florida.

Jack's daughter, Jackie, followed the family tradition in a way by going to work in the real estate department of the auction house Sotheby Parke Bernet in Manhattan: the difference is, of course, that nowadays an Astor is selling someone else's property. Her half-brother, William, having worked for the New York brokerage firm of Bache, now lives in Vermont and runs his own business consultancy, studiously avoiding the New York social scene. He once said that he was going to be the next Astor millionaire, but the best estimates are that he has not quite made it.

12 *The Last Days of Astoria*

'It's a question of almost inventing something to do which one would enjoy doing.' The words are those of David Astor, eldest son of Michael Astor and grandson of Waldorf and Nancy. They sum up the way of life of the men in the family for the last two generations.

Bill Astor had a ready-made occupation, as master of Cliveden, even though he no longer actually owned it. His younger brother, the first David, the only one of Nancy's sons who did not become a Member of Parliament, chose to become a journalist instead of a politician and became his father's successor at *The Observer*. Educated, of course, at Eton and Oxford (in his case Balliol rather than New College), he first went to work in a Glasgow factory when he came down, then in a bank and finally joined the *Yorkshire Post* as a junior reporter. Always independently minded, he stood aside from the appeasement policy his parents supported during the 1930s and warned anyone who would listen against the growing power of both Germany and the Soviet Union, having visited the latter with his parents in 1931 and supported the opposition to Hitler in the former.

In 1940 David was commissioned in the Royal Marines and shortly afterwards was posted to the new Combined Operations Command. In 1942, however, Waldorf had a serious disagreement with the *Observer* editor, J.L. Garvin, who had expressed views in the paper that were contrary to the publicly voiced opinions of the chairman and was compelled to resign. Waldorf made it clear that he wanted David to edit the paper when his war service was over, and in the meantime it was to be controlled by a man named Ivor Brown. When the war ended, David joined *The Observer* as foreign editor, taking over the chair from Brown in 1948.

Waldorf had decreed that as editor, David should also be chairman of the board, so the paper became very much his own and, despite vocal opposition from his mother, he made it a mouthpiece of moderate-radical opinion. Not that he had things all his own way as far as the family was concerned, however: when he commissioned C.P. Snow to write a profile of the late Bill Astor, his sister Pauline threw the manuscript into the fire at Cliveden on the grounds, according to a witness, that it was too 'objective' and included comments from Bill's detractors.

Some family members were rather suspicious of David's radicalism, particularly in his younger days, and went so far as to suggest that he was some sort of traitor to his class. At the paper, too, there were those who wondered just what the scion of such a patrician family was doing in his shirtsleeves at the editor's desk. One former *Observer* man tells the story that one day David appeared in the newsroom, galley proof in hand, in a state of some excitement. 'This is a very good story,' he said, waving the proof at an editorial executive. The story turned out to be the property column and it was devoted to the obtaining of a mortgage. The ex-staffer goes on: 'David said this idea of a mortgage – and he pronounced it mort-gage – was a jolly good one. When it was pointed out to him that most people had mortgages, there was nothing unusual about the story, he seemed surprised. "But surely," he said, "no one on *The Observer* has a mort-gage?"' Apocryphal, no doubt, but indicative.

Even if the paper's left-wing leanings seemed to some to be out of keeping with the background of the editor, *The Observer* captured the mood of a more or less intellectual, and most specifically London and Home Counties, audience, and in the late 1950s and early 1960s it laid fair claim to being the trendiest read on a Sunday. In time, however, the rival *Sunday Times*, with Lord Thomson's money and multifarious business activities to support it, began to make inroads into the circulation and advertising revenue of *The Observer*, and though David battled manfully against this powerful opposition for ten years, he was forced to admit defeat in 1976 and sell out to an American oil company magnate, Robert Anderson, of Atlantic Richfield, leaving himself with influence but no power on the board of directors. In 1981, however, having spent twenty million dollars on keeping *The Observer* afloat, Anderson sold it to the acquisitive, British-based conglomerate Lonrho, which added the paper to its printing company, George Outram. In return, Anderson obtained a twenty per cent share of Outram for Atlantic Richfield and the chairmanship of *The Observer* for himself. David Astor, who had opposed the sale to Lonrho, resigned from the board, ending the Astor connexion.

David's younger brother, Michael, was also something of a rebel against the family philosophy, but in a quite different way. Born in 1916, he followed the well-trodden route to Eton and New College, and then broke away, at the age of twenty-one, to live in a flat in London where he studied accountancy in rather desultory fashion. When the war came he joined the Berkshire Yeomanry, where he felt himself a bit out of place in the heartiness of the officers' mess, and after guarding the English coast against the German invaders who were expected at any moment, he eventually saw action in the wake of the Normandy invasion in 1944. It was while he was in France that he determined to be an artist, or as his friend, the playwright William Douglas Home, put it: 'He saw an art course advertised in a French town as he was driving through it in his scout car and enrolled himself.'

His dreams of an artistic life were delayed, however, for when he returned to London at the end of the war he was offered the chance of standing for Parliament in a safe Conservative seat. As he himself told it, he almost ruined his chances during an interview at Conservative Central Office when he confessed that he was in favour of nationalizing the coal mines, but somewhat to his surprise he was still adopted as candidate for East Surrey, and as such he won the seat in the 1945 election, against the Labour tide. By his account he felt guilty at taking such a course: he was not particularly interested in politics and it seemed that he was just taking an easy way out. After his election he realized, as Douglas Home said, that 'he had not the remotest chance' of ever losing his seat, and the prospect terrified him. He resigned before the next election.

Michael retained his interest in painting and found that he had some talent, but although he had many friends in the art world – and indeed was a member of the Arts Council for a time – he never attempted seriously to exploit his talent. He experimented with writing, producing in 1983 an autobiographical work, *Tribal Feeling* – which gives a charming, witty and sometimes sharp account of what it was like to grow up as an Astor – and later a creditable novel entitled *Brand*, but again he did not find a life's work in this form of expression.

'None of this should be read to mean that he was a lightweight,' William Douglas Home wrote. 'It merely means that, although he was qualified to be a salaried professional in many spheres, he much preferred the role of unpaid guide, philosopher and friend. In later years he did good work as chairman of the London Library. But it is not by his works that one should know him – since he was a non-conformist... Nor would he want it that way.'

Thrice married and the father of six children, Michael died in 1979. In a tribute for *The Times*, Douglas Home summed him up thus: 'One cannot, in my view, picture what Michael was in print... One can, of course, record his kindness and his generosity, and the great courage that he showed in his last illness. But one cannot document his charm, the twinkle in his eye and his full-blooded laugh, his sensitivity, his loyalty and his benign irreverence. All one can do is mourn their premature departure... Some said he was a dilettante. Almost certainly he would have found himself among their number. He had no illusions, least of all about himself. His sense of humour saw to that.'

The youngest of Nancy's children, John Jacob VII – known in the family as 'Jakie' – proved to be quite unlike both David and Michael in outlook. Born in 1918, Eton and New College, of course, he joined his Uncle John's old regiment, the Life Guards, at the age of twenty-one and had a distinguished war record on attachment to the Commandos and the S.A.S., receiving the military M.B.E. and, from the French government, the Legion d'Honneur and the Croix de Guerre. After the war he followed his father and mother into politics in a most literal fashion when he was adopted as Conservative candidate for Plymouth Sutton in the spring of 1946. Beaten in the 1950 election, he fought again the following year and won by the hairsbreadth majority of 710, which caused him to be featured in the 'Parliamentary Personalities' section of the Conservative

Party's *Weekly News Letter* in the spring of 1952, the year in which he was appointed parliamentary private secretary to the financial secretary of the Treasury.

But although he continued to represent Plymouth Sutton in Parliament until 1959, Jakie's chief interests have really been the same as those of his father – farming and horses. He has an extensive farm at Hatley St George in Bedfordshire, was a skilful amateur jockey and until 1975 he operated his own stud at Newmarket, founded on horses he had inherited from Waldorf. He served as president of the Thoroughbred Breeders Association, has been a member of both the Betting Levy Board and the 'Tote', and continues to maintain his racing connexion as a member of the Jockey Club. In 1978 he was knighted for his services to the Agricultural Research Council after ten years as its chairman.

Of course, the lives of these heirs of Waldorf Astor have no fixed central point now. Cliveden passed fully into the hands of the National Trust after Bill's death; the present Viscount Astor, married and the father of two children, makes his home at Ginge Manor in Oxfordshire. Similarly, the last stronghold of the Astors, Hever Castle, passed out of the family's hands in 1983. Cliveden, *The Times*, *The Observer*, and now Hever.

The present Lord Astor of Hever, John Jacob V's eldest son Gavin, struggled for years to keep his beautiful castle, but the economics of the last quarter of the twentieth century were simply too much for him. Mindful of his father's sacrifice in the face of crippling death duties, he brought up his five children (he married the daughter of Earl Haig) at Hever and even when obliged to open it to the public he and his family retained a private wing. In 1982, however, when the old place's electricity bill was running at something like £36,000 a year, Gavin decided to move out and turn over Hever to commercialism. Film makers and advertising agencies hired the castle to produce documentaries and commercials (British Airways, for instance, stood the actor Robert Morley on the battlements for a television advertisement designed to emphasize Britain's traditional glories in the minds of American viewers). The Pavilion and the Tudor Room were opened as restaurants and conference centres, and finally the castle was offered as a holiday home to anyone who could afford £220 a day. For that sum, said the land agent, 'you will stay in Lord Astor's guest suite and be waited on by his staff. If you want caviare, you'll get it. When you consider that you will get anything you want, it does come within striking distance of normality.'

But perhaps nothing ever did come within striking distance of normality at Hever: not Anne Boleyn and her family, not the counterfeit Tudor Village, not the artificially created lake and Italian gardens. The plan failed and Gavin's elder son, John Jacob VIII, to whom the actual ownership of the castle had been transferred in trust in 1974, sought permission to sell it. The asking price was thirteen and a half million pounds, to include old William Waldorf's great art and antiques collection, but in the event the castle was bought for nine million pounds without most of its treasures. The purchaser was a property company which seems to have specialized in buying country estates and reselling them at an enormous profit. In the case of Hever, however, the company says it will retain the castle as a tourist attraction.

The three thousand acre estate has already been disposed of. Some of the farms and cottages were sold to tenants, and other long-standing residents were guaranteed rent-free accommodation for the rest of their lives under Lord Astor's terms of sale. As for the collection of art, armour and other treasures, that was expected to fetch some two million pounds at auction but in fact made twice that figure.

Hever's sale, of course, attracted front page newspaper coverage in America and, with a certain irony, was even featured in the magazine Vincent Astor helped to found, *Newsweek*. Not that the glossy weekly has any connexion with the Astors now, though – one of the first things Brooke did was to sell it, along with her late husband's other favourite, the St Regis Hotel. All that remains of the man who gave the money away is the Vincent Astor Foundation, which Brooke administers as president and which, against all Astor rules, continues to give out more than it receives in income from its capital (a little under fifty million dollars at the last count).

So Astoria, in the widest sense of the term, is now fading just as the first John Jacob's dream of an empire beyond the Rocky Mountains faded a hundred and seventy years ago, though it has had a better run for its money. That an American fortune has been kept alive for as long as it has been by what is essentially an English family is not without significance: the British Astors were not only protected by a self-perpetuating class system, but they also protected themselves by their willingness to work for their living. As the fourth Viscount said recently, 'There is no question but that my children are not going to be able to sit around and live off their inheritances.' At the age of thirty-one, he is an Astor of the future, managing a couple of industrial companies and two large farms. So is David, with whom we began this epilogue for Astordom.

Aged thirty-nine at the time of writing, David farms fourteen hundred acres in Oxfordshire and talks knowledgeably about pigs, beef and dairying. At the same time, he has started an exclusive shirt shop in the fashionable Knightsbridge area of London, founded a theatrical agency which had Geraldine Chaplin on its books, become head of development of the National Theatre, and taken on the presidency of the Council for the Protection of Rural England. He also owns an antiquarian bookshop and, in 1983, raised one and a half million pounds to produce what promised to be the most expensive musical show ever staged in the West End of London.

Perhaps it is not too fanciful to suggest that the entrepreneurial spirit of John Jacob I is not dead yet among his descendants. An Astoria for the twenty-first century may even now be in the making.

Bibliography and Sources

Books

ADAMS, HENRY: *The Life of Albert Gallatin*, 1879; *History of the United States*, 1889–91.

ADKINS, NELSON FREDERICK: *Fitz-Greene Halleck*, 1930.

ALDRICH, MARGARET CHANLER: *Family Vista*, 1958.

ARMSTRONG, MARGARET: *Five Generations*, 1930.

ASTOR, BROOKE: *Footsteps*, 1980.

ASTOR, JOHN JACOB: *A Journey in Other Worlds: A Romance of the Future*, 1894.

ASTOR, MICHAEL: *Tribal Feeling*, 1963.

ASTOR, NANCY: *My Two Countries*, 1923; *The Astor Story*, 1951.

ASTOR, WILLIAM WALDORF: *John Jacob Astor*, 1899; *Valentino: An Historical Romance of the Sixteenth Century in Italy*, 1885; *Sforza: A Story of Milan*, 1889.

AVON, EARL OF: *The Eden Memoirs* ('Facing the Dictators'), 1962.

BEACH, MOSES Y.: *The Wealth and Biography of the Wealthy Citizens of the City of New York*, 1846.

BEARD, CHARLES A. AND MARY R.: *The Rise of American Civilization*, 1927.

BELDEN, E. PORTER: *New York, Past, Present and Future*, 1850.

BRISTED, CHARLES ASTOR: *The Upper Ten Thousand*, 1852.

BUTLER, J.R.M.: *Lord Lothian*, 1960.

CHITTENDEN, HIRAM M.: *The American Fur Trade of the Far West*, 1935.

COCKBURN, CLAUD: *Crossing the Line*, 1969.

COLLIER, PETER AND HOROWITZ, DAVID: *The Rockefellers*, 1976.

COLLIS, LOUISE (ED.): *Maurice Collis: Diaries 1949–1969*, 1977.

COLLIS, MAURICE: *Nancy Astor, An Informal Biography*, 1960.

COWLES, VIRGINIA: *The Astors*, 1979.

DE FOREST, ROBERT AND VEILLER, LAWRENCE: *The Tenement House Problem*, 1903.

FRAZIER, THOMAS R. (ED.): *The Underside of American History*, 1974.

GALLATIN, COUNT (ED.): *The Diary of James Gallatin*, 1916.

GATES, JOHN D.: *The Astor Family*, 1981.

GLAZIER, WILLARD F.: *Peculiarities of American Cities*, 1883.

HARRISON, MRS BURTON: *Recollections Grave and Gay*, 1911.

HARRISON, ROSINA: *Rose, My Life in Service*, 1975.

HASBROUCK, FRANK: *The History of Dutchess Country*, 1909.

HERSH, BURTON: *The Mellon Family*, 1978.

HERSHKOWITZ, LEO: *Tweed's New York: Another Look*, 1977.

HONE, PHILIP: *The Diary of Philip Hone 1828–1851*, 1927.

HOWE, JULIA WARD: *Is Polite Society Polite?*, 1895; *Modern Society*, 1880.

HOY, C.I.: *John Jacob Astor: An Unwritten Chapter*, 1936.

IRVING, PIERRE M.: *Life and Letters of Washington Irving*, 1871.

IRVING, WASHINGTON: *Astoria* (People's Edition), 1871.

JENKINS, ALAN: *The Rich Rich*, 1977.

JONES, THOMAS: *A Diary with Letters*, 1954.

JOSEPHSON, MATTHEW: *The Robber Barons*, 1934.

KAPLAN, JUSTIN: *Walt Whitman, A Life*, 1980.

KAVALER, LUCY: *The Astors, An American Legend*, 1966.

LANGHORNE, ELIZABETH: *Nancy Astor and Her Friends*, 1974.

LEHR, ELIZABETH D.: *King Lehr and the Gilded Age*, 1939.

LOTH, DAVID: *Public Plunder: A History of Graft in America*, 1938.

LUNDBERG, FERDINAND: *The Rich and the Super Rich*, 1968.

MCALLISTER, WARD: *Society As I Have Found It*, 1890.

MEDLICOTT, W.N.: *Contemporary England, 1914–64*, 1967.

MORRIS, LLOYD: *Incredible New York*, 1951.

MYERS, GUSTAVUS: *The History of the Great American Fortunes*, 1910; *The History of Tammany Hall*, 1917.

OBOLENSKY, SERGE: *One Man in His Times*, 1958.

O'CONNOR, HARVEY: *The Astors*, 1941.

O'CONNOR, RICHARD: *The Golden Summers*, 1974.

PARTON, JAMES: *The Life of John Jacob Astor*, 1865.

PLESS, PRINCESS OF: *Daisy, Princess of Pless*, 1929.

PORTER, KENNETH WIGGINS: *John Jacob Astor, Business Man*, 1931.

RIIS, JACOB: *The Battle with the Slum*, 1902.

ROSEBERY, EARL OF: *Lord Rosebery's American Journal 1873* (eds. A.R.C. Grant and Caroline Combe), 1967.

SIMON, KATE: *Fifth Avenue: A Very Social History*, 1978.

SMITH, ARTHUR D. HOWDEN: *John Jacob Astor*, 1929.

SYKES, CHRISTOPHER: *Nancy, The Life of Lady Astor*, 1972.

TERRELL, JOHN U.: *Furs by Astor*, 1973.

THORNDIKE, JOSEPH J.: *The Very Rich: A History of Wealth*, 1976.

VANDERBILT, CORNELIUS: *Farewell to Fifth Avenue*, 1925.

VANDERBILT, CORNELIUS, JR: *Queen of the Golden Age*, 1956.

WRENCH, JOHN EVELYN: *Geoffrey Dawson and Our Times*, 1955.

Newspapers and Periodicals

Britain: *Daily Express, Daily Mirror, The Daily Telegraph, The Observer, Pall Mall Gazette, Sunday Express, Sunday Pictorial, The Sunday Times, The Times, Yorkshire Post; Punch, Spectator, Illustrated London News, The Listener; The Times* house journal.

U.S.A.: *Boston Globe, Boston Herald American, Daily News, New York Times, New York Tribune, New York Herald, Sun* and other New York newspapers; *Newsweek, Time, Harper's, New Yorker, Silliman's Journal, Town Topics, Nation, Fortune.*

Documents

U.S. Senate Document No. 58, First Session, 19th Congress; U.S. Senate Document No. 90, First Session, 22nd Congress; New York Senate Document No. 36 — Tenement House Problem in New York 1887; New York Assembly Documents relating to tenement conditions in 1857, 1867, 1894; The Denning Report.

Other books, articles and documents consulted are fully described in the text.

The Astor Dynasty

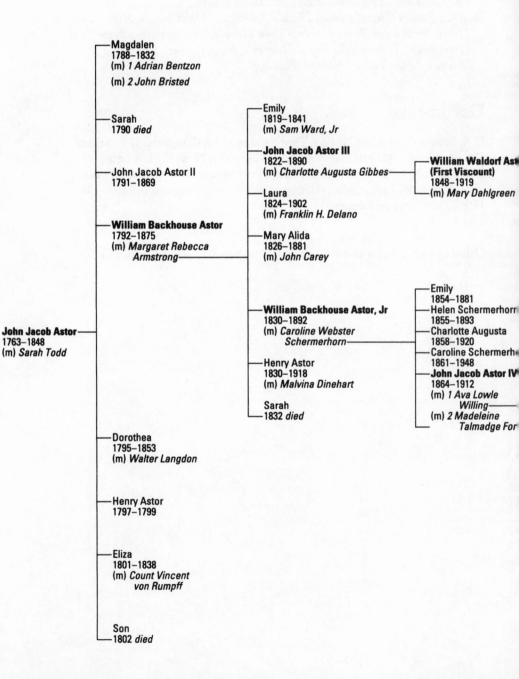

John Jacob Astor
1763–1848
(m) *Sarah Todd*

- **Magdalen**
  1788–1832
  (m) *1 Adrian Bentzon*
  (m) *2 John Bristed*

- **Sarah**
  1790 *died*

- **John Jacob Astor II**
  1791–1869

- **William Backhouse Astor**
  1792–1875
  (m) *Margaret Rebecca Armstrong*
  - **Emily**
    1819–1841
    (m) *Sam Ward, Jr*
  - **John Jacob Astor III**
    1822–1890
    (m) *Charlotte Augusta Gibbes*
    - **William Waldorf Ast**
      (First Viscount)
      1848–1919
      (m) *Mary Dahlgreen*
  - **Laura**
    1824–1902
    (m) *Franklin H. Delano*
  - **Mary Alida**
    1826–1881
    (m) *John Carey*
  - **William Backhouse Astor, Jr**
    1830–1892
    (m) *Caroline Webster Schermerhorn*
    - **Emily**
      1854–1881
    - **Helen Schermerhorr**
      1855–1893
    - **Charlotte Augusta**
      1858–1920
    - **Caroline Schermerh**
      1861–1948
    - **John Jacob Astor IV**
      1864–1912
      (m) *1 Ava Lowle Willing*
      (m) *2 Madeleine Talmadge For*
  - **Henry Astor**
    1830–1918
    (m) *Malvina Dinehart*
  - **Sarah**
    1832 *died*

- **Dorothea**
  1795–1853
  (m) *Walter Langdon*

- **Henry Astor**
  1797–1799

- **Eliza**
  1801–1838
  (m) *Count Vincent von Rumpff*

- **Son**
  1802 *died*

William Waldorf Astor
(Third Viscount)
1907–1967
(m) 1 Sarah K. E. Norton ————

William Waldorf Astor III
(Fourth Viscount)
1952–
(m) Annabelle Sheffield ——— Flora
                                 Waldorf

(m) 2 Philippa Hunloke ——————— Emily

(m) 3 Bronwen Pugh ————— Janet Elizabeth
                                Pauline Marian

Nancy Phyllis Louise
1909–
(m) Lord Willoughby de Eresby
    (Earl of Ancaster)

Francis David Langhorne Astor
1912–
(m) 1 Melanie Hauser ———————— Frances
                                (m) Dr Miles Frankel

(m) 2 Bridget Aphra Wreford ——— Alice
                                (m) Lawrence Woodward
                                Richard
                                Lucy
                                Nancy
                                Thomas

Michael Langhorne Astor
1916–1979
(m) 1 Barbara Mary Colonsay McNeil ——— David
                                         (m) Clare St John
                                         James
                                         (m) Jane de Chazal
                                         Jane
(m) 2 Patricia David Pandora Clifford Jones ——— Georgina
                                         (m) Hon. Anthony Ramsay

(m) 3 Judy Innes ——————— Joshua Paul Michael
                                Polly Michael

John Jacob Astor VII
1918–
(m) 1 Ana Inez Carcano ——— Michael Ramon
                               (m) Daphne Warburg
                               Stella
(m) 2 Susan Sheppard ——— (m) Martin Wilkinson

Gavin Astor
(Second Baron Astor of Hever)
1918–
(m) Lady Irene Haig

John Jacob Astor VIII
1946–
(m) Fiona Harvey ——— Camilla
                            Tania
Bridget Mary
Elizabeth Louise
Sarah Violet
(m) Hon. George Lopes
Philip Douglas Paul

Hugh Waldorf Astor
1920–
(m) Emily Lucy Kinloch ——— Virginia
                              Robert
                              Rachel
                              Jean
                              James

John Astor
1923–
(m) Diana Drummond ——— Elizabeth
                          Richard
                          David

William Backhouse Astor
1935–
(m) Charlotte Fisk
Mary Jacqueline

William Backhouse Astor, Jr
1959–
Caroline Fisk

(Left margin column:)

aldorf Astor
econd Viscount)
79–1952
) Nancy Langhorne
    Shaw

uline
80–1972

hn Rudolph Astor
81 died

hn Jacob Astor V
aron Astor of Hever)
86–1971
Lady Violet Elliot
  Mercer-Nairne
wendolyn Enid
89–1902

lliam Vincent Astor
81–1959
1 Helen Dinsmore
  Huntington
2 Mary Benedict Cushing
3 Mary Brooke Russell
  Marshall
a Alice Muriel
02–1956
1 Prince Serge Obolensky
2 Raimund von
  Hofmannsthal
3 Philip Harding
4 David Pleydell-Bouverie

hn Jacob Astor VI
2–
1 Ellen Tuck French
2 Gertrude Gretsch
3 Dolores Fullman

Index

Index

Index